THE PORTABLE BOOK OF
birthdays

THE PORTABLE BOOK OF

birthdays

by Dennis Fairchild and Peter Weber

RUNNING PRESS
PHILADELPHIA · LONDON

© 2003 by Running Press Book Publishers

All rights reserved under the Pan-American and International Copyright Conventions

Printed in the United States

This book may not be reproduced in whole or in part, in any form or by any means, electronic or mechanical, including photocopying, recording, or by any information storage and retrieval system now known or hereafter invented, without written permission from the publisher.

9 8 7 6 5 4 3 2 1

Digit on the right indicates the number of this printing

Library of Congress Control Number 2003093127
ISBN 0-7624-1549-5

Designed by Corinda Cook
Edited by Deborah Grandinetti
Typography: Avenir, Stempel Schneidler, and Almanac

This book may be ordered by mail from the publisher.
Please include $2.50 for postage and handling.
But try your bookstore first!

Running Press Book Publishers
125 South Twenty-second Street
Philadelphia, Pennsylvania 19103-4399

Visit us on the web!
www.runningpress.com

Contents

Introduction *6*

January *13*

February *77*

March *137*

April *201*

May *263*

June *327*

July *389*

August *453*

September *517*

October *579*

November *643*

December *705*

Introduction

"We are born at a given moment in a given place, and like vintage years of wine, we have the qualities of the year and of the season in which we are born."

—*C.G. Jung*

Early last century, Carl Jung, the famous Swiss psychologist, coined the phrase "synchronicity"—the theory that two events occurring at the exact moment in time take on the qualities of that precise moment in time. It is said that no event is an isolated happening; every thing is bonded to every other thing in some manner, linked by the commonality of that moment.

This book honors that theory. It looks at how certain patterns in place the day you were born have put their stamp on you. Specifically, it looks at patterns through the lens of astrology and numerology.

Astrology and numerology are languages of symbols. Astrology is the art of examining the patterns in the heavens and how they correlate in people's lives and personalities. It divides birthdays into 12 distinct "signs," which are broken down further into "decantes." Numerology assigns characteristics to the cosmic combos of the digits 1 through 9, and suggests traits, strengths and weaknesses for every day of the year.

Mind you, this has nothing to do with pre-destination, or relinquishing free will. Rather these are "shaping" influences.

The 366 personality profiles that follow draw upon both of these ancient arts. You will find that no two days share identical characteristics. Like you, they're special. Consider your birth date a "psychic signature," an ambiance.

The Portable Book of Birthdays is a modern tool for understanding yourself better, for learning how to make the most of your assets and compensate for your weaknesses. It also provides insights into the other people in your life. Each daily profile provides user-friendly insights about yourself, your friends, and your family.

You may not identify with everything you read, but we predict that you'll never view your birth date the same after you read this book.

Einstein expressed the idea of a structured universe by claiming "God does not play dice with the world." So take a gamble. Thumb through the following pages, examine what two of America's foremost prognosticators say about your birth date. Do your stars jive with your birth numbers? Which famous personalities share your celestial anniversary? And what do you have in common with them?

But most of all enjoy. We've already done the math, so that you won't have to do it.

Dennis Fairchild

Peter Weber

January

January 1

Whatever fields of life you graze in, your sensitive, critical and practical nature will attract the eyes of those in power, helping you go far but at a nice steady pace. Thoughtful and vigilant, and responsible in all of life's matters, you are bound to be a wise diplomat, or should try more to be. Seldom a troublemaker and blessed with a good memory, you have your own soft magnetic attractiveness and should grow out of any little nagging phobias. Boo!

Not the type that pushes and shoves, you're careful not to rock the boat among your personal pals, but you also have a keen eye for others who don't quite have their acts together. You're willing to help those who need it on a case-by-case basis. For leisure and exercise, be on the water.

Love

You are not one to rush into a romantic commitment, but you don't back off from one, either. You prefer an even, measured logical style of emotional rapport. Because you spend a lot of time by yourself, you tend to be a bit controlling or possessive with lovers. You're good at helping partners straighten out personal problems—always available with down-to-earth advice about how they can do better. After all, you're a lover, not a fighter—but you could stand to mellow out a bit!

Money

Financially, you only drive on the safe and sure road, never off-beaten-track detours. Get-rich-quick-schemes hold little interest for 1/1-borns; planning and applying foresight to long-range investments comes natural to you. Because you fear poverty, you do everything to prevent it. By understanding your faults and limitations, and correcting them, you enjoy life—and save money! Ask for advice, be open-minded, and share your opinions.

Famous People Born on This Day

Female

Carole Landis, actress
Barbara Baxley, actress
Beatrix Wilhelmina Armgard,
    Queen of Netherlands
Svetlana Beregovkina, cosmonaut
Betsy Ross, American flag creator

Male

J.D. Salinger, author
Barry Goldwater, politician
Xavier Cugat, bandleader
J. Edgar Hoover, FBI founder
Paul Revere, American patriot

January 2

Enlarging your circle of friends with your idealistic, romantic, sometimes religious ideas, you might even go a bit overboard at times. Is it your need for control that drives you to be a leading team member, a protector, and into other people's business? Noble, sometimes flippant, you want to and will be heard—marshal your flock and become a saint, perhaps. Your words can be magic, your beliefs deep, the road ahead broad and long.

An essential member of your chosen group—or any collection of people with a common goal—you excel as its representative or leader, though prone to exaggerate things now and then. Your sense of humor is biting; use it more. The grandness of big indoor halls and theaters is a natural element for you, since your life is like an opera.

Love

You communicate your needs to a partner easily—a natural 1/2-born talent, rather than a learned skill. You have a special gift for understanding others' problems, able to quickly put yourself into another's shoes. When alone, you find it difficult to do anything wholeheartedly—whereas, with a partner, your energies flourish, flow and grow. Your emotional responses are reserved and serious; however, you never sacrifice integrity for the sake of a relationship.

Money

You have a realistic attitude about money because you are a good trouble-shooter and problem-spotter. As a rule, you comparison-shop and ask questions before spending a cent. It's easy for you to keep track of expenditures, because "must watch money" is indelibly engraved on your mind. On the job, your mature 1/2-personality makes others stop, look and listen to you. Security is important; without it, you go to pieces. Gains over a long period of time appeal to your nature.

Famous People Born on This Day

Female

Christy Turlington, model
Tia Carrere, actress
Marianne McDonald, philanthropist
Penelope Jessel, political activist
Sally Rand, fan dancer

Male

Cuba Gooding, Jr., actor
Dennis Hastert, U.S. Congressman
Jim Bakker, ex-evangelist
Roger Miller, songwriter
Isaac Asimov, writer

January 3

Who knows the fire and verve beneath your veneer of practical calmness? Few do and when it seems they're not doing you justice, you are tempted to take advantage of situations more than you should, which might ultimately limit your otherwise obtainable ambitions. Ditto for your hidden romantic nature, a surprise to your respected family. Don't be betrayed by bluster or bad habits; do pay heed to your soul's sense of right and wrong.

When it comes to having fun and enjoying life's exciting leisure activities, you're always ready to go, and some of you may not want to leave, instead choosing to live the high and fast entertainment lifestyle. Why not? Watching is okay, participating is better, and you fit right in. The big city equals the big time, and the big time is where you should be.

Love

You get along well with partners who depend on you for change and variety—the social orchestra conductor of romantic unions! 1/3-borns appreciate self-expression, and you use it positively . . . even though it may upset partners and friends because you change your mind often and suddenly. Being an ardent lover, you live for the moment. Never forget the difference between idealism and realism.

Money

You drive yourself at an incredible enthusiastic pace—no one ever calls you lazy! However, by rushing hurriedly, you often waste time and vitality. You want everything "now" and indecisive coworkers irritate you. Earning money by temporary, part-time, and freelance work suits you well, because it allows you time to pursue personal pleasures, reconsider options.

Famous People Born on This Day

Female

Danica McKellar, actress
Cheryl Miller, basketball
    player/coach
Joan Chen, actress
Victoria Principal, actress
Betty Furness, consumer activist

Male

Michael Schumacher, racecar driver
Mel Gibson, actor
J.R.R. Tolkien, author
Victor Borge, entertainer
Stephen Stills, rock composer

January 4

Sit still and set goals for Y-O-U; once you're really sure, you'll reap the benefits using your exceptional skills and invisible inner strength, but too much thirst for power is risky business for you. Simply wanting something is too simple; you must earn it while sharing and being charitable too. When you're right-on, your efforts are seen as courageous, even heroic, and feel self-fulfilling. Manage defiance and determination correctly; be a lover to some, fighter to others.

Since it's not like you to be dependent on others for long, many of you are so independent that you'd be good in your own business or anywhere you have the power to put your great ideas to good use. An occasional few days of free time to put ideas in order helps, so seek isolated outdoor places.

Love

You admire strength in a lover—not necessarily physical power, but fortitude and inner stamina. Your 1/4-born personality likes companions who pull their share, don't lean on you, and who treat your relationship with respect and decorum. You have the inner perception to "see through" appearances and understand what motivates people. To you, love is not merely skin-deep, it's a long-term investment.

Money

Your financial gains come through your own merit, attention to detail, and hard work. Once you commit to a project, you never lose sight of it. You thrive on having everything in order, always analyzing, weighing pros and cons. People born on this day are noted for being discriminating and using common sense. Fly-by-night financial schemes don't fly. For you, time is money. "Pay up, or shut up!"

Famous People Born on This Day

Female

Dyan Cannon, actress
Deana Carter, singer
Julia Ormond, actress
Jane Wyman, actress
Maureen Reagan, first Reagan
   daughter

Male

Michael Stipe, singer
Matt Frewer, actor
Floyd Patterson, boxer
Louis Braille, Braille inventor
Isaac Newton, scientist

January 5

A real live wire deep inside, you're usually well-liked and sweet but reserve a sting like a scorpion for those you feel deserve it. You can control the turf and you're bound to succeed in business, sharp trader, but don't quibble over trifles: focus on the real issues whether you know enough about them or simply think you do. Lucky you can even hook up with the deeply sensual lover you imagined. But let's not do others' thinking for them, though often you should.

Not wanting to be known as someone to keep your distance from, you'd benefit from being a little warmer. Those insipid cuddling, spill-your-guts support groups aren't for you, definitely not; your own shrink is better. They'd be someone good to reason with. Any expert who shares your interests would be.

Love

An unpredictable or erratic partner doesn't satisfy your romantic game plan. Tenacious in your desires, once you set your sights on someone, you don't give up—even if you have to wait for years! Your 1/5-born influence makes you perfectly willing to let others make the initial move, but once you commit you're in it for the long run. You anger quickly, but cool off just as fast and don't hold a grudge. You contain emotional frustration and keep on plugging to make relationships work.

Money

You're always conscientious about living up to your end of a deal, rarely fearful of challenge. The 1/5-born is careful not to mix money with friends, choosing not to borrow or loan. Your approach to finances is disciplined, having no desire to upset apple carts with impulsive behavior or sudden moves. Difficult projects intrigue you because they present opportunities to demonstrate your responsible ability to persevere with exactness. You handle coworkers and the tensions that arise in employment matters reasonably, yet warmly.

Famous People Born on This Day

Female

Diane Keaton, actress
Suzy Amis, actress
Pamela Sue Martin, actress
Jean Dixon, psychic
Mabel Leigh, potter

Male

Stephen Decatur, U.S. naval hero
Marilyn Manson, musician
Juan Carlos, king of Spain
Walter Mondale, politician
Zebulon Pike, explorer

January 6

Land baron or a captain in industry, directing man and beast—that's some of you, but most born today may enjoy humbler surroundings, sharing your life with others who appreciate your earthy fortitude and solid character. Ah, the easy life, land and sky! Sports, animals, owning your own business—these hold special attraction, even gambling. All is not secure, so do be protective of possessions and resources; they cannot simply be socked away. Time waits for no one; make efforts to keep up with progress.

What goes on in your head?! You feel you have answers and usually do, and always can ask the right questions. You're also quite in touch with your desires. Your home is your ultimate refuge, and not just anyone gets invited there. Keep in touch with old friends; visit or entertain them more often.

Love

Although you are affectionate and enjoy being loved, you want to be free emotionally and otherwise. You lack energy and are rather passive, always dreaming and waiting for opportunities to come to you. Don't let the 1/6-energies make you lazy, wallowing in your comfort zone so much that you're unwilling to invest in love. Accept people as they are and appreciate their individual beauty. Because it's difficult for you to stand up for your rights, you often attract persons who are not very good for you.

Money

It isn't easy to put your financial ideas to work because you doubt that they will succeed. You don't have to accept obscurity when you are geared to take advantage of your resources! It bothers you to work without recognition, but you'll have to accept this situation until you are more confident about your abilities. You would rather be a specialist than a jack-of-all-trades. You rarely make promises you can't keep, so people respect you for your reliability.

Famous People Born on This Day

Female

Joan of Arc, French martyr
Nancy Lopez, golfer
Bonnie Franklin, actress
Kathy Sledge, singer
Capucine (Germaine Lefebvre), actress

Male

Carl Sandburg, poet
Tom Mix, actor
Khalil Gibran, poet
Sun Myoung Moon, evangelist
Lou Harris, pollster

January 7

A simple sort of beauty inside and out, others may see you as soft, certainly a fun-loving soul, somewhere in the middle between fluff and tough. What they should see is that you're gifted. More than a socialite or fashion plate, there's an artist and harmonizer inside. This blooms if you're not too self-concerned, moody, picky, or feel you deserve more. It is true: life is a stage so use it to show your loving, humane side, but keep in mind to develop a real career.

A people-person, you fit in anywhere, even with those stodgy uppity think-they're-better-than-everyone-else types. Crime and filth aren't for you—crystal and champagne are more your style. Your bed is probably pretty comfy. Bed and breakfast places are a nice break, too. Life's illusions you adore, especially a good book.

Love

Your 1/7-born ambiance is endearing to coworkers, but makes you unrealistic in affairs of the heart. You permit yourself greater indulgences than you would from a committed lover—establishing one set of rules for yourself and another for them. You don't like being tied down by anybody's rules or terms. Sometimes it is difficult for you to be objective, because of your need to explore and emotions influence your thinking so much. To learn more: ask!

Money

You have no problem letting others do what they want with their money—but yours is a different story. You're willing to take some chances to attract prosperity, but you're very careful about doing so. You are quite concerned about being right and argue very hard for your point of view. Anything that doesn't fit into your thinking you see as weakness, and may be very hard on yourself when you make a mistake. Loosen up the purse strings, as well as your personality.

Famous People Born on This Day

Female

Carolyn Bessette Kennedy, model
Kathy Valentine, musician
Katie Couric, TV news host
St. Bernadette, religious visionary
Sandra Bernhard, comedienne

Male

David Yost, actor
Nicolas Cage, actor
Kenny Loggins, singer
William Peter Blatty, author/director
Charles Addams, cartoonist

January 8

What's life without a little danger? It's dangerous and you should not get too attached to that, whether it's the ragged edge of nature, sports, or in business competition or relationships. Your logic says it will protect you, but check your past history! Be your own manager: get more organized, persistent, and build on your success. Think regal; avoid indiscretions that wear you down. Keep the channels of communication always open; talk the talk and walk the walk—balanced!

Going out on the road to work or play is something you look forward to—the world isn't big enough for you, and the more energy you find there, the more energetic you feel. Fairs and shows and lots of noise, music and singing, and a backstage pass. Knowing first aid and emergency procedures is worthwhile.

Love

You adore amusements, perks and pleasant times, especially if you don't have to invest a lot of effort. Strong, independent partners work best for you. 1/8-borns don't enjoy being alone, and it is difficult for you to like (or dislike) anybody only a little bit. However, you're a bit reserved about showing loving feelings. It's not that you're unaffectionate—you're probably afraid that people will reject you if you make the first move or don't agree. The sooner you own up to your insecurities, the sooner you'll overcome them.

Money

Unlike personal relations, you want to see real results on the job—daydreams don't cut it! You're not one to rest on laurels and are willing to give everything expected. You don't enjoy being in command and usually comply with the rules. Neither pedantic nor didactic, your ability to synthesize information and transform it into action gives you a good edge in the workplace without the need to parade your knowledge.

Famous People Born on This Day

Female

Gaby Hoffman, actress
Ami Dolenz, actress
Doreen Wilber, archer
Butterfly McQueen, actress
Fannie M. Jackson, educator

Male

David Bowie, musician
Stephen Hawkins, physicist
Elvis Presley, musician
Joseph Wiezenbaum, artificial intelligence pioneer
Walter Bothe, physicist

January 9

Imaginative, smart, and almost a genius if you aren't already, you understand it all, whether championing a cause, making the world a safe, cosmically conscious microcosm of the universe, or taking your team to the top—and so cool, calm, ultra-collected! Just doing my part, you say. Attack the problem. Do the math. Let's feel good and whip whatever. Did we mention you're attractive and orderly, but sometimes just an unmanageable handful and maybe a bit kinky-dinky?

You don't like it when people want something from you, but you are willing to volunteer if it will be truly beneficial. You have to be part of the decision-making process and should be—you do have something to contribute. You don't forget the people and how things are done. For fun, go places you've never been but wanted to.

Love

You are generous and warmhearted toward people in general, but especially toward those you love. You humbly make concessions to allow relationships to develop, and you maintain a low profile in order to avoid being rejected. You like people and don't hesitate to tell them so when they win your approval. You hope they feel the same way about you. To be happy, 1/9-born must look for Number One!

Money

Lots of what you do is based on a plan for maximizing your output, and you expect a high yield for your efforts! 1/9s can lessen feelings of inadequacy by freeing yourself from anxiety about security. Always remember that you are independent and that you can extend your field of interest when opportunity arises. You have the right to expect a reasonable return for your work. Failure to recognize your potential is a serious liability.

Famous People Born on This Day

Female

Joan Baez, folk singer
Simone De Beauvoir, writer
Phyllis Givens, medium
Gypsy Rose Lee, exotic dancer
Susannah York, actress

Male

Bart Starr, football quarterback
Chic Young, cartoonist
Richard Nixon, U.S. president
John Denver, songwriter
Jimmy Paige, musician

January 10

Finishing second place isn't in your plan, but it happens often. It's better than last place, although you'll never let that happen! Get over that "lost sheep/hermit" feeling. Having whacked your emotions, let's put the past behind and concentrate on taking care of everyday business, of family, of good health and welfare, and let Napoleon be emperor. Coloring in black and white, your soul steams always over mortality issues; consider modern remedies for handling these, champ!

Since money can slip through your fingers and others cannot be trusted to put your interests first, managing your savings and earnings is something you should not ignore, even though you need time for your many other pursuits and family. To keep connected, host a family reunion every other year. When outdoors, roll your pants up and get closer to nature.

Love

The 1/10 is intelligent and easily irritable, needing constant emotional stimulation and new, exciting experiences, which can make it difficult for anyone trying to live up to your high expectations. You categorize everybody (my "gossip friend," my "travel buddy," my "shopping pal") and insulate your and your partner's private lives from public endeavors. In order to maintain peace and harmony, you must learn how to make sacrifices, and let your lover be more than just a label.

Money

Dynamic and versatile, you have a socially savvy personality, and a keen ability to get what you want and promote your ideas. With your quick mind, natural sympathy and ability to "read" people, you have strategic skills that can be an asset to you in the business world and fields of management or psychology. Your methods of pursuing goals are always within the guidelines of sound personal convictions and ethical standards.

Famous People Born on This Day

Female

Pat Benatar, singer
Galina Ulanova, ballerina
Gisele McKenzie, entertainer
Karen & Sarah Josephson, twin
    synchronized swimmers
Dame Barbara Hepworth, sculptor

Male

George Foreman, boxer
Paul Henreid, actor
Sal Mineo, actor
Jim Croce, songwriter
Donald Brooks, fashion designer

January 11

A parent/child mixed personality, your soul has past-life connections to all types of families, from peasant nomads on dusty plains to royalty in marble palaces. A prince or princess? Not nowadays, though it would help. A writer/scholar, a teacher, a programmer—this can be you, Mr./Mrs. Philosopher. With a distinct sense of values resonating within, you truly can feel others' highs and lows. Try not to see simple things and details as cold, but as entities that you can put to very good use.

Emotional yet very much an adult even in your early years, you take things very personally, particularly feeling hurt by those evil scumbags—the opposition. Teamwork wins, so strengthen your own team by sharing and helping the key people around you, especially family members who are not your age. For fun, host your own web site.

Love

You enjoy companionship, and don't like working by yourself. Developing a philosophical perspective and overcoming a tendency to worry can help you establish emotional stability. Fortunately, 1/11-born possess charm, diplomatic skills, and non-aggressive powers of persuasion that help you attract friends and lovers. You are tolerant of others' weaknesses, believing that things will work out in time

Money

You think that you're getting ahead financially, because it's so easy for you to spend, spend, spend. The more you have, the more things you own, and the more people you meet, the better you feel. You learn quickly (although not easily), and retain what you learn. Your magical mix of social insight and emotional sensitivity ensures that, with discipline and determination, you will be successful in any career you choose.

Famous People Born on This Day

Female

Mary Rodgers, composer
Alice Paul, Equal Rights
   Amendment advocate
Tracy Caulkins, Olympic swimmer
Naomi Judd, singer
Vicki Peterson, guitarist

Male

Alexander Hamilton, U.S. statesman
William James, philosopher
Bobby Goldsboro, singer
Rod Taylor, actor
Alan Paton, novelist

January 12

Curious and reverent, cool you is fond of things "old"—or is it tradition? You make a wonderful teacher and compatriot and don't mind hard work—what hard work? You also want to escape the trappings of the past, so you are probably the most progressive person in your immediate family, and you aren't the one who sat idle through boring years of school. When will you blossom on life's stage? Whenever you want to, January 12, and start by being less cold, more friendly.

Oh, you like discovering new places and foreign customs, antiques, languages, even religion, because you like the Holy Lands. You'd go wild there, anywhere where your dreams seem to come true. A good story is heaven. Breathe! This is living, but do guard your health always at home and abroad.

Love

Curious and charismatic, your effervescent personality attracts many. However, $1/12$-born's shortcoming is being judgmental, and an inability to let bygones be bygones. Always analyzing, you rehash old issues, and constantly re-examine a lover's perks, potentials and pitfalls instead of enjoying the moment. Loosen up, and stop trying to second-guess those you care for—let your lover have a longer leash!

Money

Demonstrating your expertise and work skills is natural for you; however, you never let anybody on the job know who "you" are! Don't be embittered by any occasional setback—learn, and move ahead! Because you're rather analytical and technical-minded, you may be drawn to work in teaching, business, research or health fields. Never be afraid to show coworkers your lighter side.

Famous People Born on This Day

Female
Bernadine Dohrn, revolutionary
Liliana Cavani, cinematographer
Patsy Kelly, actress
Marilyn R. Smith, microbiologist
Melanie Jayne Chisholm, singer

Male
Jack London, writer
Howard Stern, radio personality
Tex Ritter, singer
Rush Limbaugh, radio political
    personality
Joe Frazier, boxer

January 13

Cliches were invented as advice for you: two heads are better than one, measure twice cut once, the early bird . . . "wear sunscreen." Listen! Who has time to waste?, you reply. Brash, optimistic—your conscience whispers and you believe. Maybe you shouldn't. Those tangled webs get woven. Be cautious with moola; should anyone trust you with money? Still, you'd make a good bank teller, knowing that the camera will be on you—it's like stardom!

When others have a big ego, you point at them and laugh, but notice that you have a pretty big ego, too. Since you're not one to be told what to do, we won't. We will say that others will take you more seriously if you relate to their ideas, letting them make their own crazy decisions. For fun, in games, try losing on purpose.

Love

Dynamic and strongly opinionated, you are drawn to individuals who challenge your fine and fact-seeking mind, and are able to maintain a life apart from them. It's difficult to assert yourself without causing some turmoil because all you do is plan, plan, plan. Your 1/13-personality needs an active, mature, independent lover; overly dependent partners send you scampering. Don't be too bossy to those you love.

Money

Ambition, good business sense, and a fun-filled good-spirited willingness to take the lead help you in the climb to success. You understand the beauty of power, structure and precision, and possess emotional perceptiveness. People respond to your sense of responsibility and ability to work hard. Your keen mind and good organizational skills can attract you to business and large enterprises. Sticking to a budget doesn't come natural for you, but you adhere to it, nonetheless.

Famous People Born on This Day

Female

Minne Theobald, mystic
Sophie Tucker, actress
Carolyn "Amanda Cross" Heiburn, critic
Bella Lewitsky, choreographer
Saint Collette, abbess/reformer

Male

Horatio Alger, novelist
G.I. Gurdjieff, mystic
Ralph Edwards, broadcaster
Alfred Fuller, brush manufacturer
Robert Stack, actor

January 14

Sincere and open-minded, how can anyone, reasonably, disagree with you? Sometimes they do but you're too fiery to let someone "misinformed" get in your way or subvert "the process." You have it figured. Does Faye Dunaway get stymied? Did King Richard II let a few dragons bother him? Never! Using tact and diplomacy will get others on your side; adding your special touch makes wonderful things happen.

You're a little clairvoyant, so naturally you're into other people's business, explaining that we're all in this together. If you're not into other people's business, maybe you should be, perhaps as a counselor or confidant, chiming in with your opinions on just about everything. Remember to spend time outdoors to recharge. On vacations, travel with friends, or make new ones on your way to enchanted destinations.

Love

Although you have a tendency to come off as a bit stand-offish initially, it's simply a silly defense mechanism to hide your rather "I'm afraid" thin-skinned nature. You're apprehensive about forming close emotional ties because you fear the responsibilities they bring. Always on the lookout for an "ideal" lover, you maintain an up-to-date ongoing laundry list about what you require from a lover.

Money

You are full of money-making dreams and schemes (all legal, of course!) and are a good organizer, because you need to have everything your way, and move at your speed. Once hired, you work hard to achieve your objectives, and have a deep and honest business sense. Although you yearn for recognition, you are not driven by ambition. You believe that prosperity arrives as a result of careful planning and by keeping your cool.

Famous People Born on This Day

Female
Faye Dunaway, actress
Sydney Biddle Barrow, madam/
    author
Shannon Lucid, astronaut
Ludmila Pinayeva, kayak champion
Clara Kathleen Rogers, composer

Male
Albert Schweitzer, humanitarian
William Bendix, actor
Julian Bond, politician
Marjoe Gortner, evangelist
L.L. Cool J (James Todd Smith),
    rapper

January 15

Suddenly, when your turn comes, others will look to you to take the lead, and you can. Love is a key word for you, not light love, but dignified, deep, dramatic love. So there you are—ready, willing, able—a visionary, dependable, maybe with deep pockets, maybe with a legacy to fulfill. It's not luck—you were born that way, a rough beauty. Sad to say there's karmic pitfalls: be careful to avoid an early end due to an accident, even unspeakable trouble.

Being a mere mortal, your body is not an indestructible machine, so you do need to protect your health and well-being first and foremost, then throw your body, mind, and soul into your chosen avocations, which, by the way, were not ordained at birth—it just seems that way. Never be afraid to take the lead role.

Love

Your 1/15 birth energies draw people into your personal social circle who are interested in self-improvement, exploring options and alternatives. You're optimistic, although a bit blunt. You don't make rash moves nor leap into a love affair without clear consideration. You need a lover to pamper and take care of you, rather than vice versa. You exude gentle confidence, always speak your mind, and respect the same from a partner.

Money

Gregarious and self-assured, you excel in occupations that involve logic, problem-solving, or helping the masses. Always bottom-line and to the point, 1/15s like talking and brainstorming but aren't well-suited for jobs involving emotional or medical drama. You believe that the harder you work the better the results and the greater the rewards. Choose a career that doesn't lock you into routine, or glue you to a cubicle or a desk.

Famous People Born on This Day

Female

Maria Schell, actress
Margaret O'Brien, actress
Charo, entertainer
Ella Flagg Young, first National Endowment for the Arts president
Queen Ida Guillory, Zydeco musician

Male

Aristotle Onassis, shipping tycoon
Edward Teller, physicist
Gene Krupa, big band drummer
Martin Luther King, Jr., civil rights leader
Gamal Nasser, Egyptian leader

January 16

Often starting out life in good, even great surroundings, you love to share both wealth and understanding with those with meaningful ties to you. You understand the value of freedom and are quick to catch on to new ideas and techniques, things that stir the imagination and create excitement. Rich rewards or adulation may also spoil it all, perhaps losing sight of your "self" in the process, becoming what others want you to be. To us, you'll always be you.

Some birthdays are really selfish—yours shouldn't be. Being freer than most, you are sound and dependable, sometimes a real workhorse, destined to change roles in your chosen career at least once. To raise your vitality, get outdoors and get moving, feel the wind on your face. High places—elevated—are ahead, if you're not there already.

Love

Young at heart regardless of age, you believe that there is no limit to Love. Because companionship tops the 1/16-born's want list, you're always willing to do or try anything necessary in order to keep a relationship healthy and alive. (Even though you're a bit of a snob, you hate being alone, don't you?) You are well-suited for older or mature partners—those who have been around the block and know how to fend for themselves.

Money

You hate being the one-in-charge, but follow rules very well and aren't afraid of (some) responsibility, but always draw the line when it comes to rocking the employment boat. Being part of an extended family keeps you smiling. Routine work bores you; you need to perform at your own pace, no matter how radical, or relaxed. You work best in small businesses where you're on a first-name basis with others, rather than as a faceless employee.

Famous People Born on This Day

Female

Ethel Merman, singer
Marilyn Horne, opera singer
Dian Fossey, zoologist
Laura Riding, poet
Katy Jurado, actress

Male

Jay Hanna "Dizzy" Dean, baseball
    player/sportscaster
A. J. Foyt, auto racer
Andre Michelin, tire industrialist
Edward Gordon Craig, stage art
    director
John Carpenter, director

January 17

There IS something big about you. It may be physical, or reputation, or life is very full. This may be a little too much for others to bear, but who's got time to please everyone? You have inner vitality and a need to break free of constraints. Constraints limit. Point yourself in a worthy direction, usually a profitable one, and you may wind up in charge. You can innovate, build, control, become an executive, if you learn the secrets of human nature.

At home wherever you go, you're one of those engaging personalities who learns to fit right in and get your fair share of attention. Since you shouldn't waste any of your helpful talents, don't say no when others ask you to step into more challenging roles. For stress-releasing relaxation, you like to tinker around.

Love

1/17-born are rather conservative types who need trustworthy and honest partners who are clever, ambitious, and willing to try something new. You're uncomfortable with lovers who are financially unfocused or child-like about bucks and savings, preferring wisdom and responsibility over reckless flash-in-the-pan fun. Once committed, you are a generous and kind partner who enjoys home activities and life's simple pleasures.

Money

Being productive and making profits grow keep 1/17s smiling! You're a conscientious and patient worker who hates making mistakes; you accept the lessons of the past only as a basis for continued development and prosperity. Your analytical skills and natural understanding of current trends help you excel in business. In whatever career you choose, you do your best work when independent from teams or groups.

Famous People Born on This Day

Female

Betty White, comedienne
Shari Lewis, entertainer/puppeteer
Anne Brontë, novelist/poet
Alva Vanderbilt Beaumont, women's
    rights advocate
Maia Chiburdanidze, chess champion

Male

Benjamin Franklin, inventor/U.S.
    statesman
Anton Chekhov, writer
Muhammed Ali, boxer
Jim Carrey, comedian
James Earl Jones, actor

January 18

Mind over matter—you wish it worked all the time; life would be simpler. A simple life is not for your birth date. Time is important, and not everyone is on your side. Or are they? Some say you take things too seriously, but you have to, we know, but you can do better than taking a "my way or else" attitude. You need others, and the way you get them on your wavelength is by making them happy and smile.

Your wry sense of humor should not be kept in a bottle, January 18. You could tell the teacher that a dog ate your homework and she'd laugh and still give you an "A" but only after you spent an hour after school. Patient with people, instructing others is a perfect part-time role for you, like explaining the birds and the bees.

Love

1/18-born require clearly defined, responsible and secure relationships—one-night stands don't spin your wheels. The age of a partner is irrelevant to you, although older and wiser usually wins the prize. Charming and sociable, you fit into many crowds, and have a large circle of acquaintances. An altruistic, "don't give up" attitude enables you to maintain proper perspective in your love life.

Money

Working behind-the-scenes and away from the spotlight suits you best, even though you're ambitious and versatile. You have many vocational interests, and are likely to explore a rainbow assortment of employment avenues before settling down. Always open to the opinions of others, peers view you as open-minded and capable, and employers admire your natural communication skills.

Famous People Born on This Day

Female

Constance Moore, actress
Anna Paulowna Romanov, czarina
Sylvia Pankhurst, feminist
Alison Arngrim, actress
Katia Riccilarelli, opera singer

Male

Cary Grant, actor
A.A. Milne, writer
Daniel Webster, orator
Oliver Hardy, comedian
Peter Roget, thesaurus inventor

January 19

Diversify your assets would have been good advice a few years ago when so many of you lost heavily on computer stocks, but oops, there went the hot ticket and that down payment for a space-shuttle flight! Always stick with what you do best, be it the sciences, legal field, consulting (anything but stocks), community services, or making your small private business hum. You can do a lot if you just stick with it—progress is cumulative. No drugs or alcohol, okay? Thanks.

As you thrash over all the possibilities in your head, you may mutter to yourself, as if vocalizing will clarify anything. Try to have more ears and minds involved in your conversations, please, and stop wondering about others' motives. Because you love travel and movement, horses or being behind the controls is fun, even mending things, including broken relationships.

Love

Although quite social and gregarious, you live for intimate one-on-one relationships. You are a very opinionated, willful partner, easily put off whenever anyone makes the mistake of trying to hold you back in any way. Creative and dramatic, you're very devoted and give 100% to those you love. You may not be happy in the role as major bread-winner, but you'll invest whatever is necessary in order to make partnerships prosper.

Money

Your ability to adapt to new circumstances helps you learn quickly. Versatile and spontaneous, you crave diversity and change on the job. Apply your compelling charm, social savvy and natural business sense for management, sales supervising work. The sooner you acknowledge your skills, the sooner you'll get what you want and deserve! Never lose your sense of what's possible—the sky's the limit for you regarding money matters!

Famous People Born on This Day

Female
Dolly Parton, country singer
Jean Stapleton, actress
Janis Joplin, rock singer
Alice Eastwood, botanist
Oveta Culp Hobby, news publisher/
    CEO/government official

Male
Robert E. Lee, Confederate com-
    mander
Edgar Allan Poe, writer
Paul Cézanne, painter
Michael Crawford, actor
Guy Madison, actor

January 20

Peculiar things influenced your first year of life; 29 years may pass before you're free. You may have also felt that something or someone was holding you back, but no excuses. Now let's get you to do a little positive self-motivation! It's easy and healthy—getting in touch with your heart. Luck is bound to come your way if it hasn't already, and certainly, your skills, recognized or not, are ready to take you places that will connect you to an even greater social life.

Before jumping into action, no matter how good your intentions, always get the facts first—like learn to swim before diving in to save someone from drowning. You like the steadfast, reliable roles; Mr. or Mrs. Conservative. Winter sports are healthy—particularly sitting around a warm lodge hearth-fire, all cuddly.

Love

Getting emotional stability is of paramount importance to your well-being; rejection shatters your fragile ego. You don't really care about being the "life" of the party, that is, as long as you wind up being the "loved party." You are loyal and generous, and never too rigid about your own agenda or needs. 1/20-born don't demand power in a relationship, only respect and supportive cooperation.

Money

Capable and versatile, you are a high achieving idealist. At work you are pragmatic and highly demanding about punctuality, and demonstrate your unique creative thoughts and ideas without expecting applause. Your 1/20-born ability to adapt to new circumstances is outstanding! "Time is money" for you, and you're very clever with personal finances.

Famous People Born on This Day

Female

Patricia Neal, actress/humanitarian
Eva Jessye, singer/choral director
Sybil Rosenfield, theatre historian
Joy Adamson, writer
Dorothy Provine, actress

Male

George Burns, comedian
Federico Fellini, filmmaker
Edwin "Buzz" Aldrin, astronaut
David Lynch, director
Bill Maher, TV talk show host

January 21

Helpful fresh ideas and your venturesome nature make you open-minded and somewhat fearless. Goodness and honesty usually accompany your quenelle of strong mind and usually beautiful, tall body. You get along with all genders, being graceful inside, a natural talent. A too easy life may make you indifferent so take up challenges when they come your way. Your natural "knowing" of how to win will be recognized and can take you far.

Proud to be an Aquarius, you're eager to jump right in when asked to help out, so you get kicks out of being a volunteer scout master or contributing to the pot luck. You may think of yourself as a tough cookie, but you're doughy in the middle. Getting away from your home country is appealing, so is trying to figure out those goofy foreign languages.

Love

You're a bit determined, and sagacious, always expecting a lot from a partner and the same in return. Although ambitious, you are also understanding and encouraging with others, willing to go that extra mile for the sake of love, and maintain peaceful relations. Intelligent and fairly intuitive, you prefer lovers who are street smart, social, and provide mental stimulation. 1/21s are not inclined to sit alone waiting for the phone to ring—you're open-minded and always ready to try something or someplace new.

Money

Can you say "multi-tasker"? Always on the move, you squeeze more than 60 minutes out of every hour! You're not hyperactive, although a bit spacey, and tightly wound, perhaps. Ideas come to you in brilliant bursts of inspiration, even though your follow-through may need a bit more elbow-grease attention. Being the executive or office heavy doesn't butter your bread or make you happy. You work best with teams, other people rather than solo.

Famous People Born on This Day

Female

Geena Davis, actress
Sophia Louisa Jex-Blake, physician
Gabrielle Carteris, actress
Judith Merril, writer
Katie Sandwina, weightlifter

Male

Thomas "Stonewall" Jackson,
    Confederate general
John Charles Fremont, explorer
Christian Dior, fashion designer
Jack Nicklaus, golfer
Placido Domingo, opera tenor

January 22

Bright, high-minded, and a bit too temperamental for your own good sometimes, you are one of the blessed birthdays who excels when your excellent mind gets in high gear, which is most of the time. A heavier body may be required to carry that ego around; you'll stay slimmer if your karmic ledger shows more going out than coming in. Pushing and shoving won't work for you. If all life is romance, all relationships will be steady.

Favored by the stars, many of you achieve some level of fame without even trying, seeming like walking into "it." Not all of you will, but there's something about you—make sure it's something good, worth remembering, would you? Reach out and be the helper, humanitarian, the healer, the hypocrite, hooligan—no, wait, scratch that last part.

Love

You like good old-fashioned relationships that are down-to-earth, conventional, and practical. You express your affection without great fanfare, but always employ your personal built-in lie detector for fingering insincerity in others. You would do well to choose an energetic lover who can take care of details you may overlook. You have a natural gift for inspiring change in people and are best suited for a partner who will commit and share wholeheartedly and equally.

Money

You are never happy assuming positions of power or authority, even though you're self-confident and your efficiency skills are clear and precise. You're good at planning schedules, understanding debits and credits, and priorities—you rarely take work home with you. You're not afraid of hard labor and hate it when others don't do their share. You know how to save (when necessary), and are never stingy when you have some extra dollars for frivolous fun.

Famous People Born on This Day

Female

Linda Blair, actress
Rosa Ponselle, opera singer
Ann Sothern, actress
Margaret Whiting, big band singer
Piper Laurie, actress

Male

Francis Bacon, statesman/essayist
Steve Perry, singer
D.W. Griffith, film director
Sam Cooke, singer
Lord Byron, poet

January 23

Others may take a while to get used to you and understand the courageous soul inside you. Needing plenty of space to breathe and feel comfortable, your role is to be you. Protective, strong and defiant, you can be a real champion for the cause and not affected by the elements, nor afraid to reach for the heights. Of course, crashes can occur and do, even when there looks to be rock-solid stability beneath your feet.

You sometimes have good reason to be down in the dumps, but you also have to get yourself going. Think of the glass as half full, not half empty, and make the glass half full of something sweet and delicious. Life is a beautiful work of art; land and a home a masterpiece. Leave room for others, and time for an occasional massage.

Love

You are an expressive, free-spirited lover who enjoys showering companions with gifts and attention. However, this can become quite expensive if you're not careful! You need a thrifty partner who can keep you from going overboard and to keep watch over your occasional extravagances. Because you tend to focus on the big picture, be careful not to overlook your partner's other needs. It is not enough to be generous with your attentions.

Money

You think for yourself, and don't need anyone else's opinions, but, unless you're the boss, this could cause trouble. Although you're not argumentative, you may act without considering the greater good for all parties. Whatever career you choose will require variety and mental challenge because you pick up information quickly, even though it's common for you to only glean the surface.

Famous People Born on This Day

Female

Tiffani-Amber Theissen, actress
Jeanne Moreau, actress
Dr. Laura Schlesinger, radio psychologist
Chita Rivera, dancer/actress
Gertrude Belle Elion, biochemist

Male

John Hancock, U.S. founding father
Edouard Manet, artist
Rutger Hauer, actor
Ernie Kovacs, comedian
Potter Stewart, U.S. Supreme
    Court justice

January 24

Kings and goddesses may be born this day; you're not immortal, but close. You can be precise and technical, maybe appearing stiff and cartoonish—what do they know! Your life is active and you do have executive ability, good for managing complex matters and X-ing out life's glitches. You appreciate anything that lets you travel, animal or machine, and you're particular about your diet and appearance, and about getting to the bottom of life's mysteries.

Of course there isn't time enough to do everything, but if someone can manage it, you can. You might imagine yourself as someone you're not, and create your own identity—one so much better, with power. You would have probably ended up there just being yourself, eventually. Take a personal inventory and lighten up. Always take time to improve your appearance.

Love

Intuitive and sensitive, you require emotional commitment in order to express your deep feelings. Your powerful emotions and a great desire for love crave independence and respect. Although a loyal lover, your need for comfort inclines you to settle for security rather than emotional stability and growth. Take time in order to make sure you know exactly who you want to be with. Aim to understand the shared goals of all involved.

Money

You have a spirit of enterprise, determination, and a willingness to work hard when committed to a project, which helps you greatly on the job. Your consummate skill with words can help you excel as a writer, salesperson, or negotiator. Your 1/24 personality enjoys dealing with people and loves learning. Your quick mind makes you an excellent conversationalist. However, you may be best behind-the-scenes or in a secondary position at work.

Famous People Born on This Day

Female

Nastassja Kinski, actress
Edith Wharton, novelist
Mary Lou Retton, Olympic gymnast
Vicki Baum, novelist
Tatyana M. Ali, actress

Male

Neil Diamond, singer
John Belushi, comedian
Robert Motherwell, painter
Aaron Neville, singer
Max Ernst, surrealist

January 25

Others think you can be tough to figure out and follow some rather kinky ideas that are alright to you, but could bring about troubles and many changes of careers. Drive your brain like you would your car—fast and hard but obey the rules, or else. But it's your life, you say, and you're wide awake and plenty capable; no one can accuse you of being the dullest needle in the pincushion, just don't prick the seamstress.

If your eyesight was as sharp as your mind, you'd be able to see around corners, but it isn't, so you tend to focus on the things right in front of you, here and now, perhaps exaggerating emotions, unnerving nerves. Having a regimen and sticking to schedules helps keep you balanced. Try to avoid stimulants, anything artificial.

Love

Your bright personality combined with your ability to be warm and charming is very attractive to others. You have the patience and common sense to take the good with the bad, and maintain a workable long-term relationship. You avoid rushing into an affair headfirst just for the involvement, preferring to wait for a partner whom you relate with totally and who shares mutual dreams.

Money

You are a natural diplomat at work and express yourself so gracefully that people have no bad feelings even when you have to express something unpleasant. You think objectively, as well as for yourself, and don't require anyone's approval once you understand the task at hand. The 1/25-personality has the ability to take a long view of a situation and see what is coming. Self-sufficient, you work best alone, rather than as part of a team.

Famous People Born on This Day

Female

Virginia Woolf, novelist/playwright
Corazon Aquino, Philippine president
Dinah Manoff, actress
Leigh Taylor-Young, actress
Etta James, singer

Male

Dean Jones, actor
Buddy Baker, stock car racer
Edwin Newman, newscaster/journalist
W. Somerset Maugham, writer
Robert Burns, poet

January 26

You're the perfect Aquarius prototype: lively, friendly, altruistic, progressive, unique, stubborn, analytical, opinionated, a healer and a healee, and honest nine times out of ten. Since you seldom get out of kilter, others come to rely on you for being plain old you. You don't see yourself as head and shoulders above the norm, but you are, and there's a perky aura around you, something exceptional. You definitely should continue to develop at least one of your talents.

You have refined tastes—your tastes—and probably absorb arts and music, a sort of therapy/outlet for you. You can be an emotional perfectionist and a grand speaker. Your words can be magic. Although you shouldn't, you'd be great at getting others to do things against their better judgment. For fun, try talking to animals.

Love

You may be particularly drawn to individuals who are well-known or outstanding in their profession because excellence, to you, equates to happiness. Not one for co-dependency, you enjoy those who tend to their own business and are able to take care of themselves. You appreciate a lover who doesn't discuss your personal life with others; in fact, you prefer carrying on the affair in secret!

Money

Whenever you have money, you plan what you are going to do with it very carefully, aiming to get the most out of whatever you have. To learn more, you ask questions of everyone you meet. Your mind doesn't stick to one matter but wanders far and wide over many topics. By combining your compelling charm, natural business sense, and people skills, you may be drawn to careers in public relations, teaching, sales, or publishing.

Famous People Born on This Day

Female

Anita Baker, singer
Ellen de Generes, comedienne
Angela Davis, activist
Eartha Kitt, singer/actress
Anne Jeffreys, actress

Male

Gene Siskel, movie critic
Eddie Van Halen, musician
Paul Newman, actor
Wayne Gretsky, hockey player
Douglas MacArthur, WWII U.S.
    general

January 27

That special something, you've got it. Good health, maybe not. You can get into your own special mental funk, hanging a do-not-disturb sign on your aura. Still, you should pay attention to your inner voice. Sensitivity is essential, and losing it, you lose your magic slippers. You like working with people when there's a clear, common goal; you identify highly with your social class, your brethren.

Being close to water and surrounding yourself with loyal family members definitely strengthens you, so long as you get to follow your natural calling to organize and sort out worldly woes. Basically emotion-driven, you've become a good judge of others' character, likes, and abilities. Although you may not be familiar with your own, you'll come to realize that you have your own great talents and calling.

Love

You let your friends be themselves when they are with you, and are never too demanding of their time. Your happy disposition bolsters people out of depression. You meet lovers more than halfway because you are understanding and sympathetic and possess a strong sense of ethics and social decorum. You prefer partners who are well-mannered and who conduct themselves with propriety.

Money

You proceed cautiously in everything you do, with the result that your work is always done carefully and thoroughly. You prefer long-term employment rather than three part-time jobs. Schedule and security means a lot to you. But don't be so careful that you overlook real chances to get ahead. A practical person, you don't like to make an effort unless you know it will have a long-lasting, concrete conclusion.

Famous People Born on This Day

Female

Sue Palmer, cyclist
Tamlyn Tomita, actress
Bridget Fonda, actress
Nedra Telley, singer
Donna Reed, actress

Male

Mozart, composer
Mikhail Baryshnikov, dancer
William Randolph Hearst, publisher
Lewis Carroll, writer
Troy Donahue, actor

January 28

Have you turned doing things for others into an art form? Do you ever do anything for yourself? Sure you do, but then you may feel guilty if it doesn't work out right, like in romance. Sigh! Not a perfect world, it's all relative; don't let feelings limit you, yet certainly don't stoop to rule-breaking. You're clever. That may help you rise high and bring you happiness. Not perfect happiness, but happiness that is karma's reward to you.

Reflective and responsive, you let others make the first move, then meld with them to try to improve the situation. You are a good one-on-one personality, flashy when it's called for. To better express yourself, try your hand at painting, decorating, creating—let your emotions dictate. Exercising them helps you feel peace. So do the changing leaves on a fall afternoon.

Love

Your strong emotional presence makes you noticed and prompts very quick and honest responses in others. This gives you a distinct advantage in choosing a lover because you're quicker on the draw than your competition. However, it is quite difficult to succeed in love and at the same time maintain total control over your partner, so some adaptation is necessary. You don't take love lightly; instead, you throw yourself into it with total commitment.

Money

Because of your respect for tradition and authority, combined with your ability for hard work, you know what you can and cannot do quite clearly. The 1/28-challenge is that you may accept limitations too readily and be too cautious. Bosses and coworkers respect your diligence and honesty. You're not the best with personal savings and budgets, but keep trying! You always have enough to get along, and usually you have a great deal more.

Famous People Born on This Day

Female

Colette, novelist
Sarah McLachlan, folksinger
Barbi Benton, model
Susan Sontag, author/film director
Anna Ivanova, czarina

Male

Nick Carter, singer
Jackson Pollock, artist
Alan Alda, actor
Arthur Rubinstein, pianist
Jose Marti, poet/politician

January 29

A fate-filled day and a powerful one! Your life has drama, intensity, a hunger—you are driven by something imaginary, which is just the unseen natural you. Like a magnet you attract others, good and bad, and it's boring not to be in the center of the storm. Get focused and put that energy into forms that others can enjoy and benefit from, such as legal/government professions, even acting. Keep questionable sexual conduct secret; it's embarrassing.

Gaining weight is a reasonable fear, so exercise should be part of your daily routine. Another routine would be to keep a diary of your "events" and impressions—better still, go back and read your diary—you'll be amazed how much smarter and mature you now are, or at least seem. Having your star on Hollywood's walk of fame would be a hoot.

Love

Because you understand your strengths and shortcomings, you are able to mix with people from all social groups. Because you want to understand any situation thoroughly before making up your mind, flirting and The Chase of romance excite you. You are very restless and need a lot of freedom. You like to be with interesting people, and some of your friends may be quite unusual. Ditto, with lovers.

Money

You are able to work with others and get what you want without taking anything away from them. People appreciate this and enjoy helping you. 1/29s enjoy the good life and comraderie of coworkers. You are at your best in a group and are an excellent team player. You know how to convert your creative resources into cash. Always looking for a deal, you are good with financial matters and budgets; you know how to stretch a dollar well.

Famous People Born on This Day

Female

Oprah Winfrey, TV personality
Ann Jillian, actress
Katharine Ross, actress
Sara Gilbert, actress
Germaine Greer, feminist

Male

Andrew Keegan, actor
W.C. Fields, entertainer
Tom Selleck, actor
Paddy Chayefsky, playwright
John D. Rockefeller,
    industrialist/philanthropist

January 30

How can sweet, diplomatic you be such a revolutionary? You adore working with others and there's much emotional energy fixated inside you; you have to be seen and heard. It would be nice if you were right all the time, but by golly that's not going to happen. Since you really like what you really like, do what you really like and you'll succeed. Many rules you will break, but be careful: some Y-O-U never should.

Oh how nice it would be if you could just get others to sit down and tell you all their secrets! Unfortunately, they are not open books, but you are pretty good at administering the truth serum. Anywhere there is mystery and intrigue—say, dangerous foreign lands, Russia, a boardroom, or even at a crowded dinner table—interests you.

Love

You share whatever you have with those you love, even when you don't have much. You are willing to overlook faults in your loved ones because you feel that people's shortcomings are not as important as their strengths, so you concentrate on everyone's good points. You have an enthusiasm for life that others find inspiring and catching. Since your intimate life is quite important to you, it's best to avoid the lone wolf or wallflower type of lover.

Money

You're expert at rationalizing spending money, and good at getting the lowest price! You enjoy playing games that involve your mind, such as puzzles, riddles, cards, and reading. Restless 1/30-people are born curious. Professions that involve learning new techniques or engage your hands attract you. You enjoy seeing a final product at the end of a workday. To you, dreams and dollars are two different-colored horses.

Famous People Born on This Day

Female

Vanessa Redgrave, actress
Eleanor Smeal, feminist
Tammy Grimes, actress/singer
Brett Butler, comedienne

Male

Christian Bale, actor
Gene Hackman, actor
Boris Spassky, chess master
Franklin D. Roosevelt, U.S. president
James Watt, inventor

January 31

Timing is everything and you have a tendency to rush in. Sometimes being in a hurry causes danger, or might hurt others' egos or get spouses upset. A lot of people take time to think first, or they follow orderly conventions, or maybe they don't care to hear you. When you choose the right time for action, everything will fall into place. We wonder, once you gain something can you manage to hold on to it?

A do-it-now type, you rely on first impressions and are pretty good at getting a foot in the door, but keeping up an image is not something you do exceptionally well. Still, you know that life is a lot of little battles, so you will win your share. Humor helps, so practice it. Travel makes you even more fussy. How do you get un-fussy?

Love

You make a list, construct a gameplan, and go for it, particularly in matters of love. You're not closed-minded; you merely consider yourself a goal-setter and achiever who is willing to do anything for the sake of maintaining a relationship. You communicate effectively and have a flair for dramatic delivery. You may not have many friends and loved ones, but you will always be close to those you have.

Money

You like to think big, and maintain great hope there is always a better way, another opportunity on the horizon. Coworkers admire your candid views and, most times, respect your never-ending opinions. Your viewpoints are not always optimistic but are spot-on realistic—positive yet conservative. You do good damage control and are a great systems/people analyst. You learn quite well, and what you learn you remember.

Famous People Born on This Day

Female

Minnie Driver, actress
Carol Channing, entertainer
Queen Beatrix of The Netherlands
Tallulah Bankhead, actress
Suzanne Pleshette, actress

Male

Justin Timberlake, musician
Nolan Ryan, baseball pitcher
Norman Mailer, author
Mario Lanza, opera singer/actor
Jackie Robinson, baseball player

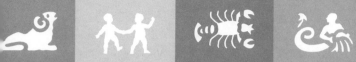

February

February 1

Heels solidly hugging the ground, your eyes look to the skies as you snatch lofty ideas, turning them into practical forms. A crusader far ahead of the crowd, you adjust and carry on, winning in the end despite the odds—was there ever a doubt? Topics that mystify others are easy-as-pie to creative, confident you, so expect opportunities to play on some of life's most interesting stages, and with the most intriguing toys.

Your toys may include fancy cameras or medical equipment or anything that lets you do things your forebears never imagined possible. Wouldn't it be terrible not to have a blender? . . . a microwave? Life would be a headache. For fun, you'd enjoy the old west, even the new west, Indians as well as cowboys, the ranch and stagecoaches, and that country slang.

Love

You enjoy the company of unusual and interesting types—ordinary friends and lovers quickly bore you. You don't expect that partners should pay constant attention to you, nor demand that a lover expect that from you, either. Possessiveness and jealousy drive you crazy. There's no room in your 2/1-life for anyone overly emotional, or who let their feelings dominate common sense.

Money

Although most would say that your thinking is neither objective nor clear, you rarely let emotions influence your business decisions. In fact, it's down-right unpleasant for you to be around coworkers who get carried away by their feelings! Although not mathematically inclined, you always seek a bottomline debit-credit balance—you love understanding how everything works as a whole. You cover the Big Picture first and then fill in the details.

Famous People Born on This Day

Female

Lisa Marie Presley, singer
Sherilyn Fenn, actress
Hattie Wyatt Caraway, first woman
    senator
Hildegarde, singer
Kate Ashbrook, activist

Male

Boris Yeltsin, Russian president
Pauly Shore, comedian
Garret Morris, actor
Clark Gable, actor
John Ford, director

February 2

Persistent, competent, and judgmental, maybe even selfish to some, you're a master at taking care of number one, bad habits excluded. Though your tastes are basic, you love caring for animals, being a friend to all of nature's creatures, and you excel in your career thanks to talents others never thought you had. You can "boss" and hold your own when faced with contradictions and multiple challenges. You manage to juggle the budget and go in style, your style, having cornered your own personal market.

Community theatre might interest you, but you're more the karaoke star—you're pretty much ready to take the stage wherever it may be, even if you don't fit the part. Home is where the heart is really isn't that appealing, unless it is like a theme park, and may be.

Love

You are friendly and awe-inspiring with friends but have difficulty forming close relationships, possibly afraid that you will lose your freedom if you become too emotionally attached. You prefer lovers who are spontaneous and independent. Although friendly and social, you value private quiet time. You attract many admirers because people like you for being yourself, and find your honesty and sensitivity inspiring and magnetic.

Money

You make up your mind very carefully, and rarely jump to conclusions. You spend as much time as possible researching every choice and weighing all points of view. (This can be very useful, but sometimes you take so long that others get impatient). Your 2/2-birthdate reveals natural investigative skills—have you ever considered a career in writing, detective work, psychology, or science? After all, you enjoy uncovering secrets—and know how to keep them!

Famous People Born on This Day

Female	Male
Farrah Fawcett, actress	James Joyce, novelist/poet
Ayn Rand, author	Alphonse Rothschild, financier
Christie Brinkley, model	Tommy Smothers, entertainer
Shakira, singer	Havelock Ellis, physician/sexologist
Nell Gwyn, comedienne	Jascha Heifetz, violinist

February 3

Your emotions will be tested, your faith questioned, even your natural kindness and courtesy mistreated; it might be true that this day attracts more trouble then most. Family and career conflicts, accidents, financial breakdowns, suspicions—it's all more than a fair, conscientious humanitarian like you deserves. Keep your faith and steer your course, make the most of education and family ties, and find yourself, ultimately, happy and in control, looked up to by those needing your help and guidance.

Since "being out there" and "living on the edge" bring the fulfillment that a cutting-edge personality like you needs, you're a natural when it comes to testing the limits of conventions. A survivor, you may find it fun to go native without going cuckoo on South Pacific islands or frozen tundra, funds permitting.

Love

You enjoy doing favors for those you admire. 2/3-born believe that love is a kind of service, and the more you do for someone you like, the better you feel. You treat people you like very well, and are willing to share everything you have. You are very loyal to your lover and friends, and always treat them fairly. Honor and integrity are important to you, and you expect the same treatment from lovers.

Money

You have a sharp mind and terrific ability for understanding ideas that aren't obvious. You're able to keep track of details and easily concentrate on long-term projects. 2/3-borns always look at the positive side, forever searching for new ways to improve things—to you, "time is money"—and are steadfast; forever seeking more efficient ways to get a job done. You easily put all the pieces together to make a whole and are good at planning and organizing.

Famous People Born on This Day

Female

Gertrude Stein, literary activist
Morgan Fairchild, actress
Edna St. Vincent Millay, poet
Elizabeth Blackwell, physician
Simone Weil, philosopher/writer

Male

James Michener, writer
Norman Rockwell, illustrator
Shelley Berman, comedian
Horace Greeley, editor
Joey Bishop, talk show host

February 4

Words are magic—any medium you choose to express yourself lets you mirror the fantastic images of life in your mind. Versatile, enterprising, ready to pepper up the conversation, you feel connected to all—the children, the critics, they are all your audience. Need to know about something, anything? Ask you. Easy to get along with and ready for the next adventure, many of you are definitely made in the Lord's image. All doors lead to opportunities, so open them.

It would be great to do something no one's done before. Think of ocean-crossing pioneer Charles Lindbergh, or even settle for Alice Cooper. But you really want to save the world, and see the need to wherever you go. You'd fit right in the clean room of a famous laboratory, anywhere new discoveries are made.

Love

2/4-born are uncomfortable with open displays of affection. You are loving, but restrained. It is hard for you to let down your hair and just have a good time, always looking for emotional support. Naturally quiet and rather shy, you enjoy being with older lovers. The more latitude and space there is in the relationship, the better. You enjoy the company of people who are not troubled with psychological hang-ups. You are a person of integrity, with high standards of behavior.

Money

Although not one to leave a task half done, you often overestimate the difficulty of a job. You learn best in a rather structured environment. Strike a balance between broadmindedness and pragmatic, realistic thinking. Idealism has a place even in the most practical minds. Since your desires come fairly suddenly and strongly, at times your enthusiasm is hard to regulate.

Famous People Born on This Day

Female

Rosa Parks, civil rights activist
Ida Lupino, actress
Constance Markiewicy, Irish patriot
Natalie Umbruglio, actress
Isabel Perón, dancer/Argentine
    president

Male

Charles Lindbergh, aviator
Dan Quayle, U.S. vice president
Alice Cooper, musician
Brandon Bug Hall, actor
Clyde Tombaugh, astronomer

February 5

Plenty of action goes on in and around you, the craftsperson, traveler, the breathless enthusiast! Stimulation is the key; putting your hands and mind on the controls lets the fun begin. You might call it work, but who are you kidding? A natural, you're exceedingly quick and strong, and probably not having to stoop to groveling for money, eventually. It bothers you to see or experience the darker side of anything, so you escape, but life is not a golf course. It needs your charity.

What's your nickname? Red? Belle? Hammerin' Hank? Your memorable name can open doors. Worry not if you don't have one; usually it's assigned by default. All things being equal, few places impress you unless it's like the view from atop the Statue of Liberty. Fascinating place for fascinating you.

Love

You have a good sense of judgment about relationships, rarely over-committing yourself or spending too much money on unions that do not pay off emotionally. Because you strive for equality with lovers, you avoid making changes too quickly, resulting in a stable, more long-lasting union. To stimulate new emotional growth, force yourself to break free from old behavior patterns and be a bit more daring.

Money

Uncharacteristic of your zodiac sun-sign, you are disciplined, careful and cautious and do everything in a structured and organized fashion. However, you may have trouble grasping an idea unless it is spelled out quite clearly and in detail. The 2/5-fingerprint urges you to learn the value of everything before you get involved. You enjoy taking ideas, and making them real and appreciated. Practical work, rather than speculative, suits you best.

Famous People Born on This Day

Female

Jennifer Jason Leigh, actress
Jane Bryan Quinn, journalist
Barbara Hershey, actress
Mary Louise Cleave, astronaut
Martha van Och-Scholl, WWII resistance fighter

Male

Henry Aaron, baseball player
H. R. Giger, movie effects specialist
Red Buttons, actor
William Burroughs, novelist
Bobby Brown, singer

February 6

What? Are you, crazy? Has anyone ever asked this after seeing some of your antics? Temper your enthusiasm with some kind of sound reasoning, and check to see how deep the water is before diving in, please? Taking care of others and not taking them along for the ride is where your true calling is, not testing fate, not partying like rock stars, unendingly. You are an odd mix, so be careful, mindful, and build a secure future honestly and fairly.

Your early environment may have been stifling so it's not likely you'll go back. Heaven knows you've seen lots of roads and places in your time. For that necessary feel of wind in your face, desert mountain activities or Everglades air boating are appealing. Your soul would glow in that glass pyramid where you enter the Louvre in Paris.

Love

When in love, you tend to do either too much or not enough. You need a partner with a steadying hand who lets you know when you're going over the edge. Much of your emotional difficulty results from crossed communication, rather than from lack of judgment. Mutual understanding will enable you both to enter new and progressive arenas of love together, rather than one partner being swept along, perhaps unwillingly, by the other.

Money

You have a very rich imagination, but must learn to control it enough to discern what is real and what is fiction. Your 2/6-temperament doesn't make you very good at math or science—not because you are slow but because you do not think that way. Employers know they can count on you to get a job done, provided that you know what is expected from you. You seek jobs that have structure because you don't enjoy improvising, or overly emotional workplaces.

Famous People Born on This Day

Female

Natalie Cole, singer
Mamie Van Doren, actress
Mary Leakey, anthropologist
April Lerman, actress
Zsa Zsa Gabor, actress

Male

Babe Ruth, baseball player
Axl Rose, singer
Bob Marley, entertainer
Tom Brokaw, newscaster
Ronald Reagan, U.S. president/
actor

February 7

A thinker who values every minute, you love to tinker and may have the annoying tendency to analyze things to tears if you don't handle your nerves better. Your heart is in the right place, usually; people listen because they know you'd never lie or cheat. It'd be nice if they returned the favor. You absolutely adore your family, their dark secrets aside. Keeping good health requires vigilance, so music, gaiety, clean outdoor surroundings, and medical knowledge are better than a pill.

Clicking your camera's shutter lets you capture the world and memories, and relating old family stories to the young ones means so much more than you'll know. Actually being at national and international monuments touches your heart, nor will you ever forget shaking the hand of a president or senator, or your first sexual partner!

Love

You are very idealistic and have many expectations about love and sex, many of which may be unrealistic. Because you set your standards high, you're likely to experience unhappiness when circumstances prove that you or your lover simply cannot live up to them. Distinguish whether your goals in love are actually attainable or whether they are merely fantasies. Be meticulous and realistic about your expectations for love affairs.

Money

You may have difficulty putting your ideas into words, retreating into a fantasy world whenever the real world seems rough. However, your feelings run deep. You see beauty in the world that others often overlook and can express this vision through writing or art. 2/7-born don't favor occupations concerning math and science.

Famous People Born on This Day

Female

Laura Ingels Wilder, author
Ethelda Bletrey, Olympic swimmer
Heidimarie Stefanyshyn-Piper, astronaut
Tina Majorino, actress
Ashley Allen, model

Male

Chris Rock, actor/comedian
Garth Brooks, singer
Sinclair Lewis, novelist/critic
Charles Dickens, novelist
John Deere, tractor manufacturer

February 8

Dreamy, imaginative, romantic, also unpredictable and wishy-washy—could you just get your emotions under control, please? Thank you. You'll be less of an easy target. Since you go with the flow wherever you go and have the nice "look" about you, smiling comes naturally, though it's not always convincing and doesn't send all troubles packing. Can we give you some dull advice to get you worked up? Escape the humdrum by focusing on a skill; it will take effort but be worth it.

You thrive in environments where there's lots of motion and comings and goings, and of course you love working with powerful people or things. Lakes and sea-lanes are a joy, but keep away from the big waves and perfect storms. A summer cottage by the lake—perfect. A home with love—sublime.

Love

You don't enter into relationships frivolously, rashly, or without caution. Once interested, you hold fast with considerable tenacity and determination. You are drawn especially to educated and refined individuals. Your 2/8-born temperament reveals a need to be very sure that your lover is at the same level of involvement in order to prevent unintentional emotional injury. Take care to avoid bitterness or harsh words—it will only hurt you both!

Money

You work patiently and privately in order to obtain answers, often retreating by yourself until you have solved the problem. However, 2/8's are very stubborn about their beliefs, forever trying to make others agree. Your strong opinions are more conventional than confrontational because you hate challenge but won't back away from one. Even though you enjoy figuring out what makes things and people tick, independent work suits you best.

Famous People Born on This Day

Female

Lana Turner, actress
Claudette Pace, singer
Marjorie Lawrence, opera singer
Kate O'Flaherty Chopin, novelist
Dame Edith Evans, actress

Male

Jules Verne, writer
John Williams, composer/conductor
Gary Coleman, actor
James Dean, actor
Jack Lemmon, actor

February 9

Noble indignation and getting fired up—you're not going to take it and nobody else should! Of course, when you're in control and living large – if you get that far and probably will—you can turn on the cruise control, soak up the luxury, self-indulge, and still tout your convictions. You will remember us wee folks occasionally, won't you? The important things, career and finances, you take very seriously. Most should. Your collection of admirers and lovers? Keep them.

Your body is your temple, so you do watch what you eat. A professionally equipped kitchen would be nice and a good place to entertain, though you can entertain anywhere by just being there. Pencil in time for these places: New York, wildlife preserves, a metaphysical trip to India, or a classic cathedral.

Love

You experience huge swings of doubt about love, sometimes feeling very confident and, other times, overly self-critical. Are you hard to satisfy? No. Difficult to analyze? Indeed. It's imperative for 2/9-born to discuss your opinions because unexpressed thoughts easily run to extremes more than ideas that are set down in words. Explain doubts to lovers and friends. Don't make hasty decisions until both parties have thoroughly examined what works for the greater good.

Money

You project yourself confidently toward coworkers. The demands you make on others are no greater than they should make on themselves. You know how to assert yourself dutifully and use your energy efficiently, wasting little of it on nonproductive endeavors. You control your temper and don't fly off the emotional handle when coworkers perform a task unimaginatively. Your dependability makes you a great team player.

Famous People Born on This Day

Female

Ziyi Zhang, actress
Mia Farrow, actress
Alice Walker, writer
Carole King, singer/songwriter
Mena Suvari, actress

Male

David Gallagher, actor
Joe Pesci, actor
Roger Mudd, newscaster
Brendan Behan, author/poet
William Henry Harrison, U.S. president

February 10

You are not a perfect 10 but may be close. Whatever you set your sights on, you pursue it seriously, intently, idealistically, and that little voice inside motivates you, or is it the stars above on this day? Maybe. You can be forceful, persuasive, and emotionally and mentally competitive, also physically firm and powerful when you make the huge effort to keep in shape. This might intimidate others, and truly, you don't want that to be your tag.

Italy. Now that's a place worth seeing. Ferraris, volcanoes, ancient and renaissance cities, the home of plumbing, opera, and the Pope. But for honor and success, look for stoic, serious people; they make good partners in business. To attract success, try to measure up to their standards.

Love

In an active relationship, you expend a great deal of energy on your partner's interests, which may be misinterpreted as meddling, depending on how you handle it. Be careful not to overdo. Although you tend to rush headfirst into affairs, make a point of stepping back and investigate where you want to go before making a commitment. You're happiest with a lover who is eager to explore anything you suggest and in your tempo.

Money

You are inclined to be apathetic and don't take advantage of assets and employment opportunities. Although you are optimistic and responsive, you don't embrace challenge. You are not a trailblazer because you lack the necessary incentive to take on arduous tasks. You prefer teamwork rather than going solo. Seek advice in order to set a proper value on your work skills. For monetary success, plan carefully, and take one step at a time.

Famous People Born on This Day

Female

Laura Dern, actress
Roberta Flack, singer
Leontyne Price, opera singer
Judith Anderson, actress
Stella Adler, acting teacher

Male

George Stephanopoulos, political commentator
Mark Spitz, Olympic swimmer
Robert Wagner, actor
Boris Pasternak, novelist
Jimmy Durante, entertainer

February 11

Your abilities and accomplishments do set you apart. Credit your intellect and a little vanity that drives you to persevere and come up with right answers. Opposition and pitfalls are reasons to build bridges—you'll need to build plenty—you cannot do it all yourself, even as strong as you are. Your inner pride means little to others; you tend to attract people who aren't sharers or who compete with you

Parties and galas, even state dinners or pot-lucks and sidewalk pageants, do get old, ditto for building a better mousetrap or playing doctor. Minding the store is just minding the store. Remedies: spend more time nurturing your children, even visit them at college and not because you're paying for it. No children? Borrow some.

Love

You have an innate good sense of proportion about what can and cannot be achieved in a relationship. Your expectations are quite realistic; therefore, you're rarely disappointed due to lack of judgment. Lovers must provide you extra challenge in order that you both feel that you are accomplishing something tangible together. Most often, you're the stabilizing influence in affairs. To a 2/11-born, love is never blind.

Money

You are a tireless worker, and give everything your full effort and attention. You go to great lengths to provide top-notch service to others and do those things that you know must be done before the urgings of fellow employees. In other words: keep away from weak-willed coworkers, aim for management or solo positions. You're confident saying "no." Deep within, you understand that you can accomplish almost anything you want.

Famous People Born on This Day

Female

Mary Quant, fashion designer
Sheryl Crow, singer/songwriter
Virginia Johnson-Masters, sexologist
Bernice Levin Neugarten, social scientist
Jennifer Aniston, actress

Male

Burt Reynolds, actor
Matt Lawrence, actor
Sergio Mendes, jazz/pop musician
Sidney Sheldon, novelist
Thomas Edison, inventor

February 12

Since no one has the right to impinge on your intellectual turf, dissuade or deceive you, you watch them closely. Listen to that voice inside—it is practical and free. Your eye is very discriminating and you may feel aloof; you are a student of the human condition, a soul participating in earthly happenings. You aim a little higher. When you set your mind to helping the less fortunate, the world is made better.

If the opportunity presents itself, you should enter stage contests—like who can shuck the most corn, or is your turtle faster than the rest. Sounds dumb, but we promise: there's nothing more of a hoot than you and your fast turtle, or having the best hot chili. What a break from fighting wars, labor disputes, and those more-serious challenges.

Love

Realistic about what you can and cannot expect from a relationship, you don't let fantasies overshadow reality. You understand yourself, are a reliable partner, and keep your feet on the ground in times of confusion. Because you are dependable and quite down to earth, your energies stabilize unpredictable or flighty companions. The age of a lover is rarely a priority, although you prefer stability, maturity, and reliability in partners.

Money

When you have extra cash, you plan what to do with it quite carefully. You handle resources well and get the most out of what you have. Although you may not earn paychecks by writing, public relations, transportation, or communication fields, your interest in how others live is huge! You have a good mind and curious nature, always asking questions. Experience has taught you to be self-reliant, and although you may be a slow learner you never forget a thing!

Famous People Born on This Day

Female
Judy Blume, author
Jackie Torrence, storyteller/artist
Maude Adams, actress
Christina Ricci, actress
Andie MacDowell, actress

Male
Arsenio Hall, comedian
Cotton Mather, witchcraft authority
Ted Mack, TV host
Charles Darwin, evolutionist
Abraham Lincoln, U.S. president

February 13

Pleasant, serene, a picture of decorum—add to that good looking, personable, steady, that describes so many of you born on this day. Plenty of love planet Venus here! Beauty, the arts, and pleasant society—you relish being there though life is not always that kind. Let someone make the mistake of breaking a rule, then you might get riled. You're stubborn enough not to let dark clouds cast a shadow on your day.

So many of you were born in the higher half of society, your lives are already brimming with colorful experiences by the time you're twenty. Pleasant to work with, you'd excel in vocations with glitter, but not the cheap, cheap glitz. Chill out down-home, outdoors, or try your hand at growing something, or photography, designing, painting, or organizing art fairs.

Love

Don't allow your lover's dreams to discolor your own desires—the 2/13's-style of expression is speaking from the heart. You are most comfortable with a partner who appreciates your honesty and directness. Always clarify your goals and desires so that your lover truly understands. Having others second-guess you drives you nuts. You expect a lot from your lover, and are willing to give 100% in return.

Money

You have a rich imagination and spend lots of time daydreaming. Sometimes it's difficult for you to be objective because your emotions influence your thinking so much. You're not interested in science and math because they seem cold and unfeeling, and their careful logic is colorless and boring. Nonetheless, you handle finances fairly well, and get the most from money by using your wits.

Famous People Born on This Day

Female
Stockard Channing, actress
Pauline Fredericks, broadcaster
Eileen Farrell, opera singer
Patty Berg, golfer
Bess Truman, president's wife

Male
Peter Gabriel, singer
Jerry Springer, TV talk show host
George Segal, actor
Chuck Yeager, test pilot
Grant Wood, painter

February 14

Valentine's Day, but you're not the dreamy romantic we think of on this day. You have zing, a sense of justice, fairness, and like things orderly, becoming suspiciously materialistic as you age. Loving things beautiful, you're not intrusive, but you are sharp-minded and critical, expressing your dislikes only behind the scenes. Blind passions, over-estimation of your role as a libertine, and raging for unpopular causes— these are weak points to avoid.

A luxury sports car might have your name on it sooner or later, perhaps sooner. Actual racing in competition would let you see if you have the right stuff or just think you do. You're a good collector of rare items, weather vanes to bird nests to hand puppets. You may want to teach college; don't say no to being a guest preacher or lecturer.

Love

You have an easy-going, low-key approach to relationships. Lovers rely on you because you stay in control of any emotional ups-and-downs. You are especially supportive to persons whose moods are steady, ones who motivate rather than waiting for you to make the first move. Your 2/14-nature suggests that you are never demanding and are quite adaptable. With your effortless natural charm, you stand out in contrast to those who dramatically struggle for center stage.

Money

Because communication is important, you are attracted to people who seem intelligent. You know how to cooperate, and do your best work with a partner with whom you can brainstorm. You enjoy a good argument, simply as an exercise of wits. Although not executive material (you have difficulty being the Bad Guy), you follow rules and tend to bottom lines. Your mindful high standards quickly understand how any situation works best.

Famous People Born on This Day

Female

Florence Henderson, actress
Mickey Wright, golfer
Betty Friedan, feminist/writer
Margaret Knight, inventor
Meg Tilley, actress

Male

Gregory Hines, dancer/actor
Carl Bernstein, reporter
Hugh Downs, TV journalist
Jack Benny, comedian
Jimmy Hoffa, union organizer

February 15

The perfect breeze makes you feel alive so it is not unusual to see you outdoors, your shirt or blouse unbuttoned, sharing conversation with your close companion. Keen instincts, natural people-skills, confidence—many of you find your way into commanding positions, but do not let over-confidence lead to arguments and estrangements; maybe others don't want to share the spotlight, nor are they required to give you your due.

Keep busy—resting on your laurels amounts to wasting your time. Study people's habits and patterns, then offer them practical solutions, not just pats on the head. Get active in government if you haven't already, in roles where you can be admired yet be useful and genuinely happy contributing. Avoid dirt and water. Ringing the opening bell at the NYSE or christening a ship or a baby—these are memorable moments.

Love

You are either too much or not enough in love. You are happiest with a partner who can moderate your energy and mood swings, someone with patience and understanding who will not be disappointed or demanding when you're feeling low. Nevertheless, 2/15s are inclined to rush into a union without foresight. You are well-suited with a lover who is older or more serious than you. Once committed, you hold fast and steady.

Money

You think big and have grand ambitions, but are inclined to always be in a hurry and, therefore, often ignore the important steps. Determined? Indeed—but not slow, nor inclined to go solo. You learn best in structured environments with others, but not so organized that you lose your freedom to think and explore. Try to learn to relax and have fun on the job! Fear of making a mistake keeps you from taking action.

Famous People Born on This Day

Female

Susan B. Anthony, activist
Melissa Manchester, singer/song-writer
Jane Seymour, actress
Susan Brownmiller, author
Claire Bloom, actress

Male

Matt Groening, cartoonist
John Barrymore, actor
Galileo Galilei, astronomer
Graham Hill, auto racer
Brian Holland, pianist/producer

February 16

A bit soft emotionally, you tend to play a likeable character, maybe even getting too caught up in the role. You admire beauty, innocence, also talent which you feel you need more of, so you have a built-in need to succeed. Insane tirades you vent. Stick with gentle pride and noble sensibilities.

A perfectionist who wants to be in touch with your body, mind, and soul, the thrill of competition appeals to you—and you're very conscious of others' opinions of you. Since you appeal to all, why not start your own business, or try out for a sports team? Bird watching, train-spotting, or art collecting are diversions you might like.

Love

You are not a demanding lover, and quickly forgive your partner when situations don't come out as planned. Your expectations are realistic, and you have a good understanding of what can and cannot be achieved in a relationship. When disappointed, you take things in stride, slowly and logically moving forward before quickly returning to second or third gear. You throw yourself wholeheartedly into unions, holding nothing back.

Money

Your mind is very active and you constantly work on being useful, efficient. Your 2/16-influence makes you a natural diplomat, expressing yourself so honestly and gracefully that no one harbors bad feelings even if you say something unpleasant. You are secure in your ideals and opinions without being too aggressive. Although you make up your mind rather quickly, you're usually right! You have a great deal of mental energy, and always keep your mind busy.

Famous People Born on This Day

Female

Lisa Loring, actress
Trina Jackson, Olympic swimmer
Gretchen Wyler, actress
Katharine Cornell, actress
Patti Andrews, singer

Male

John McEnroe, tennis player
Ice-T, rapper
Sonny Bono, singer/politician
Edgar Bergen, ventriloquist
LeVar Burton, actor

February 17

Often having a tough time deciding where you fit in—doesn't everybody?—you're a private person with a rich inner life, perhaps too private. You'd benefit by being more sociable and outgoing—communication is the key to understanding and to acceptance, which your soul needs. Many born this day can be rebellious, and what you see as valuable may not be. You may know your own strengths but need to watch your bad habits, not twittering and whitzelling as life passes by.

History and stories of good deeds interest you, and actually being where events took place lets you feel the experience. Environment is so important! You'd make a good subject-matter expert on topics you've fallen in love with, and with your good voice control, you'd enjoy a role as a broadcaster, speaker, or singer.

Love

You are a very affectionate and organized partner and expect your attentions to be returned in kind, which may be difficult for your partner. Gaining control over your lover may guarantee a continuing relationship, but it can also take away much of the freedom on which love depends. Having a lover who participates in your creative affairs will make you much more productive and satisfied.

Money

You cover a large area first and fill in the details later. Unfortunately, the 2/17s don't have much discipline with "small stuff," making you impatient about learning anything detailed or exacting. Even if your desk is messy, handwriting sloppy, and work not neatly done, you remain optimistic, open-minded, and tolerant of coworkers and job descriptions.

Famous People Born on This Day

Female

Mary Ann Mobley, humanitarian
Renée Russo, actress
Kathleen Freeman, actress
Margaret Truman Daniels, author
Mary Frances Berry, educator

Male

Alan Bates, actor
Billy Joe Armstrong, singer
Hal Holbrook, actor
Michael Jordan, basketball player
Lou Diamond Phillips, actor

February 18

There you are: a good physical specimen, usually in tight control, ready, willing and able to answer the call, to excel in the military or as a public servant, and are so loyal to the cause. Team-player, crafty in-fighter, astute diplomat—drama seems to surround you. Life is not easy so you are generally serious, appreciating wisdom and education, finding yourself in circumstances where life and death issues play out. A good family companion, they may need even more of your time.

Even on-the-go you need downtime and relaxation sometime. Stop and let go thanks to back rubs and hot baths, spas, swimming, jogging anywhere. Your ability to concentrate lets you master musical instruments; your coordination lets you dance as if possessed by demons. Enjoy mind games and testing your psychic abilities, which are substantial, right?

Love

It's a good idea that your lover likes social scenes and activity, because you tend to get depressed, or feel unfulfilled when alone for too long. You crave emotional stimulation and attention—not so much for ego's sake but merely because you're curious and quickly get bored. Choose a partner who is not too possessive, because you need entertainment, escape, and (yes, indeed) admiration.

Money

You have a clever mind, and comprehend ideas quicker than most because you're open to new ways of thinking and dislike repetition. 2/18-borns are best-suited for work that requires original or progressive ways of doing things such as design, education, the arts. Your mind breezes rapidly from topic to topic, sometimes without pausing long enough to understand. Still, you spot solutions to problems faster than most, and adore a challenge.

Famous People Born on This Day

Female

Helen Gurley Brown, editor
Cybill Shepherd, actress
Yoko Ono, artist
Molly Ringwald, actress
Toni Morrison, novelist

Male

Matt Dillon, actor
John Travolta, actor
Milos Forman, film director
Boris Pasternak, poet/author
Max Klinger, painter/sculptor

February 19

When you look to the heavens, you don't just see stars* you see stories, mysteries, hopes. You are creative; there is harmony in you—a buzz that gives you rhythm. Getting "in a zone," that's the feeling you'd like, the feeling of peace in action and oneness. You are ahead of the times, ready to pluck a solution from chaos, and often do so in the company of your tight friends. We shouldn't mention it, but do watch your diet; more importantly, develop a healthy exercise routine.

When you outgrow your childish worries, you will naturally follow your dreams and ride the crest of the wave, creating your own successes. So totally involved, you flow wherever you go. You feel comfortable in jazz clubs, underground poetry sessions, those invitation-only hidden social spots.

Love

Your intellect is often at cross purposes with your emotions, so that you either express your feelings incorrectly or they interfere with what you want to say. As a result, you may wind up so deeply involved in an affair that you cannot see what is really happening, or you may be so removed that you don't fully enjoy it. Don't burn yourself out in the initial excitement of a relationship—make it last and fully explore all possibilities!

Money

So what if others consider you impractical? After all, 2/19-borns make the world more interesting for everyone! Although not terrific with math or science, you approach your job with a fresh creativity that makes up for any lack of discipline. You have a great deal of curiosity, and patiently solve every mystery. However, you have strong opinions and hate to have anyone challenge them. Be careful how you talk with coworkers, as you tend to be pushy.

Famous People Born on This Day

Female

Justine Bateman, actress
Carson McCullers, novelist
Merle Oberon, actress
Ione Mylonas Shear, archaeologist
Frances Bairstow, educator

Male

Lee Marvin, actor
Seal, singer
Jeff Daniels, actor
Nicolaus Copernicus, astronomer
Prince Andrew of Great Britain

February 20

On your own and in your deeper inner world, there's a dream-weaver eager to participate mentally or physically in life's fast lane, though a lot of time is spent in thought, unwinding life's mysteries, color-coding relationships and issues, solving life's problems, making money . . . stop thinking and start doing! Broadminded and sociable most of the time, you have to control those moments when you turn temperamental, cautious one moment, en fuego the next.

Not pushy or overly ambitious, you'd benefit from setting goals for everything you want or have to do. Get organized. Since you don't like to be forced to sit, large crowds aren't your cup of tea, nor is patience your best virtue. Explore for gold or precious stones; hike or ride anything and absorb the earth's magical beauty before it is all gone.

Love

You're humorous, open, and candid about your feelings, seldom holding back opinions to your lover. 2/20-borns need a partner who has both feet on the ground, a trustworthy and cozy complement whose advice you can listen to. You have a compulsive sort of generosity—as a result, you may heap too much affection upon your lover, which may smother instead of nourish. Learn to pace yourself. Don't allow your deep emotions to make you lazy or to take a lover for granted.

Money

The 2/20-challenge is keeping communications with others clear. Your rational mind is strongly influenced by your imagination and ideals. You are very sensitive to those around you and often react before they say anything, which may add some confusion to your daily dealings with others. Seek employment that is well-defined and doesn't require competition. You always get the job done!

Famous People Born on This Day

Female
Gloria Vanderbilt, fashion designer
Sandy Duncan, actress
Buffy Sainte-Marie, folksinger
Patty Hearst, heiress
Cindy Crawford, actress

Male
Brian Littrell, singer
French Stewart, actor
Robert Altman, film director
Sidney Poitier, actor
Ansel Adams, photographer

February 21

When aroused, you light up and show your courage, temper, and ambition, but until then you're seen as passive, maybe too cautious, even lazy. What do they know? You're not as timid as you are moody, having deep feelings and wanting security, not satisfied until you get your share of pleasure and prestige. We suspect you're up to something good, because you are creative and capable even if you tend to change careers and romance partners often.

Clothes do make the person—the quality of your own clothes is a good indication of where you are on life's ladder. Same for your vehicles. Improve your wardrobe to improve your self-image; ditto for your home and the people in it. Create a feeling of comfortable power, and be sure to have a clean fountain or aquarium.

Love

The 2/21-mix brands you an idealist who requires that lovers live up to your very special standards. You know what you want, and specifically outline your ideals and priorities. In matters of romance, you are never vague or soft-spoken. However, you're very forgiving and value intentions more than results. Make sure that significant others truly understand you, and appreciate your wealth of fantasies.

Money

It's difficult to reach agreements with coworkers because you're rather stubborn and set in your ways. Your do-it-now and move-forward attitude is rarely influenced by feelings or intuitions. Conservative and practical—although numbers and figures are not your strength—you're well-suited for managerial positions. You keep your mind busy on the job and leave all personal stuff home.

Famous People Born on This Day

Female

Erma Bombeck, columnist
Edna St. Vincent Millay, poet
Nina Simone, singer/songwriter
Tyne Daly, actress
Barbara Jordan, politician

Male

Kelsey Grammer, actor
Sam Peckinpah, film director
David Geffen, music producer
Andres Segovia, classical guitarist
Patrick Murphy, multi-millionaire

February 22

An intriguing, altruistic, almost spiritual being, you may feel like a bit of an outsider in your surroundings, suspicious or superstitious—but that makes you more perceptive, which you usually use to your advantage in business—to meet your goals. You have a way of getting your ideas across; many born this day are good communicators, some even have strong psychic powers and leadership abilities. What you eat really does affect your physical health.

Bright, you're a bit of a politician and hold sway over others due to your organizational abilities. It is okay to dabble in government even if it's just heading up a volunteer committee or keeping a group moving in the right direction. Having your own comfortable place and family—the bigger the better—to come home to is a true joy.

Love

Your emotional honesty, complemented by a tendency to change your mind on a whim, sometimes makes you appear to others as flighty, even though you think that you're being straightforward. You're only comfortable with one who understands and caters to your habits and desires. Having clearly defined roles and responsibilities is essential for your relationships. Be exact and discreet, not frivolous or trivial!

Money

Face it: you're intensely preoccupied with yourself, always seeking approval from fellow employees and higher ups! You're mentally impulsive, a bit defensive, and don't always give coworkers a chance to answer your questions or respond to your inspired demands. You are no shrinking violet and would rather put up than shut up. You're inclined to be a little careless about financial matters and may spend more than you earn.

Famous People Born on This Day

Female
Amy Alcott, golfer
Drew Barrymore, actress
Lea Salonga, singer/actress
Ellen Greene, vocalist
Marni Nixon, singer

Male
Steve "Crocodile Hunter" Irwin
Edward M. Kennedy, U.S. senator
Robert Young, actor
Robert Baden-Powell, Boy Scouts founder
George Washington, first U.S. president

February 23

Good mannered, generous, and considered a beautiful person usually, you are a quick learner and that catches the envious, enabling eye of the rich and powerful, though you're also a dreamer and renegade and not always able to deliver as expected. Big deal. You don't mind, instead happy to do your thing, helping whoever needs it—friends or fellow professionals—and not a slave to the almighty buck. Tomorrow is another day, an opportunity, and you'll take it.

Wanting to be well-liked, you have an inbred sense of style at all levels, so building a custom motorcycle means as much as designing a building, or writing a song or cleaning up streets in a neighborhood that time forgot. For the big getaways, let beaches and ocean breezes please your heart and recharge your mental health.

Love

Don't rush into relationships: loosen up! Being impatient, you're not one to choreograph a courtship; you prefer to get down to business (and, normally, without thinking). Time and self-understanding will help you become more skillful concerning passion and enjoying the moment. Your desires come suddenly and strong—your 2/23 inclination is to strike while the iron is hot. Sit back, regroup, and unwind whenever possible. Don't scatter-shot your love life.

Money

You live to enjoy life at the fullest! You have enormous drive and ambition to achieve your goals as soon as possible and are impatient with anything that delays you. To many coworkers, your goals may be unrealistic, but you strive for them with uncanny determination. It rarely occurs to you that you will fail. Your accomplishments are acclaimed and envied. You are eager to explore new means and assert yourself in the world.

Famous People Born on This Day

Female

Sylvia Chase, newscaster
Donna J. Stone, poet
Emma Hart Willard, women's education pioneer
Sallie Baliunas, astrophysicist
Nadezhda Krupskaya, wife of V.I. Lenin

Male

Peter Fonda, actor
William E. B. DuBois, activist/author
Johnny Winter, musician
Naruhito, crown prince of Japan
George Frideric Handel, composer

February 24

Sensitive, like many born in late February, you are quick to adapt to your life's surroundings, hoping for better, but progress may have its ups and downs. Avoid feeling inferior, desperate, dissatisfied—you can be propelled to success by making sure you are where the future is unfolding, where there is learning, growth, and you can—must—find those special places. Your friendliness is persuasive, use all opportunities selectively, and be disciplined with your finances. Chin up!

Having goals is a lot easier than achieving them; promise yourself not to give up before you give it every effort. Taking classes that teach you to manage your time and resources better will keep you on the ball, too. Diving into background history on social things like family, theatre, sports, etc. that interest you is gratifying and rewarding.

Love

You lavish mucho affection on your lover, which may startle or overwhelm anyone who isn't used to, or expecting, it. It's important to you to be totally involved with your partner—you want to know (and have) everything! Casual fly-by-night affairs hold little interest for 2/24-born. Once you settle into a union, you're a model of steadfastness and often the main source of stability. Use your magnetism carefully and gently. Overdoing is a persistent problem.

Money

Planning every step on the job is essential, along with knowing when to act and when not to. You know that even with driving ambition, striving for significance is not enough unless it satisfies a clearly pictured mental vision. You are hopeful yet realistic, eager yet serious, assertive yet deliberate. Your 2/24-nature keeps you orderly, and you know how to unclutter your work life by letting go of nonessential elements that interfere with progress.

Famous People Born on This Day

Female

Renata Scotto, opera singer
Kristin Davis, actress
Paula Zahn, news anchorwoman
Linda Cristal, actress
Marta Marzotto, countess

Male

Billy Zane, actor
Eddie Murphy, comedian/actor
Steven Jobs, founder, Apple computers
Enrico Caruso, tenor
Michel LeGrand, composer

February 25

Fiery yet refined and maybe a little too heady for some, your ambitions can be met if you combine them with true skill. Often we find you in over your head, usually because you neglected the "details," but you are quick to recover but timid about making excuses. Feeling destined to be blessed by success, you usually are and rise above your humble beginnings, making a name for yourself despite many ups and downs, a result of karma's necessary tests.

A very conscientious person, you can be cynical and impatient, so you need an avocation—a discipline—that you can fine tune and try to master, getting you in a good life-balance. Set a goal of being a perfect being—and a better money manager. You may wind up living in a castle; find a modernized one.

Love

Your adventurous and articulate personality knows how to put into words the usually vague but powerful feelings of love. Loyalty and companionship are more important to you than passion. Because of your vibrant nature, you should choose a more subdued and curious partner, one who will mature and grow with you. Give yourself plenty of breathing space.

Money

Your work is very important to you, and you accept tasks eagerly, always aiming to improve your competence by performing everything exact and well. Your mentality is sharpened by an insatiable curiosity that doesn't rest until you have acquired all the knowledge you desire. 2/25-born do well in occupations such as teaching, writing, public relations, or any job that requires trigger-fast mental responses. Communication is your strong talent, so exploit it!

Famous People Born on This Day

Female

Adelle Davis, nutritionist/author
Sally Jesse Raphael, talk show host
Libby Callahan, sport pistol junior
    expert
Mary Coyle Chases, playwright
Dame Myra Hess, pianist

Male

George Harrison, musician
Jim Backus, actor
Pierre Auguste Renoir, painter
Anthony Burgess, author
Carrot Top, comedian

February 26

Fun-loving, well-liked and helpful to friends—that's what you will be once you get off your high horse. You'll attract romance and you'll become good at soothing and smoothing, too. Any strong desire for self-empowerment also includes some mistakes and injuries; survivors like you learn from these. You have a creative streak plus an able mind for things technical, mechanical—all pointing to success as long as you don't upset the powers that be.

A good way to express yourself is in writing letters and poetry where you can read and review your ideas before publishing them and paying the consequences if they're wrong. You'd benefit by having a true close friend to bounce ideas off of, but you can also do that with just about anyone, which wins them over to you.

Love

Although you live and breathe for an honest and devoted union, you often overstate your case. You voice your opinions spiritedly and concisely but not always realistically. You demand honesty between you and your lover, and above everything else, sincerity. You believe that everybody has flaws but can change, improve on their shortcomings. You strive to maintain a strong sense of ethics and social decorum.

Money

Your picture-perfect way with words and intuitive insight about schedule help you cope with difficult employment or financial problems. You're eager to learn more and more and for the chance to apply your discoveries, share your beliefs. You are very aware of the world around you, and your possibilities are unlimited. You understand your capabilities and shortcomings and are rarely at a loss for words.

Famous People Born on This Day

Female

Margaret Leighton, actress
Betty Hutton, actress
Bree Walker, investigative reporter
Madeleine Carroll, actress
Erykah Badu, singer

Male

Michael Bolton, singer
Johnny Cash, singer
Tony Randall, actor
Wild Bill Cody, Western showman
Victor Hugo, author

February 27

An "idea person" with love in mind, your magnetic personality attracts attention, often stirring the desires within others, some you'd rather do without, and should. So, you understand, moderately, human nature, the good and the bad, and cherish your special role in life's dramas. You are a professional, or try to be, with a strong desire for self-improvement, also reserving time for tenderness and caring, sometimes putting on a pouting show but surviving the challenges, a lion in sheep's clothing.

Like many born in late February, you're a perceptive soul who can feel comfortable most anywhere, inspired by the simplest human gestures, a bit of a psychic sponge. You hate waste, love nature, and actively preserve the good life. Make quality your goal, in words and in relationships. Tai chi or other mind-body-soul unifying exercises are nice diversions.

Love

Although friendly, sociable and curious, you maintain control over your emotions and don't waste time on casual acquaintances or one-night stands. You are tolerant of others' weak moments, believing that time will eventually straighten out matters. You stimulate the best in partners, and they are impressed with your kindness and affable personality.

Money

Realizing that little is ever gained by wishing on a star, you accept responsibilities as an investment in the future. No sacrifice is too great if you know you can obtain your financial wishes. Reliable, honest, and fair, you quickly gain the respect of coworkers. You earn your way and refuse to be obligated to others. Knowing that you can succeed on your own merits, you pursue your goals independently and without seeking approval.

Famous People Born on This Day

Female

Elizabeth Taylor, actress
Joanne Woodward, actress
Charlayne Hunter-Gault, journalist
Alice Hamilton, activist
Marian Anderson, contralto

Male

Ralph Nader, activist
John Steinbeck, novelist
David Sarnoff, radio/TV pioneer
Henry Wadsworth Longfellow, poet
Ariel Sharon, Israeli prime minister

February 28

An experimenter and adventurer, travel and wanderings might become a way of life, though we'd wish for more stability somewhere along the line. Over-sensitivity may cause you to go astray, perhaps taking off on some wild idealistic crusade. Keep your eye on your greater mission—a cooperative one—then your career and romance will flourish. To keep the peace, sometimes you have to concede even if you're not wrong.

Being an activist, you learn by doing. For a longer prosperous life, take better care of your health and minimize risks. You may feel protected, we'll see. Meanwhile, be a grand example for your children and do not settle for second best. Though it is not at the top of your to do list, get involved in PTA and community events—it sends a good message to others.

Love

2/28-born are late bloomers in the romance department but are always eager to experience as much love as possible. Ever the optimist, 2/28-born's greatest romantic obstacle is expecting to start at the top. Still, you get a lot out of a relationship because you invest so much—even though you prefer pampering and ease. Although pushy at times—because of your emotional nature—you relate to lovers with fairness and equality.

Money

Because linear, prolonged study is painful and demanding for your independent spirited self, you resent employers who force you to persist at a snail's pace. Learn to concentrate and apply self-discipline. In spite of this, you have the self-determination to accept responsibility, although not under the watchful eye of coworkers. You remember the lessons of the past, but have no desire to return to it. Learn to focus your attention on one thing at a time.

Famous People Born on This Day

Female
Bernadette Peters, actress/entertainer
Geraldine Farrar, opera singer
Mary Lyon, educator
Cindy Wilson, singer
Mercedes Ruehl, actress

Male
Gilbert Gottfried, entertainer
Mario Andretti, racecar driver
Linus Pauling, chemist
Zero Mostel, actor
Tommy Tune, dancer/choreographer

February 29

By accident of birth you stay so much younger than every-one else, having a birthday once every four years. Now if you just felt younger! You are not exactly the down-to-earth sort, and fate may move you around the country a bit. You're usually willing to take a chance on something new, if persuaded. You love games and sports, so good at figuring out angles, shortcuts, and taking advantage. Try not to be so stubborn and you'll be happy in your ripe old age—about 17.

You are not the lone-wolf type so fishing or knitting isn't for you—not colorful enough. A natural actor, you relish the spotlight, though your cantankerous nature makes you an easy target. You might do well in the tough guy/gal role even though you'll always be a soft touch inside.

Love

Your ideas are conventional and conservative, which means that you can be of great help to a lover who has lost his or her sense of direction. This ability comes not so much from a talent to debate issues brilliantly but from a secure inner knowledge of your realistic beliefs. You make a great effort to allow each other the right to your own opinions, thereby avoiding many pitfalls. You hate it when a lover says, "I told you so."

Money

Once you've established goals, you accurately prepare a plan for achieving them, and adhere to it. You focus on one thing at a time and direct all your resources and efforts toward that, rarely making excuses for yourself. Being fairly realistic with money, you understand how to get more bang for the bucks and are quite practical with spending. You rarely live beyond your means.

Famous People Born on This Day

Female

Edna Swithenbank Manley, sculptor
Louise Wood, Girl Scouts director
Gretchen Christopher, singer
Patricia McKillip, writer
Raisa Smetanina, Olympic champion

Male

Ja Rule, rap artist
Jimmy Dorsey, big band leader
Antonio Sabato, Jr., actor
Jack Lousma, astronaut
William Wellman, film director

March

March 1

Boys born this day can be rascals, girls eager for excitement and girl games; both are a bit stubborn and competitive, determined that their voice be heard. Stop being so touchy and learn to be comfortable around others—they're not the kill-joys you might imagine. Getting older, you gravitate toward powerful people, pridefully dedicated to your particular cause, but as the years fly by you can be worn down by your hectic pace and "try anything" attitude.

The cream always rises to the top, and you're getting up there. Being a team player will improve your social life and help you work harder to improve your own skills. Take a break from being a thrill-seeker; you'd benefit from a slower change of pace such as reading, solving mysteries, or training animals, the bigger the better, and just relaxing.

Love

Idealistic about relationships, you enter them feeling that everything will work out fine, regardless of one another's history. You want to believe "be here now" but often wind up with the same old "way we were" issues. Face it: it's very hard for you to let go. Moving forward is scary for 3/1-borns, but they can, and do. Don't let temporary objects of affection take advantage of you. Make all friends and partners prove their worth before accepting them completely!

Money

You bring wisdom and sincerity to professional interests, and express your gifted imagination in many ways that seem inspired. You prefer to assert yourself in fields that hold a reasonable promise of security because you dislike gambling or taking unnecessary chances with money. Since you are not interested in public admiration, you don't feel any obligation to gain status. Understanding finances and conservation are qualities you need to develop.

Famous People Born on This Day

Female

Dinah Shore, singer
Alberta Hunter, jazz singer
Catherine Bach, actress
Lucine Amara, opera singer
Mylie Evers, educator/politician

Male

Ron Howard, actor/director
Pete Rozelle, football commissioner
Robert Conrad, actor
Roger Daltry, singer
Harry Belafonte, singer

March 2

Instinctive and quick on your feet—and mind—you're a natural in trade or selling, maybe because there's a little ego involved in the process—yours. Switching professions and moving around benefits you—all those experiences let you acquire skills and build knowledge and connections. Besides, finding your best niche may take time. Being image conscious, you may worry too much about your own; forget the theatrics, be yourself, and don't run from responsible roles.

Nearby chaos can cause headaches and jitters, so keeping things orderly is healthy. Sweet success and life's pleasures will knock on your door more often when you steer clear of violence and the eye of the law. For vacation, why not Ireland or Iceland, or just escape the old neighborhood and do a little bargain shopping in favorite swanky commercial districts?

Love

Even though you speak with conviction, 3/2-borns don't base their life on sound reason, especially with lovers. It's easy for you to get swept away by flirtation and fantasy—after all, it's your specialty! You live for the moment without considering consequences. Beware of laying all your cards on the table because you're brutally truthful. Unfortunately, that's often not the case for others. Be happy, and keep your dance card closer to your chest!

Money

You're not afraid to work hard if your efforts are appreciated, but you often bite off more than you can chew. Be careful in your relationships with coworkers because you are inclined to take on others' duties and responsibilities at the slightest suggestion. Spending money, rather than saving, comes easy. Although rarely extravagant, budgets are boring for you. Fantasy window-shopping and cruising through mail-order catalogues keep your mind active.

Famous People Born on This Day

Female

Jennifer Jones, actress
Karen Anne Carpenter, singer
Laraine Newman, comedian
Anne Vondeling, politician
Hope Clara Chenhalls, food inspector

Male

Jon Bon Jovi, rock singer
Mikhail Gorbachev, Russian president
Desi Arnaz, actor
Lou Reed, singer/songwriter
Dr. Seuss, author

March 3

Someone special, that's you, though you may be like many born this time of year, feeling a bit out of place, unsure of yourself and your particular role. You're a "pleaser" type and would prefer constant beauty, art, and love, though you may have to work hard to afford them. So, you do have a desire to rise high; with education and hands-on experience, you can, or should. You have the quick mind for it, it's always your focus that's a bit hazy.

Since you're so easy to impress—and unpredictable and impulsive—you'll always benefit when you first get the facts, ask the right questions, and stop being a romantic "soft touch." Filled with sexy notions, why not write down your experiences and turn them into stories, even novels, even bestsellers? Make it fascinating, captivating, personal.

Love

You're moderately enthusiastic in your romantic pursuits: cautiously evaluating each potential, always willing to give another the benefit of the doubt. That's nice. However, it's important that you maintain dignity and your set of "rules" before commitment. You're easily seduced as well as seductive. It's easy for you to get overwhelmed by flattery. Make sure that you know the difference between dubious romantic fantasy and today's market value.

Money

Be wary of fellow employees taking advantage of you; just do one thing at a time and do only what is assigned—don't be a patsy for coworkers' incompetence! Generous with your time and efforts, you can always be depended upon to volunteer your services. You simply like to do things for others, but in the process may wind up on the short end of the financial stick. Set a price for your services, and make friends with the time clock.

Famous People Born on This Day

Female

Jackie Joyner-Kersee, Olympic
  runner
Jean Harlow, actress
Lee Radziwill, socialite
Beatrice Wood, artist
Jessica Biel, actress

Male

Perry Ellis, fashion designer
Alexander Graham Bell, inventor
James Doohan, actor
John McLaughlin, commentator
Ed Marinaro, actor

March 4

Like poetry in motion, you flow along, trying to avoid the dirty little roadblocks, perhaps living out your dreams, which hopefully are realistic and include others, not just yourself. Who and what you surround yourself will probably dictate the direction you go in life, usually successfully since you're a natural at staying ahead of the pack. Try to keep close to your family but know that you'll make it on your own.

Though it appears you have the right tools to succeed, still you may not feel appreciated and could be a little irritating—yes, you, perhaps becoming embroiled in emotional controversies or legalities. Think in terms of things and ideas rather than people. For an emotional eye-opener, try some offbeat roles, and walk a mile in the other person's shoes.

Love

Although you have a rich fantasy mind, you're a devoted partner and are uncomfortable playing the field. There's a "someone" for everybody, you feel. You're not inclined to settle for second-best, but not always on top of knowing what's real, hot or true. Ask the opinions of friends, elders, teachers. You have a tendency to latch on to a lover quickly and without thinking. Seek the advice of those you respect before going exclusive.

Money

Your superiors think well of you as a competent employee who isn't afraid of work, although your friends may criticize you for doing more than your share. It's fine to be of service, but you risk being exploited by those whom you serve. Social work, welfare programs, rehabilitation and therapy would be satisfying to you and helpful to others. Treat yourself to the occasional perk; don't be such a fuss-budget and worry about savings all the time!

Famous People Born on This Day

Female
Miriam Makeba, singer
Paula Prentiss, actress
Barbara McNair, entertainer
Marcella Grady Jennings, rancher
Patsy Kensit, actress

Male
Antonio Vivaldi, composer
Knute Rockne, football coach
Billy Gibbons, guitarist
Charles Walgreen, Jr., pharmacist
Giovanni Schiaparelli, astronomer

March 5

A powerful birthday—can you handle the electric emotions, the big issues, big responsibilities, tense deadlines, and competition? Of course, and do in your own way, so personably, smiling and assuring and producing results and good vibes. But, not too much confidence, please, because often you rise early in life only to slow a bit later. Right now, keep playing up your strengths, charming the audience, kicking the blues, and turning up hope.

Being alone once in a while is not a bad sign—it's time that you can spend on y-o-u. Polish up on your great artistic skills, hum a tune and relax, take your favorite pet for an extended walk. Get on the phone and get the family together for the holidays –rent a floor at a resort hotel for a special thank-you party!

Love

You either do too little or too much when in love. It's not from lack of judgment—you have distinct guidelines of wants and don't wants. It's just that you're naturally responsive to everybody and always have a very wet shoulder—damp from others' sobs. Sure, you're easy to talk with—and everybody likes you for that. Mature, stable, and independent types suit your love-style best.

Money

Over-estimating what others expect, you go to great lengths in your desire to gain approval. Do those things that you know must be done before doing anything that coworkers suggest. Learn to say no when appropriate—not an easy thing for you. Your employment attitude is admirable, so don't fault yourself for others' shortcomings. You work in hesitant spurts of enthusiasm followed by periods of mental frustration for not completing what you start. Be nice to yourself!

Famous People Born on This Day

Female

Samantha Eggar, actress
Leontyne T. G. Kelly, bishop
Mary Rose Oakar, U.S. congress-woman
Marsha Warfield, comedienne
Marcia McCabe, actress

Male

Jake Lloyd, actor
James Noble, actor
Rex Harrison, actor
Chou En-lai, Chinese premier
Dean Stockwell, actor

March 6

Getting "geared up" for tomorrow is never a problem but finding that level of perfection you so long for is. A bit of an actor and not all that confident, you're not always content in your role unless it's Mr. Shakespeare himself directing the play. Others appreciate your sunny side, so magnanimous, whispering wisdom in the boss's ear and nursing along the innocent lambs and struggling souls. Not everyone has the freedom you do nor such a distinctive, noble appearance.

A deep, fiery soul, you live in a world of thoughts and ideas; you can snatch solutions from the cosmos and make them work now. You've learned much at universities or seminaries, as an intern, or as you traveled among the enlightened. Nothing makes you happier than to have lifted another to a higher level.

Love

Although a tad quirky, you have a gentle and harmonious disposition. Optimistic about the success of your relationships, you feel reasonably secure that your trust in people will not be violated. You don't have to work hard at good intentions because your motives are always upstanding and admirable. Combined with your rich originality, you have a talent for turning sow's-ear situations into silk purses.

Money

Although you are sympathetic and kind to others, you mind your own business and don't discuss your personal life with coworkers. (Smart!) You enjoy routine and schedule and are always dependable, eager to learn from experience. You rarely overextend yourself when buying on credit, always having the money when payments are due. (Paranoic, or practical?) You're not afraid of responsibility nor do you doubt your competence.

Famous People Born on This Day

Female

Mary Wilson, singer
Elizabeth Barrett Browning, poet
Valentina Teresrova, first woman in space
Sarah Caldwell, opera producer/symphony conductor
Kiri Te Kanawa, soprano

Male

Shaquille O'Neal, basketball player
Tom Arnold, comedian
Alan Greenspan, Federal Reserve Board chairman
Rob Reiner, actor/director
Lou Costello, comedian

March 7

People should accept you for just being Y-O-U and stop trying to make you into something you're not. That's what you might say, but others wonder, who are you, really? Stop being every man or every woman and be that unspoiled, inquisitive child again. Ask questions and wear funny shoes and skip Sunday school occasionally, but still consider and encourage other people's ideas and input. Be willing without taking risks. You are pretty smart!

Since life is art and because your imagination may be on science or religion, you probably have that desire to interpret things in a unique, memorable way. What you need is a big stage and captive audience. Before grabbing the microphone, first test to see if what you're saying might be full of baloney. We want facts; skip the preachy bluster, please.

Love

Superficial emotional matters don't clutter your life. You give lovers many chances to demonstrate their understanding and express their opinions because you believe that honesty is the only policy. You enjoy partners who are not identical to your belief systems because it engages your mind and keeps you thinking, curious. However, beware of slick-talking lovers and here-today, gone-tomorrow types. You like reliability.

Money

A perfectionist, you aren't content unless you can do your very best at all times. Your instinct for self-preservation is strong and you rarely let anybody walk all over you. Granted, you're not the most confident—simply straightforward and determined. Employers recognize your strength and productivity even though you're not one to seek approval. 3/7-born want to do a good job and get it done efficiently.

Famous People Born on This Day

Female

Anna Magnani, actress
June Wayne, lithographer/artist
Janet Guthrie, racecar driver
Janet Collins, ballerina
Anne Kristen, actress

Male

Lord Snowden (Anthony Armstrong Jones), photographer
Michael Eisner, Disney executive
Luther Burbank, botanist
Maurice Ravel, composer
Piet Mondrian, painter

March 8

Daring, sometimes careless, reasonably reasonable, and probably with a head like a sharpened pencil or something that makes your face noticeable, you feel a need for attention and have some interesting stories to tell, and don't mind telling them. There is a sense of nobility about you, or are you just a bit stuck-up? Who cares! You enjoy passion in its many forms and aren't intimidated by the so-so competition.

Brave and keen, you love exploring, discovery, whether it be getting to know people or just what's out there. Step right in! Even in your challenging, serious occupation, you can joke and play; you'd make a good missionary except the natives would probably boil you for dinner! Stay out of Africa and in Hollywood or on Broadway.

Love

Although private and self-protective, you respond to the highest ideals of your lover and are enriched by him or her through your sensitive and romantic nature. You're reasonably permissive with those who fail, as long as they earnestly try to succeed. You control your deep love nature until your feelings signal that you have found a suitable partner.

Money

Not the most ardent laborer, you seek effective ways to make money with the least amount of physical or mental effort. It's not that you're lazy or afraid to take chances, however. You simply don't trust only to luck. You ponder and examine the details of every proposal and intuitively evaluate its chances for success. You give coworkers the benefit of the doubt but prefer working alone, not in group capacities. But you don't arouse suspicion or criticism from those you deal with because you rarely appear threatening.

Famous People Born on This Day

Female
Lynn Redgrave, actress
Carole Bayer Sayer, singer
Cyd Charisse, dancer/actress
Claire Trevor, actress
Lynn Seymour, dancer

Male
James Van Der Beek, actor
Freddie Prinze, Jr., actor
Mickey Dolenz, musician
Oliver Wendell Holmes, U.S.
    Supreme Court justice
Alan Hale, actor

March 9

"I'm a Pisces," you might announce, not stopping to think who you're talking to. Negligence! You don't attract trouble, you're just not making a good solid effort to avoid it. Inside, your heart is warm, your nature is sweet when not hurried, which is too often. Slow down, thoughtful Pisces.

You've had your share of hardships but carry on, developing stronger ties to your family and mate. If you're not in the medical profession already, you might volunteer, but avoid the hospital kitchen and overeating generally. Get away and put your feet up at a swanky beach resort and sip one of those drinks with an umbrella in it.

Love

You're never reckless or impulsive in romantic affairs, largely because you abhor rejection. You logically audition and "test" potential paramours. You are fearless in defending your rights, and may surprise lovers with your ruthless courage in the face of overwhelming odds. You identify with people who are not content to stand still in their development and are always eager to improve themself. You prefer mature, independent partners who pull their fair share.

Money

Although you enjoy receiving gifts, you prefer to reciprocate with favors and don't often spend money, except on yourself. You're not selfish, simply self-aware in the dollars-and-cents department. You have the knack for doing the right thing at the right time, or being in the correct place when an opportunity is presented. Always punctual, "time" means "money" to you. You don't have an "easy come, easy go" attitude concerning finances.

Famous People Born on This Day

Female
Jackie Wilson, singer
Keely Smith, singer
Irene Papas, actress
Joyce Van Patten, actress
Faith Daniels, news anchor

Male
Bobby Fischer, chess player
Mickey Spillane, author
Emanuel Lewis, actor
Yuri Gagarin, astronaut
Raoul Julia, actor

March 10

An artist at heart, a 9 to 5 personality you are not, though you are good at dressing up for any part. Cultured and perhaps raised away from your parents, you need free, uncluttered time to express yourself, beautifying the environment and contributing to society, finding your way into intelligent social circles. The body is not as strong as the mind, but you have a fire inside that lets you experience life fully, going forward in your own style.

Expressive on the outside, a firebrand within, a quick learner, you'd make a good model, even a teacher, but above all else you love shopping for the finest things so you can show how the real you feels. Take a shopping holiday every so often, or go to the old family retreat. Don't forget your camera, or to flirt.

Love

You are loyal to those you care for, and even though you may not have a wide circle of friends or lovers, you value the ones you have. You're not easily "turned on" by just anybody and are somewhat of an isolationist—act warmer and lower those nervous, self-imposed barriers! Be available when lovers need you, but don't get too caught up with your own priorities or be a nuisance when others don't.

Money

Being well-informed and staying realistic is a challenge for you, but one that you live and breathe for every day. By understanding your failings and shortcomings, you work hard to transform your weak qualities so they don't restrict or limit you and take one slow but steady step at a time. Make sure that your compliant temperament doesn't make you a dumping ground for fellow employees' demands. You know who are, even though you might have to continually remind others.

Famous People Born on This Day

Female

Sharon Stone, actress
Harriet Tubman, abolitionist
Pamela Mason, actress/writer
Shannon Miller, Olympic gymnast
Jasmine Guy, actress

Male

Prince Edward of Great Britain
Chuck Norris, actor
Bix Beiderbecke, jazz musician
Jethro Burnsburns, musician
Dean Torrance, singer

March 11

Are you trying hard enough? Are you getting out to see the good part of our world, or do you fear the bad? Indeed, you should be careful, cautious and perceptive, but don't let this limit you! You are talented; make the extra effort to become more of an expert. You're not the quitter-type; you have faith. For a better social life, like everything else, you'll have to take the initiative, even if it's baby steps.

Since others are so good at telling you what to do, you get tired of listening—what would you do if you were in charge? Don't just think, do it. Be persuasive and call up all those details, facts, and numbers.

Love

Don't fall into the trap where you think that you are responsible for your friend's and lover's sloth. Unfortunately, you tend to form romances with individuals who need you much more than you need them. Be wary of lovers who exploit and take advantage of you. You simply have to learn that you are worth more than you realize! Your love-history hints that others find you an easy mark or victim. Maintain integrity, and keep your eyes open!

Money

Once you gain proper perspective about work obligations, you plan well and get the job completed. However, your tendency to be overly accommodating is a big problem. Give attention to your responsibilities and needs before thinking about beyond–the–call–of–duty work. You understand how to budget personal finances but must learn the same concerning time and boundaries. You run the risk of exhaustion or debt unless you discipline yourself and slow down.

Famous People Born on This Day

Female
Dorothy Gish, actress
Tina Louise, actress
Eleni Gatzoyiannis, heroine
Thora Birch, actress
Letoya Luckett, singer

Male
Rupert Murdoch, media tycoon
Bobby McFerrin, singer
Lawrence Welk, bandleader
Sam Donaldson, journalist
Douglas Adams, author

March 12

A real live wire, you wouldn't want others to think you're not out there on the edge, although inside you're the struggling artist type with a plan, a goal of having lots of admirers and lovers, which you know you might not be able to handle, but don't mind trying. Winner takes all! Beside all your disagreements and quirks, you think you're a humanitarian. Maybe, but don't try playing the martyr with us . . . just make us happy.

Since rocket ships to Mars aren't a reality yet, why not a trip to the Moon? Or, how about a song or story about it? Try sitting long enough to write your novel, or pen poetry. Keep being productive, since your laurels aren't big enough to rest on, yet. For contemplation and rest, find a big shady tree.

Love

You are imaginative, inspired, and creative but find difficulty in expressing these qualities to lovers to your complete satisfaction. 3/12-born hate criticism and quickly turn nervous in the face of confrontation. Still, you rise to the occasion and try to stand up for your rights. Because you're more of a follower than a leader, you usually attract partners who are bossy or very self-important, when all you really desire is compassion and equality. Stand firm in your personal beliefs!

Money

Because you tend to underestimate your capabilities, you are easily intimidated by fellow employees who could use your generosity or ideas, and use them for their own benefit. It's one thing to be accommodating to coworkers, but being a doormat is something else! Being well thought of doesn't relieve your responsibilities and can frustrate your creative abilities. Don't try to be liked by everyone.

Famous People Born on This Day

Female

Liza Minnelli, entertainer
Lupe Anguiano, activist
Barbara Feldon, actress
Elizabeth Vaughan, soprano
Candy Costie, Olympic synchro-
nized swimmer

Male

Jack Kerouac, writer
James Taylor, singer
Al Jarreau, jazz singer
Edward Albee, playwright
Prince Henry the Navigator, explorer

March 13

Miss manners or liberator-for-the-cause, you are a smart cookie in your prime, capable of a little more soft treachery than society might appreciate. It's okay to be bizarre but not ugly, and you have a right to change your mind for any good reason. Actually, you're quite learned and slick, so even if you cannot start your own cult, you can succeed in business, usually a group-oriented enterprise.

A brain but too cool to be a nerd, tight collars are not for you, though dressing to impress has its little titillations. Honesty is not your strong suit, and now would be a good time to return all those things you've borrowed. Try this role: save the mountaintop squirrels who'll be wiped out if your investment company's telescope is built there.

Love

Security is very important to you, and you have a tendency to link up with lovers for financial advantage, although that usually means making substantial compromises. You are inclined to go along with people who are incompetent and to accept a subservient position to them. Stop it! Develop your talents, and expand your self-assurance. Refuse to be involved in relationships that make enormous demands on you.

Money

Even though it's hard for you to admit, you don't want coworkers to say that you didn't try hard enough, so you're apt to over-do. Biting off more than you can chew hurts . . . especially you, not them. You don't consider yourself weak or a patsy, but always are on the lookout for approval. You're competent and precise in your daily job responsibilities. Do what's expected of you first; then lend your willing helping hand (but not your money).

Famous People Born on This Day

Female
Janet Flanner, journalist
Corrine Boggs, political administrator
Patricia Amicome, educator
Dana Delany, actress
Robin Duke, comedienne

Male
William H. Macy, actor
Stephen Vincent Benet, writer
Percival Lowell, astronomer
Neil Sedaka, singer
L. Ron Hubbard, Scientology
    founder

March 14

Great triumphant love or sensual, steamy pits—either is fine so long as there's lots of love playing, even at work. You can get so deeply involved! And when you aim, who can say no to you? You seem so catchable, easily influenced, cooperative, even naïve. But, remember that making a habit of wrong relationships will have others wondering where your mind is at. It's on dealing, talking, timing, being your own person, regardless. Who knew?

Beating the house is almost better than chocolate; having an umbrella when caught in the rain is genius! Walking is great exercise for you—lets you think without interruption.

Love

You're careful and cautious about romance—sometimes too much so! It's one thing to be a devoted partner, but a whole different story playing the poor-me/martyr thing. You are slow and careful concerning love affairs, taking time to uncover all the facts before jumping in or making a commitment. Unfortunately, your seriousness can make you tend toward depression—feeling alone when you are not. Be careful not to over-emphasize your or your lover's flaws so much that you don't see the beauty.

Money

Your preoccupation with endless details and perfection causes you much stress. You labor over trifles, worry about unfair competition and overestimate what employers expect of you. But 3/14-borns always tell the truth—even if it's long after the fact. Even though you're a slow learner, you remember everything once it's been experienced. You crave acknowledgement and recognition but secretly fear that you will succeed.

Famous People Born on This Day

Female

Diane Arbus, photographer
Rita Tushingham, actress
Meredith Salenger, actress
Megan Follows, actress
Laura Leighton, actress

Male

Albert Einstein, mathematician
Quincy Jones, jazz composer
Michael Caine, actor
Billy Crystal, comedian/actor
Hank Ketcham, cartoonist

March 15

That's not me, you will say. How can anyone know what I'm really like? Well, it's not who you think you are, it's what others think that counts. You're full of all kinds of crazy ideas anyway, sometimes so strong-minded that you can win over any odds—usually. Gifted, multi-talented, a faithful believer—you might admit to that. You're better-liked than you believe and enjoy social interplay and being right all the time. So there.

Intense and strong enough to meet any challenges in your career, you earn the right to speak your mind and follow your special interests. If you need more, try singing, sculpting, or inventing a better mousetrap. Clear the game board—the champ is on the scene. Try not to win on technicalities. For a challenge, try picking up some real deals at auctions.

Love

Your greatest handicap is an unwillingness to let go of the past, prior mistakes, and personal history. Try to maintain a realistic emotional pace with lovers and not cut off your nose to spite your face or purposely set yourself up for disappointment. Chances are, you're harder on yourself than loved ones are on you. Instead of always being the giver, try asking for something in return. Receiving can being a very nice thing.

Money

Employers know that they can count on you to work above and beyond the call of duty, and coworkers never hesitate to ask for your help. Indeed, you're talented and generous (perhaps too much so). However, you need to invest some effort in improving self-worth and learning to say "no." It's okay to seek confirmation and applause as long as it's well-balanced and honest. You are a valuable team player—just be sure to not martyr your gifts or your time and money to the lazy.

Famous People Born on This Day

Female

Isabelle Gregory, playwright
Caroline Herschel, astronomer
Ann Rugers van der Loeff-Basenau, author
Sabrina (Salerno), singer
Caitlin Wachs, actress

Male

Fabio, model
Andrew Jackson, U.S. general/ president
Sly Stone, singer
Lightnin' Hopkins, singer/guitarist
Judd Hirsch, actor

March 16

You have a magical way of getting what you want, so you might want to wish for more of those things you need, such as a solid career or good health. Artistic, talented, sensual—you think positively and are in touch with your soul, believing that you will succeed, and you usually do. Giving is good, so you will genuinely help others. But for too many of you that fire within flares out of control, or accidents interrupt life's flow.

Environment is so important to your well-being, so you might want to look into feng shui to tighten up your surroundings. A good cleaning helps, too. Though you may be small in stature, that doesn't mean you should shy away from sports and exercise. Don't try bull-fighting; maybe diving, equestriana, dancing.

Love

You temper your love-radar judgment with tenderness, which makes you a loving, caring partner and friend. You enjoy responsibility, and rarely allow your emotions to distort or color situations. However, your suspicious independent nature makes you afraid of being entrapped, prompting you to run from commitment. You rarely make gestures of love until your partner demonstrates sincerity and honesty in caring for you.

Money

You don't fly off the handle at coworkers, choosing to cooperate rather than create chaos. 3/16s have a bit of difficulty achieving material goals, however. It is important that you learn to stand alone and secure in your independence. Because you hate being alone, it's easy for you to be overly accommodating to coworkers or overspend. You have an insatiable appetite for knowledge and are intensely determined to make everything work

Famous People Born on This Day

Female

Ruth Bader Ginsberg, U.S. Supreme
    Court justice
Patricia Nixon, First Lady
Bertha Knox Gilkey, activist
Isabelle Huppert, actress
Nancy Wilson, singer

Male

Jerry Lewis, comedian/actor
Henny Youngman, comedian
James Madison, U.S. president
Bernardo Bertolucci, film director
Erik Estrada, actor

March 17

Being popular or sexy doesn't always bring you the love and acceptance you need. On second thought, maybe it will. Regardless, you shouldn't put 100% of your time into proving your relationships. Realize that connections come first, then familiarity, then real bonding, maybe. Since others usually like you on sight, add in a diploma or polish up on at least one skill. Remember, though, your energy is limited, so only put the right things in your body.

Capable of keeping long hours, many of you are night people. Near dawn is your best time of day, so there should be a booth reserved for you at an all-night diner, with a fresh rose gracing the table. For a change of pace, take the gang RV-ing for a few glorious days.

Love

Your straightforwardness quickly informs lovers where they stand. Partners rarely consider you antagonistic, but you assert yourself under pressure and are never one to withdraw from debate. You know what makes you happy and, likewise, what drives you crazy in others. Although you consider yourself open-minded, your need for schedule and routine is voracious, and you have little patience for partners who cannot make up their mind.

Money

Although not an accusing type, you dislike being challenged by coworkers because you're used to getting your way and are uncomfortable with compromise. You're not a "know-it-all," simply an individual who has specific personal wants and nots. On the job, you read contracts clearly and always aim to be punctual. You mind your own business and respect the privacy of others. You rarely complain because you believe that "your" way is best.

Famous People Born on This Day

Female
Kate Greenaway, illustrator
Ann Wigmore, nutritionist/author
Eileen Garrett, psychic
Lesley-Anne Down, actress
Mercedes McCambridge, actress

Male
Gary Sinise, actor
Rudolf Nureyev, dancer
Nat King Cole, singer
Kurt Russell, actor
George Ohm, physicist

March 18

Born on a fate-filled March day, the stars ask that you be cautious, ever-vigilant, always checking, reducing risks. When you travel, trouble. In politics, wars. In romance, questions, although you may be blessed with the right mate. You have an old and tough soul, not afraid of the future. You see things in ways that others don't and can unwind life's mysteries, usually helped by a special gift or talent that helps you balance things out, with your loyal followers as guardians, keeping loneliness at bay.

Desiring to belong and achieve, you learn some important life lessons early, helping you realize that over-stepping boundaries, breaking rules, and recklessness come with high personal price tags. Capable of extreme hard work, you will need times for complete rest and surroundings free of danger. Roller coasters aren't for you, nor are mean people.

Love

It's not that you doubt every single person that crosses your path, but you're not one to take things on speculation. For you, there's always a better, or more effective, avenue. Therefore, love affairs quickly become testy or temperamental because you judge companions in black-and-white contrasts. It's not that you're prejudiced; you're merely a glutton for "how things should be." Explore a diet in relaxation and faith in others.

Money

You usually feel that the answers you receive on the job are never real or final (which is smart). Always questioning, you're always looking for options and alternatives—but you consider yourself merely "efficient," not compulsive. Few people have enough nervous energy to maintain your pace, so it is best for you to work by yourself. Try to slow down, and don't tackle more than is expected or reasonable. Employers and coworkers know that you're reliable.

Famous People Born on This Day

Female

Bonnie Blair, Olympic speed skater
Irene Cara, actress
Unita Blackwell, first black mayor in Mississippi
Queen Latifah, singer/actress
Vanessa Williams, singer

Male

Rudolf Diesel, inventor
George Plimpton, author
Charlie Pride, singer
John Updike, novelist
Edgar Cayce, psychic

March 19

A lion at heart, but without claws, you can be possessive, wanting family and friends close by as you go about your mission, praying for better days, clutching a rabbit's foot or rubbing Buddha's stomach for luck. Your career may take you far away, perhaps to college where you'll get over any childish sensitivity, or simply to drift in search of places where no one can question you, and there find peace of mind.

Perhaps trusting no one, you can be misunderstood—and you may be dictatorial. Rather than being caught up in your prideful emotions, try roles that let you escape your identity, let your hair down, where reputations don't count, only results. Seeing things from outside lets you see inside.

Love

Lovers feel comfortable in conversations with you because you rarely challenge or question their ideals. You have a clear concept of what's necessary for a good relationship and quickly and precisely spell out those requirements—unfortunately, many times before a prospective partner can get a word in edgewise! It's not that you're aggressive. Picky, yes. Open-minded? Maybe. Want to be in a relationship? You must learn how to cooperate in order to do so.

Money

Face it: you're thin-skinned and overreact to coworkers. You learn your job and responsibilities quickly, but you have an inclination to overdo or expect too much from others as well as yourself. Compromise isn't your best personality trait, even though you try! But you could try harder. Even in the face of frustration, you remain hopeful and strongly convinced that you can change everything. Look at things more realistically.

Famous People Born on This Day

Female	Male
Glenn Close, actress	Bruce Willis, actor
Moms Mabley, comedienne	Wyatt Earp, Old West marshall
Ursula Andress, actress	Patrick McGoohan, actor
Phyllis Newman, actress	John Sirica, judge
Shelley Burch, actress	David Livingstone, explorer

March 20

Dedicated and strong-willed, you're the humanitarian type, not made to compete with the lions and liars out there, but a tiger in your own element. You can be the champion of your cause and still be the perfect family person, even able to heal yourself in certain circumstances, it seems. Don't stoop to quibbling and fussing—you're best at hands-on problem solving. As your family grows, daughters are likely.

Fame is not out of reach for someone as progressively perky as you, and you probably have a local reputation which you should polish whenever you can. You'd like to teach others, often within your comfortable home close to the sea. The mysteries of life attract you, and you're devoted and ahead of your time. Making pies for church socials is nice, but your aim is higher.

Love

You're not comfortable with secrets, and seek up-front partners who clearly reveal their cards at the get-go. Normally, you scan ahead, peek and plot, and try to analyze outcomes before the cast of characters get their say-so. Don't second-guess your lovers or prognosticate your/their future (without this book); flow and go with it. Prospective lovers may quickly be put off by your uncensored expectations—let the hopeful other half have a say!

Money

3/20-borns are daydreamy; let's-all-get-along-together fantasies rarely over-power their day-to-day work reality. You realistically respond to outside stimuli, are socially alert and willing to pitch in when needed. However, you being a volunteer often comes with a price. You're an excellent clock-watch-er, remember favors and who-owes-whom. Your ardor to achieve and succeed is filled with passion!

Famous People Born on This Day

Female

Holly Hunter, actress
Kathryn Forbes, writer
Christy Carlson Romano, actress
Pamela Sargent, writer
Elizabeth Grille, writer

Male

Spike Lee, film director
William Hurt, actor
Sir Michael Redgrave, actor
Henrik Ibsen, playwright
Mr. Rogers, TV personality

March 21

Born on the first full day of Spring, you have a certain robust uniqueness that we'd expect, so bright, hopeful, independent. Your spiritual self-faith also means lofty ambitions, which if you work diligently toward, you might achieve to some degree or other. If you took more calculated risks or broke the mold, success may follow, but too often you are content with the status quo, good if you're in the military or a structured professional discipline, but maybe not so where you have to make decisions on your feet.

Fond of everything, it'll surprise others when you are loud, over-aggressive, even jealous. Who knew? Are you kidding us? So, you can be a tough wheeler-dealer. Why not try wheeling down the mountain on a bike or snowboard? Winter or summer, you fit in, Mr./Mrs./Ms. Springtime!

Love

You're bright, articulate and curious, attracted to the mysterious and unusual. A lover's background isn't too important to you. Unfortunately, your optimism or courageousness often creates misunderstandings or mistakes. Try to keep both feet on the ground while your head floats heavenly. It's easy for you to get deceived. Take your time in getting to know another intimately. "Trust" is one thing, "stupid assumption" is another story!

Money

Your intentions are grand, pure, and honest. However, differentiating reality from fantasy is an uncomfortable challenge for you. Once a guideline is established at work, you follow rules precisely and punctually. But being the organizer/manager isn't your strong suit. 3/21-borns work best with others and in collaborative efforts. Solo activities scatter your focus, scare you. You're a terrific follower, but not a leader.

Famous People Born on This Day

Female

Phyllis McGinley, poet
Rosie O'Donnell, talk show host
Charlotte Brontë, poet/novelist
Kassie Wesley, actress
Sabrina Le Beauf, actress

Male

Matthew Broderick, actor
Gary Oldman, actor
Ayrton Senna, racecar driver
Johann Sebastian Bach, composer
Timothy Dalton, actor

March 22

Just cautious enough, capable of great concentration, and usually well-educated, why is it some think you're grouchy or even a bit unsociable? What do they know? You think first and appreciate quiet surroundings, growing with and savoring each new life experience, carving out your own career or building your own castle. You would make an excellent doctor, nurse, scientist, clergyman, or teacher, factual and professional in whatever career you choose.

Secretly, you might be envious of others at times, driving you to compete and be better. You are also a humanitarian and do feel for the less fortunate, but you're not the type who throws money at problems and expects results. You'd get a kick out of detective work. Try telling a joke once in a while, or try an expression hobby such as singing or painting.

Love

You are clever and leave no stone unturned while pursuing your objectives, particularly concerning love. Your observations are instant and rarely leave you doubting. You have an uncanny ability to quickly size up situations, especially about material circumstances. But your "gift" lacks accuracy when matters turn to emotional evaluations. Take it slower, and develop trust in human nature; try to enjoy the ride. You miss a whole bunch when you second-guess!

Money

You're masterful in your eagerness to learn, but keep watch that you don't become a know-it-all. Employers respect your precision and devotion. You're extremely reliable and disciplined. Management and supervising roles come easy for you. However, it's a good idea to try putting yourself in someone else's shoes; life doesn't have to be a solo venture. Don't demand more from others than they're capable of giving—the same goes for yourself!

Famous People Born on This Day

Female

Ruth Page, choreographer
Ellen Glasgow, novelist
Lena Olin, actress
Betty Callaway, figure skating trainer
Reese Witherspoon, actress

Male

Bob Costas, sports announcer
Andrew Lloyd Webber, composer
Stephen Sondheim, composer
William Shatner, actor
Matthew Modine, actor

March 23

Having lots of "heart" and feeling right at home when there's peace, harmony and room for everyone to freely express themselves, you want things to run smoothly and do your part, providing hospitality and a smile. You're also a bit vulnerable and it hurts you to be taken advantage of, but it happens. A people-pleaser, you have to think first—be logical. All too often you are impulsive, careless, uninhibited, and waffle on decisions. That's just you, but others may not take it so kindly.

Rules are important, but some of yours are a little too peculiar. The phrase "this isn't rocket science" comes to mind—you treat things as if they were rocket science. Usually deeply involved in your demanding profession, you must make time to get away completely periodically, like to a desert oasis.

Love

Your romantic interests are stimulated by partners who are serious, honest and hard-working. A mature individual represents security to you; 3/23s become quickly disturbed by disorder and laziness. You don't waste time on a lover who wastes his or her time, or your time. Maintain your integrity and checklist, but try to give potential objects of affection the benefit of the doubt before judging. Don't view differences of opinion as threats.

Money

You're not comfortable having your plans or schedules challenged. You are never indifferent to the feelings of coworkers, but often become testy if others question you. Even though you freely volunteer to help beyond the call of duty, you always have a catch or loophole back-up plan. Being trustful of others is awkward for you—try working on that! Two heads can make a world of difference; aim to be more objective and cooperative.

Famous People Born on This Day

Female

Chaka Khan, singer
Joan Crawford, actress
Fannie Farmer, cookery expert
Laura Thorne, chef
Keri Russell, actress

Male

Akira Kurosawa, film director
Ric Ocasek, musician
Roger Bannister, runner
Dane Rudhyar, astrologer
Werner von Braun, rocket scientist

March 24

A good craftsperson has the right tools, so in your career you're the one that is well prepared, knives sharpened, lights on, bandages ready. No need for a how-to-do-it handbook, you instinctively know what to do, or think so. It's your passion that makes you so forceful; impatience makes you seem vain. We hope you can handle both. You'd make a good director, being an insider. You have a calculating mind and a good physical command of your body.

Not a person to mess around with and not appearing to be afraid, often we may find you at racing events—or social competitions—perhaps just hanging around and soaking it all in like a psychic sponge, getting prepared for your turn. You'd excel as a cook or chef; to please the palate is to please the heart.

Love

Although a child at heart, you respond best to mature lovers. You are impatient with trite, superficial lovers, preferring one whose life has purpose and direction. Although you do tolerate failure, you do not accept dishonesty with anyone with whom you are emotionally involved. Your way with people is charming and delightfully real, and you excel in social occasions. Your domestic affairs are a source of pleasure and contentment.

Money

You have good reasoning ability, make concessions when they seem advised, and rarely fail to discuss problems between you and coworkers. You respond to people eagerly, and your enthusiasm stimulates them to respond in kind. You don't hold grudges, preferring to keep the air clear by discussing your differences. Always punctual and practical with savings and personal securities, you are comfortable budgeting time and resources.

Famous People Born on This Day

Female
Kelly LeBrock, actress
Dorothy Irene Height, sociologist/
    activist
Elisa Felix, tragedienne
Irina Ratushinskaya, poet
Lucia Chase, dancer

Male
Steve McQueen, actor
Wilhelm Reich, psychologist
Harry Houdini, magician
Lawrence Ferlinghetti, author
Joseph Barbera, animator

March 25

Wave the banner and be the "one" that gets the job done. You're not the biggest, the brightest, the best looking, but you are a force to be reckoned with, often playing the devil's advocate, always questioning and analyzing, ever reliable and handy. Others learn to have confidence in you, and you're a good parent, though in your younger days you may have been a little gloomy and doomy.

You and the computer are a natural match; for better or worse, the Internet is a treasure trove of information and fun for you. Create your own web site if you haven't already. Good at science and math—if it's required—you enjoy having others listen to you, and know how to use tools to do the dirty work. Florida seems to be the perfect place for you.

Love

You are very effective in dealing with loved ones because you have a well-honed understanding of what makes others tick and are always ready to discuss any problem. For you, emotions must be analyzed before any conflict can be resolved. You enjoy the romantic company of one whom you can confide in and trust. Even if your partner has not achieved success, you accept anyone who has established plans for obtaining goals and whose intentions are sincere.

Money

Like a therapist or writer, you have a large capacity for evaluating and alleviating people's burdens. You are fair and sensitive to coworkers' relationships and rarely overreact when others demonstrate their failings. Because you are so eager to be well-informed on as many on-the-job subjects as possible, you are never at a loss for words. Fellow employees are inclined to work harder in your presence because your attitude encourages them—you prefer to inspire, not intimidate.

Famous People Born on This Day

Female

Aretha Franklin, singer
Gloria Steinem, activist
Sarah Jessica Parker, actress
Simone Signoret, actress
Flannery O'Connor, writer

Male

Sean "Hollywood" Hamilton, disc jockey
Bela Bartok, composer/pianist
Frank Oz, muppeteer
Elton John, singer
Arturo Toscanini, conductor

March 26

Youthful and fearless, riches and wisdom can be yours if you concentrate and put your energy to good use, trouble if you don't. In relationships, you need space; you're lean, rough and strong-willed—very good for taking care of number one and everyone else too, you think. Vocations like politics and government let your charisma shine. You seem to always understand the complexities, so your solutions are often the best.

One of the most energetic birthdays in March, you're not easy to keep up with, so it is often other people's foot-dragging that slows your progress. Self-help studies in financial management or acting would help you—usually, once you learn something, you've got to put it into action. Spend more time pleasing that special someone you love; surprise them with a trip to a place of their dreams.

Love

You're always candid and truthful, sometimes painfully so. And you're used to getting your own way. However, take steps that you don't get too carried away by criticism, or that you get too full of yourself. Just because you think "it's" a big joke doesn't mean that prospective partners will laugh with you. Listen to your words, and don't fret if you don't always get applause—remain real, conscientious.

Money

You don't let others sidetrack you from the project-at-hand but have a tendency to let impatience or envy get the best of you. Nobody likes a know-it-all! Even if you graduated with honors from Hard Knocks High School, some coworkers may be more comfortable in the bleachers and get perturbed by your blunt comments. You value your rights enough to fight for them when you feel threatened.

Famous People Born on This Day

Female

Diana Ross, singer
Erica Jong, writer
Sandra Day O'Connor, U.S. Supreme Court justice
Vicki Lawrence, comedienne
Leeza Gibbons, TV host

Male

Martin Short, comedian/actor
James Caan, actor
Tennessee Williams, playwright
Victor Frankel, psychologist
Robert Frost, poet

March 27

Perceptive, down-to-earth, a nature lover, you're a private person who really doesn't have time for other people's problems and noise. Very conscientious, you're a perfect friend, patriotic, fond of even the smallest animals, a really sweet person, but not a softy. Blessed with busy hands and a sharp mind, you're a good administrator or worker, skillful and versatile, good at the technical stuff, the perfect team player so long as you feel you're getting something out of it.

Because the mind depends on the body and the body depends on food, your health depends on eating right. Keeping your mind clean of chaos and negativity helps. For you, things have to make sense; life shouldn't have loose ends. Collecting antiques and keeping history alive are fun avocations. Gardening and farming are nice ways to relax for up-tempo you.

Love

You turn thought into action and go for the romantic gold at every opportunity. Past lovers may consider you selfish or insatiable—but you think that's their problem, and you're determined to prove anybody wrong who's not hip to your game plan. You're not selfish; you merely know what you want and what a partner has to do in order to make a union fully functional. Unfortunately, a partnership includes two people and everybody else ranks second. Time to grow up maybe?

Money

Be careful who you antagonize at work. No matter how many employment battles you have won in the past, the only way your 3/27 nature will truly win is when you try to get along with everyone. Coworkers know that you're determined, reliable, and very independent, and rarely give up in a fight. You're really not competitive because you hate to lose—just make sure that you're being noticed for the right reasons. Aim for logic rather than the limelight.

Famous People Born on This Day

Female

Gloria Swanson, actress
Mariah Carey, singer
Sarah Vaughan, singer
Annemarie Probell, skier
Xuxa, actress

Male

Quentin Tarantino, film director
Henry Royce, automobile founder
David Janssen, actor
Shaun Cassidy, musician/actor
Michael York, actor

March 28

Hanging on to money and valuables is not your strong point, so you should probably have an accountant or good companion you can count on—blindly trusting others often leads to disappointments, and you'd rather be reaching for the stars, trying out the latest trends, and winning. You love the land and protect the territory that you've come to know and love, but you're not known as the best "people-person" though you do know the ropes.

You hate to quarrel but do because you know you're right. You're right because you feel you know it's right, from experience. Times change so keep up. In all relationships, finding the common ground will make you more popular. You might want to try aviation or roles where structure is required and understood, where political correctness and rules rule.

Love

If it's true that thoughts create one's world, you may want to spend more time reconsidering the shared and sacred space of others. For some strange reason, you believe that you have hidden enemies and that you must continually look over your shoulder. Be nice, and try to objectively understand a lover's perspective. Don't be afraid to swallow your (very large) pride. Most times you let pressures build until a breakthrough is the only eventuality. Why not ask for help from the get-go?

Money

Even if you own the company, it's still a good idea to aim for cooperation and make friends with coworkers. You're determined to do everything on your own and by your rules—to a degree—but also feel deep inside that you cannot. Still, you hesitate to ask for help, thinking it a weak trait rather than human or common. Don't be afraid to ask for help, or kiss and make up. Be selective, not selfish.

Famous People Born on This Day

Female

Dianne Wiest, actress
Lucy Lawless, actress
St. Theresa of Avila
Reba McEntire, country singer
Julia Stiles, actress

Male

August Anheuser Busch, Jr., brewer
Ken Howard, actor
Maxim Gorki, writer
Dirk Bogarde, actor
Zbigniew Brzezinski, national security advisor

March 29

Heroic—that's you—perhaps the master or guru, or with your hands on something powerful. You'd make a good president, you think, but first you may want to get your own house in a little better order. Firm, courageous, direct and proud of your accomplishments, you may find your way into martial vocations or where you can excel at "the rules" and master the structure. Being before the public eye is where you'd prefer to be.

Not afraid of what tomorrow might bring, you've been known to neglect the bills and even your loved ones while you're out chasing more gold and staying ahead of the game. Helping children to develop would be a complementary role; young ones look up to you as a role model. Having an estate to come home to is your dream.

Love

There's a huge "eat, drink and be merry" ambiance to you—not meaning that you're delusional or self-indulgent. However, 3/29-borns tend to carry everything to extremes! Try to temper your enthusiasm for new relationships, learn how not to smother and overwhelm your partners. Granted, you're generous with your affections with a partner, but try not to be so overpowering or controlling. Less is more.

Money

Your no-nonsense attitude influences others but doesn't always win friends or applause from employers. Not a quiet type, you demand that your opinions be heard. But are you listening to your words before expressing yourself? Usually not. You never go into a meeting unprepared but could try harder to be more open to others' options rather than desperately cling to your presumed conclusions. Face it: you have difficulty accepting the word "no." Learn to understand the glorious beauty of "yes" or "I'll look into that."

Famous People Born on This Day

Female
Pearl Bailey, entertainer/humanitarian
Julia Montgomery, political consultant
Lisa J. Allen, TV reporter/attorney
Elle MacPherson, model
Jennifer Capriati, tennis player

Male
Sam Walton, Wal-Mart founder
Vangelis (Papathanasiou), composer
Eric Idle, comedian
Denny McLain, baseball pitcher
John Major, English prime minister

March 30

Not losing a second, you swing into action, following your head and letting others see your courage and daring—cool and calculated. Your talk isn't just chatter and you can be reasonable, using the rules to your benefit, conveniently bending them for fun or profit. You are always moving, problems shot down in rapid order. Who can keep up with you? Work on getting the best grades, and do more to meet the needs of family members and those who depend on you.

Often single, you may be a career person more than a homebody, though your family is usually quick to grow boys. You need to keep your hands and mind busy, so you often become an expert at your key interests, impressing your audience. Your reputation precedes you, so finding privacy is nearly impossible.

Love

3/30s want to be admired by friends and lovers for having a mind of your own and the courage to speak up. You assert yourself enthusiastically but impulsively. You are fearless in saying what you think but careless as well sometimes. This lack of temperance tends to put lovers on the defensive. Because you can be somewhat of a "live wire," partners come to expect the unexpected from you.

Money

Progressive in your thinking, you respect the past only for the lessons learned from it. Although you are tolerant of other people's motives, you aren't tolerant of incompetence. You expect a lot from those under you and can be vindictive toward an unqualified coworker who tries to gain a high position. Jealousy? Or are you simply insecure? Employers know they can count on you but may like you better if you weren't always so tightly-wound.

Famous People Born on This Day

Female

Celine Dion, singer
Astrud Gilberto, singer
Tracy Chapman, singer/songwriter
Anna Q. Nilsson, actress
Leslie Joan Corn, theatre producer/
    director/writer

Male

Vincent van Gogh, artist
Eric Clapton, guitarist
Warren Beatty, actor
MC Hammer, entertainer
Peter Marshall, game show host

March 31

Games are meant to be played, and you can play them very well. Sound sets the tone, so you've noticed what the right noise can make people do—dance, sing, go wild, you included—so music holds a special place in your heart. Concerned about other's well-being and your own, you like to fight for rights, wanting fairness and everyone to have a chance, just as you have had, free to experience life in spite of handicaps.

Being somewhat unsure of yourself—your personality swings depending on your surroundings—you'd benefit by having your own personalized, unique home, with a desk where your can get organized, or at least try to or hire some-one. Get away from traveling with the same-old people; next departure, try foreign places with lots of consonants in the name, like Brno, Czchechno—whatever

Love

People are drawn to your magnetic aura—like an actor or mimic, you easily take on characteristics that will please lovers and not appear threatening to them. Freedom in a relationship is very important to you, and you resist anyone who may try to fence you in. You want honesty between you and your lover and above all, sincerity. To the object of your affection, you bring much enthusiasm and optimism.

Money

Coworkers consider you dependable and inspiring thanks to your tireless effort to get a job done. Your inclination for success and the Good Life attracts you to other successful persons. Your professional potential is almost unlimited because you are not afraid of responsibility and the demands of leadership. People on their way up the ladder of achievement are those whom you can relate to meaningfully. Financially, don't try to keep up with the Joneses and spend beyond your budget.

Famous People Born on This Day

Female

Shirley Jones, actress/singer
Liz Claiborne, fashion designer
Rhea Perlman, actress
Judith Rossner, novelist
Marge Piercy, writer

Male

Ewan McGregor, actor
Rene Descartes, philosopher
Richard Chamberlain, actor
Leo Buscaglia, psychologist
Al Gore, politician

April

April 1

If there's a problem that has to be solved, you've got the answer, or at least a strong opinion. Being born on the first doesn't mean you're always number one. But you play the part superbly, and even when you clash with authority figures, they're likely to wilt, victims of your wiles and natural magnetism. You can be so serious, devoted, independent, and testy, maybe even a little sinister when it comes to getting your way.

Diplomatic and judgmental, determined yet compromising, parental yet childlike, there isn't much you cannot do when you set your sharp mind to it. Others just seem to "need" you. Sports and exercise will help keep you fit— maybe a little volleyball with the boys and girls, or make-it-up-as-you-go horseplay. Fitness equals long life. And, for romance games, read on.

Love

Possessing a flair for the dramatic, you never do anything in moderation. In order to get what or whom you want, you assert yourself fearlessly, even in the face of rejection. It is useless for anyone to pressure you to change because you resent interference. You like believing that you are the most important thing in your lover's life—and, you are! Mature, focused, responsible partners suit you best.

Money

You have a genius for asserting yourself persuasively, fearless in pursuing your objectives, and others admire your determination and persistence. Once your mind is made up, you don't change it unless the evidence is overwhelming. Coworkers recognize your enthusiasm and admire your tenacity to get the job done. Although gregarious, you're more comfortable working alone because you get easily irritated.

Famous People Born on This Day

Female

Ali MacGraw, actress
Debbie Reynolds, actress
Alberta Hunter, blues/jazz singer
Jane Powell, actress
Clara Hale, child welfare humanitarian

Male

Barry Sonnenfeld, film director
William Harvey, physician
Toshiro Mifune, author
Abraham Maslow, psychologist
Sergei Rachmaninoff, composer

April 2

Drama—that's what your life is. A little competitive, a natural attention-getter, very coordinated—your soul has that natural bounce so you are a little impetuous, especially around close friends, and not the neatest animal in the barn—maybe even a bit snippy. Everyone and everything should go your way—why not? Actually, more will go your way if you play the "pleasing game," which works both ways.

Success will find you, especially if you prepare and make an earnest effort to pursue it. Learn how to learn from your mistakes, too. If you over-bake a soufflé and it flops, blame it on the oven. Since you're a natural in the kitchen or workshop—whatever your skill center is—it may become a rewarding trade; you have that knack for delivering what others enjoy.

Love

You easily relate to all types of people and are friendly to everyone, regardless of their social status. You view everyone as unique and as an individual, and expect the same in return. Being very romantic, you have a wealth of fantasies and dreams to draw on. Your 4/2-nature helps you project your ego with finesse and articulate skill, so that when you speak, lovers are attentive. You have a strong desire to be useful to your partner, which constantly motivates you to explore new horizons and options.

Money

You are well-suited to occupations that involve novelty, where you can function on your own creative way and tempo. Your logical judgment is reflected in your material affairs. Not one to over-spend, in the face of financial adversity you remain optimistic, and always hopeful that situations will turn out for the best. Realizing that little is ever gained by wishing on a star, you accept your economic obligations realistically and as investment in your future.

Famous People Born on This Day

Female

Emmylou Harris, singer
Eleanor M. Burbridge, astronomer
Linda Hunt, actress
Karen Jane Woodward, singer
Victoria Jackson, actress/comedienne

Male

Jack Webb, actor
Buddy Ebsen, actor/dancer
Alec Guinness, actor
Hans Christian Andersen, author
Dana Carvey, comedian

April 3

Double trouble—that is what some say about this birthday! Some call you ornery, some lucky, but you know it's a skill to spot a break and take advantage of it. Since obeying the rules doesn't always get you where you want to go, why not fuss and fight and maybe complain the opposition into submission? So, you grow, and if not careful, you may grow too much physically. A tad more self-discipline helps, also seeking outside advice for managing your way down life's sometimes rough, lonely road.

Not the one to look back, you push forward, making new friends, keeping some, showing the world how dependable and cooperative you really can be. An excellent storyteller, you appreciate a good plot—your own is quite interesting. Both fire and water are dangerous elements for you—be careful around either.

Love

Once you set your sights on a love-target, you don't wait for the other person to make the first move. Your best romantic contacts are with partners who share your zest for life, who are eager to share their experiences with you and are not preoccupied with material concerns. 4/3s are very clever in devising schemes for improving love life and passion—but, never forget that it takes "two" to tango (plus, it's more fun with a partner).

Money

Because you are friendly and easy to get along with, it is easy for you to work with others—even those in competition with you. You rarely feel threatened by challenges because you are sure of what you know and rarely take on projects unless you're certain you will succeed. However, your boundless enthusiasm and ego often cause you to overestimate your capabilities and suffer occasional disappointment. Maintain your high standards and hope, but do so realistically!

Famous People Born on This Day

Female

Doris Day, actress
Jane Goodall, anthropologist
Marsha Mason, actress
Amanda Bynes, actress
Picabo Street, Olympic skier

Male

David Hyde Pierce, actor
Marlon Brando, actor
Alec Baldwin, actor
Eddie Murphy, comedian/actor
Wayne Newton, singer

April 4

Your mind just cannot stay off a diet of romance and dreamy ideas, even if the dull, dreary world around you is falling apart. It's not your style to stare trouble in the face, not when it might go away if you ignore it or let someone else handle it. Maybe they can handle it better. Still, don't wait until the last second to spring into action and save the day. Diligence, determination, and social conscience will earn you rewards.

You'd learn a lot from Bible verses—even Grimms' fairy tales—because very human stories encourage all of us to keep our sensibilities about ourselves, and our promises. Folksongs, hymns, and even rap songs have lessons. Liven up and get a little culture. Don't be an outsider. Try dancing to get a natural, healthful rhythm.

Love

Your romantic interests are stimulated by individuals who are serious, sincere, and honest. You need a lover whom you can respect and who admires you in return. Your romantic liaisons are well defined, and you expect your partner to cooperate in meeting mutual goals and are crushed if your efforts are unrewarded—mellow out and don't overdo "desire." Allow relationships to develop, without putting pressure or presumption!

Money

You don't feel confident concerning money matters, often underestimating your own worth. 4/4s must learn to temper frustration and compulsivity with objectivity. Keep peace with superiors, don't hassle them! Once you learn to moderate your insecurities and combative tendencies, you will achieve great heights. Understand what motivates coworkers to act the way they do, even when they claim a different reason or agenda.

Famous People Born on This Day

Female

Dorothea Dix, social reformer
Christine Lahti, actress
Cloris Leachman, actress/
   comedienne
Ernestine Gilbreth Carey, author
Maya Angelou, poet

Male

Arthur Murray, dance instructor
Muddy Waters, blues singer
Elmer Bernstein, film composer
Anthony Perkins, actor
Robert Downey, Jr., actor

April 5

Faithful, strong-hearted, and not short of willpower, you could probably sell iceboxes to Eskimos or talk car salesman out of their commissions, well, almost. Well-liked and noticed by the opposite sex, you'd make an excellent partner, though you must watch your associations carefully—any wrong ones can spell disaster, and lucky you certainly wants no part of that. Keep your eye on the prize—and money and resources under your control.

Ah, to be a child again … well, you are that way anyway. Idle hands mean a weak heart, so you'll want to avoid the couch potato trip. Participate in travel—biking, dune-buggies, rowing, anything that puts movement, new places, and exercise all together—and will introduce you to a lot of fun and sweat. Get a nice haircut first.

Love

You don't tolerate any restrictions concerning your romantic freedom, and constantly need to be on the move. (Do you dash about because you're afraid others will discover how sensitive you really are?) You have a wide circle of friends who adore you because of your generous and kind disposition. Nevertheless, you have difficulty forming loving relationships because you are never really certain you can fulfill the responsibilities they entail. Moderation and self-understanding are necessary in all affairs.

Money

You are curious and very informed in many matters but may lack the know-how/judgment about how to apply the data for the best results. You are neither a clock-watcher at work, nor great with a budget at home. You have an adventurous mind—normally, all that restricts you is the time and money required to develop all your ideas! Don't compare your efforts with those of fellow employees to determine your competence.

Famous People Born on This Day

Female

Bette Davis, actress
Gale Storm, actress
Agnetha Faltskog, singer
Alice B. Davis, actress
Aliza Kashi, singer

Male

Booker T. Washington, educator
Colin Powell, U.S. Secretary of State
Spencer Tracy, actor
Gregory Peck, actor
Algernon Swinburne, poet

April 6

Don't listen to your critics—what are they talking about? Don't they recognize your poise, nobleness, and quality when they see it—that you're image-conscious and more serious than most, born to succeed in business and dominate in a world that just isn't smart enough? You know fame will come and riches increase when you actually work for them. Luck is what losers bet on; you're too wise for that. The only way to beat the house is to own it or rob it.

Having all the angles covered, you are a cool customer and seldom does anyone get the better of you. Occasionally you'll catch a romantic glance; you'll know the right one when he or she comes along, hopefully. With your sound almost psychic judgment, you'd make a good advisor or doctor—very much the authority.

Love

You are forceful about making demands on your lover but not always willing to fulfill what is expected of you. You tend to make promises you can't always keep, although you may fully intend to at the time that you make them. It's a good idea to listen more before you speak. Feelings of insecurity may cause you to avoid making a commitment because you don't want to risk losing what you have

Money

It's important for you to learn how to express yourself in your financial freedom; don't be co-dependent! A bit more self-confidence could help you succeed in money matters without outside help. Coworkers sometimes use you as a means for their own gain, which makes you angry. People can climb all over you, if you allow them to. Decide on an objective, and define the goals you wish to reach.

Famous People Born on This Day

Female

Elizabeth Barrett Browning, poet
Mary Maples Dunn, college president
Ari Meyers, actress
Marilu Henner, actress
Candace Cameron, actress

Male

John Ratzenberger, actor
Ram Dass, philosopher/author
Peter Tosh, Rastafarian musician
Harry Houdini, magician
André Previn, conductor

April 7

Proud of your accomplishments and your possessions, you've earned them, and may be envied. If others were as efficient, intelligent and achieve what you do, they wouldn't have to be envious. Sociable, logical, and hearty, you're secure because you know how to use your many talents. Still, troubles with partners, business or romance, may persist. No problem: you show your smirky smile, having enough self-control to not let them get you down.

Monopoly was probably your favorite game, or you had every Barbie doll outfit along with the car, the airplane, and Ken. You're still a player, only the kid toys are gone; it's commerce and commodities and estates instead. It's a little sad. Why not try roles that let you be a kid again—a younger, fresher crowd—plus you are so much wiser!

Love

Because you are determined to have everything your way, you have a short fuse when challenged. Aim to be more compassionate with your partner, don't jump to conclusions—if someone disagrees with you, try not to reply abruptly, or with bad temper. From these experiences you will learn, and your emotions and judgment will get sharper, so that you can make loving plans for a fruitful relationship.

Money

You work hard at your career, usually doing more than is expected. You tend to bite off more than you can chew, and then desperately try to cope with situations as best you can. Your drive about job responsibilities is genuine, although you tend to make promises you can't always fulfill, even though you intend to deliver. Learn to examine financial affairs carefully before you act, otherwise you will waste a lot of time and effort.

Famous People Born on This Day

Female
Billie Holiday, singer
Yvonne Fedderson, ChildHelp
   co-founder
Irene Castle, dancer
Gabriela Mistral, Nobel Literature
   winner
Janis Ian, songwriter/singer

Male
James Garner, actor
Jackie Chan, martial artist/actor
Francis Ford Coppola, film director
Ravi Shankar, musician
Russell Crowe, actor

April 8

Sure, people can have crazy ideas and think they're immortal, but you know better. We are all one with nature—no one knows that more than you, the person who probably makes a living off our bountiful planet. Your favorite objects are usually metal. As a builder, your body and mind are the tools. You desire more and will catch pleasure once you've met your goal, filled the cupboard, and have a family that has its needs met.

Without being stingy or selfish, you take care of what's important to you, which is more important than others' opinions. We think you should follow your intuitions more, and keep score a little less. In business, your children may be your most dependable partners and workers. Pamper yourself with an occasional makeover; it improves your inner and outer image.

Love

You are drawn to lovers who have a clear idea of where they are going and what they expect to achieve. You have great respect for anyone who has the courage of their convictions, even if they differ from yours. Consequently, you maintain a good level of communication with a lover before making a commitment. For you, honesty and integrity are essential keystones in matters of love.

Money

The fear of poverty drives you to accomplish as much as you can, fully believing that your determination and persistence will guarantee success. Always willing to assume responsibility on the job, you take one step at a time in achieving excellence. Secretive about your personal life and plans, you don't share your innermost thoughts with coworkers. You are efficient in managing your financial affairs and resourceful in spending.

Famous People Born on This Day

Female

Betty Ford, First Lady/addiction
    clinic founder
Mary Pickford, actress
Carmen McRae, singer
Sonja Henie, Olympic figure skater
Elizabeth Barrett-Conner, epidemi-
    ologist

Male

Shecky Greene, comedian
Taran Noah Smith, actor
Ponce De Leon, Florida explorer
Buddha, spiritual figure
Julian Lennon, singer

April 9

Fashion, art, ego! Life should be hot and sultry, fully animated, with wild displays meant to please the eye and impress the heart. You are physically passionate, a hands-on person, not always cautious enough to stay away from trouble but confident enough to stare the tiger in the eye. Most rules are trifles. With your wild-eyed vision, you see many opportunities, perhaps exaggerating them, hoping they'll turn to gold, and do.

If people worshiped planets, you'd worship Venus. It's so entertaining, so glorious, so warm, so fertile. It's also connected to money, which might be the measuring stick others judge you by. Better to judge you by the trappings you surround yourself with. Try roles that let you feel you're liberating the world from ignorance. For fun, Mardi Gras, or throw a grand birthday celebration.

Love

You don't display your feelings until you know a person well and can determine whether the attraction is social and intellectual, or merely physical. In personal relationships, you expect lovers to be as sincere as you. Although eager to form deep unions, when your trust is violated you quickly break it off without a backward glance. Seek a lover who can provide mutual trust, sincerity, and open discussion of any problem that develops.

Money

You know how to assert yourself under pressure, and have a talent for effective communication through precise bottom-line delivery and clever use of words. Your self-discipline and determination enable you to accomplish more than your coworkers or competitors because you take the time to weigh out every detail of a problem. You're imaginative in discovering new ways to express your many creative and financial interests.

Famous People Born on This Day

Female

Michael Learned, actress
Giuditta Pasta, opera singer
Cynthia Nixon, actress
Galina A. Kulakova, Olympic Nordic skier
Keshia Knight Pulliam, actress

Male

Dennis Quaid, actor
Hugh Hefner, *Playboy* publisher
Charles Baudelaire, poet
Paul Robeson, actor/singer
Jean-Paul Belmondo, actor

April 10

Friendly, elementally cooperative, active, teetering between sound thinking and wacky ideas, you're a good one for others to dump their tales of woe on. Yech! You'd like to please all, but cannot always have it both ways, so making the right choices, at the right time, with the right people tells everyone how far up the food chain you're going to grow. Self-conscious for a reason, you have a natural curiosity, mostly about things that get you more recognition.

Willing to make sacrifices in the name of love or for a group's code, you're the one that has to plan the way out of the mess. Your outdoor adventures can wind up bewildering, your sexual bluster interesting to listen to. Remember: environment—keep the right things and right people close by; shuck the rest. Think karma, not Karmen Ghia.

Love

You are a vital, energetic, and exciting person who charms people with your infectious and personable manner. You quickly respond to people, and your enthusiasm stimulates others to respond to you as well. You are optimistic that the most difficult relationships will work out eventually, so you are not excessively preoccupied with occasional upsets. 4/10-born have great faith to rise above any of life's negative circumstances.

Money

You're imaginative, articulate, and very hopeful about the future. You study human nature, trying to learn the lessons from the past for guidance in solving the problems of tomorrow. An idealist, you are a champion for coworkers who are too timid to voice their objectives and you are shocked when you observe injustice, immediately voicing your displeasure. To you, wastefulness is appalling—life is too short!

Famous People Born on This Day

Female

Clare Boothe Luce, journalist/politician/diplomat
Frances Perkins , social worker/U.S. cabinet member
Johnnie Tillmon, civil rights activist
Mandy Moore, entertainer
Felicia Collins, guitarist

Male

Brian Setzer, musician
Omar Sharif, actor
Steven Seagal, actor
Joseph Pulitzer, journalist
Samuel Hahnemann, homeopathy founder

April 11

Unleashed, you're the fighter and the scrapper, ready to do what it takes, throwing in your body, mind and soul—and not always coming out with more than you put in! The confusion we call modern life can be, well, more than you bargained for. Faithfully you look ahead, picking up the pieces as you go, showing your humor, leaving an untidy trail, waiting for luck to strike. If only others were more reliable and sensible, and pleasure less fleeting.

Your playing is like a show: the struggling artist, the aspiring performer, life a pantomime. You flourish in polite society once you get your foot in the door and show them something new. Your physical strength can wane, and getting riled up uses so much of your precious energy, so always head away from trouble, not toward it.

Love

Your romantic and sensual needs are considerable, but you know how to contain them until you meet somebody with whom you can enjoy personal comfort. You don't threaten potential suitors' opinions by calling attention to their shortcomings. Your ease in positively expressing yourself endears you to everyone. You know how to say the right thing at the right time and are generous with praise when it is deserved (and sometimes, even when it isn't).

Money

You have a vivid imagination and easily relate to coworkers. Even when circumstances seem dismal, you always look at the bright side. You are sensitive about finances and outside influences and understand their significance. Your concern for others is boundless, and you could express this by serving people who have physical disabilities or social disadvantages. You are enthusiastic and optimistic that every problem has a solution.

Famous People Born on This Day

Female

Michele Scarabelli, actress
Ellen Goodman, syndicated columnist
Anna Magnani, actress
Louise Lasser, actress
Ethel Kennedy, Bobby Kennedy's wife

Male

Richie Sambora, musician
Lucky Vanous, model
Percy L. Julian, chemist
Oleg Cassini, fashion designer
Joel Grey, actor

April 12

Warning signs would be too simple; it takes some real persuasion, psychology, and a good dose of reality now and then to keep you headed in the right direction. 12-step programs—yes you could do that—for about 20 seconds. There's a big, complex ego inside—powerful, perhaps a healer, perhaps a catalyst, and strong sexual desires too. You can sizzle. Let's keep that secret. You're not using your psychic ability enough—it'd work better if it were for a good purpose.

Putting your life out on a limb is not good advice, still, the military, police work, medicine may be your calling, and allow you just enough independence. You'd make a good underworld mob boss, but it's better to put your revolutionary orneriness to more acceptable uses.

Love

Although your intentions are honorable, you are inclined to be a bit lazy or careless in love affairs. It's not that you're difficult to get along with—it's simply that compromise is tough for you to grasp! You have subtle magnetism, and you tempt people to want to be close to you—even though it's usually on your terms. If you meet people halfway, you'll find most of them will do the same. Understanding the romantic needs and desires of your lovers can pay huge, rewarding dividends!

Money

Overestimating what people expect from you, you go to great lengths to do your absolute best! A valued employee, you prefer jobs with flex-time, and a minimum of responsibility. You need greater self-discipline in order to funnel your creative enthusiasm into specifics. Exaggerating the importance of superficial matters, you tend to get bogged down by them. You're not great with savings because it's difficult for you to say "no."

Famous People Born on This Day

Female

Ann Miller, dancer/actress
Imogene Cunningham, photographer/painter
Jane Withers, actress
Claire Danes, actress
Shannen Doherty, actress

Male

David Letterman, late night talk show host
David Cassidy, actor/singer
Herbie Hancock, pianist
Tom Clancy, author
Riley Smith, actor

April 13

Morality, human dignity, plutocracy—big words and big ideas—that's what you want to deal with, applying mind over simple matters, and driving humankind ahead toward its ultimate destiny, or something like that. You are serious, thorough, and confident, and would like nothing better than to be the master of the plantation. A penetrating mind, you can polarize others, damaging your reputation if not for the miracles you seem to make work.

As an older soul that has more wisdom than others give you credit for, you can unlock your inner reserves by visits to historical places of power, such as seats of government and national treasures. Statue of Liberty—a minor tingle, U.S. capital—fine. The ancient streets of Rome—give you a chariot! Realistically, try improving just one other person's life at a time.

Love

You expect a lot from a partner, but always make substantial contributions in return. You are alert to a lover's potentials, stimulating them to use their gifts and talents better. You express your feelings without great fanfare, and quickly detect insincerity in others. Your emotional excitement and joy of life are the keys to much happiness. 4/13-born aim for quality rather than quantity in all relationships.

Money

You know what you want out of life, and constantly express your convictions. Education, social work, or management is well-suited for you because you're passionate about compassion, have a "feel" for social responsibilities, and a persuasion to do something about them. Through your efforts, you raise the ideals of coworkers and everyone involved. Although not extravagant, you're not good with savings or budgets.

Famous People Born on This Day

Female

Beatrix "Trixie" Schuba, Olympic
figure skater
Rosa Joyce Plesters Brommelie,
conservation scientist
Amy Robinson, writer/actress
Eudora Welty, author
Caroline Rhea, actress/comedienne

Male

Rick Schroder, actor
Al Green, singer
Samuel Beckett, playwright
Gary Kasporav, chess champion
Thomas Jefferson, founding
father/U.S. president

April 14

Watchful and choosing your words carefully, your life might be a moral drama with you at the center, taking care of number one out of necessity, stopping occasionally to point others in the right directions. Not exactly a stay-at-home family person, you might find your niche working with the masses and semi-perfect strangers. The law interests you, so does solving the human puzzle we call society, but it's not easy—being emotion-charged, you can boil over.

Edgy and a bit impatient, sometimes you butt heads with others just because you get a weird feeling about them. Let's be mellow instead—that is, if others would just behave. You can sense a power within that maybe you can't control—truth is, you can, so channel that energy in any number of productive ways, smiling as you study life's fascinating mysteries.

Love

Although you believe in love-at-first sight, and your physical desires run deep, you don't take chances with love. You relate well to responsible, mature partners, and are particularly attracted to those with well-defined goals, minimal baggage, and who want to make something out of their lives. You quickly express your feelings about those you care for, because you don't have any hang-ups about whether or not your affections will be returned. Family, and its security, suits you well.

Money

The good news: you usually know how far to extend yourself before becoming financially exhausted. 4/14-born's prosperity derives from ingenuity, time-management, and bargain-hunting. The challenging news: having unrealistic back-up plans. Don't try to be liked by everyone, or be a sucker for sob-stories. Face it—some coworkers are just plain lazy. Your sympathetic nature must be kept in check. Tend to your own business.

Famous People Born on This Day

Female

Julie Christie, actress
Loretta Lynn, singer
Sarah Michelle Gellar, actress
Belinda Quirey, dance historian
Clarice Elaine Gaylord, U.S. EPA grants director

Male

Ryan O'Neal, actor
John Paul Stevens, Supreme Court justice
Steve Martin, writer/actor
Rod Steiger, actor
John Gielgud, actor

April 15

When you sprinkle your selfless love or plant your kernels of knowledge, suddenly you're among a pleasing crop of real people, with real joys, talents, and so animated! A restless soul, your mind is always at work, looking for joy, finding inspiring words and art. An activist, you can develop answers to the world's problems—and solve your own along the way. You worry and want to win, and suffer if you don't. Lighten up, will you!

A little peppery when challenged, your defenses may hide your light side. Sure, we cannot please all people all the time, but getting others in unison will certainly increase your success rate and peace of mind. Travel to foreign lands requires you to work out the language and cultural barriers—good practice. Give yourself an "A" when you catch on.

Love

You have a fertile and loving imagination but may lack the practical know-how to use it constructively. Be more realistic; accept lovers as they are—accentuate their positive points, and minimize the negative. Mobilize your efforts, ask for assistance, and remember to say thank you.

Money

Until you learn to compromise with coworkers, you will find it difficult to achieve monetary objectives. Listen, rather than act defensively or be a know-it-all. It's difficult for you to work on a tight schedule or with strict procedures. 4/15-born are happiest when working alone; that way, you don't have to compare yourself with others. Because you are so concerned about doing good work, you are rarely caught with your defenses down.

Famous People Born on This Day

Female

Bessie Smith, blues singer
Elizabeth Montgomery, actress
Emma Thompson, actress
Marian Jordan, radio personality
Elizabeth Catlett, sculptor/
    lithographer

Male

Roy Clark, entertainer
James Clark Ross, Antarctic explorer
Thomas Hart Benton, painter
Adrian Cadbury, candy manufacturer
Leonardo da Vinci, artist

April 16

A warm birthday—not a fiery, hot one, but inner passionate warmth. Naturally receptive and trusting, you are a soft touch for religions, contrived political appeals, and mind-numbing commercialism. You're probably not so bad at promoting these things yourself, though you're a little more selective and conscientious. You also value your privacy, using it to think, invent, and recharge your body and soul. Others admire you for your accomplishments, your personal precious jewels.

Contemplative and serious one moment, determined and a step ahead the next, many would like to be your companion, married or not, as there isn't much dullness around you. Anyplace can be turned into your vacation spot; your "vision" can see though obstacles, except those you put on yourself. Try not to be bossy—it's scary when it comes from usually level-headed you.

Love

Don't be so quick to judge, or always test lovers—try to meet them halfway until you know they are sincere. Used to getting your own way, you dislike being asked what you are doing, and why. Still, you love it when partners ask your opinion, need your help. Make sure that objects of affection demonstrate their credibility and dependability before you get involved. Be true and generous to yourself before others.

Money

Keenly aware of the power of money, you plan carefully, enjoying time-honored procedures above speculation. Pension plans and future investments are as important to you as earning a living now; be alert to responsibilities at hand. Resist the temptation to freely offer yourself to coworkers. Although it may seem the best way to get them to admire you, you're likely to lose their respect. Submission is hardly cooperation!

Famous People Born on This Day

Female
Queen Margretha of Denmark
Edie Adams, singer
Dusty Springfield, singer
Mother Joseph, missionary leader
Ellen Barkin, actress

Male
Martin Lawrence, actor/comedian
Charlie Chaplin, silent screen actor
Peter Ustinov, actor
Kareem Abdul-Jabbar, basketball great
Henry Mancini, musician

April 17

A real down-to-earth type, you are the one who can make the best of limited resources and get around the obstacles—and you don't shrink from the heavy responsibilities despite odds or setbacks. It's because you have a lot of pride, and the passion to go with it. Still, expect the unexpected throughout life; your path to success is not always a clear one. Others usually will listen when you stand up and speak, seeing the benefits of having you along for the ride.

Early in life people may have overlooked you, but as time passes you are more sure of yourself, maybe even a little too sure, good at delegating and also persuasive when you want to be. Don't say "no" to leadership roles whenever they're offered; you usually have practical answers that will work.

Love

When you talk, others quickly know precisely what you mean. You never hesitate to inform lovers what does and doesn't work for you; how-ever, you're inclined to underestimate others' needs. You have strong physical desires, though you won't settle for a mere physical relationship. You need someone who is alert, exciting, and inspiring.

Money

You're filled with talented ideas—all that restricts you is the time and money needed to exploit them! Financial expectations are rarely fulfilled because you set your goals high, but you never lose hope. Your greatest fulfillment is through service to others, especially when your efforts result in lasting benefits. But beware of falling victim to coworkers or employers who may take advantage of your generous spirit.

Famous People Born on This Day

Female

Joyce Buck, actress/interior designer
Clare Francis, yachtswoman/author
Olivia Hussey, actress
Ann Shirley, actress
Teri Austin, actress

Male

William Holden, actor
J. P. Morgan, banker
Harry Reasoner, journalist
Sugar Ray Leonard, boxer
Nikita Khrushchev, Russian premier

April 18

Others may think of you as a "me first" person—what do they expect, you're usually in personally competitive situations! You have that irritating ability to expose the weak points of most anything or anybody, including potential mates, which can be a big turn-off. Bright, serious, a bit impersonal, you're well-mannered and status conscious, but can't stand to be pigeon-holed. You can be a real pain in the neck to those who get on your bad side.

You handle the technicalities well, so you're usually miles ahead of others when it comes to details—you're a good wheeler-dealer, a prima donna, too. You'd make a good investigator, but always get the facts first, and choose your targets well.

Love

As much as you dream of a perfect and loving union, you need emotional independence, and quickly flee whenever you get the feeling that someone stakes a claim on you. You aren't afraid of being yourself—you love who you are! Even partners who don't approve of your doings admire the spirit in which you conduct it! You enjoy good times, but must learn more self-control. Once you learn to temper your feelings and appetites with moderation, you'll achieve greater romantic heights!

Money

You have a quick mind and understand ideas that others cannot because you're open to new, alternative, and innovative ways of thinking. You're a concept-type person with a deep need for freedom—you hate deadlines as well as dead-end jobs. Being a team-player comes difficult (but you're trainable). Despite your emotional armor, your feelings are easily hurt when you don't get acknowledgement for a job well done. Seek an employer as clever as you are.

Famous People Born on This Day

Female

Hayley Mills, actress
Barbara Hale, actress
Lucrezia Borgia, Italian noblewoman
Melissa Joan Hart, actress
Villegas Triplets, musicians

Male

Conan O'Brien, late night talk show host
Leopold Stokowski, conductor
Huntington Hartford, philanthropist
James Woods, actor
Clarence Darrow, attorney/orator

April 19

With a burning ambition inside, you can make superhuman sacrifices to get where you think you belong in life. You are often working overtime and into the wee hours to satisfy yourself, and to please those who should be willing to reward you with a swanky position in your chosen field, usually the arts or a socially-prestigious slot. No one can say you didn't work to fulfill your ambitions. Blame your temper on always having to stretch for what you want and need.

Often very beautiful, you like a sexy image and have an earthy magnetism. You feel sorry for the oppressed, since you feel a bit that way yourself. Please yourself by designing things or experimenting with your appearance, say, with hair, clothes, or cosmetics. Getting close to the earth also makes you feel good, so play there and revitalize!

Love

You expect to be given almost everything you ask for from lovers. And you do the same in return, within limits, because you long for someone just like you. Although you may enjoy casual relationships, they never sufficiently satisfy. You know what you want, when you want it, and go after it. Never one to admit defeat, when you stumble, you get right back up and try again.

Money

Although not spoiled, you know what money can buy, and you want more and more of it! The kind of work you do isn't as important as the paycheck. 4/19-borns don't believe in failure, or doing anything halfway. You know how to make a lasting impression, and coworkers acknowledge your ambition and drive. In professional dealings, you are very honest (sometimes painfully so) and expect the same from others.

Famous People Born on This Day

Female

Jayne Mansfield, actress
Ashley Judd, actress
Paloma Picasso, designer
Gertude Vanderbilt Whitney,
    sculptor/art benefactor
Kate Hudson, actress

Male

Eliot Ness, FBI agent
Hugh O'Brian, actor
Al Unser Jr., racecar driver
Tim Curry, actor
Dudley Moore, comedian/actor

April 20

Smooth and sensual, you can attract a lot of attention, which means a variety of relationships and some that may quickly change. You also make others jealous, and why not—stylish, fit, and able to fit right in, you can trade on your many natural gifts and rise above what might have been, or your common beginnings. Power can make you impulsive, dull your perceptions, and cloud your mind; don't forget what brought you.

Contemplative and contemporary, you're a good judge of others' character, or should be. You are able to bring many of your dreams to reality, though you're usually concentrating on the here and now. You'd make a good psychic, with practice, but don't let it go to your head. Something about islands is in your fate, or a passport.

Love

You like people, and people like you as well. You are a loyal friend, and stand by loved ones for better or for worse—after all, 4/20-born are tolerant of everyone's faults. While it is admirable to help those who deserve it, be on guard against lovers who would abuse the privilege and use you as a doormat. You have a strong sense of fairness and justice, which you insist on in all your relationships. Your warmth and friendliness will always keep you well-liked.

Money

Possessions bring you pleasure—when you see something you want to own, you work very hard to get it, and will fight anyone from taking anything away from you. Although not a materialist, you believe what's yours is yours. It's not easy for you to slow down, because your mind is in constant motion. Establish definite objectives, and construct a positive plan for actuating them.

Famous People Born on This Day

Female

Carmen Electra, actress
Jessica Lange, actress
Nina Foch, actress
Betty Cuthbert, Olympic speedster
Joni Evans, New York publisher

Male

Joey Lawrence, actor
Daniel Day-Lewis, actor
Ryan O'Neal, actor
Luther Vandross, singer
Joan Miró, Spanish painter/sculptor

April 21

A quirky, seemingly noble person, you may be an enigma, being what others imagine you to be instead of being yourself. You might cloak yourself with religion, or family history, or be your job title. Maybe you feel guilty about love, or feel you aren't getting enough. You are kind of silly that way, and that slows you down. Don't be the cowardly lion: practice a little more courage, still being delicate with others' feelings. Your own feelings will be more wonderful.

Not exactly a wallflower, but passive, you would definitely benefit from roles where you're required to be more outgoing, initiating conversations and socially interactive. Dwell on the positives, please. You are a people person, after all. For a real change of pace, you should travel abroad; you'll surprise yourself with how quickly you pick up foreign languages.

Love

You prefer a partner who's a high-spirited live-life-by-the-moment type, rather than one who has a steady-as-it-goes ready-made game plan. When a lover predetermines all the shots, you flee. 4/21-born admire independence and adventure. Partners understand that they can call on you for strength in times of need, because you're willing to go that extra mile. You relate especially to open-minded people who are not preoccupied with material or physical things.

Money

Although you may believe that experience is your best teacher, you buck the establishment and go your own merry way. Working with others is satisfying for you, socially. But it drives you crazy to hurry-up-and-wait for coworkers. Independently efficient, you plan and plot before doing anything to make certain that it's initially done correctly. For you time is money; a pay-up or shut-up kind of thing.

Famous People Born on This Day

Female

Queen Elizabeth II
Charlotte Brontë, writer
Andie MacDowell, actress
Elaine May, actress/comedianne
Samantha Druce, youngest woman
   to swim English Channel

Male

Anthony Quinn, actor
Charles Grodin, actor
Rollo May, psychologist
John Muir, naturalist
Iggy Pop, musician

April 22

Outgoing and adventurous, your inner vitality urges you to travel often, to make quick decisions, and be as carefree and independent as you can. When something attracts your attention, you go for it, making new friends as you go, figuring out how things work and why. You're fearless and love a good challenge, finding luck and riches which you'll want for your later years which you've reserved for slowing down and enjoying life, if they'd just let you.

You have a good idea what others want and need, so you feel that you're a natural leader—you are, but that doesn't always spell success. Take romance, for example. After looking high and low, you may find the perfect mate is much younger or older—no matter, you're as young as you feel, and making your own breaks.

Love

You're always concerned whether or not a lover understands you, and are masterful at sending crossed signals. However, you aren't so good at interpreting the signals of others. You respect devotion and promises but are uncomfortable with emotional demonstrations. It's easy for you to take on the traits of vague or negative people. Be cautious whom you trust, but always tell the truth.

Money

It's a good idea to refrain from decision-making positions where you're responsible for others. You tend to fall for sob stories quickly and deeply, often allowing feelings to overwhelm logic. Once a schedule or duty is presented, you plow forward like a trooper. However, the minute someone weaker seeks your help, you lose momentum and need a lot of time to regroup. Let others take the lead, and be content to follow the rules.

Famous People Born on This Day

Female

Queen Isabella of Castile
Charlotte Rae, actress
Lauri Hendler, actress
Kim Elizabeth, actress
Paula Fox, author

Male

Jack Nicholson, actor
Aaron Spelling, TV producer
Immanuel Kant, philosopher
Charlie Mingus, jazz musician
Yehudi Menuhin, violinist

April 23

Be wiser, stronger, and more watchful than the average birthday—trouble has its eye on you, April 23! Beneath your distinctive exterior is a true fiery talent that cannot sit, and at times you'll have to be impatient, rough, brutally frank, and even resort to tricks to get around disharmony and others' wackiness. Life is full of lively experiences; how well you learn from them and use them tells how far you'll go.

Being an activist—not necessarily by choice—you often pick up a good cause, or a bad cause, crusade for it, then find yourself playing a bigger part than imagined. Due to disharmony, often you have to step in as the peacemaker, coordinator, be the deciding man/woman. Such high demands suggest that you'll also need much private time to recapture your cool.

Love

You're open and candid about your feelings, seldom holding back your opinions. You have a unique style of thought, especially in your response to others, and in the way you react to the suggestions or flirtations of those around you. 4/23s are compatible with a partner who has both feet on the ground; a trustworthy person on whose advice you can depend. Because you don't make impossible demands, you expect the same from lovers.

Money

You take advantage of every opportunity to show your worth on the job because you have sensational self-confidence. However, even though your ideas are terrific and inspired, your follow-through needs some fine-tuning. It's a good idea to find work where you are unencumbered by superiors and can set your own parameters. Budgets and saving money for a rainy day aren't your strengths.

Famous People Born on This Day

Female

Shirley Temple Black, entertainer/ ambassador
Bernadette Devlin, Irish civil rights leader
Valerie Bertinelli, actress
Sandra Dee, actress
Jan Hooks, comedienne/actress

Male

Max Planck, physicist
Vladimir Nabokov, novelist
William Shakespeare, playwright/poet
Lee Majors, actor
Roy Orbison, singer

April 24

Just doing what comes naturally, you say as you luxuriate in the arts—your art—and spin your own sort of accommodating magic that can put others under your spell. Who knew? Capable of hard work and surviving the challenges, you can also be hospitable, meditative, and relaxed, which puts you and others on the same page, even if just temporarily. Optimistically, you follow your own heart, always with an eye toward improving existing conditions.

Comfortably at home anywhere in the world, you have a playfulness that attracts romantic attention, but you're not a soft touch nor easily impressed, and will marry well or not at all. You might turn your home into an art museum or lab. Keep others in the loop by always sending pictures—of you. Get your healthy exercise in on the sly.

Love

You're idealistic about love, maintaining high standards for you and your partner that may not always be realistic. 4/24-born require a pragmatic partner who keeps fact and fiction separate (not your strength), someone who is sensitive yet down to earth (ditto). You go out of your way to understand your lover by immersing yourself in his or her joys, problems, and timetables. The more interaction, the more gratifying the relationship for you.

Money

Finding ways to spend your hard-earned dollars is easy for you. To you, prosperity is a physical vehicle, not a vision. You volunteer when necessary, but accomplish more when working solo. You don't deal with pressure well, and you aren't well suited for management or authoritative positions. Trustworthy and well-intentioned, you're a valuable employee and always willing to learn something new.

Famous People Born on This Day

Female

Barbra Streisand, actress/singer
Shirley MacLaine, actress
Jill Ireland, actress
Angela Burdett-Coutts, philanthropist
Yvonne D. Cagle, MD/astronaut

Male

Willem De Kooning, artist
Justin Wilson, Cajun chef
John Williams, composer
Benzion Freshwater, multimillionaire
Chipper Jones, baseball player

April 25

Sensual, magnetic, pragmatic, beautiful—it's as if you made a deal with Mother Nature—this describes most of you. People born this day tend to happily go about life, sometimes ignoring the harsher world outside, which can cause sudden showers of problems that you wake up to, then charge though. Others admire you, so always set a good example. Not calculatingly intelligent, you have a "psychic knowing" so natural that it may seem kooky.

Wanting to be accepted as a professional, you will practice and study, "mastering" it. You also enjoy the social interchange that comes in cooperative efforts, thinking in terms of "we." So, why don't "we" set aside our differences and cut to the chase? Your presence is felt in whatever you do, wherever you go. Go sweetly, press lightly, get in the groove.

Love

You dislike reruns and repeats, so once a relationship becomes redundant, you're outta there! Variety and spontaneity nourish you, and stale or unclear communication is a major source of aggravation. For you, it doesn't matter what your partner does for work—it's the after hours' creative and playful time that makes you smile! Aim for partners who are hot air balloon-like, instead of routine-loving windbags.

Money

Always maintain a strict plan over your financial affairs because your accounting skills aren't your strength. You are effective dealing with people—clients, customers—because you have a well-developed understanding of human nature. On the job, you don't take rules or responsibilities lightly, and it's difficult for you to relax when there is work to be done. You don't "sit idle" well, whatsoever.

Famous People Born on This Day

Female

Ella Fitzgerald, singer
Talia Shire, actress
Melissa Hayden, ballerina
Renée Zellweger, actress

Male

Paul Mazursky, film writer/director
Pyotr Ilich Tchaikovsky, Russian composer
Oliver Cromwell, Lord Protector of England
Al Pacino, actor
Meadowlark Lemon, basketball clown

April 26

This is one of the best April birthdays, action, excited passions, your natural well-balanced vigor catches others' attention. Some of you have an uncommon charm and facial expressions to match. You're great in your profession, plus always contributing with practical ideas and your talents. Pleasantly keeping in line with nature and the status quo, you are a trouper even if luck does desert you occasionally.

Now that we've showered you with hearts and flowers, we should mention the chance of over-revving your lifestyle, leaving relationships and romances scattered in the dust. "I'll make my own decisions," you say. Make them good ones, with good intentions and fairness in mind, please. Having another source of income would help, too. Develop it, but leave some fun weekend time for just you.

Love

Because your personal motto is "the sky's the limit" in matters of love, an emotionally secure, no-baggage type of partner suits you best. You're creative and happy-go-lucky and understand the importance of maturity. Not a footloose, fly-by-night partner, you take every affair seriously and consider it an investment. You have a natural ability to distinguish between which emotional direction is best for you, and which is not.

Money

You make a valiant effort to stay financially ahead of the game, and truly appreciate the Almighty Buck even though you can't seem to save any! You do your job well, are friendly with coworkers, and are comfortable asking for or giving help. You're an idea person who needs constant opportunities to apply yourself. You work best when you can perform at your own pace, and be creative with job descriptions.

Famous People Born on This Day

Female

Gracie Allen, comedienne
Carol Burnett, entertainer
Martha Finley, children's author
Anita Loos, author
Alice Cary, poet

Male

Jet Li, actor
John James Audubon, naturalist/
    artist
I.M. Pei, architect
Eugène Delacroix, painter
Duane Eddy, musician

April 27

Handy, quick on your feet, and to-the-point in conversations, you are more than just a talker—you are one of those mind, body, and soul types who thinks they're invincible, so you sometimes break the rules and don't always win until getting kinetic. Communication and sports come naturally, but finding your true niche will require that you get off the path of least resistance, then put together your personal puzzle pieces.

Basically, you're a lover not a fighter, and you adore social life, but not usually high society stuff. You're more the everyday person content to do your own thing, easily entertaining yourself and others, especially romantic partners. Try being the boss—you'll be surprised that you're a good one, maybe even figuring out a way to get the raise you deserve.

Love

Even though your intention is to always be truthful with your lover, your rich imagination often gets the best of you! You tend to swing from one emotional extreme to another, often letting dreams overwhelm "what is." Don't walk into a union without stating your intentions and expectations. Although you seek approval from others, never forget that your opinion counts more. Take your time during courtship. Refuse to let your passionate fantasies run rampant.

Money

An undercurrent of measured caution always accompanies your professional activities. Management and coworkers admire your honesty because you can't tell a lie, or convincingly pull the wool over anybody's eyes. You dislike balancing bank account numbers, preferring that someone else do it for you, but are always ready to tend to details that fellow employees may find obnoxious.

Famous People Born on This Day

Female
Coretta Scott King, political activist
Sheena Easton, singer
Sandy Dennis, actress
Anouk Aimee, actress
Katie Pierson, musician

Male
Casey Kasem, disc jockey
Walter Lantz, animator
Jack Klugman, actor
Ulysses S. Grant, U.S. president/Civil War general
Samuel Morse, telegraph inventor

April 28

Perfect for right here, right now, you are not the phony type; you're humane and honest, the real deal, tough but stylish, and a good judge of others' character, able to see their flaws since you're psychic, or at least in touch with your feelings. You inspire confidence when you're pleasant, so keep the shiny side up. Self-sufficient, you do gravitate to the showy "good life" and may gain weight to prove it.

A rebel, sometimes you take chances and have a "you can't touch me" swagger. Overconfident? No, but you will do what it takes to get your point across, which doesn't please everyone. Keeping the right company always helps protect you. More of a builder than romantic escape artist, you don't need weeks of time off, but you will welcome any respites from the everyday hum-drum.

Love

You delineate your desires very carefully to your partner, and treat romance as an entrepreneurial business, make changes when warranted (and profitable for you), and keep your fingers on the pulse of passion trends. Because your emotions are rarely in conflict with your intellect, you maintain objective control in fulfilling your game plan and objectives, and enjoy filling your one-on-one time with activity, preferring to be too busy than not busy at all.

Money

Even though you believe in being flexible and creative with schedules, you could stand to let fellow employees do the same. Loosen up and discuss financial matters with those in-the-know. You are diligent about paying off personal debts and bills on time, even though money managing doesn't come naturally for you. Good at planning, yes! Saving? Nope! You never cheat or steal, and always aim to learn from others, rather than be envious or intimidated. Once you set about a task, you stay until it's done.

Famous People Born on This Day

Female
Ann-Margret, actress
Blossom Dearie, singer
Ghislaine Hermanuz, architect
Beverly F. Albert, architect
Penelope Cruz, actress

Male
Jay Leno, late night talk show host
Lionel Barrymore, actor
Harper Lee, author
Francis Baily, astronomer
James Monroe, U.S. president

April 29

A sensitive soul, you need to be a caring person, pushing yourself to be better, and you're easily swayed by emotional appeals. Some of you tackle the most strenuous tasks, knowing that you must work diligently or concentrate for long hours. You're good at turning ideas and goals into concrete realities, chaos into form, and you like to experiment. Sometimes you worry too much, perhaps being indecisive, caught by the moment, but when asked to respond, you will.

Concerned about hygiene and food—the basics of good health—and also desiring to lavish yourself in creature comforts, you may turn your home into quite an eclectic place. Showcase your lifestyle—you know you're making an impact by others' homage to your home life. Consider the Chi, add the sound of water and add all the modern gadgets.

Love

You tackle any relationship problems head first and as they develop and have the fortitude to correct them. However, you tend to live by rather demanding rules, but are also willing to take any steps necessary to make your goals manifest. You can't stand disorganized or disorderly partners. More of a realist than optimist, you're best suited for mature, down-to-earth types.

Money

You're a terrific team-player, and do everything in your means to follow the rules and keep the peace. For you, it's the excitement of accomplishment rather than the thrill of competition that counts. Once you have determined what must be done, you steadily move forward. Your bills are always paid and usually on time. Neither miserly nor frugal, you're clever enough to figure out how to have some extra afterwards.

Famous People Born on This Day

Female

Michelle Pfeiffer, actress
Uma Thurman, actress
Betsey Ancker-Johnson, physicist/
    auto company executive
Kate Mulgrew, actress
Celeste Holm, actress

Male

Duke Ellington, musician
William Randolph Hearst, publishing
    mogul
Jerry Seinfeld, comedian
André Agassi, tennis star
Dale Earnhardt, stockcar driver

April 30

Praising loyalty and probably seeing yourself as a bit of a protector of your class, some might think your opinions are a little behind the times. Maybe, but your heart is kind, equally caring toward ideas, people, even animals. Your status will not always be protected, since life will always be taking you down unexpected paths—you are more capable of adapting to your changing life opportunities than you think, so don't feel tied down by circumstances.

When we listen closely, we can hear your inner emotions in your voice. You might want to try singing, or dancing, acting or any sort of public-image avocation—this will help loosen you up, build confidence, change your outlook. Get out of the house and help make good things happen in your community, and it's okay to step across international boundaries.

Love

You're clever, expressive, and extremely curious. You know who you are, and are unafraid of saying what's on your mind. Because you are so eager to experience life, and be informed on as many subjects as possible, you're never at a loss for words or something to talk about. You rarely threaten a lover's opinion with debate—you're a lover, not a fighter—and insist on maintaining open and honest communication between the two of you.

Money

Yeah, yeah, yeah—you always worry about how much "it" costs, or if you can find cheaper. It's said that "money" doesn't make the world go 'round but, for you, it's a breath of fresh air that you always pursue because financial security is very important to you. You do your job one step at a time and easily manage your employment responsibilities. But it's a good idea for you to try allowing something other than dollars to dominate your daydreams!

Famous People Born on This Day

Female

Eve Arden, actress
Jill Clayburgh, actress
Gloria McMillan, educator in space study
Kirsten Dunst, actress
Beatrix Wilhelmina Armgard, Queen of Holland

Male

Willie Nelson, singer/songwriter
Burt Young, actor
Bobby Vee teen, singer
Al Lewis, actor
William Lilly, astrologer/author/almanac compiler

May

May 1

Not big in size, you make up for it by being regal, upright, not stiff. You are also sociable and willful—a potent personal combination. Many love you—family life and children are probably very much in the picture. Most of you are true peacemakers, above common treachery—you're too thoughtful and cooperative for that. Still, there are times when your fire comes out. Watch out, world!

With strong creative urges, you like to please and be pleased, but share the spotlight? Not with you they won't! Your own person, you fit in roles as a front person or crusader, having reasonable visions of what could and should be. Fighting for a cause is a good role. A natural for travel, you'll take in the shows and nightlife at colorful distant meccas.

Love

5/1-born carefully choose lovers and friends who are straightforward, and make very few demands. It's not that you are unwilling to improvise or share responsibilities, you simply enjoy freedom and abhor co-dependence. You have a sharp tongue, and a jelly-filled heart. Strive for equality in your partnerships; do your part, and help lovers define theirs. Don't let your romantic checklist imprison enjoyment!

Money

Your fear of being taking advantage of by coworkers often gives the illusion of aloofness or stubbornness. Never lazy, you devote considerable effort to finding more efficient ways to get a job done and apply your ideas with sober inspiration. But you need to invest a bit more effort in the concept of teamwork. Although you're well suited for management and budget your money well, it's a good idea to ask for help when needed. Don't feel that you must always go it alone.

Famous People Born on This Day

Female

Kate Smith, singer
Calamity Jane, frontier adventuress
Mother Jones, labor leader/activist
Judy Collins, folksinger/filmmaker
Rita Coolidge, singer

Male

Tim McGraw, country singer
Glenn Ford, actor
Jack Paar, talk show pioneer
Harry Belafonte, calypso singer
Joseph Heller, author

May 2

There is envy swirling around this birthday, so it may be wise not to be too flamboyant as you strut your stuff—and you have plenty to strut about. Feeling a need to express your inner self, you have a creative, artistic streak, and although not a perfect people person, you fit in almost any crowd so long as you don't try to wedge your way in. The process of love and courtship is fascinating, isn't it?

Some of you are known as "high maintenance" types, so you might want to keep in mind that you'll go further faster when harmony and cooperation are the order of the day—don't demand it though. Practice making your opinions logical, not barbed, and remember that other drivers have rights too. Take a limo whenever you can.

Love

Doing your share in a relationship comes naturally for 5/2-born, but you're a bit impatient with laid-back, relaxed partners, and don't offer yourself casually to anyone. Although honest and patient, you expect a 50-50 share in responsibilities. You are an idealist, but a practical one. You do not make an emotional commitment unless there is solid evidence that the feeling is mutual and that the relationship has future growth potential.

Money

Having a coworker or boss breathing down your neck distracts you from delivering your best. Working on a team doing routine tasks, or waiting for others stifles and bores you silly. It's not that you're uncooperative or arrogant, but rather you're simply self-sufficient. You meet deadlines punctually and cleverly. Because you're inclined to be a somewhat difficult authority figure, entrepreneuring outlets with faithful employees suit you best.

Famous People Born on This Day

Female
Lesley Gore, singer
Peggy Bacon, author/illustrator
Pinky Lee, children's show host
Helen Morgan, singer/actress
Bianca Jagger, activist

Male
Dr. Benjamin Spock, pediatrician/
    author
Dwayne "The Rock" Johnson, wrestler
Roscoe Lee Browne, actor
Theodore Bikel, folk singer/actor
Axel Springer, newspaper magnate

May 3

Born into this world with a clock ticking in your head—don't worry, it's not a time bomb—you'll remain robust and forever active even late into life. Well-mannered, usually, you can turn argumentative when something or someone grates against your hallowed beliefs. In romance, you'll want to dominate and not be the precious fawn; you dislike uncertainty, game-playing, and unsettled circumstances generally.

You believe that there's something "out there"—like souls, afterlife, religion, and all sorts of stuff. If it's true, then you should give that the credit when you succeed, but we're sure you'll concede that "only you control you." To get the status you desire—and deserve—avoid the malarkey and keep to your here-and-now personal goals. You are one of those who can be a step ahead and also be a finisher.

Love

It's easy for you to separate your feelings for a lover from your personal life and needs because you're more comfortable with logic, instead of all those gooey emotions of love. Although strongly opinionated and stubborn, you're rarely arrogant or controlling. You express your likes and expectations right at the onset, while being cooperative at the same time. However, your my-way-or-the-highway manner can get out of hand, causing you to fly off the handle emotionally and create more problems.

Money

You often get into trouble taking on more than you should because you're constantly trying to prove yourself. Sure, it's nice when the boss gives you the thumbs up, as long as you remember the difference between service and martyrdom. It's not that your ego is so hungry for approval; you simply believe that your way is best! You're a trustworthy employee who doesn't mix business associates with personal friends.

Famous People Born on This Day

Female

Golda Meir, prime minister of Israel
Septima Poinsette Clark, civil rights
    activist
Betty Comden, lyricist
Marina Svetlova, ballerina
Mary Astor, film actress

Male

Doug Henning, magician
Christopher Cross, singer
Sugar Ray Robinson, boxer
Bing Crosby, singer
James Brown, singer

May 4

Though others may see you as the down-to-earth practical type—well, they're right—you're also a sharp mind, and very intuitive. Being persuasive, you'd make a good faith healer if you were not already committed to the more practical, like a job, car payments, and pleasing others who depend on you to be you. You're a helper to any partner, business or romantic, and your abrupt temper tells others not to mess with you.

A good teacher, we often find you helping eager minds and the young to learn and grow. You can explain things in such a calm, assured way—you're always credible. You know what's healthy, usually, and are probably in good shape even if you tire easy. The outdoors and eating right both help; roadside vegetable stands and natural honey await you!

Love

Your views and priorities about what you desire from a relationship are clearly defined from the start. However, if you want the union to thrive, make a special point of understanding whether your partner is getting the same satisfaction. It's easy for you to overlook the feelings of friends and lovers because your goals are rather rigid. Don't forget your significant other's feelings! Even though you always put down your foot, you embrace with both arms.

Money

5/4s don't take credit unless it's due. However, you tend to focus more on bottom lines and often overlook important details. Ask for help when necessary, and provide the same to fellow employees. Although a good people-person, you're very efficient at comparison-shopping and with personal budgets as well. You're honest to a fault and cautious, but sometimes too good for your own good.

Famous People Born on This Day

Female

Pia Zadora, actress
Heloise, author/advice columnist
Audrey Hepburn, actress
Roberta Peters, opera singer
Alice Liddell, inspiration for *Alice in Wonderland*

Male

Lance Bass, singer
George F. Will, political analyst
William J. Bennett, U.S. Secretary of Education
El Cordobes [Manuel Benitez], Spanish toreador
Randy Travis, country singer

May 5

Some see you as sophisticated, others as fussy, but all can rely on you to be steady and dedicated. Impatient when others waste time, you make a judicious leader, a confident diplomat, and a good arbitrator so long as the role doesn't go to your head. Perhaps early in life you felt it was "me against the world," and once you found the secret of productivity, you matured but still "feel" for the less fortunate. They need you.

You're not distracted by bluff or bluster—you see through that and already have a good idea of what the important things in life are. Like a Puritan, you hope to keep your soul free from bad karma. You'd make a good block-watcher. Spend more free time with your spouse—to keep balanced and for his or her helpful input.

Love

Because you express your feelings honestly, you're best-suited for lovers who demonstrate sobriety and reliability. You are happiest with lucid partners who initiate the action in your relationship, instead of only participating. Fly-by-night affairs hold little interest for you because you appreciate constancy. You are hopeful yet realistic, eager yet serious, and assertive yet compassionate.

Money

Your strong sense of discipline and diligence about getting the job done on time brings you applause. 5/5-born feel that very little that is worth having comes for nothing, so you are willing to work hard in order to obtain the brass ring (although you prefer gold.) You tend to be a bit unrealistic with spending but always pay your bills and are rarely without funds. Rather than nit-pick or complain, you roll up your sleeves and lend a helping hand.

Famous People Born on This Day

Female

Tammy Wynette, country singer
Alice Faye, actress/singer
Nellie Bly [Elizabeth Cochrane Seaman], journalist
Danielle Fishel, actress

Male

Tyrone Power, film actor
James Beard, culinary expert/ author
Rex Harrison, actor
Michael Palin, comedian
Karl Marx, philosopher

May 6

A truly independent type, you are a thinker and a problem-solver, helping your cause but misunderstood by many, so your days are not always smooth. You are not afraid of challenges and you're strong enough to persist—to bend but not break. Others rely on you—often they don't have as much self-control as you—still, you will have to earn their respect. Avoid over-working and over-stressing—get away from those who are simply rebellious.

A higher education, mastery of new high-tech stuff, and a wider viewpoint would definitely benefit you in your career, and so would surrounding yourself with experts and people "in the know." For inspiration, palaces and cathedrals have a certain power, and you'll have peace if you have your own space at home and plenty of room for study.

Love

You have strong and rather conventional ethics about relationships and about what a partner must do in order to keep you happy. You seek lovers who can help you grow and enlarge your personal world, and enjoy learning from others—even though the driver's seat suits you best. You idealize those whom you are close to, but not to the extent that you get hurt or disillusioned—especially when you discover that, like you, they're only human!

Money

You are financially restless and envious, always looking for something better, and are always alert about a lover's possessions and savings. Having security, not just money, tops your wish list. Employers recognize this, and often provide you with opportunities to show your stuff, challenging your skills and attention to facts. You accomplish a great deal when you stick to one objective because you have many skills and abilities.

Famous People Born on This Day

Female

Susan Brown, soap actress
Kim Oden, volleyball player
Brooke Bennett, Olympic swimmer
Roma Downey, actress
Lolita, singer

Male

George Clooney, actor
Orson Welles, actor/director
Rudolph Valentino, actor
Sigmund Freud, psychoanalyst
Tony Blair, British prime minister

May 7

Watchful like a cat, you pounce when trouble comes your way, decisively taking the initiative, bubbling over now and then, but just as quickly you get back on track, helping, serving. You usually act responsibly, and if you don't, then you're going against the grain, which you certainly don't need a reputation for. Balance out your inner fire with coolness.

Because of your natural pride you seldom stoop to anything, though when it's really necessary, you really are a hard worker capable of great concentration. You make a good team leader, too, so you like the role of rally-monkey for the troops, even if it's just your private circle of friends, making them happy. Take more time to make yourself happy, too, even if it means being alone.

Love

You're often in such a hurry to be loved that you forget to give lovers the chance to show their affection in return. The attachments you form are very strong because you don't take relationships casually, but you're inclined to exchange your own happiness for the sake of a warm body. Not one to rock the boat, it's easy for 5/7-born to take a backseat to a more dominant partner. You freely demonstrate your feelings and devotion because, for you, it's all or nothing!

Money

Although money is a constant dream and goal, financial planning isn't your expertise. You're a dependable and trustworthy employee, but usually go a bit overboard. 5/7s are not lazy, know how to be economical with time, and know how to get the most punch from the payroll envelope. Don't allow pettiness or jealousy to interfere with your job output. Your hopes and dreams are vivid, although not always practical.

Famous People Born on This Day

Female

Katerina Maleeva, tennis player
Janis Ian, singer
Eva Peron, dancer/Argentine
    president
Teresa Brewer, singer
Anne Baxter, actress

Male

Gary Cooper, screen actor
Robert Browning, poet
Johannes Brahms, composer
Johnny Unitas, football quarterback

May 8

You have a critical eye for understanding what's going on around you, and as a child you avoided trouble, but you were often right there to see it happen. Though your pace can be slower than most—you like to savor—you have a pretty good eye for money and where the power lies, though spending comes easy. Chasing the good life is a frolic in the park. "We all have our faults," you may say, except that you don't, as the peaceful, confident one.

With a natural love of commerce and trade, you're a good buyer and seller, though buying is infinitely more pleasurable. Your trappings can include a lot of interesting things, collectibles, and curious items that have your friends ooo-ing and ah-ing. A shopping trip to antique row is a great way to spend a weekend.

Love

You're someone to whom people naturally gravitate because you radiate a gentle aura of kindness mixed with personal strength. However, you're a deep well of emotions, and if you want a happy relationship, you better get a better grip on jealousy and envy issues! You're dependable and giving but quickly grow possessive of partners—although in a subtle, yet controlling manner. You're best-suited with a stable, reliable lover who enjoys living by schedule and routine.

Money

You enjoy logical, methodical work that doesn't require spontaneity or thinking fast, preferring defined procedures and responsibilities. You're not lazy or insecure, but when "one" doesn't precede "two" you lose it. Not one to get easily sucked into flattery from coworkers, you keep your private life separate from those with whom you work. Paranoid, or practical—who cares? You always get the job done!

Famous People Born on This Day

Female

Melissa Gilbert, actress
Beth Henley, actress/playwright
Heather Harper, soprano
Ruth Holland, journalist
Toni Tennille, singer/songwriter

Male

Enrique Iglesias, singer
Peter Benchley, author
Ricky Nelson, singer/actor
Fulton J. Sheen, church bishop
Harry S. Truman, U.S. president

May 9

Like most born in early May, you're strong, stubborn, usually with earthy good looks. But you're a lot quicker mentally and physically, though it may not show. Friendly, sweet, and flippant, you mature early in life but have to keep physically active through the years or wind up playing the weight control game. You'll always be good with your hands, likeable and fun, your mind sharp like a child's. Speak and others will heed.

Not content to sit idle, you're as much at home in your messy artist studio as you are speeding down the byways to a hot hangout, or where movers and shakers are ready to include you in their deals—in which you usually come out on top. You enjoy sports, like tennis and cycling, and you like including music in the mix.

Love

5/9-born function by logic, not feelings. Trusting others is challenging for you. You don't make friends or enter into relationships without careful consideration. More conventional than extravagant with affection, you demonstrate your love with devotion, constancy and honesty. Because it's easy for you to get stuck in ruts, refuse to allow old-thinking to clutter opportunity for growth and happiness; be open-minded!

Money

It's difficult for you to discuss personal financial matters with anybody, even a professional. You aim to be independent and to handle money matters solo. You're not a scaredy-cat when it boils down to purchasing luxuries or must-haves and rarely go over budget. You always pay your bills and resist personal loans. You're a dependable employee, on time and devoted. Still, your biggest treat is running home from the office and into your easy chair!

Famous People Born on This Day

Female

Candace Bergen, actress

Glenda Jackson, actress

Zita, empress of Austria and Queen of Hungary

Alley Mills, actress

Barbara Woodhouse, dog-training expert

Male

Billy Joel, singer/songwriter

Albert Finney, actor

Mike Wallace, newscaster

Henry J. Kaiser, builder of liberty ships and jeeps

Adam Opel, manufacturer

May 10

A fateful day in May, there is something special going on deep in your heart, perhaps a nagging left over from a past life, or maybe it's an itch that you just cannot scratch. To really make it in this world you'll need education along the way. Avoid power trips and envy, and don't be so moralistic and blindly devout. You're better than that, and should show it.

Getting away from those sheltered growing-up years will require some mental and philosophical adjustments, which once you make them, you'll be glad you did. Life is not a tug of war—it's a gentle push ahead. So, you will always go further, be happier, with kind words, reserving the tough stuff for when you really need it.

Love

Feelings rarely overwhelm or overpower your judgment, never acting in hasty, rash ways that you might later regret. But concerning matters of love, you hate dull routine. You rebel against emotional restrictions of any sort, and are repelled by anyone who tries to force their "stuff" on you. Not inclined to support a lover financially, you look for one who is respectful, responsible, and conventional. Some may find your tempo a bit slow, but it is the only way for you.

Money

You have good self-control and hate wasting time. You dislike on-the-job emotional interactions with coworkers, preferring to work alone or in a structured and organized mode. Money- and work-wise, you take care of your essentials first. Still, you're always ready to pitch in and help provided that it doesn't interfere with your productivity. You do not make loans to anyone, and rarely ask for help unless absolutely necessary.

Famous People Born on This Day

Female

Lisa M. Nowak, astronaut
Meg Foster, actress
Amanda Borden, gymnast
Nancy Walker, actress
Ella Grasso, politician

Male

Kenan Thompson, actor
Bono, rocker
Donovan, folk singer
David O. Selznick, movie producer
Fred Astaire, dancer/actor

May 11

Always starting, seldom finishing—that is probably you. Your intentions are good, and you may plan things perfectly, all the pieces in place, and suddenly you're off on a tangent, another adventure, caught in the trap of ideas, or amore, or the news of the hour. You are usually the smartest person in your crowd, or maybe you just attract the dull sorts. With effort you can reach your goals, maybe become your own boss.

Since your natural desire to be admired is always flaring up beneath your calm exterior, sex, romance, and an environment filled with lots of potential mates is a perfect spot for you. If you're a male, be an astrologer or psychic. If you're female, visit a garage or construction site. If undecided, well, you get the picture.

Love

No lover can ever call you mysterious—you toss your cards on the table so quickly that nobody ever has to second-guess your motives. You're a deep well of feelings, but tend to let them gush out all over. You prove your affection by devotion and constancy. Rejection is difficult because you're up front from the get-go. However, like many of those concise, concrete priorities of yours, you could use a bit more flexibility!

Money

It's not difficult for you to work in a planned and organized way—just the opposite! Even if a job doesn't appeal to your imagination, you bravely plug away and get the duty done. You aim to get the most bang from every buck, as well as from each hour off the time-clock! Regardless of your employment, your efficient, steady demeanor makes you a good supervisor or systems analyst.

Famous People Born on This Day

Female

Natasha Richardson, actress
Martha Quinn, MTV VJ
Nancy Greene, Olympic skier
Margaret Rutherford, actress
Martha Graham, dancer/choreographer

Male

Mort Sahl, comedian/political satirist/beatnik
Salvador Dali, surrealist artist
Irving Berlin [Isadore Balin], composer
Henry Morgenthau, Jr., U.S. Secretary of Treasury
Phil Silvers, comedian

May 12

You can ride on the crest of the wave to success, but you cannot make the wave, though you wouldn't mind trying. A real go-getter, you're an ideal worker because you can do it all, and all the while your mind is busy grinding out ways to improve things and relationships. You're also capable of crashing through language and cultural barriers, navigating your way through life's shark-infested waters.

Your idea of relaxation is getting that lover aside where you can share and chat and experience new things together. You have a lot in common, if you can find the right person who can keep up with you and complement you, like your sporty car does, and your smile.

Love

You don't waste time or words in matters of the heart—when you speak, you address bottom lines swiftly and seriously. Although you often discern the root of a problem immediately, you should approach matters with your lover more carefully and uncover solutions a bit slower—that way, your bluntness is less likely to overwhelm or offend your partner. Outline what you need to say, but allow room for discussion and debate.

Money

When there is work to be done, you get right down to business! Never lazy, always eager to finish projects on time, you're efficient and cooperative but never aggressive. (Yeah, you have a tendency to whine and complain, but only when others don't complete their end of the deal.) You learn from others' perspectives, and are masterful about incorporating them into yours. To 5/12-born, there is no such thing as "failure."

Famous People Born on This Day

Female

Kim Fields, actress
Dorothy Crowfoot-Hodgkin, chemist
Katharine Hepburn, actress
Florence Nightingale, public health
    pioneer
Mary Kay Ash, cosmetics company
    founder/president

Male

Emilio Estevez, actor
Ving Rhames, actor
Steve Winwood, musician
George Carlin, comedian
Tony Hawk, skateboarder

May 13

A bit of a rascal, your vivid imagination paints a world of passion and intensity, just waiting for you to arrive. You are optimistic, spiritual, and can flash your disarming sense of humor when you need attention. You long to establish your turf but might have to do so while wandering, since travel is almost in your blood. Being too light-minded can be dangerous, and ditto for tempting fate.

You have talent but shouldn't let obstacles interfere—sensitive you may feel thwarted by the demands of others and everyday life, which in itself is an unfolding high drama. You believe, but do your partners and lovers? Not always. So, you are out there in the high country, or on the back roads, like a symbol of freedom in motion.

Love

A good peacemaker, you pride yourself on not making excessive demands on lovers. You are understanding and forgive partners who seem to not live up to your standards or expectations. You often feel that it is better to tailor your demands to your lover's personality, instead of the other way around. This works up to a point, but don't let others fail you without putting your foot down.

Money

You have a gentle, respectable manner in how you work with people, and you consider everyone a source of inspiration rather than a competitor. You are sensitive to fellow employees' appeals for help, but only when it is a sincere request and doesn't involve a personal loan or infringe on your work responsibilities. You are growth-oriented and enjoy assuming positions of power as long as no one is breathing down your neck. Your respect for lessons of the past should serve you well.

Famous People Born on This Day

Female

Mary Wells, singer
Catherine II, The Great, Russian empress
Daphne du Maurier, novelist
Bea Arthur, actress
Betsy Finley Ashton, journalist

Male

Stevie Wonder, singer/songwriter
Harvey Keitel, actor
Ritchie Valens, singer
Peter Gabriel, rocker
Arthur Sullivan, composer

May 14

Without too much regard for rules or conventions, we find you, the little saint, being yourself, following your heart and mind, making the world a better place. So trusting, you have a weakness—you believe that the salad days will last, and so you may not plan for the future, perhaps you're stuck on some wild idealistic crusade, or you've gotten settled in chasing rainbows. In spite of your warmth and good intentions, make security for y-o-u your number one priority.

In relationships, you can get over-attached and may smother others—how could humble, naïve you do that? Because you feel that any relationship can work with work, you ignore the simple fact that not all people get along, and needs are different. Okay, we'll stop preaching if you will.

Love

You are always conscious of your lover's likes and dislikes. However, your tendency is to lavish affection on your partner, which may startle or overwhelm someone who isn't used to it. Few people are as open and direct as you. Whenever you have a problem in a relationship, you analyze it with your mind, not your feelings. Nevertheless, you live to prosper, and move ahead when lovers become lazy or unprogressive. You have the good sense and confidence to know when to move on when a relationship gets toxic.

Money

You believe that every benefit you obtain is a result of planning and your talents. You treasure the many lessons of past experiences, yet maintain a progressive and realistic outlook, eagerly embracing every day for what it brings. You view your career as a means to fulfill yourself while stimulating others to excel. Employers and coworkers know that they can trust you to get the job done well—and very well, at that.

Famous People Born on This Day

Female
Cate Blanchett, actress
Shanice [Wilson], singer
Gillian Anderson, actress
Season Hubley, actress
Patrice Munsel, opera singer

Male
David Byrne, musician
Robert Zemeckis, film director
George Lucas, *Star Wars* creator
David Duchovny, actor
Thomas Gainsborough, painter

May 15

Although yours is the middle birth date of May, there is nothing middle-of-the-road about you. There's a stately and serious quality to you, which some may see as cold or haughty, or even mean and cruel. Truth is, you're very spiritual while others are only so-so, and you do take things personally, and maybe they should too. You appreciate your family ties and cultural heritage, and you are a force to be reckoned with and not pushed around.

Many of you have earthy features and distinguished, deeper voices, and you're capable of extended concentration though you're not the studious type. Don't hide your social talents—you'll succeed in public life once you catch on to the political nuances; there's a wealth of literature to help you learn the ropes in any field you choose.

Love

Of course you dream of the ideal partner. You're not inclined to settle for second best nor for anyone who is unable to take care of him or herself. 5/15-born place high value on lovers who are aware of what pleases you, and you always make time to let your companion know exactly what makes you happy. However, it's a good idea to focus on the strengths of your mutual chemistry instead of continuously discussing your own demands.

Money

You make the most of opportunities by demonstrating your creative talents without alienating competitors, and you assert yourself positively when you encounter resistance to your plans. Because you express fairness to coworkers, you easily gain their support. You're disciplined and are a strong decision-maker. Authority figures admire your ability to stimulate dependent fellow employees to be independent.

Famous People Born on This Day

Female
Krissy Taylor, model
Lainie Kazan, singer/actress
Katherine Anne Porter, author
Bessie Hillman, labor leader
Anna Maria Alberghetti, singer

Male
Eddy Arnold, country singer
Trini Lopez, singer
Jasper Johns, painter
James Mason, actor
Emmitt Smith, football running back

May 16

Ambitions bring dangers, and the support you need is lacking—finding a middle ground without losing your head is a recurring challenge. Try to avoid being the one to dish out the trouble—realize that you have talents—you need time and space to develop them—ditto for relationships. Be sensitive without being over-sensitive.

Since wars, crimes, and unfortunate events seem prevalent on this day, it should be a personal message to you to learn ways to avoid these by preempting the causes. To champion causes like civil rights helps all humankind, though there's always a risk that it may bring trouble your way. Successful May 16s have mastered the civility game, and you shall too.

Love

"What about me?" is a constant dialogue between you and your lover or friends. It's not that you're self-centered, especially by your accounts. However, others don't always seem to fit into your comfortable little game plan for personal happiness because you have a "this-is-mine, that-is-yours" mind-set. Give your lover credit when credit is due, and don't be envious or too pushy. Work on jealousy and possession issues.

Money

The success of others spurs you on to match their accomplishments—you have an uncanny ability to size up coworkers' achievements and devise plans for recognition or monetary rewards. Although not materialistic or miserly, the only alliances that excite you are those that show financial promise. You're not prejudiced, nor do you look down on fellow employees who are in a less fortunate position.

Famous People Born on This Day

Female
Elizabeth Palmer Peabody, educator
Janet Jackson, singer
Olga Korbut, gymnast
Lily Pons, opera singer
Debra Winger, actress

Male
Pierce Brosnan, actor
Liberace, entertainer
Henry Fonda, actor
Woody Herman, jazz clarinetist/
bandleader

May 17

Most born this day are somewhat small and lightweight, but still have that great personal inner strength that can take you far in those very interesting professions and into the inner circle of some exclusive groups. Usually from common beginnings, you learned to love freedom and life's lighter moments, and tend to get caught up in earthly passions as well, which is not always good for a steady romance life, nor for settling down.

You have a gift of gab and are a natural at working with all sorts of gadgets and types of people, so you eventually put it all together and are rewarded. Don't be a softy and settle for less. You'd make a good reporter/journalist, making sure the facts are straight. All sorts of travel pleases you; pick environments that have opportunities for you.

Love

Your deep emotional nature makes you trustworthy but not always trusting of others. "For better or for worse" doesn't sit comfortably with you because you have specific needs and are always on the lookout for what's best for y-o-u. You're not attracted to passive partners, preferring more energetic and demonstrative ones who don't burden or slow you down. It takes lovers a great while to gain your trust. Treat everybody like you'd like to be treated in return.

Money

Being a realist, you know that your earnings increase when you are well-informed, try harder, and do what's expected. You're not an adaptable sort, but you easily adjust to new procedures when necessary. You are responsible and trustworthy, but a bit suspicious, always questioning coworkers' true motives. Working alone, rather than in groups, suits you best. Learn to be more aggressive in promoting your ideas and programs, and don't be afraid to remind everyone that they cannot use you for their own purposes.

Famous People Born on This Day

Female
Birgit Nilsson, opera soprano
Maureen O'Sullivan, actress
Enya, singer/songwriter
Caroline Charles, fashion designer
Vivian Moses, biotechnologist

Male
Taj Mahal, singer/songwriter
Bill Paxton, actor
Bob Saget, TV host/actor
Dennis Hopper, actor
Sugar Ray Leonard, boxer

May 18

You have some wild ideas—and you never seem fully satisfied. Not one to be hung-up by others' dawdling, your critical eye doesn't miss a trick, and you'll work and work to seek perfection—your perfection—learning lessons from mistakes. Romance might turn into a comedy of errors; there is nothing funny about that since you take almost all your relationships seriously. Things improve when you promise others their fair share. And let's be realistic about those dreams.

If you were less tough and easier to approach, opportunities might not slip by. It's a full-time job being sociable, so practice. Having a private trainer or mentor also helps you. Learning and refining, you're a winning student. Do something on weekends besides cleaning the garage.

Love

Although you lavish attention on your partner, you draw the line between money and love. You don't take chances, choosing to test the merits of a suitor before you commit. Being a realist is admirable and good, but learn to differentiate between romance and finance—after all, love relationships shouldn't solely revolve around money and security. You are happiest with a partner who is as serious as you and who is a stabilizing influence.

Money

You're frugal with time and money and have an uncanny knack for knowing how to capitalize on both. Although you think twice (at least) before investing time or money, for on-the-job advancement you stay informed and look the part in order to meet the challenge of competitors. You accept the daily trials of the workday world, knowing that you can solve any problems that come your way and earn a decent living at the same time.

Famous People Born on This Day

Female

Margot Fonteyn, ballerina
Diane McBain, actress
Sarah Miriam Peale, portrait painter
Diane E. Duane, science fiction
    author
Helen Chadwick, artist

Male

George Strait, country singer
Pope John Paul II
Perry Como, singer
Frank Capra, film director
Chow Yun Fat, actor

May 19

If you "got it" then "flaunt it!" Some people have a natural knack for flowing right in and taking an important chair—that's you. This is usually a blessing for females but an invitation to competition if you're male. Either way, there's something special about you, perhaps beauty, kinda like charisma but not quite, like a pied piper that others will gladly follow, for awhile. Be selective: some paths may not get you where you want to go.

Usually a whiz when it comes to fashion and the finer things in life, you can be caught up in the glamour—easily swayed though you think it couldn't happen to you. Since others listen, you're a good organizer. Group travels appeal to you, letting you be the ringleader—and first in line to soak up the goodies.

Love

You have plenty of energy in reserve but usually don't use it except when motivated by an equally active partner who can draw out and complement your enthusiasm. Therefore, you're happiest with a fairly demanding, constructive partner who keeps you at your highest levels of ability. For you, love is an exciting, but never scary adventure—provided that you temper your spontaneity with a modicum of wisdom and compassion!

Money

Co-workers admire your excellent reasoning ability and keen judgment—your mind is never at rest. Even people whose opinions differ from yours are quickly convinced by your arguments and won over to your position. You have a deep thirst for knowledge and an awesome capacity to accumulate information. Your gentle and easy-going personality is an asset in most professions, but you might find it difficult to cope with the abrasive elements of close and direct competition.

Famous People Born on This Day

Female

Grace Jones, actress/singer
Nora Ephron, screenwriter
Yazz [Yasmin Evans], musician
Nellie Melba [Heal Mitchell], soprano
Lorraine Hansberry, author

Male

James Fox, actor
David Hartman, TV personality
Peter Townshend, musician
Steve Ford, actor

May 20

Such a sweetheart, and if you're male, such a little GQ'er, ready for the spotlight. Self-centered but lovable, others can quickly forgive your minor faults, though they'll be talking behind your back. You can always make new friends if the old ones wear out. You're not a rocket scientist, but then who is? Always protect your eyesight, bright one. Sunglasses were invented for you.

Despite being somewhat of a fantastic person, you do wish to connect romantically with someone in the same career, though the spotlight may not be big enough for both. You know that money makes the world go around, so learning more about how to handle it is as interesting as it is profitable. You wish others wouldn't talk so fast—not as fast as you. Fun? If you're there, it's fun.

Love

To a certain extent, you may unintentionally manipulate your partner in order to ensure that you get the attention you need—passive-aggressive scenarios are easy for you, even though your intention is never to injure or hurt. However, 5/20-borns have a tendency to worry, often blabbing their frustrations to inappropriate "confidants." Remember: everybody usually gets back what they put out, and invest. Embrace your weaknesses, as well as those of your lovers, and aim for improvement and excellence!

Money

Although not driven for recognition, like everybody else you expect a little praise and acknowledgement for your efforts—and for being you! You have good control over your ego, even though it's hard for you to keep your opinions silent. Coworkers know that you are reliable and a team player. However, you need to learn how to censor or control your very strong opinions. You're masterful and loud when expressing discomfort.

Famous People Born on This Day

Female

Cher, entertainer
Mindy Cohn, actress
Fia Porter, actress
Galina Vasilyevna Amelkina, doctor/
   cosmonaut
Christina Bass-Kaiser, Olympic
   speed skater

Male

Busta Rhymes, rapper
George Gobel, entertainer
Joe Cocker, musician
Dave Thomas, comedian
James Stewart, actor

May 21

You're a perfect fit for a warm spring day—friendly, not a prejudiced bone in your body, a little dynamo of sparkling activity, surrounded by more than your fair share of friends. Holding onto things can be a pain, since you're not real good at keeping track. Being a little more orderly and less "golly gee" would help, especially to succeed in your career where you may work with valuable tools, building a better world.

A good life can turn you into a pumpkin, or at least a radish, so exercise and watching your diet as you grow older is a must. Age slows your metabolism down. Duh. A solid worker, reward yourself with steam baths, beauty treatments, even cross-country treks—and a nice soft pillow at the end of the day. Sweet dreams, sweetheart!

Love

You don't have specific priorities about what you want in a lover, so it's a good idea for you to be ever-cautious when auditioning one. Isn't it about time for you to start setting some standards? After all, a few words spelling out your expectations can make a relationship go swimmingly and prosper for all concerned. Select a partner who is not too possessive because you're used to being free, even if you don't enjoy being alone. Never underestimate your needs—TLC is for Y-O-U!

Money

Your employment requires clear guidelines and rules because you're not expert at improvising, or doing anything on-the-fly. You're a terrific team player and follower-of-rules, but not great at delegating or making decisions. 5/21-born must keep careful watch on their feelings so as not to become embittered by occasional setbacks. Learn how to budget both time and expenses because impulse-shopping and sloppy bill-paying come easy.

Famous People Born on This Day

Female
Kay Kendall, actress
Doris Mae Akers, gospel singer/
    songwriter
Annabel Schofield, actress
Fairuza Balk, actress
Peggy Cass, actress/comedienne

Male
Armand Hammer, industrialist
Mr. T [Lawrence Tero], actor
Harold Robbins, author
Judge Reinhold, actor
Dennis Day, singer

May 22

Yes, yes, we know—you're the type who gets a new book and rushes to see what it says about you first. Okay, you're kind of a courageous nut—also socially discriminating and an intellectual, or should at least give it a try. Health conscious, you might be a nurse or physician, even a farmer since the outdoors is your true second home. There isn't a device or machine you cannot handle, because you're a real craftsperson, behind the wheel of life.

Always thirsty for more, you should never go away disappointed. You'd probably make a good camp counselor, and look good in a uniform—makes you feel like a superhero. For fun, nothing beats being out in the healthy outdoors. A good communicator and a good listener, you're a hoot around the campfire or the watercooler.

Love

You're not a real serious type but are emotionally stable and cautious before committing to another. Never rash, you enter a what-is-hoped-to-be a relationship only after much thought, preferring to build momentum slowly but surely. You are tolerant with others' quirks and history, but are likely to chafe at the bit when loved ones don't share your outlook. Don't be defensive; most people are willing to meet you halfway if you give them the chance.

Money

At work, two heads (or more) are better than just yours. You enjoy comradery, gossip, and brainstorming. Capable of following instructions after they are defined, you eagerly attack projects and don't rest until they're completed. It's a good idea that you find a financial advisor, because saving for the rainy day doesn't fit in your daily regime or weather report. Although a good shopper, you are an expert at frittering away those hard-earned dollars.

Famous People Born on This Day

Female
Naomi Campbell, model
Susan Strasberg, actress
Ann Cusack, actress
Mary Cassatt, artist
Judith Crist, film/television critic

Male
Laurence Olivier, actor
T. Boone Pickens, CEO
Richard Benjamin, director/actor
Arthur Conan Doyle, author
Richard Wagner, composer

May 23

Wouldn't it be great if you could just snap your fingers and put yourself in a trance where everything works out perfectly, especially if you could put a spell on others too? Oh, but life is not always harmonious, though it's always a little more exciting when you're around and in a good mood, which is most of the time because you're basically more optimistic than most. Get the practical matters squared away first.

Planning can bring peace, so it always helps you to map out your plans of action—at work and everywhere else. You can rise to the pinnacle of success, usually without sacrificing that pleasant personality or your time for love and the arts. Socially skillful, you'd like being a hypnotist. You're tickled by mystery and suspense. When you get in a groove, you rock.

Love

You are happiest with mature but active lovers who help and encourage you to recycle your 5/23-worry-wart energies and inspire you to have fun, move ahead. It's not easy for you to forgive a lover's past indiscretions because you are fervently concerned about one's background and want to know everything. Live in the moment, rather than fret over history!

Money

In the perfect world of financial survival, you're, well, "perfect"! You work well with others who understand the work-a-day employment ropes and inspire and guide you like a school teacher. Not managerial or executive material, you enjoy being told precisely what to do and say, and how and when to act. A bit stingy with income, learn to loosen up the purse-strings and rid yourself of "poverty-consciousness."

Famous People Born on This Day

Female

Jewel, singer
Sarah Margaret Fuller, author
Margaret Hayden Rector, author
Rosemary Clooney, singer
Helen O'Connell, singer

Male

Drew Carey, actor/comedian
Scatman Crothers, entertainer
Douglas Fairbanks, actor
Artie Shaw, big band leader
Carolus Linnaeus, botanist

May 24

For someone born late in hepped-up May, you are surprisingly down-to-earth, and a good business partner or companion—love is like a business, a little. You are well aware of social rules and really, you'd make a good executive, because you're quick to turn rushing thoughts into purposeful action—orderly and dignified. Privately, you are spiritual, taking life's challenges in stride, fulfilling your karmic tests, hopefully.

Life, in general, should be good to you. Nothing should stop you from shucking any bad habits and without having to agonize over the withdrawal process like others do. You have a bit of a healing touch, so you'd make a good doctor, or counselor, though it may take awhile for others to warm up to the real you. Who knew you were so smart? Can't everyone do math?

Love

You have a tremendous capacity for empathy and kindness. You don't take relationships lightly; instead, you bulldoze into them with determined abandon, but always with both eyes open. You like bare bone, honest communication and bottom-lines. 5/24-born want everything Even Steven-balanced . . . even though it may not always be realistic or practical from others' perspectives. When you indulge the needs of others, it can provide beautiful dividends of goodwill—give it a try!

Money

Face it: you're not all that great with your savings, but love everything that money buys. You're a devoted, reliable employee who is always available in an emergency. You remember every financial boo-boo and learn from every crisis, from one mistake after another, never hesitating to ask for help, seek advice from those who know better, or who can teach you a more prosperous way to make your monies grow.

Famous People Born on This Day

Female

Patti LaBelle, singer
Priscilla Presley, actress
Victoria, Queen of Great Britian
Lillian Moller Gilbreth, psychologist
Mai Zetterling, actress/director

Male

Bob Dylan, singer
Jean-Paul Marat, French revolutionist
Samuel I. Newhouse, publisher
Tommy Chong, actor/comedian
Gary Burghoff, actor

May 25

The dark and handsome type, you're serious and thoughtful, speaking from your mind directly, streaming out amazing, useful conversation like a talking encyclopedia. Well, that's how some of you are; others of you are so businesslike that speech is doled out economically, and you should get paid for that. You don't mind arguing since you take it impersonally, though your sorry adversaries don't. The heck with them, those vulturous incompetents!

You love travel and an uncomplicated lifestyle, and usually your needs are met—you don't require millions because that is not what life is about. Still, you're capable of growing a nest egg that might make the Easter Bunny jealous, that is, if you really wanted to. Learning about philosophical topics gets you in touch with your center. That's important. Take the millions, too.

Love

You don't make a point to irritate or intimidate lovers intentionally; however, "emotional understanding" isn't your strength. Your feelings for a partner are always deep, but you tend to be more expert at denial, rather than reality. Accept the fact that you often fill those relationship baskets of yours with too many imaginary eggs. Be more understanding and clear about expressing your needs. After all, not all lovers are mind-readers!

Money

You're not a pansy or push-over, but are easily swayed by coworkers who are loud and proud (which drives you nuts). The 5/25-remedy? How about learning to be more demanding or commanding yourself? After all, fellow employees acknowledge that you're a good worker, and often do more than your share. Now's the time to put down your foot and get stricter about saying "no" when others are just plain lazy. Look in the mirror and repeat: "I am worthy, I am worthy."

Famous People Born on This Day

Female

Beverly Sills, opera singer
Jeanne Crain, actress
Anne Heche, actress
Leslie Uggams, singer
Rachel Carson, ecologist/author

Male

Mike Myers, actor
Frank Oz, Muppetteer
Miles Davis, musician
Robert Ludlum, author
Ralph Waldo Emerson, essayist/
philosopher

May 26

Outwardly smart and inwardly a bit cold-hearted, you may be destined to reign in a world of thoughts and interesting ideas. You can switch to the winning side at any time, which is good for business and necessary when the chips are down, which could be often since you may not be Miss/Mr. popularity. Since you attract a lot of romantic interest (you say you don't like it, but admit it, you do), you're likely to marry rich or marry many.

With such a rich mental life filling your head, and an excellent student when motivated, an even better teacher, you might only be able to handle ordinary life temporarily before going out on your own in search of fulfillment and excitement, perhaps writing and communicating your findings, or just getting there ahead of the crowd.

Love

Criticism makes you batty. You try to never second-guess others, and are comfortable taking things as they come. Why? Simply put: you're optimistic, and a bit spacey, perhaps, but never unaware of what's happening on any emotional front. You make your desires perfectly clear—sometimes even writing them down so that your lover won't presume. But it's easy for you to get caught up in others' unnecessary trivia or untruths. So, stop—right now!

Money

It's not that you're unrealistic or gullible, but it's a good idea that you learn to abstain from taking on positions of power on the job because it's just not where your head is at. You're popular because you don't make excessive demands on coworkers, always tolerant of their frailties. You're true blue, and devoted, and your performance is right on. However, you work best under supervision. In order for 5/26-born to make a profit, you must learn to accentuate the positive, as well as your potentials!

Famous People Born on This Day

Female

Stevie Nicks, singer
Sally Ride, first American woman
   in space
Peggy Lee, singer/lyricist
Dorothea Lange, documentary
   photographer
Mary Wollstonecraft Godwin, writer

Male

Lenny Kravitz, singer
Peter Cushing, actor
Al Jolson, entertainer
John Wayne, actor
Hank Williams, Jr., country singer

May 27

Like the rolling stone that gathers no moss, you tumble decisively through life's valleys and even up to the summits, a force to be recognized and admired by others who see that there's the heart of a giant behind your quiet, friendly exterior. You possess that special magnetism, good for romance, and your sense of drama lets you get your points across loud and clear, though you prefer the veil of secrecy and intrigue.

You have a distinctive appearance and don't mind sitting tall in the saddle. You're also an impresario and performer—not precise but you usually know your craft well enough. For a kick, find out how those snake charmers in India work—what's with that? You can charm your own "snakes" in your roles as a diplomat, technician, engineer, or problem-solver.

Love

You enjoy the excitement that relationships deliver, never having strict or rigid itineraries, just enjoyable exploration. Open-minded but not always realistic, you work well with lovers who are not static or too old-fashioned, preferring spontaneous unplanned quality time, and letting your relationship world spin about at its own merry pace. But once boredom settles in, you're out the door! A roll-with-punches partner complements your inner-child escapism best.

Money

Because you're more comfortable working in a world far removed from finances and harsh reality, you're not well-eqipped for a career in which you have to manage other people's money. You're not stupid or unmotivated, of course! However, your mind is strongly influenced by your imagination. Don't take on work responsibilities that you know you're unqualified for. Work with your strengths, don't exaggerate your shortcomings.

Famous People Born on This Day

Female
Siouxsie Sioux, singer
Lisa Niemi, actress
Amelia Bloomer, social reformer/
    women's rights activist
Isadora Duncan, dancer
Lee Merriweather, actress

Male
Vincent Price, actor
Henry Kissinger, diplomat
Dashiell Hammett, author
Wild Bill Hickok, western enter-
    tainer
Louis Gossett, Jr., actor

May 28

Emotions can get the better of you, so sometimes you surprise people with your changes of face and changes of heart. Hey, not everyone has such a range to their personality, so make the best of yours without being superficial. Realize that if others don't trust you, they've probably picked up on something or gotten side-tracked. People aside, you're a superstar at practical arts—homecrafts, construction, making a good pizza—stuff you may wish you could get away from but others appreciate.

A bit flighty, you do your best concentration without the buzz of others around you, and you occasionally come up with some flashes of pure genius, usually after you've become immersed in the topic. Because you can be egg-headed, you enjoy being a deadhead occasionally. On vacation, don't fall asleep on the beach and get sunburned.

Love

You enjoy the intellectual, mindful trappings of love because emotions frighten you. 5/28-born are happiest with straight-shooting, demonstrative, and attentive partners. You're pretty good at managing a household and maintaining your end of a relationship; it's only when the touchy-feely stuff takes over that you get paralyzed. 5/28s tend to keep their own counsel, but like to watch. You listen and assess, survey and scrutinize.

Money

You do your best work when you know exactly what is expected from you and are protected from surprise, because you like knowing what's-to-come and delight in defined guidelines. Even though you're open-minded and willing to pitch in, you're not great at improvising. Your rational mind is strongly influenced by outside circumstances. In order for you to complete a job on time, you require organization and maybe someone to crack the whip loudly.

Famous People Born on This Day

Female

Kylie Minogue, singer
Carroll Baker, actress
Julia Ward Howe, suffragist
Betty Shabazz, educator/widow of Malcolm X
Gladys Knight, singer

Male

Ian Fleming, author
Rudolph Giuliani, politician
John Fogerty, singer
T-Bone Walker, blues guitarist
Jim Thorpe, athlete

May 29

You flow like water into everything, often a tease, a flirt, a compliment-giver, a socialite, even a comedian, but respected for your ability to adapt and win just about everyone over to your way of thinking. This works for both males and females. Maybe this comes from competing with siblings. Liked by the opposite sex, still, you're likely to be cheated upon and vice versa, but you're not hurt by romance games.

You are born on an odd and fascinating day, with a powerful star shining down on you. Whoopie—lots of passion and life-action and maybe, just maybe, a respectable position at an early age. You'll also need lots of protection—there is always some disease in the wind. Pure water and mineral baths—and shade—let you cool down and really relax.

Love

You need partners who don't discuss your personal matters, keep all those secrets behind private and closed doors, and aren't too clingy or dependent. 5/29-born yearn to share time and tunes with a partner who sings the same song, drives at your speed, doesn't second-guess you, or is too bossy. You're willing to let your lover have their own life and fantasies, too—provided that he or she always returns home, and sings your blessings.

Money

It becomes unsettling for you when everyone at your job doesn't understand you or isn't your best friend. You try very hard to be friendly and cooperative, you do everything expected. However, there's this ongoing little upper-brain chatter that constantly screams: "My job IS my life!" Never forget that YOUR happiness means as much to you as to your employer's profits! However true blue and nervously sensitive you are, you meet up to all responsibilities—after all, that's what you're paid for.

Famous People Born on This Day

Female

Lisa Whelchel, actress
LaToya Jackson, singer
Annette Bening, actress
Beatrice Lillie, entertainer
Melissa Etheridge, singer

Male

John F. Kennedy, U.S. president
Bob Hope, entertainer
Patrick Henry, U.S. patriot
Al Unser, racecar driver
Anthony Geary, actor

May 30

Sensitive, yet fiery and outgoing, you're unaffected by and unafraid of the evils of life, feeling that you can and will triumph over those dirty little challenges and those unblessed ones who prey on the gifted, like you. Make sure it's not the other way around. Haven't you heard of karma? What you want is good lovin', never-ending happiness, and many successes—and you may settle for two out of three, probably.

Since you might believe that luck is a factor (it is), you have an eye on how to succeed by using timing and intuition—just plain wishing for something isn't enough; you'll have to summon some real inner magic if you think "the house" can be beaten. You have some artistic talents; a little more style would help, so would timely tutelage from experts.

Love

You're a source of inspiration, stimulation, and change to everyone you know, and appreciate receptive, easy-going partners because you have more than enough ideas for you both. Relationships mean mucho to you; you either are, or are not, a couple. 5/30-born dislike endless dialogue about responsibility, preferring a lover who's as warm, gentle, and inspiring as a sunrise. You rarely make excuses for a partner or take unexpected disappointment to heart—you enjoy the dance even more than the music.

Money

You're practical and dependable, rarely close-minded—all good reasons for coworkers and employees to like you so much! Your self-confidence needs constant attention in order to face your work-a-day world without apprehension. You respect the work ethic, value honesty, and have good morals. Being a bit on the timid side, you're uncomfortable in confrontational situations or overly responsible on-the-job positions. Bottom line: you aim to please.

Famous People Born on This Day

Female
Wynonna Judd, singer
Meredith McRea, actress
Candy Lightner, political activist
Ruta Lee, actress
Alice Sophia Stopford Green, proponent of Irish independence

Male
Benny Goodman, bandleader
Michael J. Pollard, actor
Mel Blanc, cartoon voice
Clint Walker, actor
Peter I, The Great, tsar of Russia

May 31

May's last day can feel like the very best birth date! Perhaps you're blessed with a commanding physique, sparkling eyes, or just lots of heart. Romantic and venturesome, you eye the horizon and outgrow your surroundings—you do have the ambition and brainy-ness to succeed in any number of challenging locations. To have it all, you've got to be the quiet hero—too much bluster can burst your balloon.

A good horse trader, you should negotiate your "deals" face-to-face, in earnest, so that all the cards are on the table. Letting others put the reins on you isn't something you'll sit still for anyway. Speaking of reins, you'd get a kick out of horses, especially show or racehorses. Of course, riding them can be scary. You're better as a people-person, armed with a cellphone.

Love

You express your likes and dislikes lucidly and at the moment, and do your best to create romantic, silk purse passion from all available material. Even though your imagination overflows with ideals and fantasies, you're never in a rush to get to the finish line. You take your time in love, savoring every moment. You're uneasy with clinging types, preferring passionate, imaginative improvisation over schedule or planned scenario.

Money

Do what you want with your hands, but it's a good idea to keep both feet firmly planted on the ground when it boils down to job description and deadlines. It's difficult for you to separate coworkers from personal friends; this gray line of confusion often results in problems. You're honest and diligent about work duties and are always reliable, although not particularly punctual. You do what you can, and don't over-extend yourself. Learn when to ask for assistance.

Famous People Born on This Day

Female

Lea Thompson, actress
Sharon Gless, actress
Elizabeth Blackwell, first woman
    doctor of medicine
Brooke Shields, model/actress

Male

Clint Eastwood, actor
Tom Berenger, actor
Joe Namath, football quarterback
Walt Whitman, poet
Norman Vincent Peale, clergyman/
    author

June

June 1

If you were playing cards, you'd hold them close to the vest, not wanting to take chances or give away your edge. You can be very businesslike and proud of it, and you usually get a good value for your efforts—gold trimmings and jewelry to match. Romance? Can you ever get enough? Minor tip: life is more enjoyable when you make others comfortable around you—some of you can turn them off with your aura of superiority.

You have a good eye for craftsmanship and doing things right, though you may be a bit untidy yourself—your mind is too busy on more important matters to bother with trifles. Know the rules, the tricks, and the cheat codes—pick them up at weekend seminars and quick-refresher courses—you can never have too much education.

Love

You devote a great deal of energy to your lover's interests, always planning things as a couple which may be misinterpreted as controlling, depending on how discreet you are—so be careful not to overlook or overbook your partner's needs, and don't second-guess his or her dreams! You enjoy independent-minded companions who are self-motivated, as long as they remember what makes a relationship work for you. 6/1-born are sincere about affections and not hesitant about demonstrating them.

Money

You are intelligent, optimistic, quick on your feet, and dislike routine (how Gemini of you!). More a follower than trailblazer, you lack incentive for arduous, repetitive tasks. Although gregarious and friendly, you prefer solo activities rather than teamwork or brainstorming with groups. You don't bother with coworkers who waste their time, or yours. For employment enjoyment, take things one step at a time, and function independently.

Famous People Born on This Day

Female

Marilyn Monroe, actress
Colleen McCullough, writer
Molly Picon, actress/comedienne
Alanis Morissette, singer/songwriter
Lisa Hartman Black, singer/actress

Male

Andy Griffith, actor/comedian
Morgan Freeman, actor
Pat Boone, singer
Nelson Riddle, musical conductor
Reverend Ike, evangelist minister

June 2

When others see a grasshopper, they see a bug. You see this fantastic living machine. When others see a stop sign, they put their foot on the brake. You, instead, wonder who gave anyone the authority to put it there, why is it an octagon, and by gosh, you just ought to run it! Some of your ideas are not so good but most get others thinking, so express yourself even if you come across as a dickens, or cold and calculating.

Rather shy, you'd benefit from role-playing games where you can loosen up—put on the skipper's hat, or wield a knife like chef Julia Child. Sure, you want career stability, as well as a lot less boredom in everyday routines. Don't say no to too many opportunities. A good mate, you may have a family later in life.

Love

You are great help to lovers who are vague or uncertain about their sense of direction. This talent comes from your ability to quickly analyze issues, not from a "you-do-this, and I'll do that" credo. You always allow lovers the right to their own opinions, thereby avoiding many pitfalls (mainly because you hate "I told you so's"). 6/2-born believe that it takes "two" in order to grow, even though you prefer the comfy front-seat position and last word.

Money

"Tell me what you want and I'll do it" is on your business card, probably. Once you establish goals, you prepare a precise itinerary, and don't rest until it's completed. You focus on one thing at a time and direct all your efforts towards that end, rarely making excuses or missing a deadline. Clever about money, you know how to get the best bang for the buck and have fun with spendings, as well as time. You rarely live beyond your means.

Famous People Born on This Day

Female

Betty Furness, journalist
Hedda Hopper, Hollywood gossip
   columnist
Sally Kellerman, actress
Barbara Pym, author
Dorothy West, journalist

Male

Jerry Mathers, actor
Marvin Hamlisch, composer/pianist
Stacy Keach, actor
Johnny Weissmuller, Olympic
   swimmer
Barry Levinson, director

June 3

Less talk, more action—that's what you'd like to see, as if life were a race. It is and you intend to win and you may bend the rules to do so, though you don't have to. You are bright and down-to-earth, so there is always a place for you, but you could make more of an effort to make sure it's where you can grow and eventually gain your place in the sun. Don't wander without a plan, and get away from the cheap, tawdry crowd.

You don't usually stray away from your element, so you have to learn to be comfortable in strange surroundings. Taking a vacation with you would be a lot more fun if there were fewer people to get in the way, as well as a set schedule and the option to choose the entertainment you want.

Love

Your biggest romantic boo-boo is missing out on the magic of the moment because you are always in a hurry and many times forget to appreciate it. You presume a lot from relationships and expect things to be similar to tabloids or romance novels. While fair and open-minded, you prefer pampering rather than tackling problems. Don't obsess so much about trivia because you may miss out on the golden glory of romantic right-now moments.

Money

Strict schedules are painful and demanding for you because you're repelled by snail-pace protocol, or having to do everything in an orderly sequence— preferring energetic fireworks-like tempos. You vividly remember lessons from the past and hate repeating them. Focus your attention on the end result, get into a rhythm, and just move forward. And, while you're buzzing along, find yourself an honest accountant to help you plan for the future.

Famous People Born on This Day

Female

Josephine Baker, entertainer
Colleen Dewhurst, actress
Paulette Goddard, actress
Suzi Quatro, musician
Anita Harris, singer/actress

Male

Curtis Mayfield, singer
Tony Curtis, actor
Allen Ginsberg, beat poet
Chuck Barris, game show producer/ host
Jefferson Davis, president of the Confederate States

June 4

Beauty, magnetism, so sociable—that describes many born on this special birthday. That twinkle in your eye—who can resist? Still you have a tendency to have too few scruples and too many ruses. Since people admire you, you might take advantage now and then which might be a little too visible, and the magic might wear off. Full of thoughts and ideas, you've got a business mind but an artist's ambitions—try to combine them. Work is art. Prove that you're not fluff.

Volunteering to help in projects is especially fulfilling so long as your presence isn't a distraction. Since you're in with the in-crowd, you're fond of pleasure, not really a faithful mate since you'd rather be on the go, working your mojo magic, sometimes in lush mountain valleys, a good, refreshing place for you.

Love

Realistic about what you can and cannot expect from relationships, you try not to let imaginary guidelines and fantasies overshadow reality (keyword being "try"). You cover a lot of ground in your life, not so much by being thorough but by being honest and open-minded. You are a flirtatious partner, but try to keep both feet on the ground, even though you gravitate to rather unpredictable or unconventional companions. The age of a lover is never a priority, just so long as he or she is "trainable."

Money

You have an active mind and curious nature, always asking questions. Experience has taught you to be self-reliant, and although you may be a slow learner—you never forget a thing! However, a big challenge for you is that you never learned to save money. Thinking about the future comes naturally for you, so long as it doesn't involve the bank book. Although you're not keen about budgets or financial bottom lines, you usually get the most out of what you have.

Famous People Born on This Day

Female
Angelina Jolie, actress
Michelle Phillips, singer/actress
Rosalind Russell, actress
Rosemary Joyce, model/actress
Blanch Knopf, publishing executive

Male
Noah Wyle, actor
Dennis Weaver, actor
Bruce Dern, actor
Robert Merrill, baritone
Christopher Cockerell, inventor

June 5

A keen eye and very versatile, you are bound to succeed and collect rewards along he way. Engaging but a bit egotistical, you are not the sit at home type, and wherever you go, your "sharpness" can put things on edge, usually in a fun way. You are a bit of a shining star and a favorite of the opposite sex. You'd like all the answers—don't be shy and ask the right questions! One answer is to set higher goals that include helping the world around you hum.

The night life, being in vogue, being the center of attention—you like this, and other organized surroundings where you can mix with movers and shakers, learning from their stories, making connections for profit or romance. All the hours you put in are often easy hours, which is what you need.

Love

Even though no one would consider you a social butterfly, you desire stimulating companions and are curious about life off the beaten track. Ordinary people bore you quickly. You don't expect a partner to pay attention to you during his or her every waking moment, but you also won't let your partner demand too much from you. Possessiveness and jealousy drive you crazy. You have very little interest in lovers who are overly emotional.

Money

You enjoy learning how everything works as a whole—examining and dissecting the Big Picture first, then dissecting the details, then flying by your intuitive tail! Although some may claim that your 6/5-born thinking is erratic or a bit illogical, you never allow your emotions to influence business decisions. Although not mathematically inclined, you always perform honest, straightforward work, and you don't hesitate to ask for professional help.

Famous People Born on This Day

Female
Laurie Anderson, performance
   artist
Anastasia N. Romanov, daughter
   of last Russian tsar
Rose Hill, singer/actress
Teri Nunn, singer

Male
Mark Wahlberg, actor
Kenny G, alto saxophonist
Bill Moyers, journalist
Spalding Gray, actor
William Boyd, actor

June 6

Soft, sensitive, and oh-so lovingly you flow along, your imagination filled with romantic and helpful ideas, bubbling up as you lose interest in dull mundane tasks. Usually born on the good side of the tracks, maybe even to a family who owns the tracks, you have to later prove yourself since you might be taken lightly. The arts or medicine are good fields. You are cordial, childlike, but sometimes up and down in the mental department, and probably a secret lover.

Does knowing secrets about your birthday help? It encourages you to do what you do best and grow! Higher education or a mentor builds your confidence and credibility—don't just hang with the right crowd. Be a better time manager—leave the dirty work to others—make anything you do as productive as it is fun.

Love

Although friendly, you have difficulty forming close relationships. You fear that you will lose your freedom if you become too closely attached to another. You prefer lovers who are secure about themselves, able to meet any emergency, and don't let their emotions overwhelm them. Others find your honesty and sensitivity both inspiring and magnetic. Although a bit co-dependent, you appreciate private quiet time. People like you for being yourself.

Money

You make up your mind quickly and usually stick with your decision—even though you don't carefully weigh out every option or alternative. To many coworkers, you come off as more "inspired" than "educated." Your levity and youthfulness keep fellow employees and customers smiling. It's important that you have a trusting confidant to help you in financial matters because savings and budgets are not your strong points.

Famous People Born on This Day

Female

Amanda Pays, actress
Sandra Bernhard, comedienne/
    actress
Ruth Benedict, anthropologist
Nanette Davalois, ballet dancer
Pearl S. Buck, writer

Male

Bjorn Borg, tennis player
Thomas Mann, novelist
Walter P. Chrysler, founded Chrysler
    Corporation
Khachaturian, musician/composer
Gary "US" Bonds, singer/songwriter

June 7

A wonderful day—feel life and love and be in the moment! Following your heart takes you to beauty and romance, not always the best, but fun. Life does not always reward the most talented, sometimes luck is involved—luck would be a good thing to know more about, like making your own. When things turn sour, you turn caustic. Don't! Making negatives "personal" will not endear you to others. Think a bit before speaking.

It really grates on you when things aren't going in your favor; your parade will please more if you take time to plan, are less impulsive, don't appear self-first-ish, and you spin a reasonable, fair tune. Walking a mile in the other's shoes is good occasional role advice for you. Too trusting, remember that advertisements usually deliver less than promised.

Love

For you, love is a kind of service, and the more you do for someone you like, the better you feel. You treat people very well, freely share your time, secrets and, often, your money. You are very loyal to your lover and friends and usually give more than expected. For you, "having" someone to call your own is everything; companionship means more to you than passion. Take the time to enjoy the moment—whether alone or involved.

Money

You have a sharp mind and terrific ability to understand ideas that aren't obvious to others. You keep track of details, but have trouble concentrating on long-term projects easily. Still, 6/7-born look at the positive side, always seeking ways to improve matters. For you, "honesty is the only policy, time is money." You are an efficient and loyal worker who works more for recognition than financial rewards.

Famous People Born on This Day

Female

Anna Kournikova, tennis player
Jenny Jones, talk show host
Sally B. Thornton, philanthropist
Gwendolyn Brooks, poet
Jessica Tandy, actress

Male

Allen Iverson, basketball player
Prince, musician
Liam Neeson, actor
Dean Martin, entertainer
Paul Gauguin, artist

June 8

Bad people should watch out for you since you're quite capable of turning from the soft honey-bunny into a scorpion with a revenge sting, and this applies to any relationships. You aim to please, but you also have an inner need to have it your way. What a dilemma! Channel all that hidden emotion—let off steam when you feel down; corral those sensual desires for intimacy, and don't con.

Variety is the spice of life, and you can do more than you think, so try it. Knowing the tricks of the trade—what goes on behind the scenes—will certainly impress others, and because you like to explore whatever's hidden or little-known, you'd relish the role of detective, researcher, or secret-spiller, or working your magic behind closed doors. Wear sunglasses, wear sunscreen, wear clothes.

Love

Ever hopeful, you have a tendency to plunge into relationships without thinking about consequences. You're impractically practical, cool, and conscientiously cautious. Even though you take everything in stride, you're far deeper than many know. 6/8-born need the reassurance that a lover is on the same page, and invest much time in the relationship in order to make sure that both parties are loyal. Jealous? Not really—just more needy than possessive.

Money

Some jobs require attention to small details, and others don't. Whatever job is yours, it's likely that you go for the ones with minutiae. Because you enjoy people and exploration, you do well in careers such as sales, education, and therapy. Although saving for a rainy day isn't your thing, you're always clever enough to never get caught wet. 6/8-born know that hiding from hard facts doesn't make them disappear!

Famous People Born on This Day

Female

Dana Wynter, actress
Nancy Sinatra, singer
Alexis Smith, actress
Joan Rivers, entertainer
Barbara Bush, former U.S.
    First Lady

Male

Keenan Ivory Wayans, actor/comedian
Boz Skaggs, singer
Jerry Stiller, comedian/actor
Robert Preston, actor
Frank Lloyd Wright, architect

June 9

Blessed by a star that could take you into high-stakes action careers like the military, behind-the-scenes in government (like James Bond!), or conducting the show, you have a talent for communicating and getting your point across; heaven knows there's lots of adversarial garbage you could clean up. If you had to manipulate someone, you could probably do it easily, capitalizing on emotional situations, remembering that you have what they "need."

A champion for your own cause and culture, you could expand your role by learning—stealing?—from those devils on the other side. Since your nerves are not the best, you tend to go with the flow, reserving your energy for when the chips are down—prepared to win—most of the time. You probably have plenty of children, so vacations are often with relatives in the heartland, back home.

Love

You have a practical and clear understanding about relationships, never over-stating or overcommitting yourself. You love the concept of partnerships more than romance. To those who don't know you well, you often give the impression of being a bit avant garde, unrealistic—although that's not the case. You're open-minded, but rarely eccentric. Having a partner to dance with to the beat of your personal drumbeat makes you feel complete.

Money

Uncharacteristic of your effervescent zodiac sign, you are careful and cautious about work and finances. You enjoy taking a concept and making it real. However, you have trouble with the small stuff unless everything is clearly spelled out. Practical work, rather than philosophical or speculative, makes you jumpy, but your intense belief in yourself always gets the work done. You enjoy a challenge, but know when to call it quits.

Famous People Born on This Day

Female

Natalie Portman, actress
Bonnie Tyler, singer
Mona Freeman, actress
Catherine Filene Shouse, philan-
    thropist
Helena Rubinstein, cosmetics
    executive

Male

Johnny Depp, actor
Michael J. Fox, actor
Les Paul, electric guitar innovator
Cole Porter, composer/lyricist
Dick Vitale, sportscaster

June 10

Your bright intellect draws plenty of attention, but your personal quirks and difficult environment can hinder your progress and dull your soulful fun. Education would help, but you'd probably go to some party school and only learn how to doctor up exams. You've got to "apply" yourself, be productive, and listen when we preach! You can overcome life's obstacles—try—accolades, hearts, and flowers await you. Much depends on your partners, spouse, and family members, so keep them on your side.

You'd like to shake up the world, so you're not afraid to make your own opportunities socially or in a career—sometimes it opens doors, sometimes disaster. Think like a monarch of a vast kingdom—keep everyone fed, happy, and avoid getting overthrown if you don't. Scary. For vacation fun? Foreign countries. Learn the lingo.

Love

Once a relationship turns intimate, you go through huge emotional swings—sometimes feeling very confident about romantic commitment and then suddenly, overly self-critical or fatalistic. Relax—it's common for 6/10-borns! You seek perfection in a lover because that's what you look for in yourself. Although self-confident, the Happy You only comes alive when you're in a relationship. And even then, only when you're truly in love.

Money

You project yourself confidently toward coworkers, and believe that the demands you make on others are no greater than they should make on themselves. You dutifully assert yourself and use your energy efficiently, wasting little of it on nonproductive endeavors. You control your temper and don't fly off the emotional handle when coworkers perform improperly. Your dependability makes you a great team player.

Famous People Born on This Day

Female
Elisabeth Shue, actress
Linda Evangelista, supermodel
Elizabeth Hurley, actress
Judy Garland, singer/actress
Leelee Sobieski, actress

Male
Shane West, actor
Clyde Beatty, animal trainer/actor
Maurice Sendak, author/illustrator
F. Lee Bailey, defense attorney
Saul Bellow, author

June 11

As long as you stay in good health, fit, and energetic, you'll always be up for the glorious opportunities you need to grow in status and gain riches—or should. You are a sharp tack—sometimes a little quarrelsome—ready for multiple challenges, staying on top of things. No one argues for long with you. Many of you are capable of reaching for and gaining honors, perhaps recognized by your community. Others of you travel a lot, virtually living on the road.

Social chit-chat and namby-pamby stuff is not for you—that's for lazy people, and the spotlight is overrated. You are a winner, proving it to yourself. With military precision, you can marshal your group along—having been in the trenches yourself. Spend more time pleasing your husband/wife and less wrestling with everyone else.

Love

You're sensitive and loving, caring, but restrained. Uncomfortable with open displays of affection, it is hard for 6/11-born to let down their hair in public and simply have a good time, preferring privacy and behind-closed-door kind of moments. Rather shy, you enjoy being with older people and lovers. The more latitude and space there is in the relationship, the better. You may not have many friends and loved ones, but you will always be close to those you have.

Money

Although not one to leave a task half done, you get overwhelmed by details and small stuff. You learn best in structured situations, but not so regimented that you lose the joy for exploration. You're not comfortable discussing your financial affairs and have distinctly drawn lines between friends and money. Nevertheless, your genuine personality always attracts help when needed.

Famous People Born on This Day

Female

Shia LaBeouf, actress
Christina Crawford, author
Millicent Garrett Fawcett, women's movement leader
Adrienne Barbeau, actress
Risë Stevens, opera singer/actress

Male

Chad Everett, actor
Joe Montana, football player
Gene Wilder, comedian/actor
Vince Lombardi, legendary football coach
Jacques Cousteau, undersea adventurer

June 12

Seldom at a loss for words, you are a what-you-see-is-what-you-get person, content when you feel content, satisfied and trusting in some worldly or otherworldly force that you believe keeps an eye on you. Try to break free of common vocations where you may be trapped—most of you can do much better in careers without sacrificing your likes and virtues. Wealth may increase as time passes.

When you are in your element, you want it sweet and cordial so you can harmonize with the appreciative people there. Often, your element is outdoors, enjoying nature. Or, your element is a church or school, where order and kinship make it easy to get on with satisfying your inner spiritual yearnings. No telling where the buried treasure is; look for it because it's not looking for you.

Love

Never satisfied with a humdrum affair, you view love as a special adventure. You have a positive and progressive view about relationships, needing a partner that is more than a helpmate or paycheck—you desire a dear companion whose love will grow and endure. Although a sensitive and honest negotiator, you run for the hills whenever words become harsh or angry. You enjoy mixing with well-thought-of people and leader types, even though you have no desire to be one yourself.

Money

Your terrific imagination may have difficulty transforming ideas into economic reality, often retreating into a fantasy world whenever the real world seems rough. However, you see beauty that others often overlook and can express this vision through writing or art. 6/12-born don't excel at physical labor or occupations concerning finances. Seek employment where you can be creative, capitalize on your dreams and alternative insights.

Famous People Born on This Day

Female

Brigid Brophy, novelist/campaigner
Rona Jaffe, author
Cindy Lee Berryhill, singer/songwriter
Anne Frank, Holocaust victim
Ally Sheedy, actress

Male

Jim Morris, impressionist/comedian
Chick Corea, jazz pianist
Vic Damone, singer
Jim Nabors, entertainer
George Bush, U.S. president

June 13

Fateful June 13—soaked in karma and so misunderstood. This is a challenging day to be born. Your health could be better, and seemingly, no matter how hard you try, the rewards and satisfaction just aren't enough. Maybe your expectations get in the way. You smile and know you have abilities—instructional, mathematical, and organizational to name a few. Realize you're one of those people who really does need people—then you'll be the luckiest person in the world.

Since there are a lot of tremors in the "force" around you (the fault is in your stars, not yourself), feeling dependent on others may be natural. If so, realize there's nothing wrong with dependency since we are not all created equal. Earnestly do your part to overcome adversities. Try some different paths without straining or stressing.

Love

In relationships, you either do too much or not enough. You need a partner with a steady hand and lucid mind, who tells you when you're over the edge, or out of their league. Much of your emotional difficulty results from crossed communication, rather than from lack of judgment. Mutual understanding will allow you both to grow, rather than one partner being swept along by the other.

Money

Although you have a rich insight, you need to start learning about what is real and what is fiction. You're an easy target for a con game. 6/13-born aren't great at math or science—not because you are slow but because you just don't think that way. But employers know they can count on you to get a job done. Seek jobs that don't require a lot of improvisation because you need all the structure you can get!

Famous People Born on This Day

Female

Mary-Kate and Ashley Olsen, twin
  actresses
Lois Weber, film director
Jamie Walters, actor/singer
Hannah Storm, sports journalist
Eleanor Holmes Norton, civil and
  women's rights activist

Male

Ralph Edwards, TV host
Richard Thomas, actor
Tim Allen, actor/comedian
Paul Lynde, comedian
William Butler Yeats, poet

June 14

Well-liked and depended upon, it is your quiet, thoughtful, fun-loving, and affectionate nature that sets you apart, whether you have good looks to match or not. You do need love in return and usually have it. Your home is you. To stay healthy, you need to express yourself, to get out and be seen more. Show off your craftsman-like skills or down-to-earth human qualities and excellent personal touch. You don't waste words, usually, though others do. They should listen.

A good eye for value and a bit finicky, you'd make a good mystery shopper or bargain hunter, and when cooking, you deliver up the right stuff. A smile always gets you more than a frown. A bed and breakfast would be a great weekend getaway for you; better yet, a hunting lodge for you and close friends.

Love

You're not one for slow courtship; you prefer to get down to business asap. Your desires come suddenly and strong—your inclination is to strike while the iron is hot. It's important that your partner enjoys socializing because you don't like being alone. You are a people-person and have many friends and interests. Don't shortchange your love life with a stay-at-home wallflower.

Money

You have eager, eagle eyes for money, and enjoy it to the fullest! You have enormous drive and ambition and are impatient with anything that slows your pace. To many coworkers, your goals may seem unrealistic, but you keep tweaking and fine-tuning lists and move forward with determination. It rarely occurs to you that you will fail. Your accomplishments are acclaimed and envied by many. Even when facing overwhelming odds, you assert yourself with confidence.

Famous People Born on This Day

Female

Yasmine Bleeth, actress
Steffi Graf, tennis player
Harriet Beecher Stowe, educator/writer
Margaret Bourke-White, photographer/correspondent
Dorothy McGuire, actress

Male

Daryl Sabara, actor
Donald Trump, millionaire/developer
Pierre Salinger, U.S. statesman
Burl Ives, folksinger
Jerzy Kosinski, author

June 15

With your sparkle, you shouldn't be content to play in the minor leagues. Pay your dues and move up! Feeling a need to serve the world in some way, you have to ask, what exactly does the world need? To start with, it needs you and your unique, pleasant personality, and a lot less disharmony, something you may have had to grow up in, hindering parents and all. You're too smart to let the past hold you back.

So, you seek freedom and develop your ideals. Jealousy and treachery—why can't others just behave? You make a good nurturer and teacher—given the chance—and computers and internet are useful tools—anything modern. Bad habits and vices—x-them out. You don't have the time. There's time for kites, ferrets, poems—any of life's special joys.

Love

You have good sense about what to get from a relationship—your expectations are realistic and basic. Therefore, you're rarely disappointed when things falter or halt because you're always straightforward and honest and willing to go that extra mile. Lovers must provide you emotional challenge, in order for you to feel that you are accomplishing something—you like tangible, not hopeful, results. More often than not, you're the stabilizing influence in personal affairs.

Money

You are a tireless worker and give everything your full effort and focus, (regardless of how inspired or sporadic your attention span). 6/15-born go to great lengths to provide top-notch service and accomplish what must be done before the urgings of fellow employees. In other words, keep away from weak-willed coworkers and aim for management positions or on-the-road kind of jobs. You're confident saying "no." Deep within, you understand that you can accomplish almost anything.

Famous People Born on This Day

Female

Courteney Cox Arquette, actress
Helen Hunt, actress
Brett Butler, comedienne
Janie Quigley, Olympic cyclist
Polly Draper, actress

Male

Ice Cube, rap singer/actor
James Belushi, comedian
Erroll Garner, U.S. jazz pianist
Waylon Jennings, country singer/
    guitarist
Mario Cuomo, New York governor

June 16

Rise early, move quickly—anyone born today has a long life ahead and should get started to stay ahead of the pack. They need you, you think. Well, maybe you're not that superior, but you have a pretty good idea of how to get things done fairly and profitably, probably learning from a self-made, experienced person like yourself. You add your own twist and spin, and the wheels of progress take you on down the road. Take a front seat.

You can be independent and kinky, and proud of it. You're a big thinker—big ideas and a lot of thought capacity—your brain never gets overheated from too much input. It's the output we have to watch. You'll love sailing or flying high. You could write a book if you could sit that long.

Love

Although a bit uncertain about emotions, you are an affectionate and considerate lover who expects your attentions to be returned in kind. Having control over, or the major say-so to a partner, may guarantee a continuing relationship, but it can also take away much of the freedom on which love depends. Having someone who participates in your creative affairs and isn't afraid to show his or her weaknesses makes you happy. Take issue with lovers who are not on your same wavelength.

Money

You cover a large area first and fill in the blanks later. For you, to get to the top there is no other way but to just keep on truckin'. Unfortunately, you may not have much discipline, growing quickly impatient by sloppiness, or work not done neatly. You work well when supervised because it's easy for you to get sidetracked, or misled. Set goals, and clarify your objectives; don't mistake on-the-job friendliness for honesty.

Famous People Born on This Day

Female

Laurie Metcalf, actress
Barbara McClintock, cytogeneticist
Joan Van Ark, actress
Joyce Carol Oates, author
Katherine Graham, publisher

Male

Erich Segal, author
Stan Laurel, actor/comedian
Mickie Finn, banjo player
William Fitzgerald Jenkins, science
    fiction author

June 17

The world doesn't exactly revolve around you, though it would be nice if it would. Keep promoting your people skills and out-dueling your teachers, then you may grow up to be good-looking, catch some breaks, and before you know it, you've got kids, had a couple wives, a reputation, and have lost all control. Maybe. You're unpredictable and life IS a roller coaster. Maintain your roots and stop trying to be something you can't or shouldn't.

So in-touch with your feelings, driven by them, don't forget that there are others with feelings too who need your special attention. Staying cool, under control and conscientious will open doors for you. If some are shut, no big deal, flow on to the next. Try dispensing advice—good advice.

Love

You voice your affections concisely but emphatically, often overstating your feelings about love affairs. Generous in your judgment of others, you are kind even when they disappoint you. You meet others more than halfway because you believe that everybody has flaws and can change. 6/17-born have a strong sense of ethics and social decorum.

Money

Your easy way with words and practical demeanor enable you to comfortably cope with difficult employment or financial situations. You are eager to learn, and demonstrate your skills at every chance you can. You are extremely perceptive to coworkers and know how to cooperate in order to get a job done well. You know who you are, and understand your capabilities and shortcomings. You're rarely at a loss for words, and are always available to help when assistance is required.

Famous People Born on This Day

Female

Venus Williams, tennis player
Christina C. Bakker-van Bosse,
    feminist/pacifist
Diane Murphy, actress
Phyllis Rashad, actress
Beryl Reid, actress

Male

Ralph Bellamy, actor
Dan Jansen, Olympic speed skater
Barry Manilow, singer
M.C. Escher, artist
Art Bell, radio talk show host

June 18

When you have your act together, the confidence beaming from you seems to attract others like a psychic magnet. When you're touchy and superficial, it all goes away, ditto for when you are emotionally scattered. Be more willing to pitch in and dirty your hands for the "project." To be a good learner, be a good listener—and do more than tell them what they want to hear. Some will question your motives, and probably should.

Always active, you have good hand-eye coordination, and probably a distinctive voice, too. You'd make a good musician or actor and enjoy adulation—all this opens up all sorts of interesting possibilities for romance. Flattery will get you everything. Canoeing, sailing, rowing—these are fun, especially in tandem with a well-proportioned mate, not a scurvy crew.

Love

Because you blossom in the company of others, make sure that your lover enjoys social gatherings and fun times outside the bedroom! You are inclined to wilt when occasions are quiet—stimulating conversations, and being on the go make you happiest. Being more progressive, rather than possessive, choose a partner who supports your need to be spontaneous and free. Although you believe in love at first sight, you always remember the dangers from rushing into relationships.

Money

Your clever mind quickly grasps ideas that others don't. 6/18s are good at work that requires originality, and new or unusual ways of doing things such as design, education, or the arts. Your mind moves quickly from topic to topic, sometimes without pausing long enough to understand what you have learned. Still, you see solutions to problems quicker than most. Although you're not silly with your spendings, saving money isn't your strength.

Famous People Born on This Day

Female

Carol Kane, actress
Isabella Rossellini, actress
Eva Bartok, actress
Jeanette MacDonald, actress/singer
Sylvia Porter, journalist/finance
    expert

Male

Roger Ebert, film critic
E.G. Marshall, actor
Paul McCartney, musician
Red Adair, oilman
Sammy Cahn, lyricist

June 19

Early in life you may experience difficulties which may take many years to grow away from, leaving you somewhat untrusting and skeptical—which is okay since it'll protect you from the wolves but leave the sheep bewildered. Your life path is a jagged one, with an occasional misstep putting you in risky situations, but that's kind of cool. Having the right friends will certainly help you get by, and it's important to be earnest, unbiased, open-minded, and not a stick-in-the-mud.

Your best work may be behind the scenes out of the glare of prying eyes and criticism. Since "not going out on a limb" applies to you, practice using discretion and avoid the sideshows and sidetracks. Be practical about your ambitions, philosophical about relationships. For recreation, try manipulating things with your hands, and not people.

Love

Hey there, you with the stars in your eyes: don't let a lover's desires ever dampen your dreams—always speak from the heart, and let fantasy be a part of your daily diet! You are most compatible with a partner who appreciates and supports your honest hopes, and are always clear about your feelings. You expect a lot from your partner and give one-hundred percent, once trust and guidelines are established.

Money

You have a rich imagination and spend lots of time daydreaming. Sometimes it's difficult for you to be objective because your emotions influence your thinking so much. You're not interested in science and math because they seem cold and impersonal, and their careful logic is colorless, boring. 6/19-born are valuable, respected, and dependable employees. You handle finances fairly well, and earn the most by using your wits and personality.

Famous People Born on This Day

Female

Paula Abdul, entertainer
Rosalyn Yalow, medical physicist
Gena Rowlands, actress
Kathleen Turner, actress
Shirley "Cha Cha" Muldowney, drag racer

Male

Louis Jourdan, romance actor
Blaise Pascal, mathematician/ physicist/religious writer
Guy Lombardo, orchestra conductor
Salman Rushdie, author

June 20

You take all your interpersonal relationships seriously, balancing fairness with a dose of skepticism, and usually wending your way through life with a smile, making friends when sharing experiences and sparkling in conversation with them, with relatives, and your faithful spouse. Being hard-edged is out of character, but sometimes you do reach your emotional limits, which is not healthy. Exercise and breathing loads of fresh air release the tensions and let you be more clearheaded.

A fast and loose lifestyle is not for you, since life presents enough challenges without having to drum up more. Sitting idle isn't much fun either, though having job security isn't too much to ask. Break out of routines—at least improve them—and turn on the charm. Never refuse an invitation that lets you travel, mingle, and meet new people.

Love

You have an easy-going, low-key approach to relationships. Lovers rely on you because you enjoy listening and helping others. You need a partner whose moods are steady, one who is self-assured and independent, rather than somebody who waits for you to make the first move. Your 6/20-born nature reveals your never-demanding, always adaptable nature. Because of your natural charm, you stand out in contrast to those who dramatically struggle for center stage.

Money

Because communication is important, you work best with coworkers who are intelligent and self-motivated. You're cooperative, curious, always eager to learn, and work well with others. You're not a loudmouth, bur your belief in yourself lets you enjoy a good argument, simply as an exercise of wits. Although not executive material (you'd have difficulty firing anybody!), you're not afraid of responsibility

Famous People Born on This Day

Female
Nicole Kidman, actress
Doris J. Hart, tennis player
Olympia Dukakis, actress
Lillian Hellman, writer/playwright
Anne Murray, singer/songwriter

Male
John Goodman, actor
Errol Flynn, actor
Lionel Richie, composer/songwriter
Danny Aiello, actor
Audie Murphy, war hero/actor

June 21

Lucky you—born on the longest, sunniest day of the year, but instead of being a hot blast, you're the down-to-earth type, always involved, popular, attracting love and marriage at an early age, usually. You're adaptable, too, with an opinion on everything, and capable of almost any vocation, quick to pick up the beat. A few naysayers might call you selfish, an arguer, but, hey, bug-off. You're a good friend and ally besides taking care of number one—and that's plenty good enough.

When it comes to binding a family together, you're the glue, and if called by "a cause," you'll rally behind it. Few people can do both; you make the time to. Your credible candor is good for getting people to say yes; your presence, even on vacation, assures that there's enough "juice" to succeed.

Love

You are an idealist who expects lovers to live up to very special standards—yours! You know what you want and have distinct and exact priorities. In matters of romance, you are never vague or soft-spoken. However, you are very understanding, and value one's intentions more than the results. Make sure that significant others truly understand your message and appreciate your wealth of fantasies. Always ask questions first, then listen and respond!

Money

It's difficult for you to reach agreements with coworkers because you state your opinions so enthusiastically and are so eager to move, move, move forward that you often ignore assistance—but never protocol. Nonetheless, your independent and rational mind is rarely influenced by emotions. Brainstorm with others, slow down and listen to what they have to say. Facts and figures are not your expertise.

Famous People Born on This Day

Female
Kathy Mattea, country singer
Meredith Baxter, actress
Jane Russell, film actress
Mary McCarthy, author/critic
Maureen Stapleton, actress

Male
Prince William of Wales
Michael Gross, actor
Jean Paul Sartre, existentialist/author
Daniel Carter Beard, organized first Boy Scout troop
Ray Davies, musician

June 22

A good birthdate for females, so-so for males. Females usually are blessed by wealth, beauty, style, and charm. Males might be spoiled by a lust for money and the goodies of life. Both can be the artist and accumulate treasures. Both are well-mannered, confident, and fond of trade; often overlooking faults and serious responsibilities, instead you follow your desires. Carefully choose "the others" to include in those desires—plucking the golden apple will then be easy. If not, watch out!

Work is a dirty word for you, but you're definitely willing to help if arts, finery, or money and higher society are involved. Though your closet is full already, you may want to try designing clothes—you're a natural collector and high-ticket shopper. In travel, you want to go in style—in first class is where to find you.

Love

Your tendency to change your mind on a whim makes you come off as flighty, even though your primary intention is to be straightforward about your feelings. A lover who accepts your habits and desires, and leaves you well enough alone, suits you best. Having clearly defined roles and responsibilities is essential for your happy relationships. Be exacting and discreet, not frivolous or trivial!

Money

You probably start conversations with "I" more than most, and the word "me" pops up regularly too. 6/22-borns are not egocentric, just needy for approval. You're not a shrinking violet on the job, and simply put out rather than shut up. However, you're a bit impulsive and don't always give coworkers the chance to respond to your questions or lend a hand. Your reasonably good judgment is reflected in your clear managing of money affairs.

Famous People Born on This Day

Female

Anne Morrow Lindbergh, author
Dianne Feinstein, politician/human rights advocate
Katherine Dunham, dancer/choreographer/teacher
Lindsay Wagner, actress
Amy Brenneman, actress

Male

Carson Daly, MTV VJ/talk show host
Billy Wilder, film director
Kris Kristofferson, singer/actor
Don Henley, drummer/singer
Bill Blass, fashion designer

June 23

Many socialites, including royalty, share this birthday with you, but before you get any ideas and polish your star, let's consider if that's really any advantage. It is, in business and commerce, and when champagne is flowing, but you, dear reader, may not be dipped in sacred rivers and be cuddled in the lap of luxury. Playing the part is fun—the playboy, the lover, Miss Silver Spoon, or Miss America. A lot of your appeal can be traced to your family whom you should always keep happy.

Your good memory and verbal superiority are not always noticed, nor do you use them fully in your career, though you should try to—don't secretly sell yourself short. Be determined to learn, practice, and deliver. Be entertaining as well as entertained, and use your power and control with utmost courtesy.

Love

You're either too much, or not enough in love! You are happiest with partners who accept your needs and mood swings, someone whose patience and understanding are not depressing or too demanding; happiest with a serious, older lover. You appreciate and enjoy play-time and private moments and, once committed, you hold securely and steady. You don't take affections or emotions lightly, and are philosophical and fun, yet wise.

Money

You think big and have grand ambitions but often overlook the importance of the little things, and get nervous about details. You perform well in structured environments, but not so organized that you lose your freedom to explore and experiment. Don't let the fear of making a mistake keep you from making more money, or moving forward. You're a sublime combination of cooperation and genius!

Famous People Born on This Day

Female

Selma Blair, actress
Frances McDormand, actress
Wilma Rudolph, track and field
    Olympic champion
Willie Mae "Mother" Smith, gospel
    singer/evangelist/folk artist
June Carter Cash, singer/songwriter

Male

Clarence Thomas, U.S. Supreme
    Court justice
Edward VIII, King of Great Britain
Alan Turing, mathematician
George Sax, invented saxophone
Bob Fosse, choreographer/director

June 24

Headstrong and confident, many males born today are rugged individualists, willing to speak their mind, proud of accomplishments and wanting more. Females are much better at listening and conforming, but both of you sense human emotions and may have some imbalances and worries of your own which might lead to illness or social problems. Even the too passionate and pushy you is accepted—you do mix in—but you might have to earn your spot now and then.

Happy to serve others and share in all of life's joys, expand your horizons beyond your family, develop your leadership talent at work, do what you do best and don't be roped into roles that aren't right. You have a bit of a suspicious mind; don't "blame." Be judicious, not forceful. Vacation and travel often; you need breaks from routines.

Love

Gloom and depression quickly sink your spirit. You lavish much affection on your lover, which may startle or overwhelm anyone not used to it. 6/24-borns become totally immersed with their partners—wanting to know everything, available to do anything! Overdoing or overstepping matters is a persistent problem. Casual flings hold little interest for you. Once you settle in to a relationship, you're a model of steadfast devotion.

Money

Understanding and performing every step of your job description are essential for you—knowing when to act and when not to. 6/24-borns believe that striving for significance is never enough unless it includes practical results. You are hopeful, but always realistic; eager, yet always deliberate. You constantly de-clutter your workaday life by eliminating nonessential elements that stifle progress.

Famous People Born on This Day

Female

Aadje and Rietje Lyre, Dutch twin
   princesses
Sherry Stringfield, actress
Danielle Spencer, actress
Nancy Allen, actress
Michele Lee, actress/singer

Male

Jack Dempsey, boxer
Chief Dan George, actor
Astro [Terrence Wilson], singer
Mick Fleetwood, musician
Robert Reich, U.S. Secretary of
   Labor

June 25

You emphatically share the joys, the hurts, the highs and lows of others—and are very much in tune with the dynamic world around you. You are very fair and understanding, almost always friendly and persuasive, and also quick to pick up on things that are "just not right." You are a perfect member of any team, being loyal and receptive to new ideas and tactics, though you shouldn't stay too long when things become stale or past their prime.

You enjoy tinkering and like the feeling of accomplishment when you've done your part to keep the world humming. Your larger ambitions may be toward politics, real estate, medicine, or human welfare—you'll fulfill high responsibilities, so take more challenging roles. An educational degree will help you get started. Take classes, or teach, in your spare time.

Love

Not a planner, and never demanding, you live for the moment, and forgive lovers when situations take a side-turn, or don't come out as expected. However, your goals are always clear, and you have a more-than-reasonable understanding of what is expected from a relationship. When disappointed, you take things in stride and move forward (although you never forget anyone who slights you).

Money

Your mind is always active, and you are a conscientious, useful, and efficient worker. Your 6/25-born influence makes you a natural diplomat, expressing yourself honestly so that no one harbors bad feelings, even if you say something unpleasant or bend the rules a bit. You are secure, yet flexible—never aggressive. Although you are easily beset by worry and become flummoxed when things go wrong, you know how to save the day or make it better.

Famous People Born on This Day

Female

Phyllis George, sportscaster
Dorothy Gilman, mystery writer
Carly Simon, singer/songwriter
Mirabel Morgan, author
June Lockhart, actress

Male

Henry "Hap" Arnold, general
George Orwell [Eric A. Blair], writer
Sidney Lumet, film director
Pierre "Peyo" Culliford, cartoonist
George Michael, singer

June 26

You can be everyone's everyone. No matter what culture or background you are from, you blend in, doing you part, enjoying it all, joys and sorrows, hopes and dreams. Solving problems by cooperating is your forte. But you wonder, what is your true place in life's ever-progressive drama? Rather than flowing along, set goals, and reach them by seizing opportunities that feel right for you. Don't follow trends, set them.

Timing is everything, so when you feel inner irritation, it's time to take action and institute changes in your surroundings—to look for new avenues where you can succeed and flourish. Keep a journal of when and where you do things—you'll find that there is a rhythm to life; especially watch the cycles of the moon. For fun, try singing. For exercise, you could walk forever.

Love

Don't stress out over the initial developments of a relationship—just enjoy the moment, and indulge in the possibilities! Your intellect and anticipation are often at cross purposes with your emotions, so that you either express your feelings incorrectly or they interfere with what you truly want to say. As a result, you may get so deeply involved in an affair that you don't see what is happening, or you may become so removed that you don't fully enjoy.

Money

Even though some coworkers consider you impractical, you do your job and always try to make the work-a-day world more productive and interesting. Although not terrific with numbers, you approach your job with an enthusiasm that makes up for any lack of discipline or education. You have a great deal of curiosity but are strongly opinionated—something that you should learn to mellow. Be careful how you debate with coworkers, because you tend to be inflexible.

Famous People Born on This Day

Female

Babe Didrikson Zaharias, golfer
Patty Smyth, rock vocalist
Pearl S. Buck, author
Antonia Brice, symphony conductor/teacher
Eleanor Parker, actress

Male

Derek Jeter, baseball player
Chris Isaak, singer/songwriter
Greg LeMond, bicyclist/Tour de France winner
Peter Lorre, actor
Colin Wilson, metaphysical author

June 27

Sensitive and a deeply personal person, we could probably tell you anything and you'd try it. Maybe it's because you have such a strong attachment to life and "experiences" that you're swayed by the magic of the moment. You swing into action, committed! Now, about your bad habits, shyness, and money worries. Habits are made to be broken now; don't say no to getting out of the house; get a second job or seek alternative solutions to high estimates.

You are multi-talented and as long as you stay focused, you deliver! Before agreeing to any transactions, get all the facts and second/third/fourth opinions. You're a bit sentimental about the past, so you may be interested in antiques or serve the elderly. Try to catch health problems early, you don't need to be slowed down from your full life!

Love

Although friendly and witty, you live by precise, defined rules for relationships and dislike casual acquaintances and one-night stands. You are tolerant of others' weaknesses, believing that honesty is the only answer. You stimulate the best in a lover, and he or she is impressed by your fairness. Life is never boring when you're around because you're sensitive and love to talk—but make sure that you provide a listening ear, and not only your opinions. After all, relationships are a two-way collaboration, right?

Money

You always deliver the goods—no sacrifice is too great concerning financial matters or responsibilities. Reliable, honest and fair, you quickly gain the respect of coworkers, because you do what's expected and don't stop until the project is completed. 6/27-borns are always looking for "more," but willing to follow another's lead. Nonetheless, you prefer to succeed on your own merits, prefer to pursue your goals independently and without assistance.

Famous People Born on This Day

Female

Harriet Hubbard Ayers, beauty expert/columnist
Mildred J. Hill, musician/composer
Julia Duffy, actress
Helen Keller, writer
Sally Priesand, first U.S. female rabbi

Male

Tobey Maguire, actor
Willie Mosconi, world champion pool player
Paul Conrad, comic strip cartoonist
H. Ross Perot, billionaire
Bob Keeshan, Captain Kangaroo

June 28

Rugged, robust, you are a warrior of sorts, full of enthusiasm and youth, liked by the opposite sex and desired as a companion by most everyone who gets to know you. Loyal and a "pleaser type," you approach life philosophically, having both a practical vision and a desire to be out in the world, experiencing it all. You enjoy your independence, being cool outside and fiery within (or is it the other way around?). Make the impression y-o-u want to make on people.

So what are your weak points—things you might want to consider as role changes? Others probably are too polite to say, but you can be overbearing, a spotlight hogger, and do other people's thinking for them, but you feel they need that—don't alarm them by being brusque in your tired moments.

Love

Even though your ego is no bigger than others, you are quick to grow defensive or overprotective of what you feel is right and just. You have no patience for lazy sorts who seem to wallow or beg to be rescued. Conservative by nature, you have problems letting down your barriers and opening up. The weird thing is, all you yearn for is intimacy, bare-bone honesty, and acceptance.

Money

Because of your straight-shooting manner, everyone on the job knows where they stand with you. You perform your work above and beyond the call of duty, even though you're a bit lazy and not the most innovative. To 6/28-born, "work" is a means to pay bills, making it difficult for you to marry a career. You always have a nest egg and are very determined to keep it warm and alive. Your cunning and agility inspire others.

Famous People Born on This Day

Female

Gilda Radner, comedienne/actress
Kathy Bates, actress
Danielle Brisebois, actress
Cristina di Trivulzio di Belgioioso,
    Italian princess/politician
Audrey Langford, singing teacher

Male

John Cusack, actor
Richard Rodgers, composer
John Elway, quarterback
Mel Brooks, comedian/actor/director
Pat Morita, actor

June 29

The most interesting birthday of June and maybe the laziest, too. Why? Some of you are so used to getting your own way, you can be self-indulgent, full of imagination and bravado. That's not good for your career, which has its ups and downs, but you are a fun one to "hang" with, and your desire for romance lets you easily say "yes!" You take the path of least resistance—why not? So enjoy your pleasant surroundings, cheer for your team, have fun with your toys—make sure you meet your responsibilities.

Surprisingly, you're shy inside—so much of what you do can be "show." Often others try to use you, not knowing that you are paying attention, which you do when you want to. Try doing that more. Also, make your "messages" crystal clear. For fun—sports!

Love

You know how to express the powerful feelings of love into words, and hate presumption and when lovers second-guess you. To a 6/29-born, loyalty and companionship are more important than passion or promise. Your honest and vibrant personality is best-suited for partners who are open-minded, willingly emote, and reveal their warts. You need someone who gives you plenty of breathing space—and, in return, you do the same!

Money

Having money and nice things is very important to you, and you're always trying to improve your on-the-job competence by performing everything better than ever before. Your mentality is sharp because of your insatiable curiosity; communication is your strength—so exploit it! You're most comfortable with jobs where you can learn and grow, rather than lounge in the executive throne!

Famous People Born on This Day

Female

Sharon Lawrence, actress
Little Eva [Boyd], singer
Cara Williams, actress
Joan Davis, actress
Nellie Taylor Ross, first woman governor

Male

George Washington Goethals, engineer
Robert Evans, producer
Gary Busey, actor
Fred Grandy, actor/elected official
Richard Lewis, comedian

June 30

Quickly, you fly into action, sometimes with excellent results, sometimes near-disaster. Impulse—you've got a lot of that, coupling emotion and physical fire. You'd benefit by stopping and thinking first—planning especially helps—but others are often so impressed by you, they'll follow your lead. The chaos can be sorted out later. Still, you can carry the load, not shrinking from responsibilities or commitments, and not always getting the credit you deserve.

Loyal and warm toward your children or whoever depends on you, they appreciate you and your confident, understanding approach. You're an expert at dealing with short attention spans. Others hear the emotion in your voice—something a teacher, policeperson, politician, or leader like you needs! For fun, catch the wind—kites, sailing, flying, hot-air balloon, even motorcycles.

Love

You are emotionally indulgent and understanding with lovers, but invest exacting "trial-and-error" time testing partners before you commit. "Doubting" comes natural to you, always questioning and wondering whether or not what you're seeing or hearing is true or false. You're not gullible—not at all; but it's just easy for you to get sidetracked by emotional drama or sob-stories. You're best-suited for a grown-up, straight-shooting lover who's not afraid of talking.

Money

You're lucid and alert about investments and very hard-working, even though it never seems that you have anything "extra." It's a good idea that you seek professional financial help, because saving money stifles you. Once you comprehend your job description, you are loyal to coworkers and employers. You're a slow, but steady, student and rarely rush into any job or money situation unprepared.

Famous People Born on This Day

Female

Nancy Dussault, actress
Ann Marsh, Olympic fencer-foil
Lena Horne, singer/actress
Susan Hayward, actress
Dorothy Malone, actress

Male

Harry Blackstone, Jr., magician
Eric Goetz, America's Cup ship builder
Sam Moskowitz, science fiction expert
Buddy Rich, drummer
David Wayne, actor

July

July 1

When something captures your imagination—an idea, a lover, perhaps something technologically new—you really get into it. Always busy with a plan, your analytical, active mind keeps you flowing forward, helped by rivers of physical vitality. This is bound to get you noticed by superiors who'll have to consider you as their eventual replacement. No matter what your background, you are a "fit," edging closer to that special spot of your dreams.

Not outwardly romantic, you know what you want. There is passion inside you, though you are an emotional softy. Relationships often take precedence in your life, but a good cause can also tug at your heart, so volunteering to help the weak or solve the world's problems are roles you don't mind filling. Even from a humble background, your status is bound to rise.

Love

You're not impressed by just "anyone," but not because your standards are so high, high, high. The fact is, you enjoy your own company and don't mind being alone. When in love, it's essential that you bond with someone similar. Even though you maintain a busy schedule, you are always available when a lover needs you. However, beware of getting so caught up with your own social agenda that you neglect your partner's needs!

Money

Schedules?—ugh! Being on time is challenging for you. But, like exercise, you comply, and work everything out. By understanding your failings and shortcomings, you diligently work at transforming your weaknesses so that they don't limit future income. You prefer taking one slow, steady step at a time. Insure that your relaxed, compliant temperament doesn't make you a dumping ground for aggressive employment demands.

Famous People Born on This Day

Female	*Male*
George Sand, author	Dan Aykroyd, actor/comedian
Twyla Tharp, dancer/choreographer	Charles Laughton, actor
Olivia de Havilland, actress	Carl Lewis, Olympic speedster
Jo Sinclair, author	Alan Ruck, actor
Princess Diana of Wales	Sydney Pollack, movie director

July 2

Details, details—some say you're fussy, but you're the practical type that simply can't be hung up by loose ends or wait until the last minute. Always considerate of others—there's trouble if you aren't—you have the keen intellect necessary for sorting out problems, a boon for any career you choose, usually involving people issues. Money is not your goal, and luck is not relied on but higher forces do seem to take care of you especially when you act fairly, independently, and watch your health.

Because life is precious, you take interest in health issues, paying attention to nutrition, and your inner spiritual body, too. A peaceful vacation to the seaside now and then will regenerate you, as will the hearty farm life. Need an edge? Pay attention to your dreams and the messages there.

Love

Idealistic and optimistic, you enter relationships believing that everything will work out fine, regardless of each other's past. You know that you are unique and capable enough to make any relationship prosper. Forward-moving, cooperative, and progressive commitments stimulate you—it's the living-in-the-moment that's tough for 7/2s! Due to your trusting nature, you make certain that lovers prove their worthiness early on, rather than accepting anyone's intentions on blind faith!

Money

You bring significance and sincerity to your professional endeavors, and always leave a fingerprint of imagination on everything you do. You are not interested in public recognition, even though you enjoy applause and acknowledgement like everybody else, preferring the satisfaction of busyness and good work over status. Don't allow your dislike of routine to cause unintentional, petty rifts with co-workers.

Famous People Born on This Day

Female

Lindsay Lohan, actress
Polly Holliday , actress
Luci Baines Johnson Nugent Turpin,
    President Johnson's daughter
Jerry Hall, model
Imelda Marcos, Philippine politician

Male

Richard Petty, racecar driver
Vincente Fox, President of Mexico
Thurgood Marshall, first black
    Supreme Court justice
Hermann Hesse, author/poet
Walter Brennan, actor

July 3

Do you fit in? Sometimes, but only if you care to. To some, you are the serious thinker, the worker. To others, you're the easygoing, quick to jump on the bandwagon type. You would have made a great beatnik, and usually your hair distinguishes you, maybe a goatee or a beehive. Quiet, analytical, and curt, you are not the most ambitious type, but your serene manner doesn't disqualify you from performing well above the rest.

Being too different won't endear you to family members or the boss but does get attention. You have musical talent—you can do two or three things at once. Getting down in the dumps can be cured by adventure trips, though you're not a gung-ho traveler; usually there's something to attend to near home. You'd probably hire a bodyguard if you could.

Love

Once infatuation begins to bubble, you usually do too much rather than too little. It's not from lack of judgment—although desires and dreams rule over logic and reason for most 7/3-born. You tend to get a bit confused knowing when to say "no" to lovers who request more than is necessary. You're not a wimp; you simply aim to please, and everybody likes you for that. Mature, stable, and independent partners suit you best.

Money

7/3s go to great lengths to gain on-the-job approval, but do everything without much supervision or suggestion. Your attitude is very cooperative, albeit a bit spacey, even though you never fault yourself for taking your time or rationalizing over another's sloth. You work in brilliant spurts of enthusiasm that carries through until you finish what you started. Analyze situations more precisely because you're inclined to overlook details.

Famous People Born on This Day

Female

Laura Branigan, vocalist
Andrea Barber, actress
Jan Smithers, actress
Charlotte Perkins Gilman, economist/
    lecturer/feminist
Lucy Kroll, entertainment agent

Male

Tom Cruise, actor
George M. Cohan, composer
Iain MacDonald-Smith, Olympic
    yachtsman
Tom Stoppard, playwright
Franz Kafka, author

July 4

Being born on the United States' birthday is something special—more than playing second fiddle to fireworks and flags. You do have an independent streak, often breaking clear of your family at an early age; perhaps you're a little more mature than they give you credit for. Always active, pleasant, a bit moody, you can also be critical and contradictory—you want your liberty in business, career, and in close relationships.

Being susceptible to too much heat and sunlight, you can deplete your vital energy—you are not resistant to wear and tear. You need a cooler zone where people are relaxed, professional, or share in your "cause." Use your knowledge of life's tricks in roles as a caregiver or managing other's personal affairs. For fun, go treasure hunting, where you're always finding something worthwhile.

Love

You have a rich fantasy mind, are a devoted partner, and are uncomfortable playing the field. You're not inclined to settle for second-best and believe that there's a "someone" for everybody—which, for you, translates to a mature, "been-there, done-that already"-type. 7/4-born must remember to ask the opinions of friends, elders, and teachers. You are attracted to independent, busy, and not clingy lovers with whom you can vicariously enjoy activity without too many restrictions in schedule.

Money

Authority figures respect you as a competent employee who isn't afraid to jump in when the going gets rough, even though coworkers may occasionally criticize you for doing more than your share. It's fine to be of service, but you risk being exploited by those whom you serve. Social work, welfare programs, rehabilitation, and helping others-therapy suits you well, provided that there is more mental stimulation than physical. Don't be a fuss-budget—treat yourself to something nice after a hard day's work.

Famous People Born on This Day

Female
Ann Landers, advice columnist
Abigail Van Buren, advice columnist
Eva Marie Saint, actress
Virginia Graham, actress
Gloria Stuart, actress

Male
Geraldo Rivera, journalist
Neil Simon, playwright
Nathaniel Hawthorne, author
Calvin Coolidge, U.S. president
Rube Goldberg, cartoonist

July 5

Busy, emotional, artistic, 7/5s are apt to rise quickly in status and attract a great many love interests. Youthful below your years, before you know it you've achieved honor, renown, and probably a very rewarding position of responsibility, including marriage, children, dogs. Coming from an established family also helps. Others can count on your opinions because you have that inner knack for knowing what's what.

Since "the stars" favor you in almost any endeavor you truly put your heart and soul into, you may excel in almost any field, though you'll want to avoid the truly strenuous stuff. Muscle and sweat aren't what you're about—you are the coach, trainer and the soccer mom who enables the world's games to be played. You could do a commercial for milk. You could also run the country.

Love

Even though you speak with conviction, 7/5-born don't base their lives on what's-going-on-now or topical matters—and the same applies with lovers. It's easy for you to get swept away by flirtation or fantasy because you live for the moment but often overlook the consequences. Because you rush to get to the bottom line, it's a good idea for you to take more time getting to know potential objects of affection.

Money

You aren't afraid of hard work, provided that your efforts are appreciated and compensated. But please be careful of biting off more than you can chew, or what is necessary because you're inclined to take on others' responsibilities without forethought. Settle into your job description and go about your merry way. Spending money, rather than saving, is easy for you. Although not extravagant, maintaining a budget is borrrring!

Famous People Born on This Day

Female

Julie Nixon Eisenhower, President Nixon's daughter
Meredith Ann Pierce, author
Katherine Helmond, actress
Anna Arnold Hedgeman, social activist/politician
Patsy Pease, soap actress

Male

Huey Lewis, musician
Warren Oates, actor
Jean Cocteau, writer/artist/director
Shane Filan, singer
P.T. [Phineas Taylor] Barnum, circus promoter

July 6

The whiz kid with the Coke-bottle glasses or straight-A miss priss, you'll grow into a powerhouse encyclopedia-like talent with a healthy dose of sex appeal thrown in just to make your life tantalizingly interesting. This still may not make you the most popular kid on the block, and even family members may take sides against you. Maturity will help you channel your sensitivity and surplus of "the juice" into a nice creamy.smooth career—with "power."

How can anything unfortunate dare happen to you? Sometimes it's beyond your control, but often you could have done better to head off disasters. Be wise and not just smart. A role as a teacher would befit you, though you're also the entrepreneurial type, cracking the whip, investigating and finding the pot of gold at the end of some special rainbow.

Love

You're a perfectionist when it comes to passionate pursuits—cautiously evaluating each nuance as well as suitor. The least complicated the lover, the better for you. You have a specific set of "rules" before getting personal. 7/6-born are comfy in the role of subtle seducer, rather than being the surprised seductee. You're not easily overwhelmed by flattery and know the difference between dubious fantasy and what truly flies.

Money

Because you can't stand being taken advantage of, you're quite wary making friends with coworkers—performing only on-the-job assignments, although always willing to volunteer. Even though you're a good money manager and budget-watcher, you're better at human interaction rather than facts or figures. Never a money-making martyr, you maintain reasonable rates for your services and don't respect anyone who doesn't hold up their end of the bargain.

Famous People Born on This Day

Female

Della Reese, singer
Nancy Reagan, former U.S. First Lady
Dorothy Kirsten, opera singer
Janet Leigh, actress

Male

Sylvester Stallone, actor
Dalai Lama, Tibetan spiritual leader
George W. Bush, U.S. president
John Paul Jones, naval hero
Jamie Wyeth, artist

July 7

Courageous and more intelligent than you appear, a watery type like you can just flow along, then suddenly, zap! . . . you jump on the opportunity you've been waiting for, leaving others behind shaking their heads, saying "did you see that?" You're a secretive planner—or schemer—but almost always a diplomat even if your friends and companions aren't. You'll have to watch them; they've been known to cause trouble and bring losses. When you triumph, you'll enjoy rewards.

Your mate was a good catch, and keeping up with them may be a full-time challenge—you wanted them, now you've got them. For a kick, try your hand at amateur movie making with those new digital devices. You like hanging with the in-crowd. In malls, at hot-spots, or in the woods, the hunt is on, so let's roll.

Love

You have a gentle, cooperative disposition that attracts many friends and suitors. Optimistic about love, you always try to give fellow employees the benefit of the doubt. You don't work hard at showing your good intentions because your motives are always generous and considerate. 7/7-born are tough and brave. However, it's easy for you to get blinded by the light of others' white lies.

Money

Routine and schedule-following come easy for you. You're dependable and very honest, which makes you excited to learn more and experiment. Although sympathetic and curious, you mind your own business and don't discuss personal matters with coworkers. You know the difference between a coworker and a trusted friend. You're not afraid of criticism, nor doubt your competence. Your practical nature urges you to buy with cash rather than credit.

Famous People Born on This Day

Female

Shelley Duvall, actress
Roz Ryan, actress
Michelle Kwan, figure skater
Margaret Walker Alexander,
    poet/author
Theda Bara, silent screen actress

Male

Marc Chagall, artist
Ted Cassidy, actor
Pierre Cardin, fashion designer
Doc Severinson, bandleader
Ringo Starr, drummer

July 8

With secret ambitions and a bit of devil inside, you surprise us. We thought you were so pliable and dowdy, not a vixen but folksy, not a hustler but conformer. An experimenter who stretches the limits, sometimes you do get in over your head but you'll learn with experience and fit in with the very people you were once ticked at. Some of you can be such sourpusses when "they" get you down. In relationships, remember there is no "I" in "team."

Keeping up with you is no easy task. It's no wonder that you can become a nervous wreck if you push too hard without some TLC in return. Let love flow in—it will, naturally. A good makeover would help improve your image. Of course, it's what's going on inside that really matters, so be a positive spirit.

Love

Even when monitoring your feelings (as you always do), you're alert and gracious about others' agendas. More considerate than cautious about your role in relationships, you invest kindness, even when others disappoint. You're reasonably permissive with others as long as they try and try again. 7/8-born invented denial, and turn expertly passive-aggressive when situations become confrontational. Don't neglect your own needs!

Money

Your clever curiosity constantly conjures new and better ways for making money. That is, provided you don't need to invest too much blood, sweat, or tears! Nah, you're not lazy, but patience isn't your blessing—you're better at off-the-cuff, rather than by-the-books, stuff. You always try to give coworkers the benefit of the doubt, but don't work well in teams. Don't be so independent-minded that you miss out seeing how lovely the grass is on someone's side of the hill.

Famous People Born on This Day

Female

Elizabeth Kubler-Ross, physician
Mary Johnson Lincoln, educator
Faye Wattleton, president of
    Planned Parenthood
Cynthia Gregory, ballerina
Shirley Ann Grau, author

Male

Kevin Bacon, actor
Roone Arledge, TV sports promoter
Billy Eckstine, jazz singer
Marty Feldman, comedian
John D. Rockefeller, oil industry
    tycoon

July 9

Your wiry, wavy hair gives us a clue about your forceful, pleasure-seeking, wild, dynamic nature, yet you're also the type that has their own pew in church, and loyally follows the code of your special circle, maybe holding on to relationships too long after they've run their course. Making up your own rules to fit your needs is probably not going to get you far—change your environment instead. Don't think that "everyone else does it, so it must be okay." Some things are definitely not okay.

Loving to travel, you're ready at the spur of the moment, traveling light, ready to soak up exciting, memorable experiences. Theme parks were made for you—and your family. Remember to be accountable, too. It's okay to pry into others' affairs to see if what they're up to is to your benefit.

Love

You hate cluttering your life with erratic or emotional people, but usually do. Unfortunately, you give lovers way too much leeway to prove their loyalty, and forget to warn them when enough is enough! Because you have specific expectations about each other's responsibilities, it might be a good idea to look at your union as a partnership instead of a one-sided arrangement.

Money

A perfectionist, and a lover of challenge, you're only content when you show you can do your very best. You slowly and precisely weigh out options, and your instinct to improve is as natural as breathing. You're straightforward and determined, but not especially confident (just picky). Supervisors recognize your positive strengths even though you're not all that keen about coworkers' approval. It's easy for you to fall into a comfortable routine and be a lifetime employee.

Famous People Born on This Day

Female

Courtney Love, singer/actress
Kelly McGillis, actress
Lisa Banes, actress
Debbie Sledge, vocalist
Barbara Cartland, romance novelist

Male

Tom Hanks, actor
Fred Savage, actor
Nicola Tesla, electrical engineer/
    inventor
Jimmy Smits, actor
John Tesh, new age pianist/TV host

July 10

Proud, noble, and an authority on any number of "important" topics, your genuine warmth and sincere desires are noticed and appreciated, and others court you for your personality, good looks, and maybe even your supposed wealth. You are a protector type—a crusader—always active and usually very gallant, patriotic, and respectful of family and its history. Though you can come across as pompous, aloof, it's a self-protection device; usually you are very fair with others and deserve the same in return.

You have a lot of heart, but physically your vitality level lags, so it benefits you to follow a planned, manageable schedule rather then tearing through the days and nights helter-skelter. Arising early in the morning strengthens you—set aside at least an hour in the afternoon just to relax, to make social calls, and tinker.

Love

7/10-borns' biggest romantic handicap is an unwillingness to let go of the past, and to forgive and forget. Develop a better "enjoy love right now" outlook, and don't set yourself up for disappointment about what "should-be." Express your immediate feelings and needs, redefine your desires, and be willing to change. Even though your friends know that you love to be in love, don't expect partners to be mind readers!

Money

Your coworkers know that you're generous with your time, sharing what you know, and willing to explore options. Occupations that don't require book keeping are best. For you; balancing personal finances and paying credit cards is challenging. You're always willing to give others the benefit of the dollars-and-cents doubt and are a valuable team player—just make sure that you don't relinquish your talent or time to the undeserving!

Famous People Born on This Day

Female

Jessica Simpson, singer
Camilla Parker Bowles, British socialite
Eunice Shriver, Special Olympics founder
Mary McLeod Bethune, educator
Jean Kerr, author

Male

Arlo Guthrie, songwriter
Arthur Ashe, tennis player
David Brinkley, newscaster
Marcel Proust, author
Camille Pissarro, impressionist painter

July 11

So many of you may travel far this lifetime, perhaps torn away from your home or places of comfort. Fate may press you into service, perhaps serving in government or some vital but challenging role, and probably not secure. You press on despite hardships, knowing that your character is strong, making sacrifices when called upon, collecting good karma from your successes. You could be handicapped by a health problem, so you must always consider your physical well-being and avoid bad habits.

Silver linings on emotional clouds are not always visible, but you can see them when you look, and jump into action to serve the common good, dissolving walls, and bridging the gaps in troubled relationships. If only it paid more. Learning how money works will definitely help you win the balance of payments game.

Love

7/11-born are willing to please, and always curious to explore. Because you don't handle rejection well, you gingerly test relationship waters, and are not impulsive in romantic affairs. You are compassionate yet always practical when expressing and defending your rights, and prefer mature, self-secure partners. Although you usually try to pull more than your own share of responsibilities, you don't hesitate to ask for help.

Money

You have a knack for doing the right thing at the right time, and being in the correct place when opportunity arrives. Always punctual, "time" means "money" to the 7/11-born. A good bargain shopper, you compare goods and weigh out options, never touting an "easy come, easy go" attitude about finances. However, once you reach your financial goal you tend to want more and more. Although not selfish, you always need to know what's in it for you.

Famous People Born on This Day

Female
Suzanne Vega, singer
Lisa Rinna, actress
Adrienne Barbeau, actress
Bonnie Pointer, singer
Olga Havlova, political activist

Male
E.B. White, writer
Robert the Bruce, King of Scotland
Yul Brynner, actor
Mark Lester, actor
Giorgio Armani, fashion designer

July 12

The author of your own destiny, it will be your good efforts—not family, not teachers, not luck—that tells us how far you'll go in this grand lifetime—and you can go far when you figure out that delivering what the public wants is key, not what someone or something did in the past. Even if you feel trapped by health problems, there may be unforeseen cures ahead and solutions for any problems. You are never really defeated unless adversity is permitted to unglue you.

Being intuitive has advantages, and you should develop your "sixth sense"—but without letting your imagination go overboard. Since your feelings seldom let you "settle" down, you might try meditating, or better still, getting back to nature and cutting out the modern garbage that we're meant to mindlessly consume.

Love

You tend to form romances with individuals who need you more than you need them. Don't fall into the trap where you think that you have to be responsible for your partner's silliness. Be wary of lovers who exploit or take advantage of you because some view you as an easy victim. Maintain integrity, and keep your eyes open! Learn to be comfortable with yourself, and don't be afraid of solitude.

Money

Once you understand work obligations, you complete the task quickly. However, your tendency to overlook details or be too accommodating creates problems. Give attention to your responsibilities and the little things before going beyond the call of duty. 7/12-born understand how to budget others' finances, but must learn how to do it better for themselves. You run the risk of debt unless you discipline yourself, slowing down to read all the fine print.

Famous People Born on This Day

Female

Kristi Yamaguchi, figure skater
Christine McVie, singer/songwriter
Kirsten Flagstad, opera singer
Beah Richards, actress/poet/
    playwright
Cheryl Ladd, actress/producer

Male

R. Buckminster Fuller, architect
Milton Berle, TV personality
Bill Cosby, entertainer
George Washington Carver, botanist
Henry David Thoreau, naturalist/
    author

July 13

Sociable and talkative, your friendly manner is among your best traits, promising a lifetime of people, people, people. With your quick mentality, you're ready to argue to force a fair agreement on the topic of the moment, or to enjoy romping with your brothers/sisters in arms. Concerned about others, you probably learned from your humble beginning, making the best of education and opportunities, putting you in charge as the author of your destiny and that of your family, extended or otherwise.

Optimistic and always ready to jump in, you may tire from too many loose ends, worn down by pitfalls that could have been avoided had you gotten the facts in advance. Having a peaceful, clean environment and watching your diet and exercise will do more for you than fad cures. Modernizing will work wonders at work and at home.

Love

You remember birthdays and anniversaries, even if you get the date wrong. You're conscientious, honest, candid, and don't shy away from learning. However, lovers may get put off by your blunt exactness because no one ever has to presume where you stand. It's a good idea for you to learn to go with the flow of spontaneity, try giving others more leeway. You don't fear intimacy—you simply have a long laundry list of needs.

Money

You don't let others sidetrack you from the project at hand, but you have a tendency to let impatience get the best of you. 7/13-born understand the value of time and money but could try a little harder in the punctuality department. And while you're at it, try to get better control over sarcasm, and temper! You're a positive individual, but fall easily into a "you-owe-me" monologue.

Famous People Born on This Day

Female

Danitra Vance, comedienne
Hilary Grover Barratt Brown, conservationist
Simone Veil, politician/president European parliament
Linda Ann Simon, airline captain
Tillie Ehrlich Lewin, industrialist

Male

Harrison Ford, actor
Patrick Stewart, actor
John Dee, alchemist/astrologer/mathematician
Cheech Marin, comedian/actor
Erno Rubik, invented Rubik's cube

July 14

If the world had to pick someone to go out into space and meet with alien beings, you'd be perfect. You have high ideals, you're not threatening, you're unselfish and sacrificing—a quick learner who desires to explore and serve. Aliens would probably take you with them—or jealously zap you on the spot. Closer to home, you should develop your goals and a life plan rather than wandering. You're metaphysical—a perfect guide for spiritual or natural avocations.

Life is full of roles for you to play—teacher, coach, counselor, boss, the great communicator—anything that keeps the world moving without pain, or helps society or the precious animal kingdom. Increase your great inner stamina and your status by being "in the moment"—cooperating not criticizing.

Love

Even though you stand up for your rights, 7/14-born hate criticism and are queasily uneasy with confrontation. Because you're more of a follower than leader, you usually attract partners who are bossy or very self-important, when all you really, truly want is compassion, and to be treated as an equal. You're not self-destructive or particularly weak-willed, but it's a good idea to start developing more self-confidence! Discover just how high you can fly solo!

Money

The word "doormat" is not in your job description, and although you're proud of your people skills, you're easily intimidated by time constraints and accounting expertise. But, what the hey?—you're a "how-can-I-help-you" kind of person, not a number-cruncher! You're not a major traveler, but love dreaming about exotic places; 7/14s are good teachers, reporters, and easily take charge of small companies and businesses.

Famous People Born on This Day

Female

Missy Gold, actress
Esther Dyson, computer publisher
Nancy Olson, actress
Polly Bergen, actress
Emmeline G. Parkhurst, suffragist/
    stateswoman

Male

Harry Dean Stanton, actor
Dale Robertson, actor
William Hanna, animator
Woody Guthrie, folksinger
John Chancellor, journalist

July 15

Like most July-born, you soak up experiences and knowledge by being among artisans, experts, and those who have that special something. You will also have the special something, biding your time until you feel comfortable about taking the controls. You're wise enough to make yours an easy life where thoughts rule emotions and culture is polite. Usually good looking, you have a special charm—making it pay big requires the right people around you—wrong types can be attracted, too.

We'll find you in the wrong job, wrong school, wrong hair—and you might get discouraged or sell out. Don't sell your soul—your sweetness. You should jump into environments with low stress and harmony, where the artist in you is appreciated. Get out of the Cinderella rags and show your style.

Love

Your objects of affection are always showered by your enchanting attention. You're better with fairy-tale relationships, rather than reality, but you never allow bottom line dollars-and-cents to overwhelm amore. It makes no difference whether a lover is younger or older than you, nor does his or her origin. "Loyalty" is your big thing—even though the expression " 'til death do us part" creeps you out.

Money

7/15s are competent and precise with on-the-job responsibilities—never tardy, full of excuses, or overly needy. Because you never want to hear coworkers say that you didn't try hard enough, you tend to overdo or go out of your way for approval. Biting off more than is necessary only hurts you, not anybody else. Just do what's expected of you first; then lend a helping hand—but not your money!

Famous People Born on This Day

Female
Lolita Davidovich, actress
Maggie Mitchell Walker, philanthropist
Mother Cabrini (Saint Francis Xavier), religious worker
Linda Ronstadt, singer/songwriter
Dorothy Fields, lyricist/composer

Male
Jan-Michael Vincent, actor
James Ball, economist
Clive Cussler, author
Rembrandt, painter
Jesse Ventura, wrestler/politician

July 16

Behind your smile is the heart of a hunter—a dreamy, romantic hunter of fun, good times, and adventure. Not content to be the obedient child, you need to "mix" and do at an early age, perhaps marrying young, maybe even wisely, though you shouldn't bet on it. You shouldn't bet on anything for that matter, as you are gullible and probably aren't too sure of the rules of the game. You might want to take career planning a little more seriously.

You excelled at being a teenager, so as you grow older you could return to those days by helping teens avoid the pitfalls and getting the maturing process in full swing while still running loose and independent. All people are children; they are yours to lead. Burn off your excess energy on exercise equipment or by dancing.

Love

Lovers adore you because you don't challenge them. 7/16-born have a keen awareness of what's necessary to make a relationship work and quickly relate those requirements to their partner—unfortunately, many times before anybody gets a chance to get a word in edgewise! You're not aggressive, but it's a good idea to let others do the driving every now and then. Alert and verbal lovers suit you best; strong but silent types may drive you batty.

Money

You learn quickly and keenly but have an inclination to overdo, overreact, or expect too much from yourself and coworkers. It's hard for you to relax when projects need attention or a deadline looms. Compromise isn't your best quality, even though you keep your cool. A diligent and hard-working employee, you're always hopeful about personal financial victories.

Famous People Born on This Day

Female

Ginger Rogers, dancer/actress
Barbara Stanwyck, actress
Margaret Court, tennis player
Mary Baker Eddy, founded Christian Science
Ida Wells-Barnett, human rights leader/educator

Male

Corey Feldman, actor
Michael Flatley, dancer/choreographer
Orville Redenbacher, popcorn king
"Shoeless" Joe Jackson, baseball player
Roald Amundsen, explorer/discovered South Pole

July 17

You are not a pillar of strength—you're a pillow of strength. Not a problem—with a smile you trust the winds of fate to navigate you into safe harbors where your landings are happy. You have good taste and an aura of kindness, plus enough determination to not be pushed around. High risks and contentious people are not for you, though you can blend into any crowd, for awhile. Most of you could be called "fertile" so family chores and children take up a lot of your time, which you are happy to give.

Emotional to a fault at times, you need others to provide some fire, excitement, and stability. Expand your career possibilities by trying new roles at work without stepping on others' territory. Conform without being pigeon-holed. Get to know the other neighborhood families.

Love

Your straight-speaking quickly informs lovers where they stand. Partners don't consider you antagonistic, even though you rarely back down from debate. You know exactly what makes you happy and, likewise, what drives you crazy. Although you consider yourself open-minded, your need for schedule and routine tends to inhibit or restrict spur-of-the-moment fun because your mind is always "on" and you always plan ahead.

Money

Never accusatory, you dislike being challenged by coworkers because you believe that your way is best. You're not a "know-it-all," simply an individual who has specific personal wants. 7/17-born read contracts clearly, honor obligations, and always aim for punctuality. Although you are curious about the private lives of coworkers, you keep your distance and demand that they respect your privacy.

Famous People Born on This Day

Female

Diahann Carroll, actress
Phoebe Snow, singer
Phyllis Diller, comedienne
Eleanor Steber, opera singer
Nancy Giles, actress

Male

Donald Sutherland, actor
Art Linkletter, TV entertainer/host
James Cagney, actor
Erle Stanley Gardner, author
David Hasselhoff, actor/singer

July 18

There is a little swagger in your step, a bitty bite in your voice—a little storm is brewing inside, though you will go out of your way to please others while still pressing the pace. Getting a career going is a real challenge, especially since you're accustomed to following your heart and desires without picking up much in the way of education or help. More dominating than you appear, relationships require a certain chemistry—you'll be glad you've made extra sacrifices to make true friends.

You're not afraid of hard work—it's the return on your efforts that bothers you, like the astronaut who returns to earth only to be handed a desk job. Rather than crashing through roadblocks, consider other avenues. The astronaut becomes the politician. The stagehand becomes the actor. If ill, become the healer.

Love

Your obsession with details and perfection often causes stress in your relationships, so it's a good idea to take a breath and review situations and yourself, a little bit slower! You labor over trifles, worry about competition, ex-lovers, or circumstances that are (really) not in your control, and you overestimate what others expect of you. On the positive side of the coin, you're very kind, always willing to make things better, and have difficulty telling a lie. Try to relax just a little bit, okay?

Money

You always maintain good work performance and a positive attitude and rarely fly off the handle at coworkers, choosing cooperation over cash-flow chaos. It's hard for 7/18s to understand philosophical concepts or finger future trends, but hands-on experience and repetition serve you well. You work fairly well in teams but would rather lead than follow. You have an insatiable appetite for activity and always aim to make things peaceful, although usually on your terms.

Famous People Born on This Day

Female

Elizabeth McGovern, actress
Martha Reeves, singer
Tenley Albright, Olympic figure
   skater
Jensen Buchanan, actress
Harriet Hilliard Nelson, actress

Male

Vin Diesel, actor
Hunter S. Thompson, author
Nelson Mandela, South African
   activist/president
John Glenn, astronaut/U.S. senator
Red Skelton, comedian/actor

July 19

Like a rough diamond, you will have to be faceted and pol-
ished before the real benefits of life come showering down
on you. Ambition—you have it but do be reasonable—we all
can't have it all, though you probably will get your 15 minutes
of fame. Make sure it's for something good, please. Because
you are not content to sit, you are already ahead of the pack.
To be a master, you first must learn to master.

Some great leadership and business abilities are deep
inside you—bringing them out through education will help
"qualify you" for the future. You can still be the boss of your
family and develop new roles for yourself. Others are not the
cause of your limitations—the limits are only in your mind.

Love

Always curious and sniffing about in other's business, you're not one to believe everything that's initially seen or heard; therefore, love affairs often are quizzical tests for you. Asking questions is fine and dandy, but behaving, or acting on doubt, usually isn't nourishing to anyone! Your hesitation or mistrust of others is rooted in your past. The major test for all 7/19-born is to learn to enjoy the moment, understand risk, and try to enjoy the flow of any tempest.

Money

Being an inquisitive type, you're always on the lookout for better ways to make money, feeling that on-the-job answers are never final or real. Few others have enough energy to maintain your pace or schedule, so it is best for you to work alone. Employers and coworkers may think that you're jumpy or nervous, but you consider yourself "efficient," never compulsive or overbearing. Introspection and meditation help you overcome the blues.

Famous People Born on This Day

Female

Kathleen Turner, actress
Rachel Robinson, social activist/
    humanitarian/psychiatric nurse
Rosalyn Yalow, medical physicist
Vikki Carr, singer
Sofia Muratova, Olympic gymnast

Male

Anthony Edwards, actor
Ilie Nastase, tennis player
Charles Horace Mayo, surgeon
George McGovern, presidential
    candidate
Edgar Degas, impressionist painter

July 20

Versatile, talented and well-liked, you're the fit and sporty type, maybe a little bit on the edgy side, but that makes life interesting for those around you. You have weaknesses: you're tempted to break the rules and play the blame game, perhaps thinking you're too noble for others to notice. They do notice. What you want them to notice is your sense of values and taste, your good qualities, and your eloquence, which should come naturally.

You like challenges and travel—like Edmund Hillary, the first to climb Mt. Everest A good storyteller, you need a way to reach more people, so head to the big city and get busy.

Love

Not one to believe that first impressions are correct, your fantasy mind is attracted more to what lies beneath the surface rather than what you hear or see. A lover's background is rarely as interesting as a 7/20-born's imaginary scenario. Unfortunately, your well-intended optimism often creates a misunderstanding, misjudging, and misinterpreting of prospective lovers. Learn to be a little less suspicious about matters of the heart.

Money

Although gregarious and friendly when working with others, you're a bit controlling when in positions of power. You're not afraid of responsibility, of course—after all, you're considerate, even though you easily tire of routine and hate on-the-job emotional roller coaster encounters. Although it's difficult for you to balance your checkbook, you hardly ever go in debt. Sales jobs, working with the public, are easy for you.

Famous People Born on This Day

Female

Natalie Wood, actress
Diana Rigg, actress
Lola Albright, actress
Barbara Mikulski, U.S. senator
Sally Anne Howes, singer/actress

Male

Carlos Santana, musician
Edmund Hillary, first to scale Mt. Everest
Charlie Korsmo, actor
Anthony Cavendish, banker
Nelson Doubleday, publisher

July 21

Life is a learning experience, since how far you go depends on sitting up straight, paying attention, and filing for future use all the tricks, techniques, gimmicks, and insider info you can set your eyes and ears on. It all starts with listening, but being a contented headstrong type, you might have a problem with that. You can be really devout, too, 99.9% pure believer. But you are not a pushover—get you riled and troublemakers will get all the heat they can handle.

Drawn to serious occupations that are mentally demanding, you'd make a stern but fun drill sergeant, marshaling others the way they should be marshaled, administering your sense of justice, escaping dullness and boredom, yet maintaining your privacy and time for letting your own creative juices flow.

Love

Ever the romantic, you leave no stone unturned when pursuing an object of affection. Your curiosity is quickly aroused and passion comes quickly—always eager for the chase and to make romance more exciting. You have an uncanny ability to size up situations swiftly—especially concerning others' feelings. You court lovers methodically, and always enjoy the chase. You work welll with uncomplicated, simple partners.

Money

You're a reliable, dependable employee, and coworkers and employers admire your ability to keep your head and get the job done. 7/21-born enjoy devising game plans and attacking them with precision. You're fair with everyone, rarely demanding more from others than they can deliver. Management and supervising positions are perfect for you because you adore applause, as well as perks and profits.

Famous People Born on This Day

Female

Hatty Jones, child actress
Elizabeth Hamilton, author
Henrietta Marie Morse King, cattlewoman
Kaye Stevens, actress
Kay Starr, singer

Male

Robin Williams, comedian/actor
Ernest Hemingway, author
Cat Stevens, singer
Isaac Stern, violinist
Josh Hartnett, actor

July 22

Quietly cool or chattering away, everyone in the room knows you're there, and you draw them into the conversation, liven up the party, all very busy, light, lively. Day by day you're developing your own persona, becoming your own person, improving your status and enjoying life—you do that well. Most of you are attractive, practically irresistible, still mild and caring, full of school spirit and childlike bravado. Others will look up to you, hoping that they can endure as you have, not complaining, friend to all.

Since you like to stay on top of things, and because you're a quick learner with a keen eye and talented hands, you usually succeed in whatever it is you put your mind to, but if it's not a perfect fit, you move forward to your next victory, fairly won.

Love

Because you're not good at second-guessing anyone or reading between conversational lines, you need a straightforward partner who is up-front and tells-it-as-it-is. You're very to-the-point about your feelings when in a relationship and very devoted (and, expect the same in return). Because you appreciate people from many walks of life, it's important that your partner enjoy socializing and nights out.

Money

You quickly respond to emergencies and outside stimuli and aren't afraid of responsibilities. Managerial or independent work suits you well, provided that it doesn't alienate you from fellow employees. You're not bad with facts and figures and are conservative in your spending. You're a good bargain shopper and don't spend money foolishly—a trait that you admire in friends and lovers.

Famous People Born on This Day

Female

Louise Fletcher, actress
Rose Kennedy, matriarch of
    Kennedy political family
Emma Lazarus, poet/essayist
Margaret Whiting, big band era
    singer
Amy Vanderbilt, authority on
    etiquette

Male

Willem Dafoe, actor
Danny Glover, actor
Don Henley, musician
Alexander Calder, sculptor
Alex Trebek, TV game host

July 23

It is two steps forward and one step back—you're just a little bit on the edge and tend to bump heads with the wrong people just when fate seems to be smiling on you. Many of you are homebodies and private persons, and can put on weight if you don't make extra efforts to stay industrious and active. You also have a lusty appetite for romance games, and even if you're married something on the side may be going on! Try to keep it secret.

Are you superstitious? It indicates that you really don't understand people all that well, so roles where you have to work closely with others—without picking their pockets or touching something private—help you learn human nature, body language, and cooperation, all of which help stabilize and deepen your relationships.

Love

Although a child at heart, you are well-suited for mature, from-the-heart lovers. You have no time for superficial people, preferring those whose lives have purpose and direction. Your conversation with lovers is charming, and delightfully real—emphasis on "real." 7/23-born roll with the punches and rarely hold a grudge for long. Communication and compassion rank high in regards to what makes a good partner.

Money

7/23s have good reasoning ability, know when to make concessions, and are mellow in the role of mediator. You respond to people honestly, and your enthusiasm stimulates them to respond in kind. Always practical with personal investments, you have healthy respect for time and material things, and have little difficulty putting aside for rainy days or planning future financial investments.

Famous People Born on This Day

Female

Janis Siegel, jazz singer
Betsy Haworth, deacon/minister
Kaity Tong, journalist
Alison Krauss, country singer
Gloria DeHaven, actress

Male

Bert Convy, actor
Haile Selassie, emperor of Ethiopia
Karl Menninger, psychiatrist
Woody Harrelson, actor/activist
Marlon Wayans, comedian

July 24

Life is full, colorful, full of intrigue and emotions—you don't want to be left out, so you indulge. Have a little balance, please! Inclined to see yourself as an underachiever, you can waffle—waffling is a no-no. Do you just think you have ambition, confidence? Maybe. You need not outdo the competition, but welcome more action that produces something good for others, not just fulfilling the moment. When dreaming of being the star, remember to share the spotlight.

Put on Earth to fulfill a role, start by being more dependable. You are naturally protective of your family but can neglect some simple everyday details—that's why having a partner that complements you is a good form of mutual protection, necessary for growth and prosperity, which you shouldn't waste when you find it.

Love

You have an intuitive understanding of what makes others tick—for you the emotional nature of any situation must be analyzed first, and logically. Similarly, you need a romantic partner who talks candidly and kindly, from the heart, treats others as equals, and confides in you. Even if your lover isn't successful, your understanding nature accepts anyone who is sincere, and has realistic hopes and dreams.

Money

Like a therapist or writer, 7/24-born have a keen ability for analyzing situations and implementing ways to transform any problem. You are fair and easy-going with coworkers and rarely overreact to disappointment or setback. Because you must be well-informed, you are never at a loss for words. Fellow employees work harder in your presence because you encourage them—you inspire and don't intimidate.

Famous People Born on This Day

Female
Jennifer Lopez, entertainer
Anna Paquin, actress
Bella Abzug, writer/feminist
Lynda Carter, actress
Amelia Earhart, aviatrix

Male
Michael Richards, comedian
Chief Dan George, actor
Pat Oliphant, cartoonist
Barry Bonds, baseball player
Alexandre Dumas, author

July 25

After appointing yourself to be in charge, the show begins and you joyfully relish any and all the attention that comes your way. Perhaps having to play second fiddle to other family members when you were young, you developed a personal style that now opens opportunity's doors. You brim over with that natural energy and it works wonders—when you feel good, you are good! You fit in. However, when you can't, it's a signal for change, which you definitely have the power to make.

Expression! Let it all hang out—please the eye and please the heart; better yet, please the movers and shakers! Life is art and you're the artist, and when you can make a career of that, it turns golden. Social scenes with music, entertainment, culture, and a buzz—that gets you going!

Love

Not that you're overly self-indulgent, but there's a big "eat, drink, and be merry" part of you that needs constant supervising. Like many fun-loving 7/25-born, you tend to do everything in excess. Less is more. Learn to temper your enthusiasm with new friends and lovers—don't come on too strong, or smother or overwhelm. You enjoy spontaneous partners and are always ready for a good laugh and new experience.

Money

Your live-and-let-live attitude influences others but doesn't necessarily win friends from coworkers. You have difficulty accepting responsibility and are not great about taking orders. Never a soft-spoken, silent type, you always say what's on your mind. Because you're more enthusiastic than logical, start listening to the words in your head before spouting them out haphazardly. Be open to others' ideas, rather than desperately clinging to your game plan.

Famous People Born on This Day

Female

Iman, model/actress
Katherine Kelly Lang, actress
Louise Brown, first test tube baby
Molly Bennett Aiken, founded
   Riding for the Handicapped

Male

Matt LeBlanc, actor
Brad Renfro, actor
Walter Payton, football player
Walter Brennan, actor
Maxfield Parrish, artist

July 26

The sensitive, lover type, you have the aura that attracts others, and they're not after you for your brains or money—which you might use a bit more of. You are not a pussycat—you're a lion, known to bite when you get aroused. Preferring to associate with professionals and the well-to-do, they're impressed when you show a talent in the arts, or have an inside connection—all of which you have because you hang with a strong-willed, independent achiever crowd.

Admonitions and warnings—you are just superstitious enough to heed them, though you'd rather not hear them, so we won't say anything. It's all just window-dressing anyway, and as long as you are free, you'll stay free. Kicking bad habits is easy; developing appreciated ones is your challenge. For fun, sit up front at musical events.

Love

Your romantic interests are stimulated by romantic, honest, and responsible lovers who take care of you. It's not that you're lazy, but you simply need every available helping hand, and get disturbed when partners don't devote one hundred percent to y-o-u. Maintain your gotta-have checklist, but help your objects of affection obtain theirs too! Don't be so eager to judge; after all, different folks have different strokes.

Money

You like every little thing to be the same on the job day after day and with no surprises. Unfortunately, you quickly lose your cool or get arrogant whenever things change or are challenged, becoming testy if anyone questions you. But you're more than pretty good about maintaining a personal budget, even though impulse shopping is an ongoing indulgence. Aim to develop more modesty.

Famous People Born on This Day

Female

Sandra Bullock, actress
Laura Leighton, actress
Dorothy Hamill, figure skater
Gracie Allen, comedienne

Male

Kevin Spacey, actor
Stanley Kubrick, film director
Mick Jagger, musician
George Bernard Shaw, dramatist
Aldous Huxley, author

July 27

Touchy—very sensitive—sometimes you might imagine things that aren't true about people or situations, which might protect you but leaves others wondering. Most of the time others are taken in by your gently warm attractiveness, awed when you surprise them with your special talent, coming down from your ivory tower to show that you really have something to say and contribute. When in the mood, you'll let them know you're as sexy as they think you are.

Thirsty for all the good things of life, you can be swayed by timely trends or persuaded by others who whisper the right combination of words. You'd like more important roles but they can be strenuous. Look for roles where you can be magnanimous, fair, with less competition. Not a sun worshipper, it's better to relax in the shade or the snow.

Love

You turn thought into action and go for the romantic gold at every opportunity! Some lovers may consider you too big for your britches, but you know that that's their problem, and you quickly set them straight. You're not selfish; you merely know what you want and what a partner has to do in order to make a relationship fully functional. Don't forget that a partnership includes two people; give lovers the benefit of the doubt and the right to be themselves.

Money

Coworkers know that you're determined, reliable, and very independent, and rarely give up without putting up a good fight. Truth is, you're not competitive. It's simply that you crave respect and enjoy being noticed. Personal investments are freely spent on appearances, home, and comfort rather than education or health. 7/27-born prosper from professional economic advice—even though they often rebel against it.

Famous People Born on This Day

Female

Peggy Fleming, figure skater
Maureen McGovern, vocalist
Agnes Yarnall, sculptor/artist/ author
"Queen Mother" Audley Moore,
    civil rights activist/humanitarian
Charlotte Corday, French patriot

Male

Norman Lear, TV writer/producer
Leo Durocher, baseball manager
Robert Gibb, zoo/theme park
    creator
Keenan Wynn, actor
Jerry Van Dyke, actor

July 28

Ahead of the pack, you can be a dominator, always involved and usually calling the shots, usually on some sort of mission. Sharp and usually stately in manner, you're psychically perceptive, or think you are. Leading a family is not a problem, it comes naturally, and you probably came from a well-to-do family yourself, gaining confidence, experience, and stature early in life. Eventually, your career may dominate, and there may be high risks and dangers involved; these are not a problem for you.

Even in your soft-spoken way, you are a competitive winner. You are a lion or think like one—paternal, protective, but more a lover than fighter. You go with what works, so you don't usually waste time on games, power trips, and relationships that don't work—providers provide! Appealing and persuasive, you graciously accept starring roles.

Love

It's not that you're antagonistic or overly defensive, but it's a good idea that you learn the art of listening and let bygones be, if you want to grow in a relationship. Your definite likes and dislikes often irritate partners due to your stubbornness, and your need to have the final word. Swallow your pride, and take time to examine your lover's needs. Don't let expectations or pressures cause your union to break down—aim for break-throughs!

Money

You prefer doing things your way and by your rules—just make sure that you're qualified, and not stepping on coworkers' toes! It's okay to be selective about what you say to fellow employees, but don't be so critical, please! You work best in small companies, or privately-owned establishments. Even though you tend to go over budget, and spend money on impulse, you're pretty realistic with personal spending.

Famous People Born on This Day

Female

Beatrix Potter, children's author
Jacqueline Kennedy Onassis, U.S.
    First Lady/editor
Lori Loughlin, actress
Sally Struthers, actress
Mary Jane Odell, politician

Male

Jim Davis, cartoonist
Bill Bradley, basketball player/politician/Rhodes scholar
Earl S. Tupper, invented Tupperware
Mike Bloomfield, blues guitarist/singer
Rudy Vallee, singer

July 29

A cool customer with goals in mind and a critical eye, you persuasively get what you want, perhaps having to be a lion-tamer and a "player" to get there, and making a name and career for yourself. Always consider the consequences of what you say—anything negative usually has a negative impact on someone or something else. You may be surrounded by other ambitious people, meaning that you may get knocked around.

What are you searching for? You're after an absolutely perfect someone—a soul mate not a pretender. Usually from a professional family, you grew up independently educated. Having power and wanting to use it correctly, karma suggests you try many roles in life where you'll learn what works, and apply it successfully everywhere. A perfect vacation? Anywhere, but try hanging with the old crowd back home.

Love

Because your mind is always eager for new experiences, you rarely spend time crying about what happened in the past or over old spilled-milk issues. You are best-suited for lovers who don't have a lot of old emotional baggage, drag their feet, or don't appreciate your independence and joy for life. However, they, too, must be as effervescent and happy about the future as you! Yes, indeed, "tomorrow is another day."

Money

Although you're progressive in your thinking on the job, 7/29-born get a bit bossy believing that there's a better way for doing things—plus you don't tolerate incompetence! Employers know they can count on you, but may like you better if you didn't act like such a know-it-all. You expect a lot from yourself, as well as from fellow employees. Your impulsive nature makes spending money easy, but your optimism and enthusiasm always make good all debts.

Famous People Born on This Day

Female

Martina McBride, country singer
Roz Kelly, actress
Clara Bow, silent screen actress
Patti Scialfa, singer
Elizabeth Dole, politician

Male

Peter Jennings, journalist
Geddy Lee, musician
Professor Irwin Corey, comedian
Booth Tarkington, author
Melvin Belli, lawyer

July 30

Seemingly modest, small, with good features—others do notice you and it's a bother if they don't. Maybe it's your flaxen hair, your clear skin, or your eyes. Beneath that candor and businesslike façade is a fiery, passionate heart, and a temper which you reserve for those who ask for it. Instinctive and honest, you have a deep memory, analyzing ability, and are careful not to make mistakes—good business traits. It also helps in relationships, but some might see you as high maintenance.

With a good command of your body and the right touch, you'd make a good dancer, doctor, or any occupation working with people. A good traveling companion, you usually take charge and always have something pertinent to say. You love the earth, gardening, and farms, though you don't have a green thumb and animals ignore you.

Love

Your social skills are terrific and wide-ranging. Like a chameleon, you easily and quickly mimic characteristics of lovers in order to please them, feel compatible, or appear more in command! You're truthful, but must be careful that what may seem to be a loving relationship could be merely a Hollywood-like facade. Be true to yourself, and allow your object of affection the right to do the same!

Money

7/30-born are not afraid of responsibility or the demands of leadership. Coworkers admire your tireless efforts to get a job done, but little do they know it's because you enjoy applause, glory and recognition. Living the Good Life motivates you. Money-wise, it's fun for you to try keeping up with the Joneses, having nice things. But because you live for the moment, it's a good idea to seek financial advice from those in the know.

Famous People Born on This Day

Female

Lisa Kudrow, actress
Vivica A. Fox, actress
Delta Burke, actress
Emily Brontë, author/poet
Helene P. Blavatsky, founded
    Theosophist Society

Male

Tom Green, comedian/actor
Arnold Schwarzenegger, actor
Henry Ford, auto kingpin
Peter Bogdanovich, filmmaker
Paul Anka, singer/songwriter

July 31

How dare anyone say you are stubborn or overbearing! You don't have time to waste, and life is too precious. They can keep their crazy opinions to themselves. Still, you could cut some slack now and then—try picking the right moments. Develop people skills, then inner growth and material growth will happen. Things like politics or religion are supposed to be for your benefit, not the other way around. Don't let these dictate or limit your heart, which you have more of than you imagine.

Ah! Big events, pageantry, extravaganzas—they don't happen everyday and you so enjoy being there. And you enjoy good tasting food. To answer the question, "Is something holding you back?," it's up to you to understand and unravel your own complexities; start with your many romantic relationships. See, it's easy!

Love

It's not that you're superficial or materialistic, but 7/31-born view relationships like a bank account—alert to what you invest, expecting profit and a good return. However, it's a good idea to soften your "what's-in-it-for-me?" attitude, because love is a two-way deal. Lovers quickly learn what to expect from you. You do what you say and promise, but usually on your terms. Loosen up—share, and share alike!

Money

You rarely give fellow employees the impression that you're too easy-going, or easily manipulated—you constantly remind others that you can work as hard as you wail. More responsible than ruthless, and independent-minded than determined, you always get the job done and move on. Management suits you well, although your people skills may need some tweaking. You're conventional in your personal spending and know a good nvestment when you see one!

Famous People Born on This Day

Female

J. K. Rowling, author
Geraldine Chaplin, actress
Sherry Lansing, Hollywood executive
Nico, model/singer
Evonne Goolagong, tennis player

Male

Wesley Snipes, actor
William Bennett, U.S. Sec. of Education/drug czar
Sean O'Neill, Olympic athlete
Dean Cain, actor
Gerald Anthony, actor

August

August 1

Happy-go-lucky, sociable, and probably proud of having more friends than you can count—you would never count them anyway! You are probably going far, with ample opportunities to work with others and succeed in business. Not a super-hard worker, the busy-busy worky-worky mentality isn't your style, though you are a fair administrator, always treating others without malice. Your pleasant, soothing voice mellows out your environment and attracts romance. Weak points? Not many: a little stubborn, procrastinating, and lacking zip sometimes, but so what?

No matter what culture you find yourself in, you like it orderly, with the right people, since you don't have time for chaos and distraction. A country estate would suit you fine, where there is room for everyone to stretch out and relax. You also prefer being in charge of the books.

Love

The expression, "You can lead a horse to water, but you can't make him drink," suits you well. It's impossible to stop you from running after what you want—especially concerning relationships! Although you may not win every romantic race, you're an expert at jumping over hurdles. You're strong-willed, independent-minded, and difficult to budge once you set your sights on the trophy. After all; you're the real prize!

Money

Your clever ability to adapt helps you learn quickly and easily. Versatile and spontaneous, you crave diversity on the job. You combine compelling charm, social skills, and good people sense to obtain personal success. Even though coworkers may not consider you a financial wizard, you keep your finger on the pulse of the most effective ways to get what you need. 8/1-born never forget a favor or opportunity given them.

Famous People Born on This Day

Female

Nancy Lopez, professional golfer
Tempestt Bledsoe, actress
Maria Mitchell, America's first
    woman astronomer
Yvonne DeCarlo, actress
Emilie Rose Macaulay, writer

Male

Francis Scott Key, *Star Spangled Banner* author
Herman Melville, author
Yves Saint Laurent, fashion designer
Jerry Garcia, rocker
William Clark, American explorer

August 2

One of the best days to be born on—don't spoil it! As an adult, you're refined, sociable, entertaining, paternal, and usually have that conversational gift—so you can fit in anywhere, though you're a bit of an actor and prefer the company of cultured types. You're a bit eccentric, the self-reliant individual with noticeable hair, fond of fun and frolic. A good listener when you want to be, as you're well aware that listening more helps. When challenged, you tend to be resigned and complacent.

Your "no worries–be happy" outlook doesn't mean you don't know your business. You're a tiger at making partnerships and deals, and can come out on top or jump on something else. This is not something that's taught—it's pure instinct. If possible, you'd vacation year round. Why shouldn't you soak up the good life?

Love

8/2-born sense the way that a relationship is moving, then deftly zigzag through the loaded minefields of love and emotional baggage in order to make things happy, relying solely on inner radar to guide them. You have a special gift for solving lovers' problems, and grasp situations quickly. It's difficult for you to put your heart into much when you're alone; whereas, with a partner, your enthusiasm is constant and vibrant.

Money

You're accustomed to doing what you want and are a good trouble-shooter and problem-spotter. Financial security is important to you; without it, you go to pieces. As a rule, you comparison shop before spending a cent and are always mindful of expenditures. You take achievement and success seriously, rarely leaping before looking. You know your limitations, and intelligently aim only as high as you know you can go.

Famous People Born on This Day

Female

Myrna Loy, actress
Linda Fratianne, figure skater
Bernadine Healy, health administrator
Jewell Jackson McCabe, activist
Beatrice Straight, actress

Male

Edward Furlong, actor
Carroll O'Connor, actor
Lance Ito, judge
Peter O'Toole, actor
James Baldwin, author

August 3

People enjoy your charming company, and you may sense you're stuck with the same old crowd. You'll grow out of it and move up. The important things in life will come your way either by luck, family, or associations—earlier if by your ingenuity. An eye for style, your closet is marvelously interesting. As a youth, you have an impulsive childlike quality, but as an adult you can become engaging and persuasive, though still sometimes falling for old dangerous temptations and habits.

Rallying the members of your group is a good role for you, and you'd do well in trade or commerce. You could spend a lot of time at the mall or anywhere the action is. Partying is one of your favorite pastimes. Usually very good-looking, you'd make a good role model—your smiling face gives a winning impression.

Love

When you are inspired to secure a desired partner, you throw yourself into first gear and commence an unremitting journey towards winning the heart of the targeted suitor. You love to be in love, as well as active and busy. 8/3-born crave social acceptance and peer approval. Attention, affection, and close companionship are essential to your equilibrium. Nothing makes you feel worse than loneliness.

Money

Because you fear poverty, you do everything in your power to maintain control over your money. Understanding your faults and limitations about finances, and how to improve on them, makes you enjoy life more—and profit in many ways! 8/3-born make wonderful sales people and enjoy all jobs where the challenge is immediate, and the strategies quick. Even when you encounter a momentary setback, you're always ready to try again.

Famous People Born on This Day

Female

Phyllis "PD" James, writer
Maggie Kuhn, activist
Martha Stewart, homemaker expert
Sally Benson, novelist
Dolores del Rio, actress

Male

James Hetfield, rocker
Jay North, actor
John Landis, director
Martin Sheen, actor
Tony Bennett, singer

August 4

Naturally, you can't sit still when you see unfairness, poverty, strife, and ugliness in our world, so you are in select company with those who have vision, committed to positive change. You may best evoke this change behind the scenes and away from danger. Cooperation is what's necessary—that you have learned—so think twice before biting a hand that feeds you. Your magnetic quality gets you into relationships; value others and they will value you.

A diplomat, a negotiator, investigator—these are good roles for you, where you have to be on your toes and a little suspicious—and without fault of your own! Your emotional intensity can make it hard to unwind, and although you always like an audience, it's worthwhile to think alone or to bounce your ideas off of one special companion.

Love

8/4-born have high hopes for the "perfect love relationship"—forever auditioning for that faithful someone—but are better spectators than players. You freely dish out advice but can be a bit lazy about your own self-improvement. Befriending you is easy, but it's an endurance test to be your lover. 8/4-born are capable of tremendous sacrifice in return for the special attention that they feel they need to survive. You need attention—and lots of it.

Money

Your financial gains come as a result of deliberate action and eagerness to get a job finished—thoroughly and quickly! Once you commit to a project, you voraciously attack it and get it over with ASAP, never losing sight of the reward. You keep everything in order and are constantly aware of coworkers' opinions and suggestions. You're an all-or-nothing employee; there is no middle ground for you concerning money.

Famous People Born on This Day

Female

Queen Mother of Great Britain
Helen Thomas, journalist
Tina Cole, singer
Crystal Chappell, actress
Mary Decker Tabb Slaney, Olympic
    track star

Male

Louis Armstrong, jazz great
Billy Bob Thornton, actor
Roger Clemens, baseball pitcher
Richard Belzer, comedian
Percy Bysshe Shelley, poet

August 5

Life is all about passion, and few people are as strong a believer as you are, so you come across as resolute, no stepping over the line—is that fun? Maybe. You are highly self-assured and dedicated, which will probably attract an adoring mate and maybe for quite awhile, but you might not feel entirely comfortable in your career since you are easily distracted and even irritated by others who don't buy what you're selling or don't act "right." Lighten up!

When asked to stand up and be the loyal soldier, you can do it, and you take pride in your professionalism. As a learned authority, you're a good parent or teacher. Getting genuinely involved—not just lip service—will lead to rewards in everything you do, your strength being an example for others to follow.

Love

8/5-born are understanding and encouraging, determined yet considerate—and always willing to go that extra mile for the sake of love and peace. More emotional and intuitive than intelligent, you prefer partners who provide mental stimulation but aren't complex or dramatic. You value commitment, and expect the same from your lover. You love being needed and are a good audience for partners.

Money

You always live up to your end of a business deal and expect the same in return from coworkers. You're prompt and dependable but may not excel in management positions because you're not hard-hearted enough to boss others round. 8/5-born's drive to achieve financial stability is powered by ambition to please, to win approval. You're a perfectionist at work and stop at nothing to learn more, always challenging your brain to become as strong as your heart.

Famous People Born on This Day

Female
Loni Anderson, actress
Maureen McCormick, *Brady Bunch* actress
Selma Diamond, comedienne
Sister Vince Otto, mental health activist
Mary Ritter Beard, historian

Male
Neil Armstrong, astronaut
John Huston, film director
MCA [Adam Yauch], rapper
Rick Derringer, rocker
Robert Taylor, actor

August 6

Optimistic with some fire in your eye, you have a vision and you're willing to go for it, and yes, you do take things personally! When you are warm, kind and nurturing, lasting success can walk right in. Blasting your way in probably leaves you on shaky ground, so a little more sensitivity, please, and allow time for lovers and friends to keep up! Fond of social life and adventure, there's probably a lot of stories that others could tell about you—good stories we hope! Remember: results are remembered, not intentions.

Being "touchy" makes you an individual. It just turns out that you're not exactly well-coordinated, leaving a messy path behind you. You might want to try more roles as the do-gooder. Others depend on you!

Love

8/6-born are dreamers and enjoy kaleidoscopic day—as well as night-dreaming. Love represents sustenance to you, and for you to live without it is to wilt and die. You are a generous lover and enjoy showering your partner with gifts and attention. However, this can become quite expensive if you're not careful, so it's a good idea to link up with a more thrifty partner who will keep watch over your extravagances and the bankbook.

Money

Because you are determined and strongly opinionated, you may not take on-the-job criticism very well. Careers requiring teamwork or anonymity appeal to you. Although not argumentative, you often act rashly without considering the greater good. Saving money comes with difficulty because your emotions and energy constantly tug you in different directions. Link up with others who are less enthusiastic, and you will do the accounting chores.

Famous People Born on This Day

Female

Lucille Ball, actress
Helen Hull Jacobs, champion tennis player
Louella Paisons, gossip columnist
Catherine Beecher, educator

Male

Andy Warhol, artist
Robert Mitchum, actor
Hoot Gibson, actor
Michael Burke, sports executive
Peter Bonerz, actor

August 7

Taking center stage is only natural for you. There you might be the leader, the motivator, explaining it in plain language, or just letting it all out loudly. Jerry Springer would love you. The church choir director would too if you could keep in tune. It's your enthusiasm and determination that set you apart. You want all to love friendly you, and can't understand why they don't always. Your wacky opinions aside, others can relate to you when you get results, and may even give over their hearts.

Everyone wants to be the one to push the buttons; you're the one who can do it with vigor and authority. You also love to travel, especially when you can go first class, like royalty. You're a talkative companion and can become an expert on foreign affairs, knowing where to go and who to see.

Love

8/7-born value self-expression, attention, and are compatible with a partner who will provide them with peace of mind, love, comfort and security. You are friendly but don't share confidences easily or quickly—you know the difference between idealism and realism because of past trials and error. Seek a partner without too much emotional baggage (after all, you're always on the go) because you deplore quarreling and despise arguments. Deep down, you pray for all to be well.

Money

Coworkers never call you lazy—you drive yourself at a lively, incredible pace and are always eager to escape routine. However, by rushing so hurriedly, you often overlook essential details and facts. Because you want everything "now," indecisive coworkers irritate you. Often, money is earned through temporary, part-time, and freelance work. This gives you the time to pursue personal pleasures and reconsider options.

Famous People Born on This Day

Female

Mata Hari, spy
Helen Caldicott, physician
Billie Burke, actress
Taylor Caldwell, novelist
Ann Beattie, writer

Male

Garrison Keillor, humorist
Stan Freberg, satirist
Louis Leakey, anthropologist
Carl Switzer, actor
Ralph J. Bunche, diplomat

August 8

Life can be a carnival, a circus, a big adventure—and you can be the ringleader, or at least one of the talented stars, showing no fear, delivering what you promise with a flourish—well, a few of you will crash but take the setbacks philosophically, and you may break a few hearts along the way. You're not the mushy type—unless sporty, enthusiastic, and personable is mushy. At work or play, you jump right in, making friends wherever.

The daily grind is something others do. Building dreams and spreading joy—maybe working with animals—is what you do. You are not a good loser so you stay away from that possibility. You're pretty selective of your friends, preferring the opposite sex. Moving around to where appreciative people await you, you're always at home anywhere on planet earth.

Love

Never one to fall for a "Hi, stranger. New in town?" line, nobody can pull the wool over your eyes! You have a remarkable mind for memory and are a fountain of minutiae. Tenacious about your desires, once you set your sights on someone, you never give up—even if you have to wait for years! You require that a lover be strong, pull his or her share, not lean or overly depend on you, and someone who treats relationships with mutual respect and decorum. To an 8/8-born, love is never skin-deep—it's a long-term investment.

Money

Speculation doesn't cut the economic cake for you! In order to do good work, 8/8-born must see, touch, and have hands-on experience. You don't rest on your laurels, and don't expect coworkers to either! Your ability to synthesize information and translate it into action gives you a terrific edge in the workplace, without a need to sit on the throne. Even though you yearn for attention and recognition, you're uncomfortable in authoritarian positions.

Famous People Born on This Day

Female

Robin Quivers, radio/TV personality
Esther Williams, actress
Connie Stevens, singer
Josephine Holt Bay, stockbroker
Esther Hobart Morris, suffragist

Male

Dustin Hoffman, actor
Keith Carradine, actor
Rudi Gernreich, designer
Mel Tillis, singer
Terry Nation, writer

August 9

Not a flash in the pan, you have substance, strength, and a deep, wise soul. Both a lover and a fighter, you are not afraid to speak your piece or jump on the bandwagon for a reasonably good cause. At other times you are patient and conscientious, switching gears in order to capture a special someone's attention, then taking charge of the relationship. You'd prefer working at home; you're not a carrot-chaser and probably only God is good enough to tell you what to do.

Always your own person, usually well-endowed, you can be a playboy/playgirl, getting hitched if the pot is right and rich enough, and you have an eye for that. Being wrong is embarrassing, so you're sure of yourself—it's others you worry about. Be a psychologist, not an anvil-head. Luxury baths cool you down.

Love

To you, emotional and financial security are directly linked. Your imaginative and romantic nature keeps you dreaming and hoping, rather than doing and loving. However, you tend to be lazy concerning relationships—you only live in your comfort zone, and let love come to you, rather than going out to explore. Because you have difficulty being alone, your lovers are often way too independent for your happiness.

Money

Coworkers respect your honesty, and you rarely make promises you can't keep. However, you don't understand how to save, and have grave doubts about how to make money work. The best thing about 8/9-born is their sense of integrity; they deplore quarreling, and hate being caught off guard. Thanks to your gift for empathy, you would do well in professions where you can help, educate, or take care of others—after all, that's what you look for in a lover!

Famous People Born on This Day

Female

Melanie Griffith, actress
Gillian Anderson, actress
Whitney Houston, singer
Pamela Travers, *Mary Poppins* author
Ashley Johnson, actress

Male

Deion Sanders, athlete
David Steinberg, comedian
Sam Elliott, actor
Jean Piaget, psychologist
Robert Shaw, actor

August 10

Of all August birthdays, you are probably the most down-to-earth, organized, studious, and genuinely moral character, a builder who seeks to please and impress others, and not afraid to do the hard work necessary in order to succeed. You pull your weight, but others around you may not; you're too kind and confident to have doubted them to begin with. Ignoring details can hurt your career and personal life, you believe you can make it alone, but think again.

Whether from humble beginnings or silver-spooned, you have a knack for putting the pieces together and speeding up the wheels of progress. You can use all the tricks in the book; that's what books are for. You'd love having your own home or a farm, a place where you can constantly make improvements. The Eiffel Tower is waiting for you to visit.

Love

You hate to be idle, are street-smart, curious, and socially restless. Always ready for new experiences, it's difficult for anyone to keep up with you! Although open-minded, you quickly categorize prospective lovers—but, often, before understanding the whole story. In order to maintain peace and harmony, it's a good idea for you to slow down once in a while and admit when you're wrong. You're loyal, devoted, and anxious to please and be pleased.

Money

You're comfortable with yourself, and don't mind working alone—although working in cubicles or at-home jobs drives you batty. Once you set out to do a task, you stay until (you think) it's done. You're happy to let everyone do what they want with their money provided they keep their hands off your stash! You overlook coworkers' foibles but cannot live with hypocrisy, duplicity or deception, nor can you tolerate shades of gray concerning your hard-earned paycheck!

Famous People Born on This Day

Female

Angie Harmon, actress
Rosanna Arquette, actress
Hilda Doolittle, poet
Rhonda Fleming, actress
Pepsi Nunes, marine biologist

Male

Antonio Banderas, actor
Ian Anderson, rocker
Bobby Hatfield, singer
Jimmy Dean, actor
Herbert Hoover, U.S. president

August 11

When you were younger, you probably drove your mother nuts, wanting everything perfect—your way. Your choc-o-latte milk had to be stirred just right. You wouldn't budge until you got what you wanted. You've grown up and mellowed, though you probably wouldn't go out of the house in a wrinkled shirt—unless you wanted it wrinkled. Details don't escape you, a real blessing at jobs where perfection counts and protocol is followed. Life's uncertainties and imponderables still bother you.

Mentally active and down-to-earth, you're a good listener who can dish out the facts, figures, and fun yourself. Actually, your talent knows no bounds if you persevere. You know your craft and can balance home life and career, plus other special interests—for awhile. Dining at swanky, pamper-you-silly restaurants is a kick.

Love

Getting to know you isn't easy. It's not that you're painfully shy—simply very private about sharing your inner-feelings. You're passionate about your opinions with friends, but reserved and conservative about expressing emotional intimacy, preferring to keep love private, and you have specific dos-and-don'ts that a lover must fulfill. You win romantic gold by persuasion, reason, and logic.

Money

Even though you don't enjoy being the head honcho on the job or giving orders, you are so affable and intuitive that you seem to see around corners. Your natural sympathy and innate ability to "read" people make you very gifted in the business world—particularly in social service, therapy, medical, or psychology fields.

Famous People Born on This Day

Female

Marilyn Vos Savant, world's highest recorded IQ
Carrie Jacobs Bond, songwriter
Helen Broderick, actress
Elizabeth Holtzman, politician
Arlene Dahl, actress

Male

Hulk Hogan, wrestling entertainer
Mike Douglas, TV show host
Steve Wozniak, computer whiz
Alex Haley, author
Joe Jackson, singer

August 12

It is a good thing that you're courageous and understanding, because people born this day have a lot of mean challenges to lick, not getting credit for your good works and all the blame for what appears bad. Consider it a test of your soul, for indeed, inside you have a good heart that shouldn't be influenced by bad company, poor environment, or handicaps. You are stubborn, too, and want to have it your way. Make it "a way" others can appreciate, where life is enjoyed and nurtured.

A bright spirit, you are a great companion and willing to share, but you also get opposition and distrust, which is difficult to dispel and difficult to explain. You prefer people who are on the cutting edge, who are fun-loving, thoughtful, unsettled and independent like you, going everywhere.

Love

You're uncompromising and self-indulgent, but not self-centered. You have no place in your love life for subtleties, attacking every romance with vigor, and exuding your personal sort of gentle brashness into every affair. You don't trust others easily, and take your time before committing to marriage or family life. 8/12-born are clever partners—smart and savvy but not too moderate in their demands. Irrepressible? Indeed, but never lacking compassion.

Money

Your wits and logic are sharp, your desire to do good work is real and true, but you do spur-of-the-moment improvisation too well. You learn more about yourself when working with others, rather than working solo. Aim for jobs where you can say your say, and be comfortable enough to rely on a support system to fill in the blanks. You treat coworkers with consideration and rarely affront anyone directly.

Famous People Born on This Day

Female

Dominique Swain, actress
Baroness Phillips, co-founder of
    National Association of Women's
    Clubs
Donna Michele, actress
Jane Wyatt, actress

Male

Pete Sampras, tennis champ
George Hamilton, actor
Mark Knopfler, musician
Porter Wagoner, singer
Ross McWhirter, author

August 13

Friendly, kind, and sincere, you are a revolutionary trendsetter, ready to pitch in and help others, understanding what's going on due to your refined powers of perception, proving that you're a person who will not let negativity or the past hold you back. You're also very stubborn and persuasive. Who can stop you from strutting your stuff in order to attract attention and romance, which you dearly love? Your sparkling eyes hint of a little devil inside, though you would never be violent or cheat.

With flexibility and desire, success could increase in your career, though you'll have to earn the right to be boss. Good on one-to-one relationships, try partnership roles, hooking up with people who offer stability not just opportunity. Since life is one big holiday, having your own home is the best vacation of all.

Love

Although you believe in equality, the emphasis is always on "your" needs first. You express your opinions concisely but not always sympathetically, even though you expect sincerity and honesty from the other party. The need for affection, warmth, approval, and acceptance is paramount to your love life. 8/13-born have a strong sense of ethics and social decorum, which enables them to see both sides of human behavior.

Money

Your easy way with words and social insight helps you quickly understand difficult employees and job situations. Although you may not be well-educated, you are always eager to learn. You are curious and keenly perceptive of the world around you, and with training, your possibilities are unlimited. You know who you are and understand your shortcomings—unfortunately, being a good money manager is one of your minuses.

Famous People Born on This Day

Female
Kathleen Battle, singer
Annie Oakley, sharpshooter
Lucy Stone, feminist
Ann Armstrong Dailey, founder/
    director Children's Hospice
    International
Jocelyn Elders, U.S. Surgeon General

Male
Alfred Hitchcock, director
Don Ho, entertainer
Dan Fogelberg, rocker
Gary Davidson, sports league
    founder
Bert Lahr, actor

August 14

Gazing at the world through your kind eyes, you know you're a unique person full of feelings so deep that they must be from past lives, or maybe it's your inner understanding of the preciousness of life, love, and being a genuine individual. Impressive! Enlightened and cautious, you know you have something special that others desperately want, or should want—talent and personality. Still, being emotionally driven, you'd benefit by learning and using cold common sense.

Wanting to serve, please others, and make an impact, you may go into medicine, or where your saint-like qualities bring a fair price. Getting good value for your efforts is a challenge; get prepared and use free time to gain practical knowledge, also make personal appearances and connections. For inspiration, visit cathedrals, historic places, even swanky offices of the powerful.

Love

To many, it seems that you live more for improving a relationship than yourself! Even though your feelings are easily hurt, you rarely mince words, or let anything get in the way of love. Once your sights are zoomed in on the target of affection, like Cupid's arrow, you stick around indefinitely. You don't trust easily and will search a long time before committing to marriage. 8/14s prefer mature, home-loving types.

Money

You believe in lucky stars, and see a chance for success in everyone you meet! Your people skills are sharp, and you cultivate business contacts the way that gardeners grow cabbages! Always in a hurry, you're not well-suited for work that requires attention to detail or numbers—even though you accomplish much in short amounts of time. You honor work schedules and keep a pretty good watch over personal finances.

Famous People Born on This Day

Female

Halle Berry, actress
Debbie Meyer, Olympic champ
   swimmer
Susan Saint James, actress
Sarah Brightman, singer
Danielle Steel, author

Male

Gary Larson, cartoonist
Steve Martin, actor
Russell Baker, columnist
John Galsworthy, author
Sir Walter Scott, novelist

August 15

If self-confidence was a commodity, you'd be rich! We wonder, though, that maybe you're so much of a showman with a knack for impressing others with your noble bearing, dignity, and persuasiveness that you've convinced yourself you are royalty. No matter. You have ambition, determination, and the physical vitality necessary for success, plus you can charm anyone when necessary, including the very best lovers for companionship. Always alert, always in control, always generous, an example for many.

Your vision of a perfect world would have no disharmony, just prosperity and abundance, with you contributing in an important way. There are many humanitarian roles waiting for you where you can put together your team. You're a wonderful teacher too. Even a leader needs to watch his or her health, so make time for vacations where you can completely relax and recharge.

Love

Like the ocean's undertow, it's easy for you to get swept away in relationships—you and love can be a dangerous thing! 8/15-born will do almost anything to maintain romantic equilibrium, keep the peace, or avoid making waves, which is dandy for your partner but not always for you! Be careful not to place so much emphasis on what your lover wants that you ignore your own needs. Smarten up and refuse to let your kind, easy-going nature be misconstrued as weakness.

Money

Holding down a mundane job is a problem for the over-achieving 8/15-born. Much of what you do is about capitalizing on opportunities when they're hot, always expecting a high yield for your efforts and enthusiasm. Brainstorming and making money grow come naturally for you—it may not be easy, but your inner spirit is self-sufficient and always eager for economic improvement. You expect a reasonable return for your hard work.

Famous People Born on This Day

Female
Julia Child, chef
Edna Ferber, author
Maxine Waters, congresswoman
Rose Marie, comedienne
Ethel Barrymore, actress

Male
Ben Affleck, actor
Napoleon Bonaparte, French emperor
Huntz Hall, actor
Bil Baird, puppeteer
Mike Conners, actor

August 16

Just a little bit kinky and wild—that's you. Sometimes your desires are so strong they are hard to restrain, though you usually manage. It's not easy to keep your private life private, nor will you stand for the dull, normal, easy life. You have a strong desire to prove yourself, willing to take risks and brave the ordeals, dedicated to "the cause" of the moment, always in the inner circle. There is no keeping secrets from you and your cat-like curiosity.

A playful, romantic hunter, others listen to your distinctive voice, caught up in your magnetism and good looks. You can be a charming companion, sometimes moody, and unusually knowledgeable—almost a walking computer. Don't take roles where you have to stoop or risk your reputation. Your hobbies include sports. You're also fascinated by mysteries and intrigues.

Love

Even though you are head and shoulders above the crowd, you do everything in your power to fit in. You want to be admired (but hate admitting it!), and because you don't like being alone it's easy for you to put more emphasis on a partner's comfort instead of your own. But at the same time, you can't stand clingy or overly-dependent lovers either—you're looking for a warm shoulder and companion, but one who doesn't require a lot of maintenance.

Money

The harder you work and the busier your working agenda, the better you feel. You adapt to on-the-job emergencies very well, are a terrific trouble-shooter, and have an intuitive "feel" about how to get people to work together. Your unique mix of social insight and group awareness ensures that, with discipline and determination, you will succeed in any career you choose. Even though you scrimp and save, you prove your generosity on every occasion.

Famous People Born on This Day

Female
Kathie Lee Gifford, TV personality
Madonna [Ciccone], singer
Nadia Boulanger, conductor
Angela Bassett, actress
Lesley Ann Warren, actress

Male
Timothy Hutton, actor
Robert Culp, actor
James Cameron, director
Frank Gifford, sportscaster
Robert Ringling, circus master

August 17

A step ahead of everyone, you are the courageous one who strikes out on your own, testing the limits, making even dull projects lively. A resourceful idea person, you love adventure, life, and most of all, romance. Having a family is a victory, and so is financial security since your earnings may have ups and downs. Colorfully, you over-dramatize things and dominate the scene; "no" is not an answer you'll easily accept. You will definitely be you, unforgettable, always.

Action is in the air when you're around, so the tempo picks up, often with you calling the shots. A good eye for the talent in others, you should always do well in delegating or motivating roles. You have unique tastes and probably a variety of romantic partners; let them host you on entertaining getaways.

Love

Strong, self-motivated lovers spell happiness for you. You're attracted to well-known people or those deemed outstanding in their profession because you enjoy excellence, celebrity, and everything that money buys. You don't go for clingy, co-dependent types, preferring those who confidently tend to their own business and know how to take care of themselves. Nothing makes you feel worse than loneliness.

Money

When you have money, you carefully plan what to do with it and how to get the most from every drop of your blood, sweat, and tears. Your mind enjoys learning in a wide variety of topics. Your enthusiastic personality makes you a terrific salesperson, because you have a gift for comfortable gab and can talk about anything with anyone you encounter in the workplace. You're confident and very well-equipped to hold your own.

Famous People Born on This Day

Female

Hazel Bishop, chemist
Maureen O'Hara, actress
Maureen Connally, tennis champ
Jean R. Adams, entomologist
Mae West, actress

Male

Robert De Niro, actor
Davy Crockett, frontiersman
Sean Penn, actor
Donald E. Wahlberg, Jr., rocker
Francis Gary Powers, pilot

August 18

Iron-willed, attractive, and afraid of nothing, you don't have to concede anything—that's for others to do for you. Being active and headstrong, you can out-talk, out-endure anyone, anything, anywhere. So, you're a good ally in business, really into it, and should be well paid. But you also have your loving, needful side—it's not easy to hit a good life balance point. Family members need and appreciate you—you'll be rewarded with respect and loyalty if they don't feel left out.

In relationships, take off the rose-colored glasses and first get to "know" that individual. Being genuine is good, which gets good in return, eventually. You can burn yourself out at an early age, so in middle age it's important to care for your health. To relax, trek to the mountains, but don't stray off alone.

Love

Although you may appear aloof to people who don't know you well, it's simply because you're cautious about who you share your feelings with; underneath your cool, calm surface lies a caring and considerate nature. Always searching for the ideal, you have a clear checklist for what a partner must do, or have, in order for your happiness. You consider yourself more practical rather than a perfectionist. Due to your conservative nature, beware becoming too critical with loved ones.

Money

You are full of ideas, a good organizer, and a valuable member of any team. It's challenging for you to work alone, preferring small group activities. 8/18-born don't enjoy management positions because of the paperwork involved—"paperwork" meaning "you're not good with it." You pay your personal bills promptly but have a little problem with long-term savings because you live very much in the reality of right now.

Famous People Born on This Day

Female
Vijaya Lakshmi Pandit, Indian leader
Virginia Dare, first American born
    of English parents
Rosalynn Carter, U.S. First Lady
Shelley Winters, actress
Elayne Boosler, comedienne

Male
Robert Redford, actor
Patrick Swayze, actor
Christian Slater, actor
Meriwether Lewis, explorer
Marshall Field, department store
    owner

August 19

Never one to let opportunities pass you by, you have the determination and attention to details that will help you succeed, but will others cooperate? Stepping on others' toes must be avoided even if they deserve it. It may take time before the right people—perhaps foreigners—and right pieces are in place. Use your quick tongue to make friends, not ambush them! You will learn much as you go, getting that "chemistry" going, cultivating intellectual, well-connected friends.

Your curiosity is a natural conversation starter, so when others like you and when channels of communication are open, you've noticed how things go much smoother. Roles that require a smile could get you a congeniality award—what a shock! A warning: you are a bit accident prone and danger comes in many packages. Watch for competitors.

Love

It's been said that "all's fair in love and war." You understand both games, always follow the rules, and play fair. 8/19-born don't like being alone, even though you're reserved about showing others what may truly be going on inside. It's not that you're unaffectionate—your hesitation comes from your fear of rejection, and you don't like making the first move. The sooner you own up to your insecurities, the quicker you'll overcome them.

Money

You are more efficient than lazy. However, if there's a way to cut corners, you expertly and quickly spot the short-cuts! Employers value your integrity and willingness to get a job done on time and budget—just like you do in your personal financial life. You understand the value of money and importance of time. There's something about 8/19-born that tells others straight away that you can deal sensibly with anything life places before you.

Famous People Born on This Day

Female

LeAnn Womack, singer
Tipper Gore, activist
Coco Chanel, fashion designer
Jill St. John, actress
Comtesse du Barry, mistress of
   Louis XV

Male

Orville Wright, inventor
Ogden Nash, poet
Malcolm Forbes, publisher
Gene Roddenberry, writer
Bill Clinton, U.S. president

August 20

Like a white knight or a warrior princess, you have the courage, sensitivity, and even the skill of a champion—heaven knows that you have the heart. That doesn't mean you should go asking for trouble or that the opposition will run for cover—there are complex rules to the game of success, and even if you triumph, do you get the reward? You do have your own brand of beauty and personality, loving children, animals, and the entertainment world.

Along with your natural fire, you have determination, are good in high-stakes roles in politics and fight for a cause. Sometimes you let it all hang out, neglecting to cover your back or to take care of your health. Learning more about how money works will help you manage it better and allow you to take a long-awaited adventure vacation.

Love

Young at heart, you live for entertaining, happy times. Underneath your optimism, you're a realist who believes in honesty and laying all cards on the table. Since unions and companionship top your want list, you know how to employ your social and diplomatic skills in order to maintain harmony in all relationships—familial as well as personal. Even though you believe that "two" is great company and don't like being alone, you're not overly dependent on lovers or friends.

Money

You enjoy being part of an extended economic "family" and demonstrating your skills. You work best in small companies or places where you're on a first-name basis with others rather than just a faceless employee. You maintain your calm in the face of turmoil, and your "just keep moving forward" philosophy helps you see through employment panic so as not to get scorched in the heat of the moment.

Famous People Born on This Day

Female	Male
Courtney Gibbs, actress	Robert Plant, rocker
Jacqueline Susann, novelist	Isaac Hayes, composer
Connie Chung, news anchorwoman	Al Roker, TV weatherman
Carla Fracci, ballerina	Oliver Hazard Perry, U.S. naval hero
Elizabeth Ashley, actress	H.P. Lovecraft, novelist

August 21

Well-mannered and serious, you're the practical enterprising type that believes that work and effort will bring rewards. It does. In your family, you can be the down-to-earth one doing the planning, caring for aging relatives and the roof over-head. Fun and rejoicing will come as hard challenges are met, many leading to a great rise and possible great fall—always requiring earnest effort on your part, for which you have the strength.

Preferring to play it straight and not take chances, you're perfect for roles where you're in charge of spending and resources, like investing in real estate that will later turn a big profit. Usually, you get all the facts, and you're not gullible. You like traditional things, so a cabin vacation and canoe suit you fine, but avoid exposure and catching a chill.

Love

8/21-born painstakingly pick over every detail of a relationship, or suitor. Comfortable yet cautious, your conservative personality attracts many acquaintances, but not always friends. Your definitive "like-don't like" laundry list of priorities gets constant upgrading, but you could stand to be a little less paranoid. Let bygones be; you worry too much! Don't put on false airs, or live your life second-guessing and fretting about things that may not be true or may not happen.

Money

Even at rest, you think about money and work. You always strive to succeed, and have no time for frivolity unless it helps you achieve your objective. You're not a risk-taker, preferring to be sure of what the prize is before leaping into the fire of the project. Do you save money? Well, yes, you do. Do you worry about prosperity? Yes, indeed, always. Being analytical and technically minded, you may be drawn to work in teaching, business, research, or health fields.

Famous People Born on This Day

Female
Kim Cattrall, actress
Alicia Witt, actress
Margaret Rose, English Princess
Aubrey Beardsley, artist
Ana Isabel Anderson-Imbert, physician

Male
Kenny Rogers, singer
Wilt Chamberlain, basketball player
Peter Weir, director
Roy K. Marshall, TV scientist
Clarence Williams III, actor

August 22

The worst of times or the best, there you are with your confidence, optimism, and crackling, well-chosen words, ready to help your acquaintances and family, never one to be mean or to deliberately cause trouble. Your heart is in the right place so you can be counted on for an honest opinion and honest effort, and you often lend a fine "artist's touch." You can be overly critical too, and emotions do affect your health, which you should always monitor, being careful of your diet.

Not the type who can smash through obstacles, little things can hold you back if you don't have goals and priorities in mind. Practice a diplomatic, firm approach and be a self-starter. Opportunities increase when you widen your social circle, but remember: more action, less talk. Oddly, forests help you think and are incredibly healthy.

Love

Dynamic, independent, and strongly opinionated, you require a responsible and mature lover—clingy, dependent partners send you running out the door! You don't like taking risks in relationships; you need to be assured of the "prize" before you play. Impermanence and compromise make you uncomfortable. You prefer a world where the emotional-ephemeral doesn't exist. Don't consider unions like a business arrangement—respect its unique beauty!

Money

Ambition and a willingness to take the lead help you climb the ladder of success. More economical than egocentric, you admire structure, power, and precision, and are terrifically perceptive. People respond to your sense of honesty, responsibility, and dependability. You do every small task in very big ways. You start a task and labor at it until the job is done. Because you are strong, and persistent, nobody should stand in the way of an 8/22!

Famous People Born on This Day

Female

Tori Amos, singer
Cindy Williams, actress
Dorothy Parker, writer
Valerie Harper, actress
Theoni Vachliotis Aldredge, costume designer

Male

Layne Staley, singer
Ray Bradbury, writer
Jacques Lipchitz, painter
Claude Debussy, composer
John Lee Hooker, blues guitarist

August 23

Excited and enthusiastic, there's a straightforward quality about you that people like. Your good coordination gets you started early in life—you show a talent, usually in the arts. Continually developing your mind, body, and spirit, you become a wonderfully sensual individual; if not, then you might appear over-emotional or fitful, a wallflower. You're close friends with a few select people, a loyal love-mate, always particular about your appearance, conscious of making a good impression. We like you.

Your romance life affects how you feel, so you might consider if there is too much drama there and not enough on life's other aspects. Work can be therapeutic since it gets your mind in a productive gear, and a continuing education will definitely improve your prospects for success. You probably wouldn't mind yakking it up with a psychologist or sailing on the Love Boat.

Love

You think quickly on your feet, are a versatile conversationalist, and keep up with topical headlines. However, you have a problem with control because you don't do anything halfway. You take love seriously, and you toss yourself into flirtations and relations with total commitment and abandonment. Keep that big mouth of yours open, and always ensure that you're both on the same wavelength! Your notion of love combines ambition and social advancement, rather than entertainment.

Money

You're hyper-ready to get a job completed, work hard, and know what you can and cannot do. However, your enthusiasm often finds you accepting gigs before considering the extent of what's necessary; being cautious isn't your strength. Nonetheless, bosses and coworkers respect your diligence and honesty. You always have enough personal savings to get along—and usually a great deal more. You make a point of honoring your commitments.

Famous People Born on This Day

Female

Nicole Bobek, figure skater
Norah Ellen O'Neill, pilot
Shelley Long, actress
Barbara Eden, actress
Vera Miles, actress

Male

River Phoenix, actor
Kobe Bryant, basketball player
Rick Springfield, rock vocalist
Mark Russell, political satirist
Gene Kelly, dancer

August 24

Perfection is not something that's high on other people's wish lists, but it can be on yours. It can bother you that we aren't as conscientious, efficient, and particular enough about all pulling together or solving the world's problems, or at least keeping our promises. You are a little scattered too, but when you do concentrate and aim, you usually hit your mark. Since you're so smart, we'd expect you to be richer, but that's not your priority; quality of life is.

Facts and figures are second nature. So are the birds and bees and so is being "right"—that makes for some interesting dating experiences. That aside, try roles as a mastermind or instructor, and genuinely prepare for promotions at work. Health spas visits and good check-ups should be part of your routine.

Love

Your concepts about love are more practical than fanciful. You're optimistic and positive about your romance, but don't take risks. For an 8/24-born, you know that a union of convenience seldom lasts and stifles both of you—so, you usually stop before "it" could injure you. You don't require a lot of social activity; you simply want "your" lover available and constant. Your uncanny hunches perceive dishonesty through almost any disguise.

Money

Your creativity fares well in occupations that involve logic, rather than quick-thinking. Forever idealistic and loyal, 8/24-born enjoy working in teams and collaborating in group efforts provided that they can assume the role as "teacher," but not as executive big shot. With your appreciation of the ever-changing Circle of Life, it is vital to choose a career that offers progressive options and futuristic alternatives (even if you don't invest in those credos personally).

Famous People Born on This Day

Female

Marlee Matlin, actress
Anna Lee Fisher, astronaut
Karen Keskulla Uhlenbeck, mathematician
Anita V. Figueredo, physician

Male

Steve Guttenberg, actor
Mason Williams, writer/musician
Cal Ripken, Jr., baseball iron-man
Max Beerbohm, writer
Duke Kahanamoku, Olympic swimmer

August 25

The "yes sir/no sir" world is not for independent, good-looking you—being self-sufficient and free to sample all the delights that life has to offer. Negativity is not in your vocabulary, and you will not let the bad guys get you down, nor are you tied to the past. Sex is a topic of special interest; should we go into that? It takes a very reasonable argument to get you to ever change your mind, since chances are you're on target to begin with.

Fiery yet well-mannered and coolly in control, you usually establish yourself as an expert in your chosen profession. It isn't like you to be silly; you're easily embarrassed and a private person. Doing a duet with anyone is an off-beat fun role. Antiques, collectibles, and cool cars are also a kick.

Love

It's difficult for you to give lovers a lot of leeway or the benefit of too much doubt, because you don't take risks or act on impulse. You expect suitors to share equally in a relationship (and maybe even a bit more), because lazy liaisons make you flee fast. You are unerringly faithful and sentimental about friendship and family matters. Your worst failing in a partnership is your inability to see yourself as others do: strong-willed. For this reason, you abhor criticism. Nonetheless, you always try harder and harder.

Money

You are capable, practical, and versatile, but not particularly ambitious. You probably have a long laundry-list of job skills and employment history—the reason being, you simply don't like doing the same old thing over and over because you bore easily. Working behind-the-scenes and without a spotlight suits you best. "To work" is only natural to the 8/25th-born. Once you set about a task, you stay until it's done.

Famous People Born on This Day

Female
Claudia Schiffer, model
Clara Bow, actress
Ruby Keeler, actress
Althea Gibson, tennis champion
Anne Archer, actress

Male
Sean Connery, actor
Leonard Bernstein, conductor
Tom Skerritt, actor
Kel Mitchell, teen from the hood
Elvis Costello, rocker

August 26

Always busy and full of ideas and "possibilities," you are a hands-on type who gets things done quickly, and also quite capable of mischief in romance—you're not the "one mate for life" type. Up-to-date on the latest trends and styles, your sharp opinions are persuasive; a better team player than soloist, you're not the self-consumed executive type.

Your full heart has a place in it for a little of everything. It's what's going on upstairs that leaves us wondering. Versatile and quietly critical, your likes and dislikes may change until you find the right niche—this takes some time, so avoid being caught in nowhere roles with nowhere people. Usually health conscious, you're physically fit and get a lot of power from arising early and fresh air, so sessions of outdoor exercise are recommended.

Love

Your humble and honest ego is happiest when being the silent, loving part of a relationship, rather than its bright, shining star. You don't do well under pressure; indecisiveness is your biggest challenge. You are easily swayed and often have trouble making up your mind. You're comfortable hovering and observing from the shadows and sidelines. You are loyal and giving, and require a strong, but kind, companion.

Money

Versatile, energetic, and unstoppable, coworkers admire your assertive attitude about devotion to do good work. You're not afraid of criticism and go the full distance to realize a project. On the job, you are efficient and positive, and freely share without expecting applause—only honest feedback! Your ability to adapt to emergencies is outstanding. You listen and assess, survey and scrutinize. It's hard to catch an 8/26-born napping!

Famous People Born on This Day

Female

Joanne Gail Abbott, MTV executive
Geraldine Ferraro, politician
Peggy Guggenheim, art patron
Alison Steadman, actress
Jan Clayton, actress

Male

Macaulay Culkin, actor
Branford Marsalis, jazz saxophonist
Ben Bradlee, editor/journalist
Steve Wright, actor
Christopher Isherwood, writer

August 27

An "activist"—that's you—mindful of worldly concerns, so often your life is dedicated to service, improving the community, or simply being helpful to friends and "the cause." Possessing good judgment, you are almost always truthful and precise, disliking anything disorderly or contemptible. Taking chances is not your style, and there are only a few of you who are not squeaky clean. Once your mind is set, you won't let a little irritability or obstacles get in the way.

More than most, you take a high degree of responsibility for yourself, and will work to make close relationships more perfect. If you are not out there already, you might enjoy roles that take you outdoors more or among the people or natural environments. You'd make a perfect office manager. Talking to famous people would thrill you to no end.

Love

"Love at first sight" is a bit of a problem for you because you don't initially see people as they are. Impatience and emotional confusion about commitment is an 8/27-born's shortcoming. This temperament makes you best-suited with lovers who are straightforward and uncomplicated. However, because you're a sucker about flirtation as well as fantasy, you must constantly review relationships.

Money

You have a good and clear understanding about current trends, what's hot or not, and are fairly realistic about your personal finances—"fairly" being the key adjective here. Because you're compassionate and eager to learn from others, it's easy for you to fall for a sob story, volunteer for overtime, or do more than is called for. Your by-the-book nature is more linear than intuitive. 8/27-born understand and enjoy the true meaning of teamwork.

Famous People Born on This Day

Female

Mother Teresa, humanitarian
Martha Raye, actress
Catherine Marshall, editor
Antonia Fraser, biographer
Alexa Vega, actress

Male

Tommy Sands, singer
Ira Levin, author
Lyndon Johnson, U.S. president
Samuel Goldwyn, film magnate
Paul Reubens, actor

August 28

Dependable, trusting, moral, and a perpetual student of life, it's surprising that we don't find more of you running the show. You probably have a unique name, like Rokie. Busy solving the usual problems, you might not see the big picture—more ambition would help. You have genuine talents to contribute, you work well with others, and you're quite capable of turning out practical and durable advice, and results. Check the scorecard and see where you might handsomely profit by fulfilling a need.

Getting out to see the world and expand your horizons sounds like simplistic advice, but making the scene provides you with wider vision, ideas, and adventures. You're probably doing too much of the mundane work around the old plantation. Let others pamper you—trick them into it if you have to.

Love

You are kind-hearted and curious, but have difficulty forming close relationships. (Is it because you're afraid that you might lose your freedom to do as you wish, and when?) You prefer lovers who are family, home, and work-oriented, rather than adventurous or always on the move, away from the house and you. People admire your grass-roots honesty. Although friendly and always willing to help, you value private quiet time.

Money

Getting to know you is pretty easy! You make up your mind very carefully, rarely jumping to conclusions. Even when on the job, you're a bit of a loner, spending a lot of time considering each choice and weighing out every point of view. You enjoy uncovering secrets, know how to keep them, but aren't comfortable working in positions of power, or in those with too much responsibility. Coworkers can always count on you to tell it like it is.

Famous People Born on This Day

Female

LeAnn Rimes, singer
Shania Twain, singer
Vonda N. McIntyre, author
Rokie Roker, actress
Elizabeth Bayley Seton, humanitarian

Male

Jason Priestley, actor
Daniel Stern, actor
Scott Hamilton, Olympic ice skater
Jack Kirby, cartoonist
Johann Wolfgang von Goethe, poet

August 29

The award for the most unique August birthday goes to you. You're one of the most pleasant and revolutionary, a real wild card, also a sort of purist. You have plenty of talent and persuasiveness, too, flocking with other birds of your feather. Generally peaceful, orderly, you are not the type that settles down easily, preferring your kinky freedom. You are a good friend once we get to know you. Having someone watch over your affairs is a good idea.

While you may not want to be tied down in relationships, you simply must have companionship and some sort of cause to champion. You certainly don't want to be known as ordinary. Try roles that go to the limits in the arts, but without breaking society's rules. Go west to relax; be in the rain for inspiration. Wear sunscreen.

Love

As talkative and sociable as you are, you have a real block about expressing your true feelings. You keep to your own counsel but aren't overly shy—it just takes a great while for people to earn your trust. You never feel alone. Even when you're not involved in a relationship, you maintain a busy social agenda. Try treating others as you'd like to be treated in return. 8/29-born work best when coupled.

Money

Your ability to put yourself in other people's shoes, combined with innate organizational and social skills, always keep you one step ahead in the economic game of life. Ambitious and versatile, you need variety and freedom on the job in order to maintain interest. You never let private matters interfere with paychecks—you always keep personal separate from business. You choreograph every detail of your life to run smoothly.

Famous People Born on This Day

Female

Rebecca De Mornay, actress
Wyomia Tyus, Olympic speedster
Ingrid Bergman, actress
Olive Ann Beech, aircraft industry
    executive
Isabel Sanford, actress

Male

Robin Leach, TV host
Elliott Gould, actor
Richard Attenborough, director
Charlie "Bird" Parker, saxophonist
Michael Jackson, singer

August 30

Anyone making a deal with you should read the fine print—not that you'd take anyone for a ride, it's just that you can be a sharp trader. You can also be a lot of fun to be around, and you seem quite at home in almost all social situations. Moderate, unprejudiced, polite and cooperative, who can say no to you? If life is a game, you are definitely a top player. Still, you can be taken advantage of, so you've learned about that "fine print."

Considering your inner desire to protect, serve, and enjoy, you might like a role in politics, medicine, or social services—if the pot is right. Your sense of humor and your clear, open mind usually put you in league with movers and shakers who help you succeed—there's nothing wrong with a healthy assist!

Love

You acknowledge your strengths and shortcomings, and easily mix with others. You are more socially savvy than restless but get bored quickly, and require lots of freedom. You prefer interesting, busy, well-respected partners; some of your friends may be considered quite unusual. Never at a loss for words or things to do, you enjoy the company of active individuals like yourself. Nonetheless, you prefer to run things rather than take orders.

Money

You work well with others, and get what you want without taking anything away from fellow employees. Even though you tend to be a bit bossy, coworkers appreciate and enjoy helping you. 8/30-born enjoy the Good Life, and teamwork. You are at your best in group endeavors, and always willing to lend a helping hand. Financially, you are always looking for a deal, are good with budgets, and know how to get your money's worth.

Famous People Born on This Day

Female

Cameron Diaz, actress
Peggy Lipton, actress
Mary Shelley, author
Shirley Booth, actress
Joan Blondell, actress

Male

Michael Chiklis, actor
Fred MacMurray, actor
Ted Williams, baseball legend
Timothy Bottoms, actor
Jean Claude Killy, Olympic skier

August 31

Talking with you can be like talking to two people at once—your mind is like a computer gone astray. Some of your ideas have us thinking "are you kidding?" Maybe you are, or maybe you're just being nice. Nothing escapes your interest and there's very little you cannot master, including romance when you calm down and get serious. Keeping promises and credibility earns others' trust and admiration.

You love nature. You love travel. You love talking, so take any opportunities for roles where action and movement are involved, with an eye on safety and profit. A ride on the space shuttle would be great—you could also do the driving, run the communications, mix the Tang, and fix the thing if it broke.

Love

You plot and plan, make lists and schedules, and constantly construct game-plans in order to ensure that a relationship goes smoothly. 8/31-born are perspicacious, shrewd, and not easily fooled. Your intelligence is penetrating; your mind is cautious and skeptical. You may not have many friends and loved ones, but you will always be close to those you have.

Money

You're an analytical thinker who believes that there is always a better way to improve money matters, and always a more prosperous opportunity on the horizon. Coworkers admire your progressive but practical ideas and respect your opinions. Your views are not always optimistic but are spot-on realistic—positive and conservative but also futuristic. You conduct good damage control and are a great trouble-shooter. You learn well, and what you learn you remember.

Famous People Born on This Day

Female

Debbie Gibson, singer
Gina Schock, rocker
Marcia Clark, District Attorney
Maria Montessori, educator
Marva Nettles Collins, educator

Male

Richard Gere, actor
Van Morrison, singer
Dan Rather, news anchorman
William Saroyan, novelist
Chris Tucker, actor

September

September 1

Few are as busy and adept as you at wheeling and dealing and getting all on your "to do" list done. Your keen mind helps you cut through red tape, and being a good judge of people—also careful and a bit secretive—you are a diplomat in the making. Life's mysteries and inside secrets aren't secret to you; you'll get used to them during your rollercoaster rides of love and romance. Not one to wait, you should always plan ahead. Turn on your magnetic charm always.

Leisure time for fun and games is actually quite healthy for you since it reduces inner tension. Try roles as a teacher or instructor; the bonding with others is also healthful. Travel is adventure, and you like exploring and finding the out-of-the-way paradises and secret passageways to fun.

Love

You're the last of the redhot diehards—both sectarian and fanatical about what you believe in, and what's required from someone who wants to be your lover. But you never rush headfirst into an affair just for the involvement. Even so, you have the logic and common sense to take the good with the bad and create a long-term union.

Money

You are a natural diplomat and express yourself on the job with such graceful exactness that people rarely harbor bad feelings about you even when you have to relate something unpleasant. Self-motivated, you think about the greater good of the company (as well as yourself), and don't require approval or orders to get the job done. Self-sufficient, solo work suits you best, rather than teamwork.

Famous People Born on This Day

Female

Gloria Estefan, singer
C.J. Cherryh, author
Yvonne DeCarlo, actress
Lily Tomlin, actress
Elizabeth Carpenter, journalist

Male

Johann Pachelbel, composer
Conway Twitty, singer
Edgar Rice Burroughs, author
Tim Hardaway, basketball player
Seiji Ozawa, orchestra conductor

September 2

Who knows what secret desires you're keeping in your heart? It's probably not a good idea to let others know any of your secrets! In total control—you wish, until your heart melts when someone sweet and attractive comes your way. When others need something now, they can turn to you—hard work, sacrifice, complexity are not problems but challenges, where your mind triumphs over matter, and we can all drink from the cup of sweet success, then later spin the tale to please eager listeners.

Since you don't stray too far off course, others depend on you, especially family and friends. You'd prefer a more independent role—like Ernest Hemingway—with your own hideout in the Florida Keys, or anywhere away from the humdrum and pointless toil. Life should be something special—you truly are.

Love

Never demanding of a partner's time, you're happiest when lovers do their own thing and are not dependent on you. You know what you want from others and what you'll give in return. Always responsible and honest in commitments, you simply do not like being entangled in lovers' chores and schedules, preferring partners who are able to take care of their own business—that is, provided they pencil in some private lovin' time for the two of you. You're more practical than romantic.

Money

You proceed cautiously, carefully, and thoroughly on the job, preferring long-term employment rather than sporadic or part-time work. Schedule and security mean a lot to you. But don't be so careful that you overlook real chances to get ahead. A practical person, you don't commit or invest until assured that there are concrete benefits. You're efficient with savings, although a bit miserly. 9/2 are born with the foreknowledge that if setbacks occur, you can always stage a handsome comeback!

Famous People Born on This Day

Female	Male
Salma Hayek, actress	Lennox Lewis, boxer
Christa McAuliffe, astronaut	Keanu Reeves, actor
Linda Purl, TV actress	Jimmy Connors, tennis star
Eileen Way, actress	Mark Harmon, actor
Marge Champion, dancer	Terry Bradshaw, football player

September 3

Do you hear a calling? You could be a saint—or sinner! With such deep feelings and a penetrating mind, there is a lot of good you could accomplish, or a lot of mischief you could perpetrate! A self-starter, you have an imagination and the talent to turn visions into reality, helped by very natural friendships that become lasting relationships. Not a sit-still type, fear is not a conscious factor, though you should be more cautious than you usually are!

Since you will get more from a smile and a kind word than from gloom and criticism, make it a point to rule the role, not vice versa. Others expect you to be your usual perfect self; use your fire to light the way, not burn bridges. To recharge, be outdoors, explore but keep on your clothes.

Love

Because you possess a healthy ego, you need a lover who is equally self-assured and independent, although impulsive partners don't turn you on. Being a devoted friend, you invest lots of personal time in your circle of pals, but it's not necessary that your lover hang out with your chums—after all, everything you do is premeditated, and everybody is assigned their own special place in your datebook and life.

Money

You're not a prima donna or egomaniac, even though coworkers quickly notice when you enter a room. 9/3-born are strongly opinionated, enterprising, determined, and work hard. Your quick mind makes you an excellent conversationalist, because you enjoy figuring out what makes people and things tick. However, you're best-suited for behind-the-scenes jobs because you prefer that everything flows along the course of your chosen direction and speed, rather than conform to others' itineraries.

Famous People Born on This Day

Female

Kitty Carlisle Hart, actress
Marguerite Higgins, journalist
Sarah Orne Jewett, novelist
Eileen Brennan, actress
Valerie Perrine, actress

Male

Charlie Sheen, actor
Ferdinand Porsche, inventor
Alan Ladd, actor
Michael Huffington, oil millionaire
Mort Walker, cartoonist

September 4

When something captures your attention, you lock in and the chase is on! If it's adventure or includes members of the opposite sex, even better! If it's sports or something classy or has animals, then you're up for it. Some say you're forgetful even undependable, but it's because something terrific is on your mind. You will try to keep "in focus" if you remember to, we hope. We can usually say "we told you so" when you're in a rocky romance.

Since something akin to fun seems to be always swirling around you—and because no one knows what you'll say next—you make a good teacher or project manager who won't let "the class" drag its feet. Horseshows and racetracks—or big civil events—attract you; don't get too carried away by the ambiance.

Love

9/4-born are generous with their affection and invest a lot in relationships. Devoted and determined, you overlook faults in your loved ones because you feel that people's shortcomings are not as important as their strengths—always the optimist, you concentrate only on a lover's assets. Your kindness is inspiring, but can also be intoxicating to partners, make them lazy, because you often give more than your share.

Money

You're naturally curious about how to best profit from time and investments and have a bit of a gambling streak. You enjoy hobbies that engage your mind—like puzzles, riddles, cards, or reading. Professions that involve exploration and analysis, uncovering secrets, or engage your hands do well for you. You enjoy seeing a final product at the end of a work day. You prefer to make your way alone, working happily at a job which allows you freedom rather than confining routine.

Famous People Born on This Day

Female

Ione Skye, actress
Phoebe Cary, poet
Mary Renault, writer
Dawn Fraser, Olympic swimmer
Mitzi Gaynor, actress

Male

Donald McKay, U.S. naval architect
Nigel Bruce, actor
Edward Dmytryk, director
Paul Harvey, radio commentator
Damon Wayans, actor

September 5

Like a warm breeze on a pleasant late summer day, your sunny presence is enjoyed. Everyone knows when you're around, ready to hear your opinion or the inside scoop—be on their toes or they might miss something. You excel as a parent, getting Johnny to pick up his socks and clean his room—and he's your husband. Still, you are a soft touch and easily taken advantage of. Your favorite word is "yes." Agreeable, but you do reserve the right to do the opposite.

Traveling in style is the way to go, but you'll go in whatever way you can. You'd enjoy a leisurely railroad trip, leaning out the window, but theme parks are more your speed, though you wonder what germs the crowds are carrying. You might have some natural luck at games, temporarily.

Love

You clearly and quickly define the priorities and what you need and expect from a relationship from the get-go. You're a determined "full steam ahead"-type of person, so it's not unusual for you to overlook the feelings of friends and lovers, but never with malice—you simply have a habit of focusing more on the union, instead of the two individuals involved. You adore intrigue, the chase, the seduction. But don't be in such a rush that you ignore your significant other's feelings!

Money

You enjoy speculating and analyzing financial options in order to improve profits and productivity, and are very efficient, but never at another's expense. However, you tend to focus more on bottom lines and overlook details. Money-wise, you're good at discovering bargains and tending to personal budgets. Though supple of spirit and understanding, you enjoy controlling others and do well in positions of authority.

Famous People Born on This Day

Female
Cathy Guisewite, cartoonist
Carol Lawrence, actress
Raquel Welch, actress
Cari Shayne, actress

Male
Louis XIV, Sun King of France
Freddie Mercury [Bulsara], singer
Arthur C. Nielsen, TV market
   researcher
Bob Newhart, actor
Jesse James, outlaw

September 6

If we had to pick one person to manage our millions of dollars, it'd be hard to turn you down. You're credible and businesslike, and we like your down-to-earth nature, and you still have that dramatic flair and a noble aura. People appreciate that you can keep promises, though you don't make wild ones, and you're pretty fair when making the rules. No wonder superiors like you, and subordinates, too—so graceful, charming, and usually too busy to waste precious time.

Since you're pretty well-equipped—vitality-wise—to run the show, you might find that committees—like at your bowling league or garden club or coffee-klatch—are good places to practice being the mover and shaker. You usually have an answer, and you should never wait to have a pop quiz with potential lovers. One thing, though: your wardrobe. Ugh.

Love

9/6-born are deeply passionate, driven people. Your adventurous spirit makes you a bit impatient with lovers who function at relaxed, slower speeds. Although reliable and always true-to-your-word, you do things at a fast and determined pace, and you're inclined to overlook important details about your partner or relationship. Lovers quickly understand your effervescent energy, but also may get put off by what appears to them as reckless or being too full of yourself. Make time to clear the air immediately whenever confusion appears.

Money

You struggle bravely with getting things done, often being inspired by setbacks and stimulated by adversity. You meet deadlines precisely and cleverly, but have a little problem with teamwork and working closely with others. Having a coworker or boss breathing down your neck keeps you from giving your best. Managerial positions suit you best because you enjoy a bit of power—but keep watch over your ego, because you're a strict taskmaster.

Famous People Born on This Day

Female
Rosie Perez, actress
Jane Addams, social reformer
Jane Curtin, actress
Lisa Thorsen, singer
Swoosie Kurtz, actress

Male
Jeff Foxworthy, comedian
David Allan Coe, musician
Earl of Cawdor, British large landowner
Anton Diabelli, composer
Joseph P. Kennedy, diplomat

September 7

What a world this would be if you were in charge! You would stop all that monkey-business, including your own, outlaw all bad habits, except your own, and we'd all live happily ever after. But, sometimes when the elevator door opens, instead of going up to success, you get the shaft. What a shame for someone so selfless, devoted, talented and correct. Don't be stiff; be a people person. Make the world your extended family.

A self-starter with a no-nonsense approach, you are the one who knits together all the elements into one big—something. In romance, you might not be on the same wavelength; listening and not rushing helps. You'd do well in public careers, and for fun get behind the wheel, any wheel.

Love

It's easy for you to separate your feelings for a lover from the practical necessities required to keep a relationship functioning fully. You're a bit compulsive about responsibilities in unions, but never controlling. You express your likes and expectations lucidly, and expect the same in return. However, your know-it-all streak occasionally gets out of hand causing you to sulk, run away, or unfairly criticize a partner's wishes. Ease up; aim for cooperation, not confrontation!

Money

To you, nothing is impossible—unfair, perhaps, but never unattainable. Your on-the-job ego doesn't yearn for approval as much as that you believe your way is best. You have the punch, drive, and belief in yourself to make things work—although it's a bit difficult for you to stick to a personal budget! You're a trustworthy employee who prefers not to mix business associates with personal friends

Famous People Born on This Day

Female

Chrissie Hynde, rocker
Julie Kavner, actress
Grandma Moses, painter
Jean Blackwell Hutson, curator
Elizabeth I, Queen of England

Male

J.P. Morgan, financier
Richard Roundtree, actor
Buddy Holly, singer
James Van Allen, physicist
Elia Kazan, movie director

September 8

A live wire who has a "lot" going on, you don't care who you call company as long as they don't smell and you can't see holes in their socks. Sometimes fussy, you don't know all but do know more than most. Can anyone tell you what to do? You can be the life of the party or suck the energy right out of the room, by accident. Unless worries get in the way, you're adept at following the path of least resistance—easy romance, easy money, why not?

Are you a health nut or just a hypochondriac? Both could be roles; don't take them too seriously. Do something with your hands besides cracking knuckles. Not a strongman type, instead you outwit the opposition—then split! Simple success tips: be honest and take care of business.

Love

You think with your brain but act from the heart. Your determined, solid-as-a-rock nature makes you trustworthy but not always trusting of others. "For better or for worse" doesn't sit well with you (there's gotta be a better way for you to get a bit more, right?). You prefer passive partners; those who don't slow you down, or interfere with your emotional itinerary. You are infinitely approachable and open to discussion, as long as you get the final word.

Money

9/8-born rarely succumb to impulsive, must-have buying spurts. You don't let anyone take advantage of your savings or investments. Being a self-motivated realist, you believe that your earnings will increase only if you are well-informed and ready and willing to go that extra mile—which you are! You are responsible and trustworthy, but grow suspicious of coworkers who don't perform their duties. Working alone, rather in groups, suits you best.

Famous People Born on This Day

Female

Pink, singer
Patsy Cline, singer
Heather Thomas, actress
Grace Metalious, author
Virna Lisi, Italian actress

Male

Jonathan Taylor Thomas, actor
Peter Sellers, actor
Sid Caesar, comedian
Willie Tyler, ventriloquist
Richard the Lion Hearted, King of England

September 9

There's probably not a dishonest bone in your body, but mentally you have some wild, crazy thoughts running loose—that's what makes you so interesting. Not everyone thinks like you do—if they think at all. If you wanted to, you could probably have a mental conversation with a grasshopper, though most of the time you're focusing on more practical things like saving the world, tidying up your physical temple, and not harshing any mellows. You know what we mean, right?

No one likes to get away from all that technical mind-numbing stuff at work more than you. To escape, what do you do? You go to a noisy, crowded, mind-numbing place, calling it entertainment. Last week's music and news don't cut it with you, but you do appreciate how clean Disneyland is in the morning.

Love

You carefully choose lovers and friends who won't clutter your life with their must-do list or make make huge demands on your time. It's not that you are unwilling to help or share—you simply get turned off by co-dependent and unfocused folk. As you are disciplined and organized, you may ignore relationships because of the responsibility involved. Refuse to let your romantic checklist of demands imprison everyday, right-now enjoyment!

Money

Your distaste of being dependent upon coworkers often gives others an impression of aloofness or stubbornness. Never lazy, you devote considerable effort to find efficient ways to get the job done faster and better, and are often inspiring in the way you apply them. But you should try investing a bit more effort in understanding teamwork. Although you're well-suited for management and budget your money well, know when to ask for help!

Famous People Born on This Day

Female

Angela Cartwright, actress
Jane Greer, actress
Sara O'Meara Sigholtz, social reformer
Sarah Snell Harder, human rights activist/president AAUW
Sonia Sanchez, writer

Male

Henry Thomas, *actor*
Adam Sandler, actor
Michael Keaton, actor
Otis Redding, singer
Hugh Grant, actor

September 10

You do love the earth; better still, the farmer's market, any market for that matter. Things—we've got to have things, and nobody knows/handles/fondles/manages "things" better than you. People? You handle them well, too. Animals? Yep. And you're not afraid of hard work, either, it's just that somebody else can do it. You make friends quickly—you're cooperative and probably more than attractive, but you cannot be possessed unless the price is right, and it seldom is.

Green is a great color for you—not to wear, but to grow, like plants, crops, money. Your clothes aren't rags, unless you want them to appear that way to be cool. For fun, you'd like to go exploring and mingle with natives, language barrier aside. Travel light and watch your valuables. As usual, you'll find treasure at bargain rates.

Love

You get all warm and fuzzy when not restricted by a lover's emotional demands, thirst for the novel, and are always willing to explore elbow room latitude in love. You express your feelings honestly and directly; your ego is very healthy but rarely overwhelms. 9/10-born are as passionate about their own personal needs as they are realistic, and willing to try something new. Undefined, noncommittal, fly-by-night affairs hold no interest for you.

Money

You rise to great heights by advancing square-by-square at your own languid pace. 9/10-born believe that very little that is worth having comes for nothing, and you work hard. You diligently labor to get the job done well and on time. However, you tend to be a bit unrealistic with your personal spendings; not extravagant or foolish, but willing to pay for instant must-have gratification rather than analyzing, comparing prices.

Famous People Born on This Day

Female

Amy Irving, actress
Allison Daughtry, actress
Susan Gautier-Smith, producer
Judith Banister, demographer
Yma Sumac, singer

Male

Ryan Phillippe, actor
Chris Columbus, director
Arnold Palmer, golfer
Charles Kuralt, newsman
Jose Feliciano, singer

September 11

Every cloud has a silver lining, and every situation is a success story in the making, and if others really knew what's going on inside your creative mind they'd offer praise instead of frowns and bad vibes. Bad vibes—that's other people's problems. You'd rather take life easy, enjoy it, soak up the joy, appreciate the good things like apple pie, grandmas, triple coupons, votive candles, maybe one of those vibrating easy chairs. You're not lazy—you just know the shortcuts and tricks of the trade.

The Statue of Liberty is a pretty neat place to visit, so are babbling brooks winding through meadows, and having your own zoo. You like to think, plan, consider the possibilities, and like roles where you can cut through red tape and all sides come away happy. Happiness is liberty.

Love

9/11-born are non-confrontational, compromising, and easy-going. You maintain good control over your feelings and don't act rashly, but are repelled by dull, short-sighted people. You refuse to be tied down by emotional obligations and rebel against anyone who tries to push their stuff on you. Not inclined to financially support a lover, you are more compatible with responsible partners rather than clingy, needy types.

Money

You don't deal well with on-the-job debate, preferring to work alone in structured and organized capacities. Nevertheless, you're always ready to pitch in and help—provided that it doesn't interfere with your productivity. Money-wise, you believe that there's a time, place and budget for everything. You tend to your responsibilities first and offer assistance afterwards. Your bank account is usually well-balanced, and you are conscientious and clever with spendings.

Famous People Born on This Day

Female

Ariana Richards, actress
Kristy McNichol, actress
Donna Auguste, computer designer
Lola Falana, singer
Betsy Drake, fitness expert

Male

Harry Connick, Jr., singer
Moby, musician
Brian DePalma, director
D.H. Lawrence, English writer
O. Henry, writer

September 12

"Why can't we all just get along?" We all get confused, and facts get blurred, and we can feel overwhelmed—that's when our good self should come out, strong but not offensive. In the meantime, the clock ticks, never waiting for anyone, hoping that you'll be the one to come through in a pinch, with love and caring.

You probably have a valuable collection of something. It's good to have spare time to let your mind escape from mundane pressures, to attend to your health, or have a job that isn't laborious. You may wonder, will I be a success? You will; line up trusty allies to share it.

Love

People warm to you and admire your edifying style. You're an easy-going and imaginative lover, but a daunting adversary. You have precise expectations about relationships and what it takes to make you happy; honesty and equality are essential. Ultimately, your biggest challenge is to simply abide, but not necessarily to prevail. You mastered the art of passive, enduring resistance (and insistence) at an early age. You have an engaging way of stalking your prey, and keeping all those ducks properly lined up.

Money

Although not materialistic, you're always on the lookout for something bigger and better, rarely satisfied with what is or with what you have. Having security, more so than money, is a major objective in your life. Employers recognize this and often provide opportunities for change, challenging your skills and precision. Because you have many skills and abilities, you accomplish a great deal when you stick to one objective at a time.

Famous People Born on This Day

Female

Linda Gray, actress
Rachel Ward, actress
Maria Muldaur, singer
Irene Joliot-Curie, physicist

Male

Paul Walker, actor
Barry White, singer
Joe Pantoliano, actor
Mark Knopfler, rocker
Jesse Owens, Olympic champion

September 13

This is a fruitful, brave day, and when at your best, you are giving, sincere, confident, and not afraid to speak your mind, using your range of voice to illustrate your story. Why do some say you are vain, contradictory—what sort of trouble are they up to? You probably don't want to know, so you keep them at short arm's length while you fulfill your duty, every move graceful, helping make those in your circle happy. The child inside believes the impossible is possible.

It is obvious that we're put here to fulfill a purpose of some kind, so your soul relishes roles where there is self-improvement and bonding. You may be "into" the health field, or somewhere saving and helping those who cannot help themselves. Make pride work for you; the same for the cast and crew.

Love

Perimeters and parameters, rather than goodwill and good faith, are necessary requirements for your love relations; otherwise, you drift aimlessly, get duped, or become way too defensive. 9/13-born are not naturally street-smart—you like rules, schedules, dates. Once committed to a union, you are stalwart and tenacious, devoted and deliberate about your affections. As virtue and right-eousness are very important to you, you're rarely malicious or partake in gossip.

Money

Employment with specific rules and procedures is easy for you. It's not that you're lazy or dull-witted; the fact is, you have a great grip on order and logic, rather than speculative or social venues. Not one to get easily seduced by coworkers' flattery, you keep your private life separate from work. You're more practical than paranoid, especially concerning personal savings. Your rainy day nest-egg is bright and always on your mind.

Famous People Born on This Day

Female

Fiona Apple, singer
Jean Smart, actress
Jacqueline Bisset, actress
Judith Martin, writer
Claudette Colbert, actress

Male

Ben Savage, actor
Milton S. Hershey, manufacturer
Walter Reed, U.S. Army surgeon
Mel Tormé, singer
Fred Silverman, broadcasting
exec/ABC/NBC/CBS

September 14

A busy time of year and a busy birth date, when things are analyzed and decisions made and relationships become tighter—all these things you do well. Also during this time the sun gets in your eyes and people rush, so offering a good word and a helping hand and other gestures of love are much appreciated. Yes, others notice your strengths, your talents, your distinctive style, and your good timing, your caution—you're a wise voice in a changing world.

The past and present seem to come together in you—neither young nor old, moving steadily, charming everyone, sending that little twinkle in your eye out to a special some-one—or someone who could be that special someone. Traveling together, you'll enjoy each other's stories, making fun of the road signs as life flies by.

Love

9/14-born learn about love and heartbreak by repeating things over and over again, rather than from emotional spontaneity. Although quite cautious about new experiences, you're never insensitive or inconsiderate. However, unconditional love is challenging for you, and you are best-suited with older, more settled-down partners. Don't let old-thinking stifle opportunities to help you grow happier in love.

Money

Business and pleasure mean two different things to you, and you don't discuss personal financial matters with others even with a professional. You're a diligent, independent worker who prefers doing things solo, and are an honest and dependable employee. You're not a scaredy-cat about spending money because you enjoy "things" and always pay your bills on time. "Doing things by the book" is your security blanket

Famous People Born on This Day

Female

Kate Millett, feminist
Joey Heatherton, dancer
Faith Ford, actress
Margaret Sanger, leading crusader
   for birth control
Zoe Caldwell, actress

Male

Sam Neill, actor
Clayton Moore, actor
Callum Keith Rennie, actor
Nicol Williamson, actor
Ivan Pavlov, physiologist

September 15

Brave, enthusiastic, and maybe even a bit boastful, you're ready to put the pedal to the metal for fun, profit, even for work. The nine-to-five routine is for others; you have your sights set on loftier goals, your satisfaction, your brave new world. Anyone who wants to come along for the ride is welcome! You are also a pragmatist—a problem-solver—and letting obstacles off easy is not your style, so, determinedly and persuasively you wrestle with destiny, soon to be the winner, not giving in.

Some say the boy who winds up with the most toys wins, but what good are they if you don't use them? You can drive machines into the ground, sending labor-saving devices to labor-saving heaven. Roles where you have to master today's digital toasters and internet-ready cellphones are, well, intriguing. Shocking, too.

Love

You don't mince words with lovers about matters of the heart—when you speak, you express yourself clearly and precisely. Although you discern situations quickly, almost intuitively, your candid bluntness has a tendency to overwhelm partners. Meticulous by nature, 9/15-born detest slapdash or halfhearted relationships. Beware of coming off as too bossy or all-knowing to loved ones.

Money

You get right down to business when there is work to be done. Never lazy, always eager to get agendas completed on-time, you're efficient and co-operative but never aggressive. However, you have a tendency to whine or complain, but only when others aren't holding up their end of the agreement. Management is a natural for you because you're a tireless employee. You keep your checkbook balanced and never ask employers for financial help.

Famous People Born on This Day

Female
Penny Singleton, actress
Agatha Christie, writer
Fay Wray, actress
Margaret Lockwood, actress

Male
Prince Harry of Britain
Tommy Lee Jones, actor
Oliver Stone, director
Jackie Cooper, actor
Merlin Olsen, football player

September 16

Your goal isn't to make a tiny niche where you can put your feet up and let someone else pick up the potato chip crumbs. You've got an itch inside and someone must scratch it, and by golly, there's got to be more to this life than you're currently seeing. You'd prefer the company of sophisticated people who are "set" and flaunt their Sunday best or Monday corporate pajamas. If loose ends dangle somewhere, you'll jerk them—but don't trust luck to protect you from fallout!

Fun and laughter is good medicine, and you see the value of a sense of value, turning life's ironies into beneficial lessons. You can get discouraged, too. That's usually due to your impatience and competitive nature. Consider safe roles for channeling that.

Love

You don't intimidate lovers intentionally—it's just that emotional control and discretion aren't your strength. You never leap into an affair blindly or without examining the situation a hundred times. However, you tend to fill up relationship baskets with too many eggs at once and get frustrated when events don't materialize as planned. 9/16-born love to build a homey nest, and invariably keep packs of domestic animals or plants.

Money

You are strong-minded (and a bit demanding) on the job, always expressing your own priorities first, yet unafraid to make concessions, and negotiate where you cannot win. When confronted with an impending hurdle, you may find it hard to concentrate, and bolt to where the grass looks a shade greener and there are more folk to love you. 9/16 usually want to make and keep lots of money and are known to marry "well."

Famous People Born on This Day

Female

Madeline Zima, actress
Jennifer Tilly, actress
Karen Horney, psychoanalyst
Lauren Bacall, actress
Janis Paige, actress

Male

David Copperfield, magician
Mickey Rourke, actor
Peter Falk, actor
B.B. King, bluesman
Allen Funt, TV host

September 17

Everybody's sweetheart—that can be you, ready to leap into exciting, racy relationships, indomitable but so sociable, always with a passion for the game, a dependable team player and gentle, firm leader. Genuinely a loving person, soft-hearted, you are also peppery enough to be the trendsetter. Your personal magnetism is hard to resist. Just daring and inquisitive enough, you'll come up with the right answer at the right time—can you tell we like you?

Unless you lose your poise—your composure—others see you as the cool customer, which can lead to success in many esteemed professions. Your good memory helps, and secretly your heart yearns for close personal relationships; you'd make a good parent and do take the time. Parades and pageantry please you; life is not a demolition derby.

Love

Although you enjoy schedule and predictability in a relationship, you never make excessive demands on your lover. You are very understanding and don't expect everyone to live up to your standards or dreams. A good negotiator, you know how to gently tailor your demands to your lover's personality instead of the other way around. You dislike emotional outbursts, always looking for peace, not problems.

Money

You have a realistic, respectable rapport with coworkers, considering everyone a source for inspiration rather than a competitor. Because you are responsive to others' needs, it's easy for you to gain favor and recognition—or at least attention! You believe that everything can change for the better and are open-minded about "there's always a better way to do something." You're comfortable in groups and take orders well. Because you don't like being a harbinger of unwelcome news, you're not well-suited for executive positions.

Famous People Born on This Day

Female

Karen Straker, jockey
Cassandra "Elvira" Peterson, actress
Anne Bancroft, actress
Mary Stewart, novelist
Dorothy Loudon, actress

Male

Wade Robson, songwriter
John Ritter, actor
Roddy McDowell, actor
Ken Kesey, author
Stirling Moss, racing legend

September 18

Sugar-coating won't persuade you, and diplomats' promises or romantic whispers barely raise an eyebrow. Money might help, but you prefer that others mind their own business and yours is private, though they should take your advice if you'd just give it. Few people are so correct, courteous, and long-sighted intellectually, and still privately affectionate as a cuddly kitten as you. Headstrong and no-nonsense, you prefer solid relationships, since dependability leads to growth and satisfaction.

Your words aren't cheap, so friends, family, and associates find it easy to love you once they get to know that you're not the little emperor. Loving nature and the arts, you cherish roles where you can help the innocent. The right foods and the right exercise are very important—good looks mean good self-image—and so is not harboring bad thoughts.

Love

You don't like surprises or taking chances, and often test companions. Being a realist is admirable and good, but being paranoid is not. 9/18-born grows quickly impatient and morose with rejection or heartbreak. You are happiest with a lover who is as serious as you about commitment, and who is a stabilizing influence. Don't shy away from changes that may be stimulating because you consider them too much trouble.

Money

You always think twice before spending money, are punctual and dependable with your on-the-job responsibilities, and devoted to every mission. Coworkers and employers know that they can count on you. You're frugal with time and money and have an uncanny knack of knowing how to utilize both. You accept the daily trials of the workaday world, convinced that you can solve any problem that comes your way—or at least know when to admit defeat, if you can't.

Famous People Born on This Day

Female

Jada Pinkett Smith, actress
Joanne Catherall, singer
June Rosemary Fisher, teacher
Agnes DeMille, choreographer
Greta Garbo, actress

Male

Lance Armstrong, cyclist
James Gandolfini, actor
Frankie Avalon, singer
Jimmie Rodgers, singer
Jack Warden, actor

September 19

Great birthday for romance, marriage, and sex, and you're a bit of a whiz in the business world, too, because you can be such an operator! Delightful in conversations once you get by any shyness, others may sense your shrewdness, but you are hard to please and a step ahead, perhaps still thinking and dreaming of that perfect partner. To some, you're a tough pill to swallow even if the doctor recommends you. Certain others may see you as a free ride they can latch onto. Are you the catch of the day?

Blessed with wit, a gift for conversation, and a sharp mind, you could fulfill roles as a writer, politician, or mediator. You'd also make a perfect shopkeeper or small business person, charmingly serving the public, surpassing your contemporaries, extending your reach to the stars.

Love

You openly display your cards on the table in order that lovers don't second-guess your motives. You're upfront and definite about your desires, never hesitant saying what you think. You show your affection by strong devotion and uncanny eloquence. You have a good memory for details such as anniversaries and personal matters, and know when to and when not to debate. As long as both parties are honest, you're a happy camper.

Money

You enjoy working in a planned and organized capacity, always knowing what's expected from you and fellow employees. Even if a job doesn't appeal to your imagination, you plug away and get it done. You wear your iron-clad principles on your sleeve and practice what you preach. "Time is money" to you, and you know how to get the most bang from every buck, as well as how to manipulate each minute on the timeclock!

Famous People Born on This Day

Female

Alison Sweeny, actress
Twiggy, model
Mama Cass Elliott, singer
Joan Lunden, TV hostess
Trisha Yearwood, singer

Male

Jeremy Irons, actor
Paul Williams, songwriter
David McCallum, actor
William Golding, novelist
Mike Royko, journalist

September 20

Excited and full of anticipation, you rush to read something about yourself, believing that any tidbit will help, maybe something to talk about, or the wisdom of Solomon. What you really want is hope and an edge; what you need is more confidence and stability, which you get by finding, pleasing and working with key people around you. You are quite skillful, versatile—more positive reinforcement helps. Figure out ways to reinforce yourself, and voilà!

Being a person who can wear a lot of different career hats, you should pick roles that you'd like, not always what the environment, friends, and want ads bring along. Never really idle, you have a gift for talking—ah, there's a key thing to talk about—gifts! For fun, be fun, share fun, and make good first, lasting impressions.

Love

You don't settle for second-best, nor a lover who's unable to take care of himself or herself. You place high value on partners who support you unconditionally and without lots of strings attached or old baggage. Many 9/20s worry about their image and care immensely about how others feel toward them. Accentuate mutual interests and each other's strengths, rather than name-call or whine.

Money

Your controlled-but-gentle spirit helps you make the most of opportunities without alienating competitors, and you assert yourself positively when in the face of resistance. You don't beat around the bush about finances or doing what's expected of you, and are a strong advocate of truth and hard work ethics. Although you prefer jobs that keep you in the background, authority figures admire your people skills—perhaps it's time to leave the cubicle and get out on the floor?

Famous People Born on This Day

Female

Laurie Spiegel, composer
Debi Morgan, actress
Dr. Joyce Brothers, psychiatrist
Sophia Loren, actress
Anne Meara, actress

Male

Crispin Glover, actor
Gary Cole, actor
Jelly Roll Morton, composer
Upton Sinclair, writer
Mungo Park, explorer

September 21

Quirky and never seeming to stop growing, you are quiet, smooth, and insightful to talk with, perhaps showing your religious feelings/spirituality. More intuitive and superstitious than the norm, you have strong feelings about social problems, licking them time and time again. Sex isn't your major concern, though it can be on your mind a lot. You'd like to contribute to a good life for those around you, and friends become family and family, friends.

Forward thinking and able to put ideas into form, you often find your way into key positions, like architects of reality. Whoa! A real workhorse and thinker, remember to be flexible, too, because as you know, we all fail occasionally. Education is a good field for you. Frolic in the new West.

Love

You're not blunt or short-sighted, but few are as open and direct as you. Whenever you have a problem in a relationship, you pick it apart and analyze every nuance with your mind, never your feelings. You dislike dramatic or overly emotional partners, preferring those who are mature, remain cool, and in control. Your innate good sense knows how and when to de-clutter your love life—or, when to get out when the gettin'-time is good!

Money

To you, everything good is a result of planning ahead, setting goals, and remaining unattached to disappointments or delays. You treasure and learn from past experiences, comfortably capitalize on every work opportunity, and have a progressive yet realistic outlook about the future. Employers and managers know that they can trust you to get the job done well, and usually under budget. You are clever and always willing to put your shoulder to the wheel.

Famous People Born on This Day

Female

Ricki Lake, talk-show hostess
Faith Hill, singer
Fannie Flagg, actress
Ann Elder, comedienne
Serena Scott Thomas, actress

Male

Stephen King, writer
Larry Hagman, actor
Leonard Cohen, songwriter
H.G. Wells, author
Bill Murray, actor

September 22

Is your piece of the pie not big enough—is something shadowy holding you back? Not you! This is your time, this is your place—Y-O-U, the versatile, adaptable one who, through life's experiences, builds momentum, gaining here, finding a big opportunity there, always with emotion showing in your face, ready to hatch a plan, determined to meet challenges and toy with the good life. Like a rock—no, a rolling stone—no, a magic pebble washed up on the beach of life. . . .

When you're with friends, there's excitement. You don't talk about girl-meets-boy stuff, you're the hands-on type who can mix it up, gets hooked-up, and not just in social roles but in your profession, too, where you'll make a name for yourself—a good one, we hope. Sometimes your willpower and judgment may take shortcuts.

Love

Not only do you feel things deeply, but you're also very empathetic and observant about people's quirks and habits, and highly gifted for rhetoric. 9/22-born have powerful desires, but also have difficulty expressing them because you don't like rejection or rocking the status quo boat. So, to compensate, you grow secretive or spin white lies whenever conversations become intimate or question your personal philosophy. Learn to be yourself, without fear of judgment.

Money

The financial successes of others inspire you to match their accomplishments (after some initial pangs of jealousy, of course). 9/22-born have an uncanny ability for sizing up others' achievements and, afterwards, devising an even better means for prosperity and profit. Never one to prejudge, you live by the credo: "It's not what you know, but who you know." Perhaps it's time to know yourself better?

Famous People Born on This Day

Female

Joan Jett, rocker
Debby Boone, singer
Anna Karina, actress
Tai Babilonia, U.S. figure skater
Martha Scott, actress

Male

Scott Baio, actor
Andrea Bocelli, singer
Paul Muni, actor
John Houseman, actor
David J. Stern, NBA commissioner

September 23

You're very romantic, soulful, and noble. You have it an aura of decency, vigor, love of justice, and an understanding that life is what you make it. So you carve your special niche, cajoling and dealing, taking your special talent to the next level, or using it publicly. Independent and courageous, playful and magnanimous, you live the buoyant lifestyle you dream of. You'll work hard to overcome early obstacles, eventually making your family proud.

Usually you stay single, then suddenly you decide to let a special someone capture you. You're kind of tricky that way—in many relationships. And if the mood swings, you know you'll survive. Wide open spaces will recharge your worn body and mind, so will a closer look deep inside, finding a star in the making.

Love

To a certain extent, you manipulate your partner in order to get the attention you need—even though your intention is never to cause trouble, hurt, or injury. You have a tendency to be a blabbermouthy worrywart, revealing secrets or frustrations without thinking. You may act independent, but underneath the cool 9/23-facade of self-sufficiency, you live for the love of family, friends, and longtime companions.

Money

It's nearly impossible for coworkers to tell you what to do or how. You are a monster of professional integrity and aplomb. Doing things "your" way works quite nicely, thank you very much. You appreciate praise and acknowledgement for your efforts on the job, but are neither timid nor too humble to ask for it. Instead, you plug away, doing what's expected and usually without too much complaint.

Famous People Born on This Day

Female

Louise Nevelson, sculptor
Mary Kay Place, actress
Romy Schneider, actress
Carole Lombard, actress
Victoria Woodhull, publisher

Male

Bruce Springsteen, rocker
Julio Iglesias, singer
Ray Charles, singer
John Coltrane, jazz saxophonist
Jason Alexander, actor

September 24

Under-achieving is not what you want on your report card, so you'll figure out some cool ways to please the onlookers, but mind you, nothing like hacking into the school's computer to change your grades, or shady tricks like that. No, you can earn it fair and square by putting your mind to it, begrudgingly making the little sacrifices. You have deep feelings of love, which others don't always see, but they notice your generosity and fairness. You are blessed with just the right tools to succeed almost anywhere.

Switching sides and changing opinions is your right, though generally you are loyal to the cause and your key relationships. Others should take you more seriously, but when it comes to cutting loose, partying and enjoying life, you're the best, perfectly dressed and never a wallflower, uptown or down.

Love

Optimistic and romantic but never quite realistic, you have dreamy concepts about relationships, are always on the go, and prefer unplanned quality time rather than the organized or scheduled. Once boredom sets into a union, you're out the door! Ever restless, you'll try almost anything once (or twice) in your constant search of The Perfect Lover. A free-spirited, easy-going partner works best for you.

Money

Following a rigid schedule or doing repetitious work drives you crazy. You're brilliant at brainstorming, sensational at sales, teasing and titillating others for talk and tribute. Even though you pay your bills every month, you're not too pro-like with personal savings. Although you appreciate the nice things of life, you're by no means materialistic or greedy. It's not easy for you to see how your input affects situations.

Famous People Born on This Day

Female

Theresa Merritt, actress
Catherine Burns, actress
Linda Eastman McCartney, singer
Sheila MacRae, actress
Barbara Brilliant, TV hostess

Male

Jim Henson, Muppeteer
Anthony Newley, actor
Jim McKay, sportscaster
F. Scott Fitzgerald, author
John Young, astronaut

September 25

Creative, industrious, dramatic, and well-liked, you are the pleasantly dedicated type who is like a quality blend of valued human traits, but is not superficially flashy. You'd make a good doctor and you're health conscious having learned that your physical stamina may not match your mental zest. Still a hard worker, you may be known more for your career—you are drawn to competitive fields and will have to prove yourself, so aim and study well; education is key to your success.

Since you can be so practical and have the angles covered, we can rely on you for dependable advice. You turn on a surprising amount of charm in the right company, and vital issues concern you. Vacations are for relaxing, so you avoid the crowds. A friend's wonderful ivy cottage would be right for you.

Love

You always test the waters before plunging into a relationship, cautious about sharing your feelings upfront. Never rash but always hopeful, you enter a union only after much consideration, building momentum and clout slowly and surely. You're rarely verbally abusive (and never physically cranky), even when frustrated. Your drive for self-improvement keeps you quite tolerant of a lover's quirks and needs. Make love, not war.

Money

At work, two heads (or more) are better than singular noggins. You enjoy on-the-job brainstorming, socializing and camaraderie. More than capable of following instructions, once defined, you eagerly attack the project and don't rest until it's completed. It's a good idea to find a financial advisor, learn to budget, and save for a rainy day. You are an easy victim for impulse-buying, or frittering away all those hard-earned dollars. Snatch a lover that has good financial latitude and loving leeway!

Famous People Born on This Day

Female

Catherine Zeta-Jones, actress
Heather Locklear, actress
Cheryl Tiegs, model
Barbara Walters, journalist
Juliet Prowse, dancer

Male

Will Smith, actor
William Faulkner, novelist
Michael Douglas, actor
Mark Hamill, actor
Christopher Reeve, actor

September 26

Perky and usually more than attractive, you could be a role model or poster boy/girl, attracting all sorts of interested parties. You're not too interested in romantic sideshows, though. You have your own goals to think about, and an eye on having a secure relationship with all the trimmings—nice digs, comfortable wheels, stylish rags, and don't forget sunglasses so that you won't be recognized. Did we mention "staying in shape" and that "the sky is the limit" and you're like "poetry in motion?"

You have a practical, down-to-earth side, and the outdoors certainly appeals to you, maybe even a role as the farmer in the dell. Orchards and rolling hills let your heart soar; never hesitate to show your creative side. You've gotten dragged into enough senseless intrigues, so you should rely on proven experts.

Love

You enjoy the intellectual trappings of love because strictly sensual, overly emotional affairs make you jumpy and grumpy. A good conversationalist, you're never at a loss for words and are open-minded, and optimistic. You're happiest with demonstrative, attentive take-charge kind of partners—not dependent types. Your youthful curiosity enables you to enjoy everyone, regardless of age; you rarely set your standards too high.

Money

You aim to be useful to everyone you deal with, which motivates you to constantly broaden your knowledge. 9/26-born are happiest when their own skills are exploited to their fullest. Although you're good at improvising, you work best when you know exactly what is expected, preferring employment with defined guidelines and structure. You work well with others, and your tact and diplomacy are so great that even competitors admire you.

Famous People Born on This Day

Female
Julie London, actress
Olivia Newton-John, singer
Linda Hamilton, actress
Mary Beth Hurt, actress
Judith P. Appelbaum, editor

Male
Johnny Appleseed [John Chapman],
    frontier nurseryman
T.S. Eliot, poet
George Gershwin, composer
Jack LaLane, fitness guru
Marty Robbins, singer

September 27

Possessing that legendary sense of justice that Libras are known for but few have, you're one of the gifted birthdays: distinctive-looking, friendly and tasteful, and you can be a real favorite when you want to be. It's your earthy magnetism and your keen instincts. Lending a shoulder to cry on, you need and give lots of love, and you can be swayed, though you're not the one to let emotional baggage slow you down. Instead, you look forward, helped by the stars.

Lucky you may not have to work, though you could be the office personality or the organizer—people usually trust you. Getting down, dirty, or pushy isn't your style; being understanding is. Roles in arts or crafts let you excel, since keen-eyed you enjoys being a people-pleaser. Get away to beautify your body and soak up luxuries.

Love

Love is meaningless to you if it doesn't lead to commitment or marriage. You don't take relationships lightly; you plummet into them with total abandon and with both eyes open. You are creative, sympathetic, tender, and affectionate and go to great lengths to do everything necessary to protect the union and make it grow. You desire open and honest communication—but abhor debate and arguing.

Money

You're a devoted, dependable employee who is always available to pitch in and help. You uncover inventive avenues for igniting enthusiasm in others, so that everyone recognizes their own potentials. You would do well in such fields as personnel research, education, or therapy. Analytical by nature, you instinctively know how to make everything flow smoothly, and coworkers are comfortable with you.

Famous People Born on This Day

Female
Barbara Howar, reporter
Jayne Meadows, actress
Rosa Lewis, hotel owner
Kathy Whitworth, golfer
Sada Thompson, actress

Male
Meat Loaf, rocker
Shaun Cassidy, actor
William Conrad, actor
Arthur Penn, director
Sam Ervin, Watergate committee chairman

September 28

Chemistry—you have it, not the mad-scientist kind where you cast spells but the light, lively, sociable kind where you can mingle and bond with almost anyone you choose to, winning, if necessary, with friendly persuasion and positive energy, reserving the hard words for when you're really ticked. You can be the workingman's workingman or the high society flyer, and may only be held back by not being discriminating enough, not seeing the need to move forward.

Imaginative and industrious, plus attractive, you're a desirable partner, though you may be at your best when left to work alone, connecting to the cosmos. You are a romanticizer, so roles where you can influence public opinion suit you. A dreamy home in a vacation paradise may be in your future, a showcase of you.

Love

Even though you want more than anything to be attached to somebody you can call family, you're far from easy to live with! 9/28-born need partners who let you drive at your own speed and don't second-guess or demand too much from you. Clingy, dependent lovers make you crazy; you expect others to be as independent and sincere as you. Though you are eager to maintain relationships, when your trust is violated you immediately break it off without a second thought or backward glance.

Money

The mind of the 9/28-born is fertile and full of hidden resources. You're able to solve the trickiest problems quickly and act wisely in an emergency. Because you are a bit tight-fisted and meticulous about money, you will almost always succeed at careers that involve ruse or calculation. You're efficient and thorough in everything you undertake, often attempting the impossible, trying to please everyone who needs you.

Famous People Born on This Day

Female

Gwyneth Paltrow, actress
Mira Sorvino, actress
Brigitte Bardot, actress
Janeane Garofalo, comedienne/
    actress
Frances Willard, social activist

Male

Ed Sullivan, TV host
Al Capp, cartoonist
Marcello Mastroianni, actor
Edward Herbert Thompson, arch-
    aeologist
William S. Paley, president of CBS

September 29

Syrupy sweet and sentimental, you can play the role of the struggling artist, Bohemian-ing it up, doing your thing and impressing your audience—or you can be the career professional and champion of the cause. You have to express yourself, like a guru sometimes, so you're always "on." Getting paid for it is, well, the challenge. You have a sort of universal love, and many of you have really hot partners, temporarily, since you're shrewd enough to feel you can do better.

Swimming with the sharks or the noble whales, you need some type of security screen or safety net around you. With the right people, you are a surprisingly good deal-maker, if you can avoid being haughty and be more down-to-earth. Taking romance/adventure vacations will please your partner, plus you can check out the other prospects.

Love

You express your likes and dislikes easily (and often), which endears you to many. Even though you are overflowing with romantic ideas and fantasies, you never "hurry" love. You take your time getting to know a partner, savoring every moment. You're uneasy with clinging types, preferring passion and imagination over schedule and scenario. Affection, tenderness, and devotion are the only drugs you need—and you'll do anything for your daily fix!

Money

Even though you have exceptional judgment and understanding, you lack strength in managerial skills and work best under supervision. You are popular with coworkers because you don't make excessive demands, always tolerant of their frailties. You desire the "good life," nice things, comfortable surroundings and good Feng Shui. 9/ 29-born have difficulty with a life of austerity that allows only the barest essentials.

Famous People Born on This Day

Female

Natasha Gregson Wagner, actress
Greer Garson, actress
Elizabeth Cleghorn Gaskell, novelist
Madeline Kahn, actress
Lizabeth Scott, actress

Male

Bryant Gumbel, TV host
Lech Walesa, Polish patriot
Gene Autry, actor
Stanley Kramer, producer
Miguel de Cervantes, author

September 30

In touch with your inner emotions and potent desires, you can be a crafty devil and you don't mind being a rumor-mill topic. Scandal equals publicity—who cares about what the mangy critters think about you? You have your own ideas and you're busy pursuing them, perhaps ultra-secretly. You love intrigue and exploration, and even push yourself to the limits in pursuit of your goals—good ones, we hope. Sometimes you side with the underdog just to ensure fairness.

Not much escapes your keen eye and calculating mind when you get "focused in," including the private lives of others, which you could control if you wanted to. Roles where you must be responsible and obey the rules are good learning experiences, helping you gain emotional equilibrium. Flying makes you edgy, but hopping a tramp steamer would be fun.

Love

You're the source of inspiration, stimulation, and change in every affair and have more than enough ideas for both parties. 9/30-born do not enjoy the fireworks of argument, preferring discretion to belligerence. You keep your head during a crisis and are loyal to friends and family. You're rather shy, a warehouse of self-discipline, and best-suited with calm sorts of lovers who don't get carried away by impulsive notions.

Money

You relate to large groups, dislike power or dominion over others, and are open-minded—all good reasons for coworkers and employees to like you so much. Although not too keen with details or numbers, you value honesty, maintain good morals, and aim to please. You like financial security, and know how to live well on budget. You don't want success for yourself, but you love being the power behind the throne.

Famous People Born on This Day

Female
Jenna Elfman, actress
Marilyn McCoo, singer
Fran Drescher, actress
Angie Dickinson, actress
Deborah Kerr, actress

Male
Johnny Mathis, singer
Truman Capote, author
Buddy Rich, drummer
Robby Takac, singer
Dirk J. Bush, mathematician

October

October 1

Not only are you born on the first, you feel like the first—underneath your placid exterior is a fountain of emotion that, conveniently, buoys you up—and at times pulls you down deep. You've learned to manage your life challenges with grace and courage, and being an "action now" person and good secrets keeper, you are a natural at being the understanding sweetheart and a great supportive friend. You can make major career shifts with ease, following your changing heart and fortunes.

The company you keep is very important, so having a top-notch team—be it family members or professional associates—will keep you pointed in the right directions, with less confusion and less energy-sapping scrambling for the almighty buck. Play roles where you have to be alert, fair, confident, humanitarian. Practice modesty and honesty, too.

Love

Earnest, well-meaning, and super-compassionate, 10/1-born feel the pain of others more than they do their own. However, once a relationship turns intimate, you go through enormous emotional swings—sometimes feeling very confident about commitment and, suddenly, overly self-critical or fatalistic. You seek perfection in a lover because that's what you expect of yourself, and you're not one to hold a grudge or seek revenge.

Money

You control your temper and don't fly off the emotional handle too often, and project yourself confidently, yet personably, toward coworkers. You know how to assert yourself dutifully and use your energy efficiently, wasting little of it on nonproductive endeavors. Even if you don't enjoy your profession, you're always conscientious and tenacious. Your consideration for others makes you a great team player.

Famous People Born on This Day

Female
Annie Leibovitz, photographer
Julie Andrews, actress
Annie Besant, social reformer
Stella Stevens, actress
Faith Baldwin, novelist

Male
Mark McGwire, baseball player
Randy Quaid, actor
Richard Harris, actor
Jimmy Carter, U.S. president
Walter Matthau, actor

October 2

Vitality is not a problem since you have more than most, but a little more genuine help from your close companions will help ease pains from woes that you seem to have more than your fair share of. Having the right mate and right environment means a lot; with your cheerfulness and casual easy-to-please lifestyle you'll always have plenty of chances to connect with people. Use biorhythms or astrology to pick out the best. Don't take friends' advice without double-checking first.

Friendly and philosophical, you can be a true speed demon on projects. Your industriousness lets bosses lay more work on, usually for not enough pay. A higher education would help you earn more, and you would excel in the right school. Don't shy away from roles with higher responsibility. For fun, anything racy has a special appeal.

Love

You devote a great deal of energy to your lover's interests, always planning things as a couple, which may be misinterpreted as controlling, depending on how discreet you are. You're more clever than strong-willed; a survivor, rather than fighter, and understand the beauty about kissing-and-making-up. You are secretly preoccupied with what others think of you and usually aim for a low profile. Don't second-guess your lover's needs!

Money

You are intelligent and quick on your feet, but dread "change." More a follower, rather than trailblazer, you enjoy working with others, rather than solo and never commit to anything you cannot do. You're cooperative but tend to hold grudges when things don't jive with your agenda. Even though you love luxury, you rarely push your luck or overspend, and are responsible with personal finances.

Famous People Born on This Day

Female

Lorraine Bracco, actress
Donna Karan, fashion designer
Jill Powell, actress
Tiffany, singer
Persis Khambatta, actress

Male

Sting, singer
Don McLean, songwriter
Rex Reed, movie critic
Groucho Marx, actor
Mahatma Gandhi, spiritual leader

October 3

All the special projects you've been on and all those places you've been provide you with plenty of interesting things to talk about. Life is full of unique surprises, and it's no accident that independent, inventive, adventuresome you is there for them. This includes forays into the great outdoors or sports and also your favorite topic: romance. You can be fiery and fearless, even shocking sometimes, naturally a hunter or huntress, all part of what's happening.

Will your fond dreams become realities? Sometimes, but it will take more than wishful thinking. You're already good at making people connections, but please try having more patience as you fit together all the important puzzle pieces, including dressing for success and doing something about your appearance. You have a message. For impact, deliver it in an acceptable style.

Love

You expect a lot from a lover but give them one-hundred percent once that trust and guidelines are clearly established. You need a partner whom you can respect, is tactful, and has a strong character. Emotionally drawn to persons who are educated, bright, and cheerful, you can relate best to a partner with definite goals, and who has a realistic gameplan to achieve them. You're repulsed by vulgarity and disturbed by disorder.

Money

You have a rich imagination and spend lots of time daydreaming. Sometimes it's difficult for you to be objective because your emotions influence your thinking so much. You're not interested in science and math because they seem cold, unfeeling, and their careful logic is colorless, boring. 10/3-born are valuable, respected, and dependable employees. You handle finances fairly well, and get the most from money by using your wits.

Famous People Born on This Day

Female

Neve Campbell, actress
Gwen Stefani, singer
Kathryn D. Sullivan, astronaut
Angeles Alvarino Deleira, biologist
Gertrude Berg, actress

Male

Eric Von Detten, actor
James Herriot, veterinarian
Chubby Checker, singer
Lindsey Buckingham, guitarist
Gore Vidal, author

October 4

Behind your down-to-earth, pleasant appearance is a tough customer—a real dynamo that believes strongly in what you are doing, determined, almost always looking ahead. Your possibilities are endless, and since people naturally like you we'd expect you to "come through" and never let us down. Your focus is not always on you, though you're very good at taking care of number one; you will stand up and defend a good cause, or the weak, or even anyone who'll pay you.

A creative thinker, you are also more of a private person than you seem, content to develop your own plans and thoughts, then spring into action. Choose roles where you have a gameplan, but throw in your bubbling spontaneity to add excitement. You are strong physically but need rest when things don't go your way emotionally.

Love

10/4-born believe that two heads are better than one, and are rarely, if ever, the aggressor. A believer in positive thinking, you encourage lovers to express themselves, try a little harder, and examine matters differently—as well as getting them to enjoy and explore the beauty of commitment! You respond to people truly, sincerely, and personally, and your honesty stimulates them to respond to you the same.

Money

Your ability to think twice before you act helps you to avoid many on-the-job complications. You easily focus on one thing at a time and direct all your efforts towards that end, rarely making excuses or missing a deadline. Once goals are established, you follow the itinerary and don't rest until completion. Realistic with spendings, you rarely live beyond your financial means. Thanks to your gift for empathy, careers where social progress can be made suit you well.

Famous People Born on This Day

Female

Alicia Silverstone, actress
Susan Sarandon, actress
Anne Rice, writer
Hattie McDaniel, actress
Elisa Bialk, writer

Male

Charlton Heston, actor
Alvin Toffler, writer
Armand Assante, actor
Damon Runyon, writer
Buster Keaton, actor

October 5

Many born on this day are a bit of a devil, sometimes feeling justified in taking advantage, thinking that you deserve more and others don't. You can dish it out though others wouldn't expect it from "friendly" you. Don't be tagged a wolf in sheep's clothing, and yes, it's not easy to be mellow and handle negatives. Consider it your challenge to meet your true inner calling—to help, serve, and cooperate with others for the good of all, doing so without smothering or simply marshalling them.

Because you're calculating and ambitious, roles in the high-end of business can certainly bring rewards once you get asked into the boardroom. Strengthen your vitality by trying positive, traditional roles, usually in orderly environments, like in church. You need lots of fun, too, so make lots of time for it!

Love

You have difficulty forming close relationships because you fear that you will lose your freedom if you become too closely attached to another. You prefer lovers who are able to take care of themselves, who are independent, and emotionally mature. Others find your honesty and sensitivity both inspiring and magnetic; subterfuge and deceit are intolerable to you. You are painfully sensitive to what others think of you.

Money

You analyze things very carefully and rarely jump to conclusions, preferring to spend as much time as possible researching choices and weighing every point of view. This can be very useful, but sometimes you take so long that coworkers grow impatient because of your cautious thoroughness. Your innate curiosity enjoys uncovering secrets—and you know how to keep them! Discipline, reserve, and sharp powers of observation are native to the 10/5-born.

Famous People Born on This Day

Female

Kate Winslet, actress
Karen Allen, actress
Glynis Johns, actress
Yvonne Braithwaite Burke,
    congresswoman
Autherine Lucy, first black student
    to break color barrier

Male

Guy Pearce, actor
Mario Lemieux, hockey player
Ray Kroc, founder of McDonalds
Larry Fine, comedian
Donald Pleasance, actor

October 6

All born today won't be famous, though you definitely make an impression on people. We want to say there's a certain "electricity" about you since one of the early developers of our electrical system was born today. It would be more accurate to say you're a visionary and a builder, an all-mindful, detail-conscious person with a knack for getting things done, which doesn't sound real romantic, though you're an excellent mate who just needs your time.

Cautious and perceptive, you can be counted on for an honest opinion, often mixing in psychic impressions with your down-to-earth experiences. You can be a little too set in your ways, too, so you might want to ask others what personal improvements they would want you to make. Swallow that pride! Re-connect and re-focus with family members, or vacation in the Swiss Alps.

Love

You have a wonderfully seductive and charming way with words—always personable, sincere, and honest. You treat people kindly and are willing to share your time and knowledge (and many times your money)—the more you do for someone you like, the better you feel. Always upfront with lovers and friends, 10/6-born usually give more than expected. Honor, integrity, and helping others mean everything to you.

Money

You have an inquisitive mind and terrific ability to grasp ideas that aren't obvious to many coworkers. You understand (but don't always remember) details, enjoy the vistas of long-term planning, and are always willing to explore new ways to improve finances. For you, "honesty is the only policy, and time is money"—so, you act open-mindedly and with loyalty, objectively negotiating so that everyone gets a fair deal. You never sacrifice integrity for economics.

Famous People Born on This Day

Female

Gloria Lane, educator
Anne Bashkiroff, activist
Shana Alexander, journalist
Janet Gaynor, actress
Julianne McNamara, gymnast

Male

Reginald Aubrey Fessenden, inventor
Thor Heyerdahl, explorer
Henry Chadwick, baseball pioneer
George Westinghouse, inventor
Le Corbusier, architect

October 7

Courteous, worldly, and more shrewd than others give you credit for, you may be ttracted to people in humanitarian or scientific careers, where your casual, cooperative personality—which is appreciated almost anywhere you go—lets you contribute positively. You're smart and instinctive, able to summon up all your education and experience to rise to the occasion, overcoming the odds and hardships, molding relationships that will or should last, always keeping the world moving forward.

If you're not comfortable with your "crowd," then it's time to break loose and get busy being the helper/people-person that's in your heart. You're not the kind that can drop everything and switch careers, but to expand your horizons, you can try roles connected to your career. You also need down-time and a fly-away vacation after periods of hard work and strain.

Love

You enjoy emotionally-demonstrative lovers; "ordinary" or "laid-back" ones bore you quickly. You don't demand that partners pay attention to you every waking moment, and you don't let anybody do the ho-hum thing to you either. Possessiveness and jealousy drive you nuts. You have very little tolerance for strong, silent lovers who hold back their feelings, and who are unsocial or close-minded.

Money

Although nobody would ever say that your thinking is logical or clear, you never allow your emotions to influence money or business decisions. In fact, it's downright unpleasant for you to talk with others about your personal-finances. 10/7-born always seek honest, straightforward bottom lines, but are not mathematically inclined. You enjoy knowing how things works—but not as a whole; usually exploring the big picture first, and then the details.

Famous People Born on This Day

Female

Toni Braxton, singer
Ludmila Tourischeva, Olympic
   gymnast
Judy Landers, actress
June Allyson, actress
Spring Byington, actress

Male

Yo-Yo Ma, cellist
John Cougar Mellencamp, rocker
Desmond Tutu, South African
   Archbishop
R.D. Laing, psychiatrist
Louis S.B. Leakey, anthropologist

October 8

Libras are known to be a step ahead in the quick-brains department, but you are double that! You handle the tough assignments with ease, and you're inventive, altruistic, industrious, able to ad lib, usually with a strong physique and breezy yet firm temperament, free to follow whatever attracts your attention. Yet, because your tough, noble reputation precedes you, you can attract dumb enemies and jealousy. Do not take them lightly even if they respect you.

Mechanical things and computers come naturally to you, just as your ability to chat and persuade does. You relish roles where you give out inside secrets or train others, though you could excel in government or scientific roles, too. Flying is fun but dangerous; ditto for thrill rides. Go for softer sensual pleasures; include spas and mineral baths on vacation schedules.

Love

The 10/8-born only reaches life's cruising speed once they've found true love. One big romantic boo-boo is that you tend to miss out on the magic of the moment because you are always in a hurry or thinking three steps ahead. As talkative and as sociable as you are, you have a real block about expressing your feelings. At first glance, you may appear open-minded and adventurous, but you're actually very conservative—and require a devoted, down-to-earth partner for happiness.

Money

Strict schedules are exhausting and boring for you because you don't like dancing through life at snail's pace or others' protocol. You learn and remember lessons of the past—and hate repeating them, or anything for that matter. Focus your attention on just one thing at a time, and move forward at your own comfort and pace. It's also a good idea that you find an honest accountant to help you with personal budgets and maybe educate you about spending beyond your means.

Famous People Born on This Day

Female
Sigourney Weaver, actress
Stephanie Zimbalist, actress
Rona Barrett, gossip columnist
Janice E. Voss Ford, astronaut
Sarah Purcell, actress

Male
Matt Damon, actor
Chevy Chase, actor
Jesse Jackson, civil rights leader
David Carradine, actor
R.L. Stine, writer

October 9

Imagination is not something you should let run wild, though it is one of your best features, along with your easy-going, childlike nature. You're not suited for hard work—you'd like to not work at all—so you follow your artistic or musical talents to where there are pleasant, appreciative people like yourself, engaged in a common cause without commotion and drudgery. Good artists copy, great artists steal. Ill-chosen words can get you into trouble, and obeying the law is not something you're known for.

Due to your emotional nature and lusts, your energy is easily depleted, so sooner or later you'll be paying major attention to your physical temple and kicking all bad habits. Needing peace and quiet, choose roles where you work one-on-one, not in large groups. For vacation? Rest and reading, but rowing on still waters is very good.

Love

Realistic about what you can and can't get out of a relationship, you try never to let imaginary romantic standards overshadow reality. You are a loving partner and keep both feet on the ground during times of confusion. Even though you are lucid and fair, for some strange reason you often gravitate to irrational, illogical partners! The age of a lover is never a priority, although you need one who is mature.

Money

Many 10/9-born are slow learners—but, even so, never forget a thing! Each employment experience teaches you to be more meticulous and self-reliant. You like making things happen behind the scenes and are always open-minded about finding better ways to make the hour last longer than 60 minutes. You are helpful to coworkers, yet when asked to do a favor or overtime, you always set the limits before tackling the task.

Famous People Born on This Day

Female

Sharon Osbourne, MTV personality
Jean and Liz Sagal, twin actresses
Aimee Semple McPherson, evangelist
Harriet Hosmer, sculptor
Helene Deutsch, psychoanalyst

Male

Scott Bakula, actor
John Lennon, singer
Zachary Ty Bryan, actor
Jackson Browne, rocker
Robert A. Rushworth, X-15 test pilot

October 10

Loving beauty and refinement, you see success as harmony and material gains as the rewards of your good karma—however, getting the world to operate and think the same way will be a herculean task, but you'll contribute in your own genuine way, forgiving others for their faults while sparkling with joy and sacrificing for both of your families—your personal one and the world outside. You're likely to marry rich—your sensitive artist personality is much desired!

A mellow purple-ish gold aura hints that you are a royal but somewhat complacent type, and others can sense that you're easy to be taken advantage of, and do. Those cop dramas are on TV for a reason—to scare you into covering your backside! For fun, shop for delights and antiques. For profit, sell! For joy, sail!

Love

Because love easily consumes you, you always try to weigh out options logically, and rarely plunge into a relationship blindly or recklessly. You have tremendous tenacity, and live and breathe for the greater good of your partnership. 10/10-born always need to keep their finger on the same partnership page, because you tend to attract perspicacious and shrewd lovers. You're far deeper than many may ever acknowledge.

Money

10/10-born are independent thinkers and generous with money but not too realistic with personal investments—an eternal victim to compromise or intimidation from peers. Your opinions are conventional, rather than controversial because emotional displays frighten you. Although you're not terrific executive material, you're a good secret-keeper, comfortable working at a casual pace, and like solving problems on your own.

Famous People Born on This Day

Female

Mya, singer
Jodi Lyn O'Keefe, actress
Helen Hayes, actress
Priscilla L. Williams, social activist
Tanya Tucker, singer

Male

John Mobley, NFL linebacker
Ben Vereen, actor
Brett Favre, NFL quarterback
David Lee Roth, singer
Thelonious Monk, musician

October 11

It would be nice to look at others and see what they are think-ing, and you can almost do it! You have a deep soul and a penetrating curiosity, in addition to the good Libra traits—engaging, sociable, an individualist—and you have an extra dose of courage, so you're not the namby-pamby type who's trying to talk their way through life. Plus, you're very industri-ous, not content to rest on your laurels. It's no wonder that you succeed in unusual occupations—it all makes sense to you.

You're not the fiery smash-your-way-to-the-top type, and often you settle for less, kindly waiting your turn. When it comes to love, you're usually very committed but need space and lots of support. Just out of curiosity, find out what's really behind the waterfall. Get on a game show and win.

Love

10/11-born exude confidence and competence and are sensitive and lov-ing, but uncomfortable with open displays of affection. It is hard for you to let down your hair in public and just have a good time, preferring privacy or behind-closed-doors time. Rather shy, you prefer the companionship of older people and lovers. The more latitude and space in a relationship for you, the better. You may not have many friends and loved ones, but you're always faithful, and honest.

Money

Although nobody expects anything but the best from you, and you never leave a task half done, 10/11-born are easily overwhelmed by dollars-and-cents stuff. You're articulate and nimble-minded and have a smooth-talking manner. You function best in structured situations, but not so regimented that you lose the joy of exploration. While always considerate, you maintain strict boundaries between you and coworkers.

Famous People Born on This Day

Female

Eleanor Roosevelt, First Lady
Michelle Trachtenberg, actress
Joan Cusack, actress
Dottie West, singer
Natalie Jay, actress

Male

Luke Perry, actor
Elmore Leonard, writer
Henry John Heinz, food manufacturer
George Williams, founder YMCA
Leste Bowie, trumpeter

October 12

With so much passion going on inside, it's no wonder that you're one of the most uptempo, ethereal birthdays of October—a real live wire who has depth and probably a lot of sexual things going on. We won't get into that. God would make a good friend for you, and there is probably that little messenger talking to your conscience. Realize that inventive, hopeful you has cooked up another way to be chatty. Have a mission but get off your high horse.

Running the show appeals to you, so you can be very good at making and enforcing rules. As a child, you experimented, perhaps cutting your own hair. Nowadays, you might want to travel back in time to the old country.

Love

You have a practical and lucid philosophy about relationships, rarely over-committing yourself or spending too much money on anybody or on anything that may hurt you in the long run. To many who don't know you well, you often give the impression of being a bit avant garde, unrealistic—although that's not the case. You delight in dancing to the beat of your personal drummer and enjoy company with similar tastes.

Money

You love taking on-the-job ideas and tweak and gamble and make them real, but are very hesitant and conservative about toying with personal finances and investments. Routine and linear work, rather than philosophical or creative, makes you jumpy, but you always get the job done—and usually on-time! You enjoy mental challenges, but always know when to call it quits.

Famous People Born on This Day

Female

Susan Anton, actress
Marion Jones, runner
Abigail Kingsley Alling, executive
Daliah Lavi, actress
Jean Nidetch, nutritionist

Male

Luciano Pavarotti, tenor
Dick Gregory, comedian
Hugh Jackman, actor
Elmer A. Sperry, inventor
Ned Jarrett, auto racer

October 13

More freedom, less work, more money, save the world! These are your rallying cries, but it is not revolution you want, it's better perks. You matured early, but settling down is not of much interest to you, so off you go chasing rainbows, overtaxing yourself, barking up the wrong trees, and being too naïve about romance. Still, you have chatty enthusiasm and are a fast learner, a guarantee that you'll get 15 minutes of fame if not more.

Trendy, faddish, and hip—it's not that you're trying to be cool, it's just that the status quo is so oppressive, you need your space to be your own person. Roles where you get special training or unique skills can help stabilize your flimsy career; college was probably a party. Living in an island community would suit you.

Love

Your personal life is never a romantic novel, and you're not the most realistic in matters of love or sex—argumentative, but in a charming, winning manner. You really, really try to be open-minded and progressive, but you tend to bend yourself out of shape if lovers don't live up to your dream scenario. Now's a good time for you to distinguish whether your outlook and goals about love are actually attainable, or merely fantasies.

Money

It's hard for you to put your ideas into practical form because you live in a fantasy world—not a sci-fi unrealistic one, but not day-to-day real, nonetheless! Still, you see beauty around you that others ignore or overlook. You keep a low profile, and try your best to stay sober about personal goals—ever eager for the reward. You're not driven, nor overly ambitious; simply, a "I want to have this" kind.

Famous People Born on This Day

Female

Nancy Kerrigan, Olympic skater
Marie Osmond, entertainer
Margaret Thatcher, British Prime Minister
Lady Jane Grey, Queen of England for 9 days
Laraine Day, actress

Male

Paul Simon, singer
Jerry Rice, football icon
Cornel Wilde, actor
Sammy Hagar, rocker
Yves Montand, actor

October 14

A lot of strange and unusual things happen to people born today, and it's not always easy being you. To some, you are fussy and particular; to others, you seem gregarious and campy, but we soon get to know that you're smart and sly, able to shift gears when necessary, landing on your feet, always with cheery optimism and pizzazz. You may change masters but you never lose your heart, which you have learned to protect.

You are drawn to where the action is, like proverbial bees to honey. The so-called normal life doesn't cut it, although when you do go home, you can settle down. Roles as a lecturer, specialist or troubleshooter fit you—if you don't become a pop celebrity first. For fun, hook up with the gang for a road trip, barnstorming your way anywhere.

Love

Always questioning your self-worth, you feel that usually you do either too much or not enough for your lover, right? It's a good idea to rope one who's strong, tells it like it is, and treats you with equality in return. Many of your relationship difficulties are due to crossed emotional signals, rather than fact or reason. You continually worry about whether or not your lover is devoted and are prone to crazy fantasies or escapism. Be more secure, not so solipsistic!

Money

You have a very rich imagination, but must learn to control it enough to discern what is real and what is fiction. Your 10/14 temperament doesn't make you very good at math or science—not because you are slow, but because you do not think that way. Employers know they can count on you to get a job done, provided it is spelled out and not speculative. You seek jobs that have structure because you don't enjoy work that limits your mind by the dry rules of logic.

Famous People Born on This Day

Female
Natalie Maines, singer
Katherine Mansfield, writer
Udo Kier, actress
Hannah Arendt, political scientist
Lillian Gish, actress

Male
Dwight D. Eisenhower, U.S. president
Ralph Lauren, fashion designer
William Penn, Pennsylvania founder
Paul de Keyser, storyteller
e. e. cummings, poet

October 15

Success seems to have its eye on you—why shouldn't it: you seem so universally linked-up wherever we find you, with your earthy magnetism and no-nonsense approach, plus you have loads of determination to go with your particular charm. Facts and numbers make perfect sense to you, and you don't mind standing up and taking charge, just don't waste it on the little stuff—aim high and be particular about connecting with the right people. Your rewards will be handsome.

Roles in the arts, real estate, or legal profession fit you, but as time passes and you accumulate experience, you may find yourself near the top of the ladder, maybe a little dizzy from the height, but you'll get over it. For fun, lavish yourself in luxuries to convince yourself you've arrived.

Love

You're not one for slow courtship; once your sights are set, you rush forward and get right down to business (and normally without thinking). Your desires come suddenly and strong—your inclination is to strike while the iron is hot. 10/15-born hate confinement of any sort; their need for freedom and insatiable thirst for the novel make them unwilling to accept restriction or the word "no."

Money

Charisma, ambition, and enormous drive are your strong suits, but you quickly grow impatient with anything that holds you back. However, if success knocks at your door, you're well-advised not to open up until you summon your accountant to stand by. To many coworkers, your game plans may be a bit spacey or unrealistic, but you push forward with determination. In spite of overwhelming odds against success, it rarely occurs to you that you will fail.

Famous People Born on This Day

Female

Sarah Ferguson, Duchess of York
Penny Marshall, actress/producer
Linda Lavin, actress
Tanya Roberts, actress
Helen Hunt Jackson, novelist

Male

Emeril Lagasse, chef
Lee Iacocca, automaker
Mario Puzo, novelist
John Kenneth Galbraith, economist
John L. Sullivan, boxer

October 16

No one can tell you what you cannot do since they have no idea what you're capable of, and it is a lot. Carefully, you will step over and redraw the boundaries to your liking. In your formative years, you felt a yearning that you can improve things or do more—learning that others might try to hold you back. To get attention you must be better, delivering more quality, outshine the competition, be a diplomat as well as the humble, warm, shining star.

As a gifted defender of liberty, you can be clairvoyant, or at least have a deep understanding of human operations. In the flower-filled meadow of love, you like the romantic lead, love being the ultra-ultimate experience, its pleasure filling your senses. So, you won't travel alone as you explore the culture and the country.

Love

You have good sense about what you can and cannot do in a relationship. Your expectations are realistic and basic; therefore, you're rarely disappointed if things falter because you're always straightforward and honest. Lovers must provide you emotional challenge in order to feel that you are accomplishing something—you like tangible, not hopeful. More often than not, you're the stabilizing influence in personal affairs.

Money

You are a tireless worker, have good concentration, and give every project your full attention. 10/16-born are self-motivated and do what must be done before being told, and always go to great lengths to provide top-notch service. You're confident saying "no," believe that you can accomplish almost anything, and are well-suited for management positions or where you can work totally on your own.

Famous People Born on This Day

Female

Kellie Martin, actress
Ellen Dolan, actress
Angela Lansbury, actress
Lorraine Sweeny, communications
    specialist
Suzanne Somers, actress

Male

Tim Robbins, actor
Eugene O'Neill, dramatist
David Zucker, director
Oscar Wilde, writer
Noah Webster, dictionary editor

October 17

Behind your friendly, inoffensive smile and your relaxed manner is an imaginative genius, even a daredevil at times, and a flighty, engaging personality. You can be proud, conservative, tactful, and mentally sophisticated, and can hold your own in conversations with anyone because your mind is on ideas and possibilities. You're not intimidated. You're not superficial, you're just busy, and a fun romantic partner. You can go a million different career paths, usually successfully since you won't let grass grow under your feet.

Your sharp competitive mind makes you a good writer, talker, instructor, and quite an actor too. Single-person sports appeal to you, and parachuting from an airplane would be, well, a breeze. Sitting still and listening wouldn't be. Romantic vacations would be wonderful if you didn't get distracted, your mind wandering off on another tangent.

Love

You are an affectionate, considerate, and imaginative lover who's not afraid to show your vulnerable side to partners—for you, relationships are all-or-nothing! 10/17-born are security junkies and deeply concerned about being well-sheltered and living in a peaceful environment (and hopefully with a lover)—even if it's outrageously demanding of your time. Your single biggest flaw is your talent for acting impetuously, rushing off half-prepared.

Money

You cover a large area first and fill in the details later. Unfortunately, you don't have much discipline—easily sidetracked and always impatient with routine or detailed tasks. Even if your desk is messy, handwriting sloppy, and work is not done neatly, you remain hopeful for a rescue. You're a languid dreamer whose aim about financial matters shifts about with ease, following no particular rhyme or reasonable pattern.

Famous People Born on This Day

Female

Margot Kidder, actress
Mildred Knopf, civic contributor
Rita Hayworth, actress
Jean Arthur, actress
Priscilla Lanford Buckly, editor

Male

Eminem, rapper
Alan Jackson, singer
Evel Knievel, daredevil
Montgomery Clift, actor
Jimmy Breslin, NY columnist

October 18

Who says they know the real you? Each of your close friends has a different idea; it seems you can adapt to whatever standards, talk their language—you have personality dexterity. You enjoy mental intrigues, also putting on a show, being the natural actor type. Fate is something you shouldn't test too much, since your natural good fortune isn't failsafe. Accused of being devious, you're just independent, probably having a mate who takes care of you like one of the kids.

Not all born on this date may be playing without a full deck. Most of you are generous, no-nonsense charmers who love love and leisure, and are quick to raise your hand because you have an answer. Roles where you show your versatility with people and your expertise with objects and ideas could become unique careers.

Love

You voice your opinions concisely, always realistic about matters of love. Generous in your judgment of others, you are kind even when they're disappointing. You meet people more than halfway because you believe that everybody has flaws and can change. 10/18-born have a strong sense of ethics and social decorum. You give, and expect, honesty and sincerity with anyone who captures your heart.

Money

Your easy way with words and pleasant demeanor allow you to cope quickly and generously with difficult employment or financial problems. You are always willing to learn something new as long as it doesn't require lots of numbers or memorization, and you enjoy demonstrating your skills at every chance. You know who you are and understand your capabilities and shortcomings. You're rarely at loss for words and are always ready to lend a hand.

Famous People Born on This Day

Female

Laura Nyro, singer
Pam Dawber, actress
Melina Mercouri, actress
Fannie Hurst, novelist
Isabel E. Allen, biostatician

Male

Jean-Claude Van Damme, actor
George C. Scott, actor
Jesse Helms, U.S. senator
Chuck Berry, rocker
Peter Boyle, actor

October 19

Handling money isn't something you're particularly good at, but doling out advice like you were an inside trader or gossip columnist is. Cool customers like you can diplomatically work your way up the career ladder, but romance isn't so dependable, though you have an eye for beauty and sexuality and may be pretty attractive yourself. You could marry the boss, but where's the freedom you need? People should be careful what they say about you; you're pretty good in an argument when aroused.

What can we say that you don't already think you know? You're capable of deep concentration and hard work—you can talk others into doing the latter. Try roles as an advocate or spokesperson; the world is your office. Old age and strife are always after you, so take vacations to relax and rejuvenate often.

Love

Make sure that your lover likes social gatherings, because your radiant charm is inclined to wilt when occasions get too quiet. Stimulating conversations and being on the go keep you happy. More progressive, rather than possessive, you require an open-minded, gregarious partner who's not intimidated by intimacy or your independent nature. Although you believe in love at first sight, beware of rushing into relationships!

Money

Your clever mind quickly grasps ideas that others don't. 10/19s are good at work that requires originality or innovative and unusual ways of doing things like design, education, the arts. Your mind moves quickly from topic to topic, sometimes without pausing long enough to understand what you have learned, even though you spot solutions quicker than most. Although you're not silly with spendings, saving isn't your expertise.

Famous People Born on This Day

Female

Amy Linker, actress
Jeanine C. Riley, singer
Annie S. Peck, mountain climber
Johnetta Betsch Cole, educator
Georgia Montgomery Davis Powers, politician

Male

John Lithgow, actor
Peter Max, artist
Jack Anderson, columnist
Robert Reed, actor
Evander Holyfield, boxer

October 20

It is worth it to write things down and take notes—getting organized and meeting schedules isn't something that comes naturally to someone as mentally and emotionally busy as you—and you have your goals and promises to keep! Don't worry, almost all of you have a fantastic cast of supporting characters around you, ready to help poor little you get out of a relationship jam, or buy something, or go out on the town to meet Mr. or Mrs. Right, if you haven't already.

A positive, winning environment does wonders for your soul, though too much work and competition can put you on the sidelines. Learn to pace yourself and find the level of vitality that's right for you. How much is that? Depends. Get away from dependent situations when you can, and spend more time on Y-O-U.

Love

You have an easy-going, low-key approach to relationships. You are well-suited for a partner whose moods are steady, one who is self-assured and independent, rather than one who waits for you to make the first move. Your 10/20-nature keeps you approachable and adaptable, rarely demanding. With your effortless natural charm, you stand out in contrast to those who dramatically struggle for center stage.

Money

Because communication is important to the 10/20-born, you're best-suited to work with intelligent coworkers who are self-motivated. You're productive and active, kind and charitable with your knowledge and time. You live for cooperation, and perform best with coworkers with whom you can brainstorm. Still, you enjoy a good argument, if only as an exercise of wits. You're a peripatetic soul who requires change and movement.

Famous People Born on This Day

Female

Princess Michiko Shoda, Japanese
  royalty
Anne Murray, country singer
Anna Neagle, actress
Frances Kellor, reformer
Arlene Francis, actress

Male

Tom Petty, rocker
Art Buchwald, columnist/
Bela Lugosi, actor
Arthur Rimbaud, poet
John Dewey, philosopher

October 21

The saying "You've got to have heart" certainly applies to you, since you have it. Many of you are daydreamers and idealists who love romance and friends. Inspired by humble causes, you go about life with a philosophy in mind, or religion, believing that all experiences mean something, that there is a special bonding in your family. You can be moody, worrisome, a homebody that might gain weight since you are not overly-active. Not exactly a psychic, you are good at "reading" people due to your cautious nature.

We find you in pleasant social situations like coffee shops, there reading a book, sometimes nursing a cold or whatever—you're susceptible to what's in the air, so having the right comfy personal environment is important. Try roles involving money; manipulating helps you understand wealth, something you need.

Love

You are an idealist who expects lovers to live by very special standards—yours! You know what you want and have clear, exact priorities. 10/21-born are never vague or soft-spoken to lovers. It's difficult for you to tell a lie, even though you're not a keen lie detector about others. (You have your faults, but you hide them very well!) You're terrified of loneliness and disorder and keep a good close reign over your emotions.

Money

It's difficult for you to reach agreements with coworkers because you state your opinions so enthusiastically and are always on the move and often ignore protocol. Nonetheless, your independent and rational mind is rarely influenced by feelings. It's a good idea for you to try slowing down, and listen to what coworkers are saying. You're more intelligent and curious than ambitious.

Famous People Born on This Day

Female
Judge Judy Sheindlin, TV judge
Joyce Randolph, actress
Carrie Fisher, actress
Ramabai Dongre' Medhavi, social
reformer
Ursula Le Guin, writer

Male
Dizzy Gillespie, trumpetter
Alfred Nobel, scientist
Jeremy Miller, actor
Elvin Bishop, guitarist
Samuel Taylor Coleridge, poet

October 22

Likable and magnetic, you might be one of the very fortunate suave beauties, and when you develop your artistic talents or stand up for your cause, others do more than just notice you. What do they have in mind? Hmm. A little vulnerable and easily influenced, you like exploring the secrets of life, not wanting to miss a beat, yet sometimes raising doubts and jealousy by being quirky and independent. Still, the public listens. You're a better spokesperson than a spy.

Not a ditzy lightweight, you have deep feelings and can be gently persuasive. Roles where you showcase your loving side and keep a firm foot in the real world help your reputation and chances to gain long-term success and security. Marriage may help, too. Living near the ocean is healthful, but not too much sun.

Love

Your tendency to change your mind on a whim makes you come off as flighty, even though your only intention is to be straightforward about your feelings. You're most comfortable with a lover who accepts your habits and desires and leaves you well enough alone. Having clearly defined roles and responsibilities is essential for your happy relationships. Be exacting and discreet, not frivolous or trivial!

Money

You probably start conversations with "I" more than most, and the word "me" crops up regularly in dialogue. 10/22-borns are not egocentric but are quite needy for approval and enjoy working in teams and with others. You're not a shrinking violet on the job, even though you're inclined to compromise, rather than stating your case or rocking the employment boat. You're an eager-beaver type and never empty-headed!

Famous People Born on This Day

Female

Annette Funicello, actress
Henriette Wyeth, artist
Sarah Bernhardt, actress
Joan Fontaine, actress
Catherine Deneuve, actress

Male

Jeff Goldblum, actor
Tony Roberts, actor
Timothy Leary, professor
Brian Boitano, figure skater
Karl Jansky, physicist

October 23

Beneath your friendly, active, seemingly casual and fun aura is a thinker, with aspirations and the tactical ability to reach them, and very dedicated to a career, often more than to family. Impatient with obstacles, you talk your way around them using practical logic—bluffing doesn't work. Sometimes you're like a new baby crying for attention—which you'll get. An individualist like you gets others thinking, percolating. You're down-to-earth enough for dealing with details as well as that big picture.

Working with a good supporting cast helps since you don't have a lot of aggressive fire, just passive pizzazz. Personal not competitive sports are more your style for exercise, and you need your quiet, meditative times to make up for when you're going full blast. Enjoy romantic dates and candlelight more often, and hold hands. Warmth is wonderful.

Love

You're either too much or not enough in love—and may suffer from the blinding light of your own brilliance. You demand that partners accept your mood swings and not be too demanding. 10/23-born are happiest with serious, older lovers. You live for special private moments and, once committed, you remain loyal and steady. You never take affections or relationships lightly, and don't let emotional problems follow you into bed.

Money

You're inspired, outspoken, and think big, but often overlook important details. Spontaneous and independent, the fear of making a mistake never stands in the way of taking action. However, you learn best in structured environments, but not so organized that you lose your freedom to experiment. Even though you prefer to make rules rather than follow them, coworkers acknowledge that you are serious and trustworthy.

Famous People Born on This Day

Female

Brooke Theiss, actress
Margaret Fuller Ossoli, feminist
Anita Roddick, cosmetic manufacturer
Gertrude Ederle, swimmer
Sarah Hale, activist

Male

Weird Al Yankovic, singer
Pele, soccer icon
Michael Crichton, novelist
Johnny Carson, TV talk show host
Ang Lee, director

October 24

Life must have meaning, so you have to feel that you're contributing, which you always are. Step back occasionally and assess the real benefits, and don't paint yourself into a corner. You are very practical and determined and don't mind lending out your heart and soul—you don't want others to say you didn't try. Tension and competition sap your vitality, so you learn early about planning ahead and keeping communication lines open—being adaptable and not fussy—and getting it in writing.

Medicine and health fields may offer you excellent roles for growth and advancement, but any role where problems have to be consistently resolved is fine, even in the magical world of high-tech, or where ideas and your sharp thinking merge. For vacations, take to the great outdoors—back to nature—safely.

Love

You lavish affection on your lover graciously and often, which may startle or overwhelm someone not used to it. 10/24-born bond with their partners immediately and intuitively, and figure out the pluses-and-minuses of the relationship potential in record speed. However, overdoing and overstating matters can be a problem for you because you tend to act before thinking. Even though you're inclined to be a bit cranky, after you settle into a commitment you're a model of steadfast devotion.

Money

Following routine, planning and plotting, and knowing when and when not to act is as natural as breathing for you. 10/24-born don't do anything unless there is a promise of reward. Always more productive, rather than provocative, you're sincere about job commitments and expect honest compensation in return. You hate clutter in your workaday life and quickly eliminate nonessentials that inhibit your profits.

Famous People Born on This Day

Female

Sarah Josepha Hale, author
Susan Leigh Still, astronaut
Denise Levertov, poet
Karen Austin, actress
Belva Bennett Lockwood, activist

Male

Kevin Kline, actor
F. Murray Abraham, actor
David Nelson, actor
Clarence M. Kelley, FBI head
Moss Hart, playwright

October 25

Wherever you go—and you should go far—you have learned to be duly diligent, checking every angle and possibility, seldom making a misstep or rocking the boat. Some think you are slow—you're thoughtful and careful, contemplating first, never bullied, then acting decisively and fairly. You enjoy life, too; dull routines are not something an individualist like you can stand unless it includes a lot of freedom to call some shots.

Because you're a good analyst or researcher—and with your eye on pleasing others—roles where you can influence others positively, like astrology or any eye-opening practice, suit you. Delving into the mysteries of life or meditation hold a certain appeal, so does folksy wisdom. The winds of fate may blow you far from home, and when you return, you've grown and have been missed.

Love

Your needs and desires are clear and defined, and you have a reasonable understanding of what is expected in a relationship. You easily forgive lovers when situations don't come out as expected and let bygones be. You take emotional disappointment in stride and always jog forward. You know how to cooperate and display yourself in a relationship, and are clever at conjuring up novel ways to attack any problem.

Money

You are a conscientious and efficient worker; a natural diplomat who expresses yourself so honestly that no one ever harbors bad feelings, even if you say or do something unpleasant. You are secure and flexible in your ideals and opinions—never aggressive, archaic, nor static. Although you make up your mind rather quickly, you always wind up profiting from your natural intuition. Idle time is not comfortable for you; you enjoy being of service, staying busy.

Famous People Born on This Day

Female

Tracy Nelson, actress
Anne Tyler, writer
Helen Reddy, singer
Minnie Pearl, comedienne
Marion Ross, actress

Male

Pablo Picasso, artist
Richard E. Byrd, admiral/polar
    explorer
Rob Halford, singer
Leo G. Carroll, actor
Georges Bizet, composer

October 26

If you can't make your own luck, nobody can! You have an airy, light approach, cheerful and childlike, plus some pretty powerful people skills and much-appreciated artistic talents. You have depth and will take the extra steps when asked, often helping brothers, sisters, and friends, turning disharmony into harmony. Problems should happen to others, not you, but there can be opposition when you cross cultural barriers or those imaginary lines.

Since you see that we should all have opportunities to enjoy life in its various forms, roles that include diversity and communication draw you, but you'll need to develop more discipline and spunk if you are to last until the big paydays—you have been known to jump the fence easily. On vacation, you might drop in on some of your associates, ready to chat and exchange memories.

Love

It''s hard for you to kick back and just enjoy the comforting beauty of a relationship. You always are planning, scheming, and plotting activities—you rarely reside in the "here and now," usually jumping ahead without the consent of loved ones. You work harder than anyone else to make a relationship work; one thing is certain: you're always willing and able! Idleness and a lover's ignorance are your enemies.

Money

Granted, some coworkers may consider you quirky or impractical, but you always perform your job efficiently and vitally. 10/26-born are ebullient but a tad stubborn; and, although not too savvy about math or science, you complete your obligations with a unique creativity that makes up for any lack of discipline or previous know-how. You are proud, yet passionate about money-making, arrogant, yet oddly modest, about obtaining your goal.

Famous People Born on This Day

Female

Lauren Tewes, actress
Mahalia Jackson, singer
Jennifer Roberson, author
Georgette Amowitz, choreographer
Jaclyn Smith, actress

Male

Cary Elwes, actor
Pat Sajak, TV host
Bob Hoskins, actor
Jackie Coogan, actor
Leon Trotsky, Russian revolutionary

October 27

How dare anyone call you reckless or out of touch! Few are as keen-witted and courageous, and so what if you have a few dings, and no, you are not required to put on a show, though when you do it's quite a display. A fast learner and quick with your hands—good for a surgery or tickling the keyboard—you are also quick with stinging words and being brutally frank. You take your responsibilities seriously—can you manage enough time for family, love, and career?

Success is usually earned and you're crafty enough to earn it. If you need guidance it's not hard to find. Others listen because your words have a certain magic and audacity; roles where you are behind the microphone are, well, interesting. Flighty by nature, you love and need the great outdoors.

Love

10/27-born are blunt and exacting and believe that honesty is the only policy. You stimulate the best in lovers, and they are impressed with your bottom-line strong-mindedness and love of discussion. Nonetheless, you live by very strict guidelines, always questioning anybody or anything who appears to be too good to be true. Life is never boring when you're around—but, please make sure that you offer an objective listening ear and not just your opinions!

Money

You patiently accept responsibilities and always deliver the goods (although not always on time). Reliable, honest and fair, you earn the respect of coworkers because you always do what's expected and don't stop until a project is done. Knowing that you can succeed on your own merits, you prefer to work independently, rather than on a team. You're not afraid of starting out small in order to rise to the top, and are diligent and self-motivated.

Famous People Born on This Day

Female

Carrie Snodgress, actress
Sylvia Plath, writer
Nanette Fabray, singer
Ruby Dee, actress
Teresa Wright, actress

Male

Roy Lichtenstein, artist
Simon Le Bon, singer
John Cleese, comedian
Theodore Roosevelt, U.S. president
Dylan Thomas, poet

October 28

If there is a perfect Scorpio, you're a candidate. Fearless and sure, you believe you'll succeed not fail, and once you get fixated—on an idea, a romantic partner, a goal—you hold tight, persevering even if you have a few rough edges—even if your looks don't match the role—you can re-create the role. Inside, you are fiery, passionate, and have "the juice." Others sense your magnetism and see your self-discipline—and give you respect.

Not one to go halfway, you can soak up knowledge and turn into a real expert, often in life-and-death occupations, so roles in medicine, military, or police sciences interest you. You'll also want to try lighter roles, and may be interested in history or collecting, being a life scientist, but love and attachment will put you securely at ease.

Love

It's tough for you to listen to another's side of the story, because you feel that everything revolves around you. Most often, your ego is larger than that of your lover, and you become quickly defensive about what you feel is right and just (for you) and consider compromise difficult. Obstacles spur your energies, adversity gives you incentive. A 10/28-born rarely lies and acts openly and without guile.

Money

Coworkers always know where they stand with you. Even though you're a bit of a loud-mouth and difficult task-master, you can always be relied on to do good work, and above and beyond the call of duty—but, in return, you expect others to be just as exacting and responsible as you. Try to learn the beauty of teamwork, and learn how to ask for help, when necessary. Don't let short-sightedness stifle your financial successes.

Famous People Born on This Day

Female

Julia Roberts, actress
Dody Goodman, comedienne
Edith Head, costume designer
Cleo Laine, actress
Jane Alexander, actress

Male

Joaquin Phoenix, actor
Bill Gates, Microsoft founder
Jonas Salk, medical researcher
Dennis Franz, actor
Charlie Daniels, singer

October 29

At first glance, who would know that pleasant, well-mannered you is actually a fiery catalyst, mentally on the go and full of restless energy? You have deep feelings and sensitivity, also definite tastes, a code of values, also a liking for unique and expensive, precious items, so you may accumulate wealth eventually, though you're not always successful in your careers, but smart enough to change to a better one, believing that you shouldn't settle for something that isn't quite right.

Tactful, persuasive, you have your own interests in mind first and foremost, and you prefer to take the lead in relationships. Roles where you are the power behind the throne suit you, but you desire more of the spotlight although there are more risks and opposition. Metaphysics is fascinating since you like knowing and using secrets.

Love

You hate presumption and when lovers second-guess you. For you, lucidity and honesty are more important than passion or expectation. 10/29-born's noble personality is best-suited for partners who are open-minded and provide you plenty of breathing space. You have very little patience for subtleties or vapid nuances, because you're strongly opinionated and think you know best. Find a lover who will let you roam from square one to square three whenever, and if, you want.

Money

Financial security means buckets to you, and you're forever improving, regrooving and moving forward into prosperity. You get bored quickly with trivial chit-chat, and enjoy working alone. Your insatiable curiosity never rests until you understand every in-and-out. You're more relaxed working in the shadows, rather than radiating responsibility from the executive throne. Discovering and uncovering secrets is your strongest talent—so exploit it!

Famous People Born on This Day

Female

Winona Ryder, actress
Finola Hughes, actress
Fanny Brice, comedienne
Melba Moore, singer
Kate Jackson, actress

Male

Richard Dreyfus, actor
Bill Mauldin, political cartoonist
P.J. Oppenheimer, diamond trader
Johann Olav Koss, speed skater
Neal Hefti, orchestra leader

October 30

Traveling light, you're attracted to the action, not afraid of competition so you wedge your way in, fighting and politicking if you have to, showing that you're a force to be reckoned with—with plenty of ability, fitness, and savvy. Impressive! From high-society or not, you would much rather avoid the sniveling masses and others who don't have your level of self-esteem. We wonder: for someone who seems so invincible, so often at the right place at the right time, where is lasting romance?

Others soon learn that you have courage plus a sharp mind, so roles with challenge and adventure can be offered to you, though you should be careful not to be caught up in scandal and kukka-lucka ideas. Entertainment and "the scene" appeal to you, and travels to far-off action spots are your best vacations.

Love

Like the typical game of cat-and-mouse, you cleverly maneuver lovers into their position, allow them ample trial-and-error time, and then test and tease them before you accept or believe them. Doubting comes as naturally to you as breathing. You always question whether or not what you're experiencing is true or false; you're not gullible—not whatsoever. You're best-suited for an uncomplicated grown-up who has easy-going attitudes and a pure joy for living.

Money

You deal reasonably well with personal investments, even though it seems to you that you never turn a profit. Happily, you're smart enough to never make loans to friends or family, and you do everything in your power to pay off your monthly bills on time—which is good! Rarely ruthless, and never power-hungry, you enjoy building up benefits without too much sweat or aggravation from others.

Famous People Born on This Day

Female

Kristina Wagner, actress
Andrea Mitchell, newscaster
Ruth Gordon, actress
Ruth Hussey, actress
Grace Slick, musician

Male

Henry Winkler, actor
Robert L. "Hoot" Gibson, astronaut
Harry Hamlin, actor
Ezra Pound, poet
John Adams, U.S. president

October 31

Halloween is not so bad, you have learned, since it's all a joke and a put-on, though you are pretty self-sensitive, maybe a bit of an ego, and not as childlike as some would like to think. You can be a stern, uncompromising dictator—good for working with children who need discipline, but not with adults since you'd rather fight than switch. Surprisingly, many leaders are born today—like you, they're smart cookies with keen eyes and passion for romance.

When you were young you got your way, stubbornly clinging and demanding attention, training the adults. Getting away with that is not so easy later, though usually your good looks and credentials will open doors to many interesting roles, often in institutional, structured settings. Getting away from chaos and pressure is essential for regaining your inner balance.

Love

Even though no one would consider you an incurable romantic, you do take relationships very seriously. You deeply analyze a partner's likes and peculiarities, but cannot tolerate anybody having secrets! Indeed—you can be a bit of an emotional bully, or verbal fighter when angered or scared, although your optimism usually dominates. Plus, you have a silly, bad habit about always testing a lover's loyalty. Stop that!

Money

Because you're a touchy-feely, sensual kind of person, it's common for you to spend money without considering long-range consequences. You long for luxury and to be rich, but maintain realistic good-enough sense (or paranoia) that you always remain reasonable. You're independent-minded and don't mind working by yourself—knowing that the early bird's worm will always be yours.

Famous People Born on This Day

Female

Deirdre Hall, actress
Juliette Gordon Low, Girl Scouts of America founder
Jane Pauley, TV journalist
Barbara Bel Geddes, actress
Dale Evans, actress

Male

Dan Rather, news anchorman
Ad-Rock, musician
Michael Landon, actor
Rob Schneider, actor
John Keats, poet

November

November 1

Lighten up and stop being so serious, will you? Must you always have things your way? Most of you do—not only do you know the insider tricks, you're smart enough to not share them unless you're paid handsomely. A thinker, you are not exactly overconfident, but you are loyal, a real problem solver in business, and respectful of family and things traditional.

As a teacher, scientist, or analyst, or when dealing with facts and figures, you usually excel, but you should get into more roles that call for people skills. Whatever you do, you do it in your own recognizable style, and some of you look so good in black. In your free time, explore the big city where there's big money.

Love

You're not easily impressed, always quizzing others like a caffeine-crazed attorney. So, you either need a lover who can comfortably turn a deaf ear to your hot air queries, or a partner who simply goes about his or her own merry way. 11/1-born are dreamers and brooders—they just can't help worrying that something isn't just so. However, after all the Q&A, and once committed, you remain a loyal and very devoted companion.

Money

You deal with responsibilities fairly well, although following a rigid schedule or working with numbers is challenging to you. Nonetheless, you comply—always analyzing your strengths and shortcomings, and always alert about positively transforming any weaknesses so that they can never inhibit your income. Although it's easy for you to get caught up in daydream fantasies about money, you take one slow, steady step at a time on the job.

Famous People Born on This Day

Female
Barbara Bosson, actress
Betsy Palmer, actress
Jenny McCarthy, TV personality
LaTavia Roberson, singer
Kim Krizan, writer

Male
Lyle Lovett, singer
James J. Kilpatrick, columnist
Robert N. Rapoport, social anthropologist
Robert Foxworth, actor
Stephen Crane, novelist

November 2

The high-wire act that many of you perform is very admirable, but you had it all figured out so there isn't as much risk as it seems. You're one of those "blessed" birthdays, always knocking on success' door, proud of your family and children, ready to blaze your own trail, usually puncture-proof and a bit high-handed—remember what happened to Marie Antoinette? When motivated, you're a whiz in business, so very industrious and down-to-earth, almost always able to put the puzzle pieces together like magic.

A cool customer, many of you become capable administrators and judges, always sharp-eyed and keen, sometimes showing your biting wit. Your soul has been around the block; the occult and hidden mysteries may interest you as something more than parlor games. Visits to ancient lands and the pyramids would be worthwhile.

Love

Idealistic and always cautious, you enter relationships believing that every-thing will work out fine, regardless of one another's past. Forward-thinking, progressive-minded lovers stimulate you the most; old-fashioned types who live-in-the-past drive you batty! Your suspicious, imaginative nature doesn't accept anyone or anything on blind faith. You never settle for mediocre or second-best.

Money

You never let anything get in the way of getting your work-mission accom-plished by the end of a day, and enjoy solo employment over teamwork. In order to be happy on the job, you need to demonstrate your imagination and not be bothered by details, facts, or figures. You are not interested in public recognition (although you enjoy applause and acknowledgement, like everyone else), preferring the satisfaction of financial security over status.

Famous People Born on This Day

Female

Shere Hite, author
Ann Rutherford, actress
Marie Antoinette, French queen
k. d. Lang, singer
Stefanie Powers, actress

Male

Burt Lancaster, actor
Daniel Boone, frontiersman
George Boole, mathematician
Patrick Buchanan, politician
Ray Walston, actor

November 3

Busy as a bee, you're in a race to build a better world—hustling to come out on top and smart enough to be several steps ahead of the competition. If not, then you had better get going; you can be a real dynamo once you get a taste of success and its rewards. Expect trouble when the truth leaks out about questionable deals and your romantic wanderlust, but you're always able to rebound and come up with the right words like "I'll make it up to you."

Sports and competition are natural elements for you, so you're usually pleased with your individual results; don't have too much "I" for the team. Prudence and patience are virtues, and roles where you can learn from them are worth taking. Since you can have fun anywhere, life is a vacation.

Love

Always the fantasy fanatic and believer in someone-for-everyone, you leave no possible stone unturned when pursuing an object of affection. Your passion is quickly aroused—always titillated by the teasing, one-on-one seduction, and other games of love, while always keeping the romance "dance" exciting. You have an uncanny ability to size up suitors, and jive best with mature, strong, but uncomplicated partners.

Money

You're a reliable and disciplined employee who works well during emergencies, and everyone admires your ability to keep your head atop your shoulders and finish the job! You love devising game plans and schemes, and attack each of them with precision and vigor. Although strongly opinionated, you always play fair. Because you never let anything get in the way of getting the job done, management and supervising positions suit you well!

Famous People Born on This Day

Female

Anna Wintour, editor
Kate Capshaw, actress
Lulu, singer
Kathy Kinney, actress
Roseanne, actress

Male

Dennis Miller, comedian
Ken Berry, actor
Charles Bronson, actor
Larry Holmes, boxer
Walker Evans, photographer

November 4

Imagination is a wonderful thing, and when your determination and technical abilities are factored in, you're a pretty handy, helpful person to have around. You're self-sufficient, clever, probably take to new things like computers without having to be shown twice. With your natural willpower and credibility, we expect you to meet our expectations and be a good protector of your own position, family, and romance. You're smart enough not to let power trips mess up your near-perfect universe.

Fighting for a cause or being a humanitarian—or revolutionizing your corner of the world—these are roles you'll take pride in since you empathize with all people, knowing that information is essential for growth to happen—we can count on you. For fun, visit and get acquainted with the Old West and whisper to horses.

Love

Your feelings get easily hurt, always a victim of extreme highs and lows. And, once you get interested in a lover, you usually do too much, rather than too little! It's not from lack of judgment—it's just that you're easily confused about when to say "yes" or "no" to a lover. You're not an emotional wimp; you simply aim to please, and everybody likes you for that. Nevertheless, you would do best with a strong, mature, and stable partner.

Money

11/4-born go to great lengths to gain approval on the job and perform every task without much supervision or suggestion. Your opinions are always clear and real, although your healthy ego finds you a bit defensive. Try to invest more time analyzing work details, because you're inclined to overlook the small (but important) stuff. You work in brilliant spurts of enthusiasm that carry through until the job is done—at least to your satisfaction!

Famous People Born on This Day

Female

Loretta Swit, actress
Doris Roberts, actress
Courtenay E. Benson, broadcaster
Darla Hood, actress
Markie Post, actress

Male

Ralph Macchio, actor
Martin Balsam, actor
Art Carney, comedian
Walter Cronkite, newsman
Will Rogers, entertainer

November 5

Airy and uncomplicated, who can't like you—a shiny personality, though life is not so simple. You'll be the friendly, casual diplomat, willing to share and cooperate, perhaps not watching that some of your human connections are not the best, even unscrupulous, but not you. Usually, your mate is very close to your heart, and you've made a good choice—two heads are better than one. When it comes to wheeling and dealing, you usually come out on top.

Knowing what things are worth, you could sit in the bank president's chair, but your personal commitments come before money. Roles where you help people appeal to you, and your own desires are secondary—usually. A ranch with plenty of animals would make you happy; you'll keep that perfect lifestyle dream alive until you've made it a reality.

Love

You have a terrific, rich fantasy mind and are a devoted partner—after all, once committed to a relationship, 11/5-born rarely mess around. You don't like being overlooked or considered unimportant. You are attracted to active, non-clingy, independent lovers with whom you can enjoy spontaneous intimate activity without interfering with each other's duties. You project an image of masterful courtesy and reserve, coupled with charisma.

Money

Authority figures respect you as a competent employee who is never afraid to roll up your sleeves and pitch in when the going gets tough. Social work, welfare programs, rehabilitation therapy, and helping others suit you well, provided that the stimulation is more mental rather than routine or physical. But try not be such a fuss-budget, always worrying about personal savings—treat yourself to something nice after a hard day's work!

Famous People Born on This Day

Female

Irene Dunne, actress
Elke Sommers, actress
Vivien Leigh, actress
Tatum O'Neal, actress
Patricia K. Kuhl, scientist

Male

Art Garfunkel, singer
Roy Rogers, actor
Bryan Adams, singer
Joel McCrea, actor
Eugene V. Debs, labor organizer

November 6

A structured, "mother-may-I" environment is not for some-one so debonair and trendy as you. Most born today are so attractive, showing your tasteful side, flashing your eyes, your talent flowing freely. You are a people-person who thinks nothing of sacrificing to help others in need, and trusts that you will be taken care of, usually attracting a happy mate who handles the messy business, like bills, leaving you free to pursue your career, life's pleasures, even the interesting occult.

Music—with singing and dancing—may be a part-time role, or even a career, since you love being human and love love. Surrounding yourself with other talented people is pleasing, of course, and many of you are asked to be the "front person" or teacher, taking others under your precious wing. For relaxation, visit the countryside often.

Love

It's easy for you to get swept away by flirtation or fantasy, because you live for the moment or the future instead of right now, and tend to overlook obligations and responsibilities. Because you're always in a rush to get happy, it's a good idea for you to take more time during courtship, and constantly redefine relationships. Although you give the impression that you're strong and independent, your skin is thinner than others would believe.

Money

You aren't afraid of hard work, as long as your efforts are appreciated. But be careful of biting off more than you can chew or is necessary, because you are inclined to take on others' duties and responsibilities without much thought. Just learn your job description, understand coworkers' responsibilities, and then go on your merry way, or improvise. Spending money, rather than saving, comes easy. Although not extravagant, maintaining a budget is borrrring to you!

Famous People Born on This Day

Female

Sally Field, actress
Rebecca Romijn-Stamos, actress
Maria Shriver, newscaster
Lori Singer, actress
Lisa Fuller, actress

Male

Ethan Hawke, actor
Charles Dow, Dow Jones co-founder
James Naismith, basketball inventor
John Philip Sousa, composer
Adolphe Sax, saxophone inventor

November 7

Passionate and determined, you can be the one with the ulterior motive, a romantic plan, and a secret life. As a child, you probably learned to appreciate the art of persuasion, and still may be superstitious and illogical, your imaginative mind getting you into trouble. Vices and gambling are not for you, but crusades and causes are since they fit your revolutionary spirit. You can feel so immersed! To friends you are faithful, as to yourself.

Ancient wisdom seems so cool, so travels to holy places would interest you, as would knowing the secrets of life, or a trade. Getting over your fears means not being so shy, and you'll find that you have a way with people, able to inspire or add hope. For yourself, you believe that meditation helps, but water is your healing element.

Love

You're precise and picky about romance—cautiously evaluating every nuance, as well as suitor. The least complicated the lover, the better for you. 11/7-born have a specific set of "rules" before getting personal. For you, being the subtle seducer, rather than a surprised seductee, turns you on. You're not easily impressed, and understand the difference between dubious fantasy and what truly makes you fly.

Money

Because you won't allow yourself to be taken advantage of, you're very wary about fellow employees—always professional and performing what is assigned. Even though you're a good money-manager and budget-watcher, you excel at human interaction, versus facts and figures. Not paranoid or a martyr, you maintain a clear head, and respect coworkers and the work ethic.

Famous People Born on This Day

Female

Joni Mitchell, singer
Marie Curie, scientist
Joan Sutherland, singer
Alexa Canady, neurosurgeon
Lisa Canning, TV hostess

Male

Jeremy and Jason London, twin actors
Al Hirt, trumpeter
Billy Graham, evangelist
Dean Jagger, actor
Christopher Knight, actor

November 8

If love is a game, you can be the ultimate competitor and survivor, flirting and toying, then moving in for the commitment when you feel the chemistry is right. You are a natural actor; although you are basically soft-hearted you are not mousy—more like a lion. Inclined toward the creative arts and entertainment, do not "be" caught up in your role and miss out somewhat on deeper personal experiences. Where others see ink blots, you see angels, lambies, roadkill, or something descriptive.

Being more down-to-earth would probably not be too fun, so you often turn your life roles into games, sometimes profitably. Others are surprised to find that there is more to likeable you than they thought—there's talent and a chance-taker. You enjoy dressing for the part. For fun, take a riverboat cruise or see the South.

Love

Your engaging understanding of human nature and social situations attracts many friends and lovers. Optimistic about unions, you always try to give others the benefit of the doubt. It's easy for 11/8-born to turn around potentially explosive situations with your clever tongue. However, it's also quite easy for you to get blinded by the light of others' good intentions or white lies. Never a doubting-type, it's a good idea to test romantic waters before plunging headfirst or without thinking!

Money

Following a strict routine and schedule comes easy for you. Although sensitive, sympathetic and considerate of coworkers, you mind your own business, and don't discuss personal matters, understanding the difference between employees and intimates. You're not afraid of criticism, nor doubt your multi-talented skills. Your practical nature urges you to pay cash, rather than credit.

Famous People Born on This Day

Female
Roberta Hazard, admiral USN
Margaret Mitchell, novelist
Esther Rolle, actress
Dorothy Day, humanitarian

Male
Jack Osbourne, TV celebrity
Christiaan Barnard, surgeon
Joe Flynn, actor
Morley Safer, newsman
Leif Garrett, singer

November 9

Regal and ambitious, sometimes you can be too smart, too trusting, and too cute. But we like that and how you naturally assume control, or try to, and come across "big." Sometimes you rise to fame but holding a fortune may be a tough chore even for someone so courageous, sweet, and independent! Go out and get it, you think to yourself; don't let jealousy or bias stop you. No one needs to do your thinking for you! Reach for the stars and guard your precious, passionate heart.

Having a skill and a purpose benefits you, so higher-education does help and also a little luck; look beyond friends and lovers for that—understand what's inside you first. Roles where you can show your excellent people skills helps. For kicks, boot a bad habit, or visit tropical islands.

Love

You monitor your feelings, and are always alert and gracious about others' needs. More compassionate than cautious about another's responsibilities in one-on-one relationships, you are kind even when others disappoint. You're reasonably open-minded and rational about others' shortcomings, as long as they're sincere and honest. However, 11/9-born invented denial, and quickly turn a passive cheek whenever situations turn confrontational.

Money

Your clever curiosity is always on the lookout for new and better ways to turn a profit—that is, provided you don't have to invest a lot of time! Patience isn't your strength; you're better at doing on-the-job duties off-the-cuff rather than by-the-books. You give coworkers the benefit of the doubt, but don't work well in teams. Don't be so full of yourself that you overlook expert assistance or guidance.

Famous People Born on This Day

Female

Florence Sabin, scientist
Hedy Lamarr, actress
Mary Travers, singer
Dorothy Dandridge, actress
Anne Sexton, poet

Male

Nick Lachey, singer
Lou Ferrigno, body builder
Carl Sagan, astronomer
Tom Fogerty, rocker
Lewis Lewin, toxicologist

November 10

Some say that a birthday today can be tough to handle—more troubles and challenges seem to come your way—but if anyone can avoid disaster it's you, though you have to try to avoid it. Generating sparks, all of you have loving hearts, even if misunderstood by others who simply cannot see inside. You have control, you're perceptive, and with the right attitude, you endure and succeed, but there will be fire along the way.

Impatience is not a virtue; you could be a better time manager and more cooperative when you are focused, so a healthy, less-chaotic environment will let your sunshine through, and get you away from the fight-or-flight feeling. You will do quite a bit of moving and traveling, eventually finding a perfect niche, admired as a sweetheart of a human being.

Love

11/10-born are old-fashioned, fairly conservative types, who don't clutter their lives with erratic, emotional people. You give lovers lots of leeway to prove their loyalty, but know when enough is enough! Because you have exact expectations about (what you think should be) one another's contribution to a relationship, it's a good idea to develop better observational and listening skills—simply because you need someone strong enough to do things on their own rather than an attractive suitor who is overly dependent.

Money

Menial tasks repel you; 11/10s are perfectionists, and only content when doing their personal best. You consider every option slowly, and are motivated to excel and be successful. You're straightforward and determined, but rarely egocentric—you don't need to be adored, admired (only paid well). Although not inclined to seek approval, supervisors recognize your positive strengths. You are comfortable doing more than the job requires provided that it sets a good example for subordinates, or will beat the competition.

Famous People Born on This Day

Female
Mabel Normand, actress
Donna Fargo, singer
Mackenzie Philips, actress
Jane Froman, singer
Ann Reinking, actress

Male
Richard Burton, actor
Martin Luther, religious reformer
Roy Scheider, actor
Claude Rains, actor
Tim Rice, lyricist

November 11

When you enter the room, everyone knows you're there—you simply cannot be ignored, ready to take control if you have to. You are daring, smart, even cunning, and still down-to-earth—often landing you in responsible, decision-making positions. A favorable birthdate for social advancement, you are more a thinker than a talker, but when you talk, your words have authority. You'd benefit from not being harsh and inflexible—others should instead see you as well-heeled, educated, and worthy of respect.

To say that sex is not important to you would not be true; you have been known to have "affairs" now and then—maybe just to show you have that old magic. Saturday night on the town, Sunday in church. For vacations, you prefer to travel by land, perhaps meeting that special someone for another romantic fling.

Love

One of 11/11-born's biggest romantic handicaps is an unwillingness to let go of the past. Develop a more be-here-now outlook about love, and don't set yourself up for disappointment because of what-used-to-be—chances are, you're harder on yourself than loved ones. And, don't expect partners to read your mind. Explain your needs, define your desires, and reconstruct what needs changing. After all, you always (try to) play fair!

Money

Your fellow employees acknowledge your generosity and expertise, and willingness to explore options. However, balancing financial records, or understanding economics is quite challenging for you. You quickly give others the benefit of the doubt and are a valuable team player—provided that undeserving or lazy coworkers don't expect you to do their job. The achievement of objectives makes your day!

Famous People Born on This Day

Female

Abigail Adams, U.S. First Lady
Daisy Bates, activist
Ernestine Anderson, singer
Demi Moore, actress
Barbara Boxer, senator

Male

Leonardo DiCaprio, actor
Jonathan Winters, comedian
Kurt Vonnegut, Jr., writer
George Patton, U.S. military man
Pat O'Brien, actor

November 12

Are you trapped, feeling that you're not going anywhere, maybe in a low-end job? It is too easy to settle for less— what you need is more fire—a controlled burn—and to get in the game and play to your strengths! Put the past behind you and chase the future—envision your place in large organizations like unions, corporations, or government, but not in social situations where the wolves howl. Still, don't be part of the herd—your daring determination and love could go to waste.

Emotionally like a bull in a china closet, maybe you are a little awkward, but you should fix that, not fight it. Roles that include responsibility for animals or to promote the common good are perfect; your artistic flair needs to be expressed, fired-up by the exciting sights as you travel.

Love

11/12-born are willing to please, always ready to explore, but don't handle rejection well. You gingerly canoe through relationship waters, and are never impulsive when the subject is "romance." You are compassionate, yet always practical, when expressing desires and defining your needs, and are well-suited for mature, honest and loyal partners. Although you willingly pull more than your share, you're a bit timid to ask for help, or when talk turns into debate.

Money

You have a knack for doing the right thing at the right time, and being in the best of any place when opportunity starts scratching at your door. Always punctual (at least, you try to be), "time" is "money" to you. A good bargain shopper, you compare prices to value and weigh options—never living by an "easy come, easy go" attitude about finances. Even after obtaining one monetary goal, you quickly plot and eagerly attack a new game plan for the next!

Famous People Born on This Day

Female
Elizabeth Cady Stanton, activist
Nadia Comaneci, Olympic gymnast
Grace Kelly, actress
Kim Hunter, actress
Jo Stafford, singer

Male
David Schwimmer, actor
Neil Young, rocker
Al Michaels, sports commentator
Auguste Rodin, sculptor
Sammy Sosa, baseball player

November 13

At your best with family, neighbors, and in harmony with nature, you love to talk, so how can someone so enterprising, liberated, seeming so intellectual and gracious be such a heartbreaker, or have your own heart and hopes dashed? You definitely have feelings but remember: not everything is going to work out as you see it in your mind's eye. Make reasonable efforts to see things honestly from the start. For your growth and prosperity, first acquire the tools for success.

Some say it's somewhat easy to take advantage of you. Schmooze you with the right words, you melt. Get your dander up, you'll fight. Always look for the ulterior motives and be value conscious. Responsibility roles with money are good practice—always have more coming in than going out. Get someone else to pay for your vacations.

Love

You tend to form romances with individuals who need you more than you need them. Don't fall into the trap where you think you have to be responsible for your partner's weaknesses or silliness. Be wary of lovers who exploit, take advantage of you, because many consider you an easy target. Maintain integrity, but keep your eyes open, and your personal planner closed tight! Nonchalance and martyrdom don't suit you.

Money

Once you understand work obligations, you complete the task quickly. However, your tendency to overlook details or be too accommodating creates problems. Give attention to your responsibilities and the little things before going beyond the call of duty. You understand how to budget others' finances, but aren't so good about your own. You run the risk of financial struggle or debt until you understand how to discipline yourself, slow down and read all fine print.

Famous People Born on This Day

Female

Hermione Badderley, actress
Whoopi Goldberg, comedienne/
    actress
Jean Seberg, actress
Linda Christian, actress
Joan Haanappel, figure skater

Male

Joe Mantegna, actor
Robert Louis Stevenson, author
Oskar Werner, actor
Garry Marshall, producer
Christopher Noth, actor

November 14

Many born today are in well-to-do families, a big plus that not all of you have, but you do have the benefit of good health, a friendly personality, and usually acquire your own wealth and status, but holding on to it may not be easy. You're a smart cookie, a quick learner—not that you need to go to school except to make connections and fit in with the upper-crust crowd and the gym squad. You are industrious and a mover-and-shaker when not consumed by fun and lust.

Your mind is a step ahead, sometimes stepping off the deep end, but you're a good swimmer. You need a dynamo for a partner, not just eye candy. You're pretty mellow for almost any role, though sports are a good way to vent and strengthen your will and body.

Love

You have an intuitive understanding about time, and (sort of) remember birthdays and anniversaries, even though you may get the date wrong. You're honest, candid, and never shy away from getting to know someone new. However, lovers are often put off by your bluntness, because you state your personal case—likes, dislikes—so fervently and fast! Try to learn to go with the casual flow of the moment, and give others a chance to breathe. You don't fear intimacy—you simply have a long laundry list of needs that you always feel need immediate attention. Your lover should be self-secure and calm, because you're so determined, volatile, persuasive, and dynamic.

Money

You really try hard not to let others sidetrack you from a project-at-hand, but you have a tendency to let impatience get the best of you. And while you're at it, aim to get a better grip over sarcasm and your temper! Although you're a positive individual—more eccentric than egocentric—you have a tendency to ignore the needs of others.

Famous People Born on This Day

Female

Claudia Archibald, parapsychologist
Clara Fasano, sculptor
Veronica Lake, actress
Rosemary DeCamp, actress
Phyllis Avery, actress

Male

Yanni, musician
Aaron Copland, composer
Brian Keith, actor
Claude Monet, painter
Robert Fulton, steamboat inventor

November 15

The good life, the arts, even science or anything that benefits humanity call out to you—answer positively in your highly personal way! Active, appealing, and somewhat fickle, which is your right, you have that provocative sort of heady magnetism that suits you for the world of thoughts, ideas, not the world of alien abductions, though it may feel you may be from another planet. Indeed you are a breed apart, the champion of many good causes.

Answers, you want answers. You're pretty good at making the best of opportunities; your status can grow thanks to marriage or hooking up with the right crowd. Connections count, as does education. Career is unpredictable; you're not versatile but enjoy early success. Getting in touch with the common people and cultures is joy.

Love

Even though you're never without companionship for very long or hesitant to stand up for your rights, 11/15-born hate criticism and confrontation. Because you're more of a follower than leader, you usually attract partners who are bossy or very self-important, when all you really desire is compassion and honesty. You're not self-destructive or weak-willed, but should try to develop more self-confidence and practical understanding about relationships!

Money

Because you tend to underestimate your capabilities, you're easily intimidated by strangers and can be taken advantage of without even seeing it. You try very hard to please coworkers, and must remember that it's impossible to be liked by everyone. It's one thing to be accommodating, but being a doormat probably isn't in your job description! Even though you're always willing to lend a helping hand, you rarely lend money.

Famous People Born on This Day

Female

Georgia O'Keeffe, artist
Petula Clark, singer
Zena Grey, actress
Anni-Frid Lyngstad, singer
Joanna Barnes, actress

Male

Sam Waterston, actor
Ed Asner, actor
Joseph Wapner, TV judge
John Banvard, painter
Felix Frankfurter, Supreme Court Justice

November 16

Alive with feelings and emotions, you can be the intuitive type—well, actually, you may only think you're intuitive, but a good guesser nonetheless. You can flow along through life, following your credo, steering clear of trouble—you're adaptable, easygoing, and like a psychic sponge, searching for the power within your soul, watching for karmic reactions, sometimes being a bit touchy, but we won't go into that. Hardships and unhealthy environments are not for you since negatives can dissolve away your long-term vitality.

So many of you are found in essential life-and-death, sink-or-swim roles, administering aid to the ill, injured, or family members; even your well-chosen words are soothing. Life has rhythm and you're attuned to it, or should be. To lighten your load, you need long, relaxing vacations, beaches and warm breezes, and watch your weight.

Love

You shower your object of affection with attention, and always intend to be a caring partner and friend. Relationships flow with ease and in a mellow tempo, never letting anger or intense emotions run amok. However, your 11/16-suspicious nature fears obligation and entrapment, usually prompting you to hit the road and run away when unions show signs of confinement.

Money

You're competent and precise with job responsibilities—never tardy or blaming. Many admire your steel-trap thinking and marvel at your ability to see both sides of a situation, to abstract emotion and balance your conclusions. Employers never think that you don't try hard, so you tend to overdo or go out of your way for approval. Biting off more than is necessary only hurts you, not anybody else. Do what's expected of you, first; then lend your willing helping hand—but not your money!

Famous People Born on This Day

Female

Alice Adams, sculptor
Oksana Baiul, Olympic figure skater
Lisa Bonet, actress
Martha Plimpton, actress
Elizabeth Drew, journalist

Male

Guy Stockwell, actor
Daws Butler, actor
Clinton Golden, United Steelworkers
    of America founder
Burgess Meredith, actor

November 17

So good at "going with the flow," sometimes we don't notice that you're steering the ship, sometimes into the teeth of another of life's storms, not always encouraging us with observations like "Lifeboats?! We don't need lifeboats." You shun the limelight and idle adulation—you're a private, sensitive person, in touch with your "self" and your karma, which can get rugged up now and again, so you summon up courage, never selling out, fair to all, beating the odds, sacrificing to help those who need it.

Knowing that your soul is in touch with the essences of life, you can be mellow and over-emotional. Your influential parents helped you, though your own offspring may get off track or grow apart. Leave room for roles where you can help heal your family. For offbeat fun, learn to fly airplanes.

Love

Lovers adore you because you rarely challenge their ideals or intentions (key word being rarely, not never). You have a lucid awareness of what's essential for a relationship to work and clearly define and relate them to a partner. Even though you're not an aggressive type, it's a good idea to let others do the driving every now and then and explain their two cents' worth of intention. Alert and verbal lovers suit you best; overly passive, silent types get you comatose on the get-go.

Money

You learn quickly and keenly but tend to overdo, overreact, or expect too much from yourself and coworkers. It's hard for you to relax when projects need attention or deadlines loom. Compromise and slo-mo tempos aren't your strengths, even though you always try to maintain your cool. A diligent and hard-working employee, you always aim for victory and to get the job done well.

Famous People Born on This Day

Female

Grace Abbott, social worker
Winson Hudson, activist
Lauren Hutton, actress
Libby Newman, painter
Daisy Fuentes, actress

Male

Danny DeVito, actor
Lorne Michaels, producer
Gordon Lightfoot, songwriter
Isaac Hanson, rocker
Martin Scorsese, director

November 18

Easily charged-up at the mention of something provocative, you are a live wire, and thank goodness you seem to have it under control. You are more cultured than most and appreciate values, history, achievements, and celebrity—you're also optimistic, well-read and probably well-educated, sincere, and often asked into cooperative ventures and adventures, sometimes developing your own career, seeing yourself as powerful, which you are. Public recognition may be in your future. You are already public-spirited.

Strong, subtle, and domineering when necessary, you're not afraid of challenging roles since you have political and other ambitions. Organize the library—no problem. Run for office—what fun! Meet a foreign leader—naturally. Raise a million for charity—what's your cut? Do housework—not! Take a group of select friends on a European holiday—or just throw a wild party.

Love

Your straightforward manner of expression quickly informs lovers where they stand with you. Opinionated and secure about your needs, you don't run away from debate, and partners rarely consider you antagonistic. You simply know what makes you happy, and likewise what drives you crazy. Although you consider yourself open-minded, your need for schedule and routine tends to inhibit spur-of-the-moment fun because your mind is always thinking about tomorrow or planning ahead.

Money

Although never lazy or accusatory, you hate being challenged because you believe that your way is best. You're not a know-it-all, simply an individual who has specific personal wants and nots. You read all contracts clearly, honor obligations, and always aim for punctuality. Although you are curious about the private lives of coworkers, you demand that they respect your privacy. You are a wise counselor and give candid, considered opinions.

Famous People Born on This Day

Female
Dorothy Dix, journalist
Dorothy Collins, singer
Margaret Atwood, author
June Havoc, actress
Brenda Vaccaro, actress

Male
Alan Shepard, Jr., astronaut
Eugene Ormandy, conductor
Kevin Nealon, actor
Johnny Mercer, lyricist
George Gallup, opinion pollster

November 19

Full of fun, noble ideas, and good graces, there has to be some deeper meaning to life, so you're into religion or a worthy cause, not willing to be told what to do unless it comes from the top, your ambitious eye looking for a fitting, respectable place where you'll call the shots. Others may not exactly understand where you're coming from but they'll catch on. You feel destined for good things so you rarely break a promise or miss your mark.

You can be the star also a calculating force behind the scenes—the fire plus the savoir-faire—the know-how. Roles where you champion for the good of the people or try a unique approach suit you. Once you decide, your mind is fixed. With so much intensity, take breaks to rest often, and fix your hair.

Love

It's imperative that you keep open all lines of communication with your lover all the time, because of your obsession with "your" time schedule, "your" daily details, and "your" must-do needs. You can't help nitpicking over trifles, worrying over small stuff and constantly re-examining everybody's agenda that is either not in your control nor yours to begin with. On the positive side, you're always considerate about others' feelings, try to make things better, and have difficulty telling a lie (although you're masterful at spinning convincingly gentle untruths).

Money

You always aim to do good work, try to keep a positive attitude, and rarely fly off the handle at coworkers—usually choosing cooperation and being concise, over chaos. Because you're . . . um, a bit eccentric, it's hard for you to understand philosophical and conventional concepts. Nonetheless, you work well with others, but would rather lead (but not be the Big Shot) than follow. You have an insatiable appetite for activity and always aim to keep things peaceful.

Famous People Born on This Day

Female	Male
Jeane Kirkpatrick, political scientist	Ted Turner, media mogul
Indira Gandhi, India prime minister	Dick Cavett, TV talk show host
Jodie Foster, actress	Calvin Klein, fashion designer
Meg Ryan, actress	Larry King, talk show host
Kerri Strug, Olympic gymnast	Tommy Dorsey, big band leader

November 20

Impulsive, front-running, and sometimes antagonistic and usually opinionated, not everyone trusts you, but someone as creative, bright, good-looking, and sporty as you may not need to please everyone—you should have plenty of friends and connections already. Cleverly leaving the hard work and details to others is better, so your repertoire includes schmoozing superiors and insider tricks, all of which others may resent; that can hold back your growth.

Family ties are helpful stepping stones to success; you really don't take a shine to outsiders, instead putting much of your energy into just being who you want to be. Roles where you crusade for a good cause widen your horizons, though you're the type to go to court to fight a parking ticket. Attending parties lets you shine; keeping those close family ties strengthens you.

Love

For 11/20-born, love affairs are usually quizzical tests or endless mysteries that you feel you must solve—because otherwise nobody will get any rest! (Why is it that you always seem to be busier or more bothered with everyone else's needs, rather than your own?) Demanding data about a partner's history is smart and real, but living in a relationship fueled only by doubt won't nourish anyone. Never forget that you're an essential component in the "takes-two-to-tango" scenario!

Money

Being a restless, inquisitive, curious type, you're always on the lookout for more effective ways to make a buck and turn a profit. Your work-history may be varied and sporadic, but no one can ever call you lazy or uncreative! Although you have good people skills, you have little patience for lazy, sloppy coworkers. You never give up when there are opportunities for a bill to get paid, a bargain to buy, or a lovely new light at the end of a credit card tunnel.

Famous People Born on This Day

Female

Judy Woodruff, news analyst
Bo Derek, actress
Sean Young, actress
Veronica Hamel, actress
Kaye Ballard, actress

Male

Mike D, singer
Dick Smothers, comedian
Robert F. Kennedy, U.S. Attorney
     General
Alistair Cooke, TV host
Richard Dawson, TV game show host

November 21

Blessed with plenty of personality and pristine perkiness, you're usually at the head of the line, unsinkable and ready to go, a bit of a hero and a devil. Maybe you are mentally superior—you can walk the walk and talk the talk and manage your way upward, avoiding the troublemakers, your calculated enthusiasm making it hard for others to react negatively. You're not the innocent type—you'd make a good spy/confidant. Some of your antics are worthy of James Bond.

Many of you are attracted to the adventure and intrigues of the military life or hear the higher calling of religious or philosophical roles since you're persuasive. You love to travel and quickly pick up foreign tongues because you hate not knowing what's going on. For fun, explore forbidden zones and religious places, and hide behind sunglasses.

Love

Not one to believe that first impressions are necessarily correct, your terrific fantasy mind is attracted more to what lies beneath the surface appearance, rather than what you see or hear. A lover's background is rarely as interesting as your imaginative scenario. Unfortunately, your well-intended optimism often creates misunderstanding, misjudging, and misinterpreting prospective lovers. Learn to be a little less suspicious in matters of the heart.

Money

Although gregarious and friendly, you tend to become quickly commanding when placed in positions of power. You're not afraid of responsibility—after all, you live for bottom lines and end-results! But as an intuitive employee, you're not too keen about budgets and financial projection. Although it's difficult for you to balance a bank account, you rarely owe anybody much of anything.

Famous People Born on This Day

Female

Marlo Thomas, actress
Goldie Hawn, actress
Henrietta (Hetty) Green, financier
Bjork, singer
Juliet Mills, actress

Male

René Magritte, surrealistic artist
Voltaire, philosopher
William Beaumont, surgeon
Ken Griffey, Jr., baseball player
Harold Ramis, director

November 22

Do you hear the good life calling you? It's saying enjoy me, buy me, I'll pamper and thrill you! So many of you will enjoy a better lifestyle, go to the best schools, dress for the best parts, filling your house with treasures, love, and conversation, then bursting out on the world in search of adventure, testing life's fast lane, always making snap decisions, staying free, usually with the companionship of someone as interesting as they are attractive. Just don't be careless—injuries will result.

Life should be light-hearted but you've learned that often it isn't. You need more roles where you uplift others and show your productive, artistic side—and your natural style, since others see you as a role model. Vacations can be long and frequent, or should be, and far from work and worries.

Love

Because you're not too good at second-guessing anybody, or reading between any of those boy-and-girl lines, you require a straightforward and straight-thinking partner who tells it as it is, warts and all. You always try to be precisely to the point about your feelings, and what you expect from a relationship right from the start. 11/22-born need to be entertained, they love attending social events, and like people from many walks of life but quickly grow bored.

Money

No one considers you a penny-pincher, even though you respect everything that money buys—you simply don't spend anything extra, period! You tend to your on-the-job responsibilities efficiently, thrive on improvisation, and cope with things as they come. You're not too bad with facts and figures, are a good bargain shopper, and don't spend money foolishly. You're intelligent, curious, and practical to a fault.

Famous People Born on This Day

Female

George Eliot, novelist
Billie Jean King, tennis player
Mariel Hemingway, actress
Jamie Lee Curtis, actress
Geraldine Page, actress

Male

Charles DeGaulle, French president
Hoagy Carmichael, actor
Wiley Post, aviator
Rodney Dangerfield, comedian
Stephen Geoffreys, actor

November 23

Dull moments are history when you're around, and we wonder what you're up to since you're hard to predict. One moment you can be the practical visionary, artist, or lover, then the next you'll be a rascal, mixing it up in rough-and-tumble fashion, saying and doing contradictory things—it's hard to take you seriously, which you would dearly like. You'll take chances in romances and marriages, trying to find Mr./Mrs. Right.

Parties and social life are awaiting you, and your warming smile can cut the chilliest chill, though not everyone warms up to you right away. A bit of a risktaker, you can stir the pot and test emotions, though you should be sharpening your image, not chumming along. You need to get unmuddled, so quiet vacations are best if the silence isn't unbearable.

Love

Although a child at heart, you respond best to mature, down-to-earth lovers. You have no time for superficial people, preferring those whose lives have purpose and direction. Your way with lovers is charming and delightfully real—with the emphasis on the word "real." 11/23-born roll with the punches and rarely hold a grudge for long. Communication and compassion rank high in regard to what makes for a good partner.

Money

You have good reasoning ability, know when to make concessions concerning your cash flow, and are comfortable in the role as mediator. You respond to people honestly, and your enthusiasm stimulates them to respond in kind. Always conservative with personal investments, you have a healthy respect for time and material things, and have no difficulty putting aside for rainy days or planning future financial investments.

Famous People Born on This Day

Female
Rita Rossi Colwell, oceanographer
Ellen Drew, actress
Salli Richardson, actress
Susan Anspach, actress
Nadia Gray, actress

Male
Boris Karloff, actor
Robert Towne, producer
Bruce Hornsby, singer
Harpo Marx, actor
Jerry Bock, composer

November 24

Many born today are pilots; you love the speed, the travel, and responsibly manage the job no matter what it is you do. When not required to be serious and powerful, you let your hair down and can be quite charming. Sentimental and a bit possessive, you love family life. You're also a bit psychic, and your estimations are usually right on. In the habit of controlling situations, you seldom abuse or take advantage of others—it'd break their hearts.

If you concentrated more on moving up in your career, you'd probably soon be a millionaire, but you're too busy being sidetracked by your various interests, including romance. You're also very tight in your beliefs; you'd benefit from roles where you see things from the other side, too. A good book and warm fire are very relaxing.

Love

11/24-born hate arguing and will do almost anything to maintain peace and not make waves. You need a romantic partner who talks candidly yet kindly from the heart, treats others as equals, and confides freely in you. Even if your lover isn't financially savvy, your understanding and compassionate nature is complemented by sincere partners with down-to-earth hopes and lucid dreams.

Money

Like a therapist or writer, you have a keen ability for evaluating situations and discover efficient methods for transforming problems into profits. You are fair and easy-going with coworkers, and rarely overreact to disappointment or setback. Because of your curious nature, you're always well informed and never at a loss for words. Your open-minded ambiance encourages fellow employees because you inspire, don't intimidate.

Famous People Born on This Day

Female
Geraldine Fitzgerald, actress
Lilli Lehmann, singer
Frances Burnett, novelist
Katherine Heigl, actress
Chen Lu, Olympic figure skater

Male
Dale Carnegie, author
Bram Stoker, author
Scott Joplin, composer
Howard Duff, actor

November 25

When it comes to achievement, we can count on you to rise to the occasion. With your sensitivity and vision—always looking for solutions—so many of you become wizards in business, and with your knack for fun, physical activity, and your loyal nature, being around you is a pleasure. It is no wonder so many of you enjoy success, marriage, and a large family. But you have weak moments, too, when you over-react and impulse takes over—the moon's position may have a lot to do with this.

Everyone likes travel, excitement, and entertainment, but these things mean more to you especially when you partic-ipate. You are practical, and roles where you communicate, teach, mold, and design are good for your heart. Inactivity isn't allowed so you usually stay physically fit. It's upstairs we wonder about.

Love

Nope, it's not that you're self-indulgent, but there's a huge "eat, drink, and be merry" part of your makeup that needs constant supervising—like many fun-loving 11/25-born, you tend to do everything in excess. Learn to temper your enthusiasm with new friends and lovers; don't come on too strong, smother, or overwhelm. You enjoy spontaneous partners and are always ready for a good laugh and a new experience. Remember: less is more.

Money

Your live-and-let-live attitude influences others but doesn't always win friends of coworkers. You have difficulty accepting responsibility and don't follow orders all that well, either. Not a soft-spoken, silent type, you always say what's on your mind and have a bit of a problem with punctuality. Because you're more enthusiastic than exacting, try listening to others' ideas rather than desperately clinging to your game plan and time schedule.

Famous People Born on This Day

Female

Helen [Gahagan] Douglas, politician
Christina Applegate, actress
Amy Grant, singer
Carry Nation, activist

Male

John F. Kennedy, Jr., publisher
Joe DiMaggio, baseball player
Ricardo Montalban, actor
John Larroquette, actor
Karl F. Benz, auto manufacturer

November 26

Sometimes you'll wake up in the middle of the night, with an idea or an urge, and so your mind goes to work, writing and figuring and churning, sometimes solving the world's problems, sometimes your own. You're also excitable and will push the envelope, but taking every precaution, usually. Others see you as disciplined, cultured, and well-mannered—formal clothes should suit you fine if "casual you" would wear them. Oddly, some of you are cat people, others dog people.

Some of your best work is done in solitude, but that doesn't mean you're lonely. That confident voice inside is always on overtime, plus you're on an intuitive channel that ties you to the universe. Hmm. Roles that involve people and languages suit you. Like most born in November, you do a lot of traveling or wandering.

Love

You're stimulated by nurturing, responsible lovers who enjoy taking care of you. It's not that you're needy or lazy—you simply like as many helping hands as possible at your beck and call, and are put off by partners who don't devote one hundred percent to you. Be careful not to get so caught up in your fantasies or the excitement of courtship that you lose your foothold on terra firma! Stay clear-minded while smiling.

Money

You like every little thing to be the same on the job day after day, and with no emotional surprises. When work goes as expected, you perform every task responsibly and without complaint. Unfortunately, you lose your cool when anything changes and turn testy if anyone questions or challenges you. Even though you're pretty good with personal budgets and bank books, impulsive-buying comes easy!

Famous People Born on This Day

Female

Sarah Grimke, reformer
Sojourner Truth, abolitionist
Francoise Gilot, painter
Elizabeth E. Bailey, university dean
Tina Turner, singer

Male

Robert Goulet, singer
Eric Sevareid, newscaster
Charles Schulz, cartoonist
Rich Little, impressionist actor
Samuel H. Reshevsky, chess grand-master

November 27

Outgoing, confident, and almost as much of an invincible expert as you think you are, we should call you "the energizer" since you have plenty of energy in reserve, also all the verve and nerve you need to keep you pointed toward the top. You are resourceful, and when you're educated and have experience under your belt, you're a perfect partner in business and maybe even in romance—you usually go for the more attractive mates. Wanting independence and to "shine," you won't be hemmed in.

Roles where you are the hunter or sportsperson come naturally to you—that applies to your career: you can be the traveling executive, the agent, perhaps speaking a bit of several languages, or just being on the road, eyeing the horizon, aiming for the stars, and worshipping with your heart.

Love

A bit of a flirt, you run for the romantic gold at every opportunity. Past lovers may consider you too big for your britches—nevertheless, that's their problem, and you quickly set them straight. You're not selfish; you merely know what you want and what a partner has to do in order to make a relationship fully functional. Always remember, a partnership includes two people; give lovers the benefit of the doubt and the right to be themselves.

Money

Coworkers quickly recognize your drive, independent mind, and determination to never give up without a good fight. The truth of the matter is that you're just always hungry for more attention and respect—you're not real competitive, you simply hate losing! Personal profits are invested in health, home and comfort, rather than education. You prefer improvisation and creating new ways of making money, rather than laborious routine.

Famous People Born on This Day

Female

Terri R. Adams, educator
Frances Swem Anderson, scientist
Robin Givens, actress
Caroline Kennedy Schlossberg, attorney
Jayne Kennedy, sportscaster

Male

Bruce Lee, actor
Jimi Hendrix, rocker
Buffalo Bob Smith, TV host
Bill Nye, TV host
James Agee, author

November 28

An expert shopper, there is plenty of material girl—or boy—in you, also strong romantic desires. You love a lot of things—the land, home, soft green grass under your feet, flowers and honey, even the nightlife—whatever you're into, it is full commitment, and winning. A good education helps you win, too. Allured to anything filled with culture, pageantry, and excitement, you have more happiness than you realize, a flair for the dramatic, and won't be interfered with.

Being at the right place at the right time is usually a matter of luck, but you seem to have a knack for finding an "opportunity" and may make a fortune from it, or a name. Another thing to watch is your weight. You're proud of your appearance though it matters more to you than others.

Love

If you really want a relationship to grow, it's a good idea to explore the art of listening. You're not antagonistic or overly defensive, but your stubborn likes and dislikes have a tendency to irritate partners because you always feel that you must have the final word. You're not easily duped, because you're suspicious by nature. Swallow your self-defensive pride, and make time to examine your lover's needs.

Money

You don't give coworkers the impression that you're a pushover or easily manipulated, because you constantly display your personal bite in between your rather loud bark. You're an all-or-nothing employee, and, to you, there is no middle ground. You're more responsible than ruthless, always get the job done, and then move along your way. Managerial positions suit you well, although your people skills may need some tweaking.

Famous People Born on This Day

Female

Helen Kinney Copley, newspaper
    publisher
Phyllis Jenkins, agent
Nancy Mitford, novelist
Anna Nicole Smith, TV celebrity
Scarlett Pomers, child actress

Male

Jon Stewart, comedian
Judd Nelson, actor
Ed Harris, actor
Paul Shaffer, TV band leader
Randy Newman, songwriter

November 29

Win or lose, you're a true optimist, learning from your miscues, reveling in your triumphs, often taking one step forward to two steps back—or is it two steps forward, one step back? A personality heavyweight, your mind looks to the heights, contemplating the meaning of it all, dancing with angels. Concentrate more on the here and now—you'll earn yourself and family a brighter future. Your confidence and composure will bring success; speculation and getting talked out of it are the pitfalls.

Having learned early to play the game of life for keeps, you put a lot of consideration into any roles you take. You'll go with what works, historically, then improve on it. For excitement, you might want to take the controls of an airplane, something fast that will scare the dickens out of you.

Love

Because new experiences are exciting to you, you rarely spend time worrying about what never happened or shed tears over spilled milk issues of the past. 11/29-born are best-suited for lovers with minimum emotional baggage and who are decisive and optimistic about change. It doesn't matter to you whether or not a lover is older or younger—just so long as they are progressive and willing to try new things!

Money

Although realistic about job responsibilities, 11/29s are a bit bossy and don't tolerate incompetence. Employers know they can count on you, but may like you better if you didn't act like such a know-it-all. You expect a lot from yourself as well as from fellow employees. Your effervescent, impulsive nature makes it easy for you to spend money, but your honesty and enthusiasm always keep watch over what is owed to whom!

Famous People Born on This Day

Female

Louisa May Alcott, novelist
Madeleine L'Engle, writer
Cathy Moriarty, actress
Kim Delaney, actress
Ellen Cleghorne, comedienne

Male

Howie Mandel, comedian
John Mayall, musician
Chuck Mangione, jazzman
C. S. Lewis, author
Busby Berkeley, choreographer

November 30

Some days have a history for being more troublesome; it is up to you to make this birthdate run smoothly. Life can be a rollercoaster ride, with peaks and valleys, twists and turns, and the loose change may fly out of your pockets. Agitation can get on your nerves and affect your health, plus you may have learned it's worthwhile to keep an eye on your backside. All the trouble aside, you are a survivor, turning adversity to your benefit, proving the naysayers wrong, leaving you with some real stories to tell.

Because the earth can crumble away under your feet, and ambitions become demons, you should avoid dangerous roles and items—like recklessly talking about things, not handling them. Enough scare tactics—we just want you to stay around for awhile because we like you!

Love

You have common-sense-like intuition and a down-home intellect, easily understanding the hidden meanings of human problems almost before they arise. However, you tend to live a love life second-guessing others, predicting and reacting to their reactions even before they get a chance to speak! 11/30-born are repelled by lovers who lack enthusiasm or live in the past. You wear your iron-clad principles about relationships on your sleeve because you hate to be alone.

Money

Living the good life motivates you to work hard. 11/30-born are not afraid of on-the-job responsibility or the demands of leadership. Coworkers admire your tireless devotion—but do you perform because you like doing good work or because you enjoy applause and recognition? Money-wise, you freely (but not foolishly) spend money on nice things, and usually on yourself or the home.

Famous People Born on This Day

Female

Shirley Chisholm, politician
Virginia Mayo, actress
June Pointer, singer
Kaley Cuoco, child actress
Joan Ganz Cooney, producer

Male

Winston Churchill, English prime
   minister
Mark Twain, author
Dick Clark, TV host
Robert Guillaume, actor
Ridley Scott, director

December

December 1

You're a special number one. First, you're incredibly smart—your mind is like a computer with no shortage of memory. Second, you have an incredible personality—so talkative, persuasive, so natural when you want to be. Third, you're very dedicated once you find a cause, a reason, something special and challenging that someone so fiery and clever can make work that others can't. You've arrived when the big bucks roll in—when all the pieces to the magic puzzle that is your life fall into place.

The normal life just isn't for you—after all, you have that magic intuitiveness. You hate to suffer, to be restricted, and so you exercise your freedom and help others find theirs. The big city, with all its opportunity and variety, is where you ought to be.

Love

"What about me?" is constantly ringing in your head. It's not from lack of self-worth or esteem, mind you—you simply, and honestly, believe that yours is the best way. Unfortunately, that doesn't leave much room for a lover's concerns. You always have a specific gameplan cooking atop every burner, and have a bit of a hard time adapting to any occasional cold water that may stifle the heat. Make sure to give your partner some say-so as well as some loving leeway.

Money

Others' successes inspire you to excel or do better than their accomplishments—12/1-born have an uncanny need for recognition and reward. Although not a cheapskate or clock-watcher, you only get excited with alliances that promise financial gain. You're not prejudiced, nor do you frown on fellow employees in less fortunate positions. It's just that, for you, the Almighty Buck and Numero Uno rule!

Famous People Born on This Day

Female

Mary Martin, actress
Bette Midler, actress
Julie Condra, actress
Emily McLaughlin, actress
Charlene Tilton, actress

Male

Richard Pryor, comedian
Lou Rawls, singer
Woody Allen, actor
Lee Trevino, golfer

December 2

If a ringleader is needed, you are the perfect volunteer. When the serious work needs to be done, you're on top of things. Winning? . . . you will find a way. Noble and perceptive, who wouldn't suspect that you're one step ahead, a trailblazer, physical dynamo and a smart diplomat? Your family admires you—they know what's good for them. As the leader of any group, you're a natural and don't need a uniform to give you authority. You'd rather be a trusted friend.

Many of you fulfill life roles as public servants even though you're a rebel. Structured environments help keep you calm, but you need to keep moving and being involved too, so computers and hi-tech environments let you make breakthroughs quickly. You excel at games, but for a real adventure explore the Old West.

Love

Because you're optimistic and not comfortable about debate, you prefer like-minded lovers who don't place demands on you and know how to take care of themselves. It's not that you are unwilling to help, it's just that you despise co-dependence, and hate being tied down even though you cannot stand to be alone. Nevertheless, friendship is your extra point, and you do your part to keep peace and uphold all relationships.

Money

Never lazy, you devote considerable effort to finding more efficient ways for getting the job done and are inspired in the manner you apply them. But you need to invest a bit more effort in the concept of teamwork. Your fear of not getting your job done because of slow or uninformed coworkers often gives the illusion of aloofness or stubbornness. Although you're well-suited for management and budget your money well, it's a good idea to learn when to ask for help or lend a hand.

Famous People Born on This Day

Female

Monica Seles, tennis star
Julie Harris, actress
Britney Spears, singer
Lucy Liu, actress

Male

Stone Phillips, news host
Charles Ringling, circus promoter
Georges Seurat, painter
Michael McDonald, singer
Ric Felix, rocker

December 3

Why can't we all just get along? We can, it's just figuring out the right way. Remember that we are not all equal, and others have their own lives to live, too. Though a lot of things can set you off, it's not all your doing, of course. People born today do have more challenges than normal—and more "good" is expected from you, including more patience and sharing, and self-understanding of what makes you tick.

With cartloads of karma to work out, you will make a lot of adjustments and perform a lot of different roles in your lifetime. That will include romances, which cannot be possessed, just enjoyed. Emotions are powerful things, but not an excuse—learn not to let yours work against you, especially when you're supposed to be enjoying leisure times and love.

Love

12/3-born don't quite get the concept of unconditional love and tend to be impatient with laid-back, unfocused partners. You don't offer yourself to a lover, friend or family casually, at least not without an attached string or two. Although honest and patient, you expect a 50-50 split in responsibilities. You are an idealist, but a practical one, and won't make an emotional commitment unless there is solid evidence that the feeling is mutual.

Money

Having a co-worker or boss breathing down your neck keeps you from doing your best. Working on a team performing routine tasks or waiting for others stifles and bores you silly. It's not that you're uncooperative or arrogant— you're simply being efficient. You meet deadlines punctually and cleverly. Entrepreneuring venues with few employees suit you best. Unfortunately, you tend to spend money like a drunken lottery winner!

Famous People Born on This Day

Female

Ellen Swallow Richard, scientist
Anna Chlumsky, actress
Holly Marie Combs, actress
Daryl Hannah, actress
Julianne Moore, actress

Male

Ozzy Osbourne, rocker
Andy Williams, singer
Jean-Luc Godard, director
Bobby Allison, auto racer
Bucky Lasek, pro skateboarder

December 4

Work is not one of your favorite words, so you are usually making a living doing something fun—you'd have fun all the time if you could, and why not? So easy-going, your mind can wander off into idea-land. Meanwhile, bills don't get paid—what happened to taking care of number one and saving the world? Others may point to you and say "Look what happens when . . . " Get a little more organized, and polish your image, too.

Morals and morality—and health and accidents—play a role in the crazy drama that is your life. You are not too egotistical, or lofty, or ethereal, at least one of your feet is on the ground—it's just you. Try writing down a list of good and bad things you do each day. Exaggerate only a little. You might become a writer.

Love

It's not difficult for you to separate your feelings from your relationship responsibilities. Although strongly opinioned and a bit stubborn, you're never controlling. You soberly express your needs and expectations and usually emphasize cooperation. However, your "my-way-or-the-highway" attitude gets out of hand occasionally, because your temper control switch is very sensitive to partners who are needy.

Money

Because of an innate need for you to prove yourself to others, you often take on more than you should. Sure, it's nice when the boss acknowledges or gives you the thumbs up, as long as you understand the difference between applause, job description, and martyrdom. You manage your personal finances pretty well, and are a trustworthy employee who keeps business discussions and coworkers separate from friends.

Famous People Born on This Day

Female
Deanna Durbin, singer
Joanne Battiste, artist
Tyra Banks, model
Marisa Tomei, actress
Lila McCann, singer

Male
Jay-Z, rapper
Max Baer, Jr., actor
Vassily Kandinsky, painter
Jozef Sabovcik, ice skater
Jeff Bridges, actor

December 5

Hopes and dreams mean a lot to you, so beginning early you choose a direction, seek higher education for it, try to make the necessary connections, learn to manipulate, eventually land a great job, then decide you'd rather do something else. You'll stick with it, sure, but you'll also develop something secret on the side—something to fulfill your need for adventure and intrigue—testing your intuition and power, which you have a good supply of.

You are more reactionary than logical, but do have a good sense about what is right for the immediate situation. Roles where you have to be accountable—though you're not wild about that—will help you keep focused and get the boss's attention. For vacations abroad, you'd enjoy Italy or cruises to far-off places of mystery and romance.

Love

Your priorities about what you expect from and will give to a relationship are quickly and clearly defined from the initial flirtation, but not too negotiable. However, if you want the union to thrive, it's a good idea to make a special point of understanding your partner's needs as well! It's easy for you to overlook the feelings of friends and lovers because your goals are ingrained, and rather rigid. Don't forget your significant other's feelings!

Money

You always do what's expected from you on the job and don't take credit unless it's due. However, 12/5-born tend to focus more on bottom lines, often overlooking important details. You're honest about learning from your mistakes and not afraid of criticism, are a good comparison shopper, and pretty realistic about personal budgets. Learn when to ask for help when necessary, and provide the same to others.

Famous People Born on This Day

Female

Joan Didion, novelist
Morgan Brittany, actress
Lady Huxley, author
Carrie Hamilton, actress
Margaret Cho, comedienne

Male

Walt Disney, cartoonist
Jim Messina, rocker
J. W. "Corkey" Fornof, stunt coordinator
Little Richard, rocker
Fritz Lang, director

December 6

There is no shortage of fire and ambition inside you, even if you are small, so you easily make good first impressions and achieve short-term aims, but we wonder where you'll be a year from now. Will you be trapped in a low-status job or wandering from place to place, content to be you without making the right changes for real growth to occur? That's not you, so clear your head; set reasonable goals. Break free—upward.

You can be a real hustler and have the vitality to master almost any talent, particularly music, which you're pretty hip on. Roles where you teach others or con them out of their stupid habits might interest you, plus you're hip on the newest stuff and are pretty creative. Burning out and tension can lead to problems; a temporary change of scene helps.

Love

Because you express your feelings freely, often and honestly, you're best-suited for lovers who relate in kind. You are happiest with active, self-motivated partners who initiate action or stimulate change in your relationship, rather than only wait or merely participate. Fly-by-night affairs hold little interest to 12/6-born because you appreciate constancy. You are hopeful yet realistic, eager but serious, plus assertive and compassionate.

Money

Your optimistic and diplomatic drive to get the job done on time keeps you happy, and pays the bills. 12/6-born believe that everything worth having comes from effort and diligence, so you work hard and reap the rewards. You tend to be a bit unrealistic with personal spending, but are rarely without funds. Rather than nitpick or complain to coworkers, you just roll up your sleeves and then dance to the bank.

Famous People Born on This Day

Female

Eve Curie Labouisse, author
Rose Schneiderman, labor leader
Lynn Fontanne, actress
Agnes Moorehead, actress

Male

Dave Brubeck, musician
Ira Gershwin, lyricist
Wally Cox, actor
Bert Geoffrey Achong, inventor
Tom Hulse, actor

December 7

Pinning you down or categorizing you is not allowed since you believe firmly in your power to achieve whatever it is you set your mind to. People are attracted to your activism and verve, but some will learn that you have a fiery touch, too, and not to step over the line. You don't mind being the star or painting your own picture of how life should be—that's your prerogative and you exercise it right or wrong. That independence may put a strain on romance and deep relationships, though.

Keeping focused and "finishing" are not your strong points, so roles that give you freedom plus keep your feet on the ground—being practical and reliable—help you learn to recognize trouble before it gets out of hand. You enjoy holiday celebrations and getting out on the road in style.

Love

You have strong, but rather conventional beliefs and rules about relationships, and what a partner has to do in order to keep you happy. You seek lovers who stimulate you, help you grow and explore the outside world, and are comfortable sharing time behind the steering wheel. Once committed to a relationship, you give sound advice and are not afraid of taking risks, but probably never to the extent that anyone gets hurt.

Money

12/7s are always financially hungry for "more" and forever on the lookout for bigger and better everything. However, security, rather than money, tops your must-have list, even though you're very aware of others' possessions and savings. Employers recognize this dreamy, inspired nature, and usually give you opportunities for improving finances, challenging your skills and stimulating your attention. You prefer to work with others and accomplish a great deal by sticking to one project at a time.

Famous People Born on This Day

Female

Willa Cather, novelist
Mary Stuart, Queen of Scotland
Ellen Stewart, actress
Ellen Burstyn, actress
Martha Layne Collins, governor

Male

Aaron Carter, singer
Harry Chapin, songwriter
C. Thomas Howell, actor
Ted Knight, actor
Eli Wallach, actor

December 8

Walking on the wild side, sometimes in the rain, you can be like a pied piper, enticing friends and lovers to come with you, seeking adventure, running wild and taking everything life has to offer. Some of you are more down-to-earth, settling into careers where you show your handiness and organizational abilities, and that you're equal to the boss. Recreation and entertainment take up a lot of your time, and something divine will protect you, perhaps.

It's a surprise to find that others are better at some things; you may wish to tone down a bit and listen, which you can do naturally—drugs and such can really do you wrong. Roles as an entertainer come naturally; you're good at getting the ball rolling, but not stopping it. For fun, visit foreign lands; you may choose to live there.

Love

Because you don't take relationships casually, the emotional attachments you form are very strong, and you rarely fall in love too quickly or easily. Make sure partners have your best interests in mind because you sometimes ignore yours for the sake of peace. A passive but effervescent person, you're not one to rock the relationship boat, which makes it easy for you to slip into the backseat to a more dominant partner. You don't quickly commit to a lover, but when you do it's all the way!

Money

Although it's a 12/8-born's constant dream and desire, saving and making lots of money isn't your expertise. You're a dependable and trustworthy employee, and always do what's expected, but very little extra. It's not that you're lazy—you're just more disorganized than economical about time and responsibilities, more laid-back than a push the payroll-envelope sort. Your hopes and dreams are vivid, although not always practical.

Famous People Born on This Day

Female

Patti Page, singer
Dorothy Mae Ballard, activist
Kim Basinger, actress
Teri Hatcher, actress
Mary, Queen of Scots

Male

Jim Morrison, singer
David Carradine, actor
Flip Wilson, comedian
Sammy Davis, Jr., singer
James Thurber, humorist

December 9

Loving, caring, and a bit of a soft touch, few would guess by looking at you that there is a passionate, huggable side, but when they see you with your mate, they'll understand. You can be very firm in your beliefs, your commitments, though there can be something tragic in romance—something to cry about. With an ambitious eye to the future, you dream of the day when you'll be the leader or land baron, and may settle down long enough to accumulate wealth, land, and resources instead of using them.

You can play the tough guy/gal roles, and grow up quickly, but your spirit won't grow old. When your sights are set on something, stand aside, world. Cooperative roles will widen your horizons—others appreciate that you'll share the spotlight. Traveling with groups keeps you from being bored.

Love

People gravitate to you because you radiate a gentle natural type of warm, personal strength. However, you're a deep well of emotions, and in order to maintain a happy relationship you have to get a more mature understanding about your feelings. You're dependable, and giving, but get easily possessive of partners—but never in controlling fashion. You're best-suited for a stable, predictable, straightforward lover.

Money

12/9-born prefer logical, methodical work that doesn't challenge the emotions, preferring defined procedures and formal schedules because you tend to lose your cool whenever "one" doesn't precede "two." Not easily impressed by coworkers' flattery or their personal dramas, you separate your private life from paycheck pals comfortably and intuitively, and always get the job done!

Famous People Born on This Day

Female

Dina Merrill, actress
Grace Murray Hopper, computer
    innovator
Margaret Hamilton, actress
Leonie Fuller Adams, poet

Male

Donny Osmond, singer
John Malkovich, actor
Beau Bridges, actor
Kirk Douglas, actor
John Milton, poet

December 10

Someone has to light the fire to get things—and people—going. You're the spark that can do it. Drifting along through life is not for you—there have to be goals, purpose, a guiding light—and you are not afraid of work because you will definitely be rewarded. You are a builder and mover and shaker—a do-it-yourselfer—with a fine eye and high standards, your own critic, and others need not apply.

So full of compassion—yet calculating and objective—you usually hit your mark. Telling you what to do has to be done tactfully, so your partners are often mellow professionals, and you supply the cultural umbrella and make the decisions. If we may suggest, a trip to India or the colonies might be worthwhile. Can you get some time to get away?

Love

You live and let live and function from logic, rather than feelings, because issues of "trust" are challenging for you. You don't make friends or enter into love affairs without careful consideration and evaluation. More exact than extravagant, you demonstrate your affection through devotion and constancy. Because it's easy for you to get stuck in relationship ruts, you mustn't let stale or outdated behavior thinking deter future growth.

Money

It's difficult for you to talk with others about personal finances—even with a professional! You have your own unique way of budgeting a bank account and your personal investments, and learn best from hands-on trial and error. You're not a scaredy-cat when it boils down to purchasing big-ticket items, and rarely go over budget. Even though you're not too punctual, you're a dependable employee and true blue about follow-through. Nevertheless, your most valuable luxury is retreating from the office and into your comfy easy chair at home!

Famous People Born on This Day

Female

Susan Dey, actress
Emily Dickinson, poet
Gloria Loring, singer
Nia Peeples, dancer
Dorothy Lamour, actress

Male

Kenneth Branagh, actor/director
Chet Huntley, newsman
William Lloyd Garrison, publisher
George MacDonald, author
Melville Dewey, Dewey Decimal
System creator

December 11

Imagine you in your lab coat, working studiously till dawn, trying to unlock the answers from your test tubes and gadgets, or see yourself·under a cold white light writing your thesis, crafting words that no one can resist. You are a genius of sorts, eloquent, enthusiastic, often questioning authority or dictating what will be. Never be discouraged because the world needs you to help us along. In romance and close relationships you can be a clinger, hopefully clinging to the right people.

Public service roles seem to fit you since you're amenable, dedicated and not the kind to take advantage and goof off. Thinking before you speak will help you avoid embarrassing faux pas; generally you say what bosses like to hear, and you pick up foreign languages easily, which comes in handy during your many travels.

Love

Volcanic emotional eruptions rarely cloud your judgment, and it's uncommon for you to treat anyone without consideration. However, dull relationships agitate and bore you; you hate emotional restrictions of any sort, or irrational, forceful lovers. Even though you're a bit eccentric, you live by your word and promises, and expect the same. Because 12/11-born have difficulty financially supporting their lovers, they often seek partners with good income and comfortable nest eggs.

Money

You have good self-control for getting a job done and not wasting time. You refrain from personal on-the-job interaction, preferring to work alone and in a structured fashion. You take care of your essentials first, but you're always ready to pitch in, provided that spontaneous requests don't interfere with your productivity. You never make loans to anyone and rarely ask for help unless absolutely necessary.

Famous People Born on This Day

Female
Annie Jump Cannon, astronomer
Teri Garr, actress
Grace Paley, writer
Donna Mills, actress
Brenda Lee, singer

Male
Rider Strong, actor
Nicki Sixx, rock guitarist
Jean-Louis Trintignant, actor/director
Max Born, German physicist/quantum mechanics
Carlo Ponti, film director

December 12

"Life is a cabaret," so the song says; you might even whistle that tune. Imagine, locked in a dance theatre 24/7! You'd like a little less chaos, a quiet break now and then—but you'd handle the sizzling night life longer than most! What about romance? You could agonize over it when it doesn't work out, perhaps frequently, then decide it's their problem and off you go on another adventure, back to the cabaret—or workplace—where you feel at home.

You are a quick study, quick to try your luck, and quick to bend the rules, too. Most obstacles melt away with a little effort, though you're not the type to go after the hard stuff anyway. Traveling comes naturally and you're at home wherever you touch down, sighing with relief that you've landed on your feet.

Love

You're a deep reservoir of emotions, and lovers rarely have to second-guess you, because you always (and quickly) toss your cards on the table. However, some of those concise, concrete priorities of yours could use a little more flexibility! More blunt than outspoken, you get right to the point—and for you, "love" means everything. You're devoted, open-minded, and never give up when times get tough, even though you prefer to have fun, instead of frantic!

Money

Although you're quick on your feet, you like to work in a planned and organized fashion. Even if a job doesn't appeal to your imagination, you diligently keep your "time is money" nose to the grindstone and get the duty done. Regardless of your occupation, your efficient, conscious demeanor makes you a good supervisor and systems analyst as well as good team player.

Famous People Born on This Day

Female

Helen Frankenthaler, painter
Cora Lee Johnson, social activist
Hermione Gingold, actress
Connie Francis, singer
Dionne Warwick, singer

Male

Frank Sinatra, singer
Bob Barker, game show host
Edward G. Robinson, actor
Emerson Fittipaldi, race car driver
Edward I. Koch, TV judge

December 13

Hopefully you weren't born on a Friday—not that it really matters, you are already more superstitious and suspicious than you let on, not helpful when it distracts you from the more important issues, even coming between you and friends and lovers. Strong, willful, and quick, you do know how to use your body like a wonderful tool and can be charming too, but some of your ideas are, well, we expected better and more congeniality too—don't we deserve it?

Power isn't in taking—power is putting in, so roles where you contribute are better for your karma—and help you avoid resentment. A good word, a nod of approval—you do get more with sugar than with spice, even from the wrong elements and usual suspects. Time spent in the desert will get your old self back.

Love

You don't mince or waste words with loved ones—when you speak you quickly and efficiently address all issues at hand when they develop. Although you discern the root of a problem immediately, it's a nice idea that you remember to treat lovers with a bit more compassion and sensitivity. You constantly offer advice but aren't the best at listening. Mature lovers, rather than unrefined ones, suit you best.

Money

When there is work to be done, you get right down to business and leave no stone untouched! Never lazy but a tad picky about "your" schedule, you're always eager to learn something new, and are efficient but never aggressive even though you tend to whine. You're masterful about adapting and transforming ideas into action. To the 12/13-born, there is no such thing as "failure" or having too much.

Famous People Born on This Day

Female

Wendie Malick, actress
Christie Clark, actress
Genevieve Page, actress
R. A. MacAvoy, science fiction author
Lillian Roth, singer

Male

Ted Nugent, rocker
Dick Van Dyke, actor
Van Heflin, actor
Carlos Montoya, guitarist
Jamie Foxx, comedian

December 14

Taking things too personally is an art form for some of you, feeling that you're better and deserve more—that you over-pay your dues. There is such a thing as having too much passion, taking too much care of number one, and maybe your aim isn't so good. Don't you just hate to be preached to? Good, because that's just how you sound, often. Whacko rules and power trips aren't acceptable, so why bother—all that will happen is that you'll wind up alone.

Now that we've got your attention and you promise to behave, let's go have good, unstructured fun. Escaping from work always puts you in a better mood. If you don't wind up behind bars first, talking with a good shrink could help if you let it, and don't write a bad check for their advice you'll ignore.

Love

As a good peacemaker, you pride yourself on not making excessive demands on lovers. You worry about being perfect, strive to be liked, to be acceptable company, and do the right thing. You are understanding about partners who don't, or simply can't, live up to your expectations—but also know when to discard and de-clutter those who hold you back. Your respect for lessons from past relationships serves you well.

Money

You have a gentle, respectful manner when working with people, and consider everyone an extended family member rather than a competitor. You are sensitive to a fellow employee's appeal for help—but only when it is sincere, won't infringe on your work responsibilities, and doesn't involve a personal loan. You are growth-oriented, and enjoy positions of power as long as no one is breathing down your neck.

Famous People Born on This Day

Female

Margaret Chase Smith, politician
Lee Remick, actress
Patty Duke, actress
Shirley Jackson, novelist
Abbe Lane, singer

Male

Spike Jones, comedy bandleader
Nostradamus, astrologer
Charlie Rich, singer
James H. Doolittle, USAF general
Edward L. Tatum, molecular geneticist

December 15

Just think: you were almost born on Christmas! That would be fitting—you'd make a good religious person: pious, brave, and optimistic, full of compassion and charitable deeds, keeping rhythm with all activity around you. That is you, right? There is a challenging catch: not everyone shares universal love and you may be a bit of a target, too busy helping others to defend yourself. Plus, you're very susceptible to cold and illnesses—your health needs careful attention—and fate may force you to change residence often.

Though you might not believe it, you're quite intuitive, even psychic, so in business and trade you have an edge, capable of astonishing others with your accomplishments and practical imagination, playing your part convincingly. A warning: waters and dark places aren't safe. Travel only when the stars approve.

Love

12/15-born figures out a suitor's likes and dislikes quickly, and accurately. However, you have a tendency to lavish affection on partners, which may startle or overwhelm anyone who isn't used to it. Few people are as open and direct as you. Whenever you have a problem in a relationship, you analyze it with your mind, not your feelings. You have the good sense and confidence to know what to change or when to move on when a relationship turns toxic.

Money

Everything that you obtain is a result of planning, and sensitivity to co-workers or what's necessary. You treasure the many lessons of past experiences, and have a progressive but realistic outlook that eagerly embraces every day, and what it brings. You consider finances as a means to fulfill yourself, and an avenue to allow you to stimulate others to excel. Employers and coworkers know that they can trust you to get the job done well—and very well at that!

Famous People Born on This Day

Female
Edna O'Brien, writer
Annie Pujol, TV hostess
Betty Smith, novelist
Helen Slater, actress
Melanie Chartoff, actress

Male
Don Johnson, actor
Tim Conway, comedian
J. Paul Getty, oil tycoon
Alan Freed, DJ who introduced
    term "rock-n-roll"
Jeff Chandler, actor

December 16

Bright, eager and indomitable, not much escapes your attention, and when you are in love, the world glows. Whoa! There is a fiery temper, also a heart of gold, and passions that take you where bright lights and glitter can cloud your usually excellent judgment. Often, you live beyond your means, flowing toward the easy life, trusting that better days are ahead. They are if you keep putting your abundant energy into your work. You should be your own boss.

Your talent, often in the arts and music, would go to waste if you didn't apply it more, so part-time roles in groups that share your same cultural passions shouldn't be passed up. Ah! Remember vividly the joys of earlier times; recapture them whenever you can. Trips to places of natural beauty and glamour always inspire and enrich you.

Love

You're quite conventional about your personal needs, and do that extra mile on the love train, but don't invest a thing unless motivated by a partner who is equally responsible and enthusiastic, who is eager for new experiences. You're happiest with a fun-loving goal-oriented partner who keeps you on your toes, and inspires you. For 12/16-born, love is an exciting, rather than scary, adventure—however, once it gets boring or routine, you're outta there!

Money

Co-workers admire your excellent reasoning ability and keen judgment—your mind is never at rest. Even people whose opinions differ from yours are quickly convinced by your arguments and detailed game-plans. Saving money isn't your strength, but being responsible is. You have a deep thirst for knowledge and an awesome ability to apply data quickly and intuitively, even though you have difficulty dealing with repetition and win-lose situations.

Famous People Born on This Day

Female

Margaret Mead, anthropologist
Jane Austen, novelist
Liv Ullman, actress
Lesley Stahl, reporter
Catherine of Aragon, Spanish
    princess

Male

Beethoven, composer
Noel Coward, actor
Arthur C. Clarke, author
Henry Clarke, fashion photographer
Steven Bochco, producer

December 17

Even if your eyesight isn't the best, you see the world—in your mind's eye—more vividly than most, and you have that burning desire to enjoy not just what everyone else thirsts for, but also to be a faithful friend and perfect lover. It's not surprising that you are well-liked and blend in anywhere, but when your hard-edged opinions and temper come out, all that can change. You're not as good at talking your way out of things as you are getting into them, including misunderstandings over love.

Your high ideals and independent nature take you down life paths that include some interesting, unforeseen opportunities—you're better at "being there" than most. Your favorite word is "yes" but you are clear-sighted and willful enough to say no. Don't say "no" to active adventures and diving off waterfalls.

Love

To a certain extent, you know how to subtly manipulate partners to ensure that you get the attention you need. Passive-aggressive lovers bore you, although your intention is never to control or hurt. However, 12/17-born have a tendency to worry, frequently spouting their frustrations to inappropriate acquaintances. Everyone wants a good return on their investment—whether emotional or economical. Embrace your weaknesses as well as a lover's, and always target improvement and excellence!

Money

Although not driven by applause, you enjoy recognition and acknowledgement for your efforts. You keep your ego under control, even though it's hard for you to keep silent. Coworkers know that you are reliable and are a team player. However, you have to learn how to censor those very strong opinions of yours! Your mouth isn't any bigger than anybody else's, but your bark loudly competes with your always-ready bite whenever you get upset.

Famous People Born on This Day

Female

Vanessa Zima, actress
Milla Jovovich, actress
Sarah Dallin, rocker
Giulla Boschi, actress
Julia Meade, actress

Male

Willard Frank Libby, inventor
Arthur Fiedler, conductor
Bill Pullman, actor
Eugene Levy, comedian
William Safire, political columnist

December 18

Too busy pursuing your hopes and dreams, there isn't time to worry about others, so you usually do succeed because you aren't easily sidetracked. Others should take care of themselves, just as you do. When duty calls, you summon up all the people skills you need, tackle the task with tact, having learned good and bad lessons from experience—you're evolving into a real executive! You're not a big time waster—there are plenty of obstacles and you're serious about overcoming them. Even in the heavens above, you are blessed by a business star.

Tedious roles are not for you. Even if you travel a lot already, pencil in short vacations to the real out-of-the-way places, but remember there always seem to be lesser, vulgar people sniping at you, trying to pull you off the high road.

Love

You're an easy-going, let's-all-get-along-together, footloose kind of lover who's as uncomfortable with loud-mouths as well as quiet solitude. You're open-minded and very humorous, too. But 12/18s are such live-by-the-pants kinds of people who react without thinking that long-range matters cause problems in relationships. A focused, mature partner who reacts well to change and emergencies suits you best.

Money

You need clear guidelines and rules about every job description, because you're a better team player than solo act. You need specific guidelines and rules to follow in order to get the job done because you're not great at making decisions. 12/18-born must learn not to let sudden changes in schedule or set-backs become frustrating. Learn how to budget your time and expenses, because impulse-shopping and sloppy bill-paying come naturally for you.

Famous People Born on This Day

Female

Katie Holmes, actress
Gladys Cooper, actress
Christina Aguilera, singer
Betty Grable, actress
Anita O'Day, singer

Male

Brad Pitt, actor
Steven Spielberg, filmmaker
Ossie Davis, actor
Stone Cold Steve Austin, wrestler
Roger Smith, actor

December 19

If there's a tingle in the air, you feel it—you're easily excited by anticipation and just being there when something momentous is about to happen—something that will be etched in your memory. Walking the jet-way to the airplane: suspense. Thinking about having children: seizure! Job interviews: torture! Pricking your finger: infection! Maybe you are accident-prone.

Despite whatever troubles may come your way, after the mandatory angst, your optimism and forgiving nature shine through, and you promise never to have it happen again. Your health and even your crazy ideas can hold you back, but little can hold you back from cutting loose on that dreamed-of vacation.

Love

You view relationships like a business deal—always checking debits and credits, negotiating. Never rash, you enter a what-is-hoped-to-be a long-term relationship only after much thought, preferring to build momentum slowly but surely. You are tolerant with others' quirks and demeanor but are likely to chafe at the bit when loved ones don't share your outlook. Stop being so defensive; most people are willing to meet you halfway if you give them the chance.

Money

At work, two heads (or more) are better than yours alone. You enjoy comradery, gossip, and brainstorming. Capable of following instructions after they are defined, you eagerly attack every project and don't rest until completion. It's a good idea for you to find a financial advisor because saving for the rainy day isn't in your consciousness. Although a good shopper, frittering away those hard-earned dollars comes easy.

Famous People Born on This Day

Female

Maria L. Sanford, activist
Cicely Tyson, actress
Alyssa Milano, actress
Jennifer Beals, actress
Edith Piaf, singer

Male

Robert Urich, actor
Ralph Richardson, actor
William De Vries, surgeon
Richard Leakey, anthropologist
Tim Reid, comedian

December 20

Telling you to do something takes bravery; physically getting you to do it takes an act of Congress. But, when you say something, we had better jump, and quick, and we should have read your mind and then in zombie-like fashion played our parts in your life drama. Okay; we can do it so long as we think we're helping you, and you do need help, just like everyone else. Everything has to go at your pace—a bit slow until the race starts.

Drawn to less rigorous activities and vocations—you'd make a great badminton player if you could see better—you do take your duties very seriously, seeing details that others, darn them, missed. When you do get outdoors (if it's not raining) and fill your lungs with fresh air, you feel super, simply inspired!

Love

You are happiest with a logical, mature, and loyal lover who will put up with your worry wart meltdowns, and inspire you to have fun, move ahead. 12/20-born observe the world from their comfy little space on earth, meticulously scrutinizing their own and others' behavior. It's not easy for you to forget past indiscretions because you are so fervently concerned about a lover's history. Live in the moment rather than recycle old worries!

Money

Not managerial or executive material, you prefer being told exactly what to do and say, and how and when to act. You work well with others who understand the work-a-day itinerary of the job and will guide you like a school teacher. Number-crunching accounting types of employment make you uneasy—probably because you're not too good at managing your own, even though you always have more than enough. Loosen up the purse-strings on personal budgets, and get a better grip over your "poverty- consciousness" thinking.

Famous People Born on This Day

Female

Maude Gonne, Irish nationalist
Hanna Fromm, activist
Hortense Calisher, writer
Dianne Arndt, artist

Male

Uri Geller, psychic
Harvey S. Firestone, industrialist
Dick White, head of British secret
  service
Max Lerner, columnist
John Hillerman, actor

December 21

Sweetness should be your middle name, since under that wry, fiery exterior is a thinking heart and a soul in search of happiness. Will you get the chance to reach for the stars and come back with a pocketful of rainbows? Some lessons about human nature and how things really work have to be learned first, and you'll learn them if not tied down, or settling for less. Sacrifices for love, security, and a happy home may have to be made.

You do have a way of getting people to cooperate, and you're a good manager when you want to be, though you're not usually the tough guy/gal. You don't need to be told what clothes to take on vacation since you're planning to buy clothes when you get there—so you won't look like another wacky tourist.

Love

You have tremendous empathy and kindness, don't take relationships lightly, or blindly bulldoze into affairs with dyslexic abandonment. No matter how socially savvy or respectable you think you are, 12/21-born are rather insecure, worrying about what others think, wondering if others respect you, scrutinizing your and everybody else's behavior. Love is a biggie for you—but it should also be an exciting source for joy and exploration.

Money

Your self-confidence needs constant attention in order to function without fear in the work-a-day world. You respect what's expected of you and the work ethic, value honesty, and have good morals, but being more easygoing rather than timid, you're uncomfortable in confrontational situations or overly responsible on-the-job positions. You work contentedly behind the scenes, creating, inventing, and following plans.

Famous People Born on This Day

Female

Jane Fonda, actress
Alicia Alonso, ballerina
Chris Evert Lloyd Mills, tennis champion
Florence Griffith Joyner, Olympic runner
Henrietta Szoldi, Zionist leader

Male

Keifer Sutherland, actor
Ray Romano, actor
Samuel L. Jackson, actor
Frank Zappa, rocker
Phil Donahue, talk-show host

December 22

Being born on the shortest day of the year must mean something—less sunlight—unless of course, you're in Australia, Argentina, or South Africa, where you'll be roasting. You're a dignified, spiritual, and reserved type, maybe psychic, and a lot stronger inside than you realize. A real bundle of emotions can get the better of some of you, though most of you are lucky—not in everything, but you may become millionaires and famous even while shunning the spotlight.

How well you feel depends on your mate, and you're not known as a charismatic dynamo on the social scene—too busy making your other ambitions come true. You are loyal to partners and friends. Out on your own, you feel at one with the world.

Love

You're an uptight type of lover who doesn't emotionally, or ever, intentionally, intimidate a lover—and, hopefully, the same is true of him or her about you, too. But because it's so hard for 12/22s to turn off their fantasy mind, don't presume that your partner is a mind-reader! Your feelings about relationships are conventional, but not always logical. On the surface, you appear optimistic and buoyant; and, on a graded scale, you are. But in matters of intimacy, you scare easily. You need someone who keeps you comfortable when you let down your hair and are being yourself.

Money

12/22s are not pushovers but are easily swayed by coworkers who are louder or prouder—which drives you nuts! Since fellow employees know that you're a good worker, and you usually do more than your share, develop more confidence about saying your say, and just do the job! Although you perform what's expected from you, you're better at following orders and the rules, rather than barking them.

Famous People Born on This Day

Female
Lady Bird Johnson, First Lady
Diane Sawyer, investigative reporter
Barbara Billingsly, actress
Dorothea Jordan, actress
Doris Duke, tobacco heiress

Male
Robin and Maurice Gibb, singers
Gene Rayburn, game show host
Rene-Robert La Salle, explorer
Justin McCarthy, Irish politician
Hector Elizondo, actor

December 23

Are you ever really satisfied, or must you always change things to your liking, always rushing, impatient, independent? When you point your finger, you mean it. You have a lot going on upstairs—you can be a real brain if you want to be—a pioneer, sometimes a tough cookie. It's no wonder so many of you are leaders and trendsetters, and when you get the romance thing figured out, you may make some special someone very happy if they'll let you.

Not many famous women are born on this day, so if you're female, chances are—with a little effort—you can hit the Top Ten List of December 23 movers'n'shakers. Anyone born today is not satisfied with common roles; you'd be wasting your time if you weren't pushing your limits, including during active leisure times.

Love

You're not rugged or romantic, and criticism makes you flee. You don't second-guess others, and take things as they come, but grow quickly comfortable with unpredictability. You proclaim your desires perfectly clearly—most times in writing so that your lover can't presume. It's easy for you to get caught up in a lover's trivia and untruths. Stop it—right now!

Money

You're not unrealistic or gullible, but it's a good idea for you to abstain from on-the-job positions of power because it's not your strength. You're an honest, popular employee because you don't make excessive demands on coworkers, always tolerant of others' frailties. However, you work best under supervision. Accentuate your positives rather than profit-making traits.

Famous People Born on This Day

Female

Susan Lucci, actress
Harriet Monroe, poet
Madame C. J. Walker, cosmetic
    mogul
Elizabeth Hartman, actress
Ruth Roman, actress

Male

Eddie Vedder, singer
Harry Guardino, actor
Jose Greco, flamenco dancer
Dick Weber, bowler
Harry Shearer, actor

December 24

It is no accident that you arrived on this busy day, with so much anticipation and fervor, and thank goodness you have intelligence and wits—and plenty of vitality—to carry you through the 364 other days. Many see you as dignified and scholarly, and most of you have paid your dues to earn a reputation—hope it's a good one. You have a smoothness—a sharp, organized mind—and never talk out of turn. Give yourself more credit as sexy.

Roles where you speak before the public would be an exciting change for normally reserved you, and letting out some of your insider secrets will have everyone listening, drooling over your sage advice. It's not easy to pick a perfect vacation for you—you'd rather fly the plane than put your feet up in first class.

Love

You enjoy the excitement that relationships deliver, never seeking a fixed itinerary—only enjoyment of the moment. Open-minded but not always realistic, you work well with lovers who are not static or rigid, preferring unplanned quality time. However, once boredom sets in, you're out the door! A roll-with-punches partner complements your need to escape from the real world. You're a lover, not a fighter!

Money

Because your everyday world is far removed from that of finances and schedule, you're best-suited for jobs that are more social, spontaneous, or inspiring to others. Because your rational mind is strongly influenced by your imagination, you punch the time-clock forever unsure about your talents. Never take on responsibilities that you know you can't perform. Work with your strengths, rather than dreams or shortcomings.

Famous People Born on This Day

Female

Ruth Chatterton, actress
Ava Gardner, actress
Mary Higgins Clark, author
Stephanie Hodge, actress
Mary Ramsey, singer

Male

Ricky Martin, singer
Kit Carson, explorer
Paul Tagliabue, NFL commissioner
Howard Hughes, tycoon
James Prescott Joule, physicist

December 25

Yes, you were born on Christmas and all that, but you ARE one lucky person! Really. Your luck in love and gambling is legendary even outside the North Pole. Most see you as a kind, orderly, noble person, active, self-assured, a real go-getter and a nice catch for some lucky lover. You revel in life's pleasurable pursuits and finer things, including sports. A little vain, but we forgive you. After all, you are lucky, and your children are above average.

Famous people from all walks of life are born today; you'll get there too if you get out of the hood and get in the game. Roles where you nurture people along—or where you pick up a specialized skill—get you in the groove. You don't need to follow the sun for warmth—there's plenty wherever you are.

Love

You enjoy logical, mindful relationships because emotions make you uneasy. 12/25-born are happiest with alert, attentive partners who help and support you. You're wonderful at managing a household and fulfilling your part—it's the emotional touchy-feely scenarios that frighten you! Try relaxing, explore your needs, and let the music move you.

Money

You do your best work when you know exactly what is expected from you, with no surprises, because you need (and love) clearly-defined guidelines. Even though you're friendly and kind, you're not great at improvising. Your rational mind is strongly influenced by outside circumstances. In order for you to complete a job on time, you require guidance or someone to loudly crack the whip.

Famous People Born on This Day

Female

Clara Barton, humanitarian
Evangeline Cory Booth, social
    reformer
Barbara Mandrell, singer
Sissy Spacek, actress
Annie Lennox, singer

Male

Jimmy Buffet, entertainer
Rod Serling, writer
Humphrey Bogart, actor
Conrad Hilton, hotel mogul
Sir Isaac Newton, scientist

December 26

If someone had to run the world, it would be you. First, you're a bit gullible, so we could talk you into granting us lots of favors. Second, you're kingly—or queenly—noble, protective, all-seeing as you gaze over your minions. Third, you're a friendly, witty character, and we want a ruler who can tell a good joke. Fourth, people naturally like you, and you've got a good balance of business acumen and personality. When you aim, you usually hit your target—or an innocent bystander.

Roles where you are the power behind the throne are good, too, like secretary Rosemary Woods who conveniently garbled her boss's (President Nixon) incriminating tapes. Get that boss to give you a blank check to vacation anywhere in the world!

Love

Partners who do not discuss personal and emotional matters make you crazy; you need one who listens and doesn't judge, and who keeps your secrets locked behind closed doors. 12/26-born must be in tune with a partner who lets you drive at your speed, won't second-guess you, or is too busy for personal stuff. You respect others' choices—provided that they come home on time, say their say while they were away, and sing your blessings.

Money

You're responsible, work well with others, and do what's expected—but you need a bit of applause or acknowledgement to cavort with customers and be part of "what's happening." Because you hate working alone, and cubicle-confined jobs make you sad, working with others keeps you happy. Your somber 12/26 penchant doesn't live for acknowledgement, but you really, really like knowing that you're doing good work and are not overlooked.

Famous People Born on This Day

Female

Susan H. Butcher, dogsled driver
  champion
Lucy Faithfull, activist
Lynn Martin, U.S. Secretary of Labor
Joyce Jillson, psychic
Victoria Racimo, actress

Male

John Walsh, TV host
Phil Spector, record producer
Alan King, comedian
Steve Allen, comedian
Richard Widmark, actor

December 27

When you were young, you were a bit shy, already busy with your own ideas, then you grew up to be achievement-oriented, lovingly protective, and a bit eccentric. Actually, you have a lot more good traits and some hidden ones, too. Many see you as reserved, orderly, cautious, but you are honorable, judicious, and dependable, always ready to fight for what's right, and so you're a good parent, breadwinner, and probably a lot smarter, stronger, and prettier than your mate.

Since you'd rather be right, a lot of you go against the grain, sometimes upsetting the powers that be. Don't they know you're too self-assured to bend to others' potato chip–thin whims? Roles where you teach or lecture let you share your wise gifts. Give yourself an "A," then disappear for a secret rendezvous with a special someone.

Love

You're uneasy with formal, follow-the-rulebook, or clinging partners, preferring passionate improvisation, live-for-the-moment types. Even though your imagination overflows with romantic ideals and fantasies, you're never in a rush to reach the finish line. 12/27-born need and admire responsible, true-blue lovers with solid follow-through. For you, love means honoring and savoring the moment, rather than hopeful good intentions.

Money

You separate coworkers from personal friends and are honest and diligent about work—always reliable and punctual. You come through and do what is expected, and know when to ask for assistance, always keeping both feet firmly planted on the ground concerning job responsibilities and deadlines. Although you work well with others, you're happiest performing independent gigs.

Famous People Born on This Day

Female

Marlene Dietrich, actress
Norma Rae Beatty Ashby, broadcaster
Heather O'Rourke, actress
Cokie Roberts, newscaster
Tracy Nelson, actress

Male

Gerard Depardieu, actor
John Amos, actor
William Howell Masters, author
Louis Pasteur, bacteriologist
Oscar Levant, actor

December 28

Life isn't moving fast enough for you, so naturally you gravitate to more challenging roles, putting your whole being into it—heart, mind, and soul. You're a bit of a magician the way you magically get things done, and there isn't anything you can't figure out, or pretend to. One thing that really helps is your good memory—maybe also your good looks. In a debate, who can argue with you? This doesn't describe you? Well, you'd better get with it then, Mr./Mrs./Ms. Know-it-All.

You'd relish a role as an artist, donning the funky artist clothes, splashing paint, and grinning a devil-may-care grin. Secretly, you do have a swagger, though you're still conservative enough to keep a straight face, reserving smiles for all those sexy beings you find attractive, especially at hot vacation spots—Monaco, Berlin, Amsterdam, Muskogee.

Love

You're uncomfortable with lovers who are financially unfocused or childish, preferring wise and responsible partners rather than reckless ones. Once committed, you are a generous and kind partner who enjoys life's simple pleasures—even though you enjoy a little extravagance every now and then! 12/28-born are best-suited with reliable, conservative, trustworthy types who are ambitious and willing to commit for the long run.

Money

Being productive, and making a profit, keeps you happy. You're a conscientious and patient person who hates making mistakes; you learn from and accept the lessons of the past as a means for future prosperity. Your analytical skills and natural understanding of current trends help you excel in business. In whatever career you choose, you do your best work when independent from teams or groups.

Famous People Born on This Day

Female

Anne Legendre Armstrong, ambassador

Janet Hough Bryant, author

Maggie Smith, actress

Nichelle Nichols, actress

Terri Garber, actress

Male

Denzel Washington, actor

Cliff Arquette, comedian

Stan Lee, comics artist

Sam Levenson, humorist

Woodrow Wilson, U.S. president

December 29

If you didn't get bored so easily, you probably wouldn't be trying to enjoy life as much as you do or looking for adventure (sometimes in questionable places), or campaigning for a cause, or brainstorming about the topic of the minute. You like playing those games your gender enjoys, often with close friends, keeping an eye out for trouble, since you're said to be a pessimist. But, when you find your niche and the bennies start rolling in, hallelujah! Now all you need is that perfect mate, or an imperfect one.

No one enjoys the good life as much, and you have always done much as you please, following your natural interests. It's said that you can't be a prophet in your own land, so expand your horizons and find out there's more out there than you imagined.

Love

You're constantly exploring solutions for personal and sensual happiness, and have the impetus and courage to tackle emotional problems head on, and the fortitude to ensure that they are just and correct. More of a realist than optimist, you're best-suited for mature, down-to-earth types. You don't like being alone and must always (re-)consider romantic options. 12/29s are more determined and sagacious than others.

Money

You're a terrific team player and do everything within your means to follow the rules and keep the peace. For you, it's the excitement of accomplishment rather than the thrill of competition that counts. Once you have determined what must be done, you steadily move forward. Your bills must always be paid and usually on time. Neither miserly nor frugal, you're clever enough to figure out how to have some extra afterwards.

Famous People Born on This Day

Female

Mary Tyler Moore, actress
Madame De Pompadour, mistress
    of Louis XV
Marianne Faithful, singer
Paula Poundstone, comedienne
Kimberly Russell, actress

Male

Jude Law, actor
Jon Voight, film actor
Charles Goodyear, inventor
Pablo Casals, cellist
Ted Danson, actor

December 30

Unlike others born around this time of year, you're a live wire, ready with an opinion and a snappy line, usually including the word "yes." Impressing people means opening opportunity's doors, so you're a good mixer, though often mixing yourself into unworkable love affairs, deals with the wrong people or the wrong idea, but also good times and fun—especially if that includes someone attractive. You also have a special spot in your heart for family and home, and they do love you there.

You can flip-flop on a whim, but when you're focused on success at work, you usually deliver. Roles that aren't going anywhere aren't for you, still you will sacrifice for those who need your loving help. For a kick, fly a hot air balloon, then drink champagne if you come back to earth.

Love

You're bright, expressive, and extremely curious (as well as romantic and needy). You know who you are and are not afraid to say what's on your mind. Because you are eager to experience life and be informed on as many subjects as possible, you're never at a loss for words or for something to talk about. You rarely threaten a partner's opinion with debate. Above all, you insist on open and honest communication between partners.

Money

You worry about how much "it" costs or how you'll pay for it. But you always discover a solution or loan. Right? It's said that money doesn't make the world go around, right? Nonetheless, financial security is very important to you. You do your job precisely and one step at a time, and manage your employment responsibilities. Don't give up your daydreams for dollars! 12/30-born esteems honesty and wants to be valued as fair and just.

Famous People Born on This Day

Female
Sister M. Lawrence Antouin, college
    president emeritus
Tracey Ullman, actress
Patti Smith, rocker
Laila Ali, boxer
Skeeter Davis, singer

Male
Tiger Woods, golf phenomenon
Rudyard Kipling, novelist
Jack Lord, actor
Bert Parks, Miss America host
Michael Nesmith, songwriter

December 31

As the darling of all the birthdays, you can be so sad and sentimental, sensitive to a fault, in love with love and if you stay loving, all love's promises will come true. Mother Nature is precious to you, and you have a natural knack for seeing to it that the innocent, as well as the brave, are taken care of. Your laughter and charm are healing; others appreciate that. It can be hard to make decisions; it's important to surround yourself with others who offer honest, sound advice.

A good provider and practical, you're not the rough 'n tumble type, so hard and dirty roles are not for you. Others could take advantage of your good nature; fortunately, you can almost see into others' hearts. For fun, go where your artistic side gets a kick-start and ideas.

Love

You are uncomfortable with open displays of affection, but you are loving. It is hard for you to let down your hair and have a good time, always seeking emotional support. Naturally quiet and rather shy, you work best with older lovers. The more latitude there is in a relationship, the better. You enjoy the company of people who are not troubled with psychological hang-ups. Not one to interfere in the lives of others, you demand that others give you the same consideration.

Money

Although not one to leave a task half done, you often overestimate the difficulty of a job. Your 12/31-birthdate reveals that you work best in structured environments, but not so regimented that you lose the freedom to think or explore. Idealism has a place even in the most practical minds. Since your desires come suddenly and strong, your enthusiasm is hard to regulate. Nevertheless, you are a person of integrity, with high standards of behavior.

Famous People Born on This Day

Female

Odetta, singer
Diane Von Furstenberg, fashion
   designer
Sarah Miles, actress
Donna Summer, singer
Rosalind Cash, actress

Male

Val Kilmer, actor
John Denver, singer
Ben Kingsley, actor
Anthony Hopkins, actor
Rex Allen, singer